EAST OF EMPIRE

STANFORD BRITISH HISTORIES

Edited by Priya Satia

East of Empire

**EGYPT, INDIA, AND THE WORLD
BETWEEN THE WARS**

Erin M.B. O'Halloran

STANFORD UNIVERSITY PRESS
Stanford, California

Stanford University Press
Stanford, California

© 2025 by Erin M.B. O'Halloran. All rights reserved.

This book has been partially underwritten by the Peter Stansky Publication Fund in British Studies. For more information on the fund, please see www.sup.org/stanskyfund.

No part of this book may be reproduced or transmitted in any form or by any means, electronic or mechanical, including photocopying and recording, or in any information storage or retrieval system, without the prior written permission of Stanford University Press.

Printed in the United States of America on acid-free, archival-quality paper

Library of Congress Cataloging-in-Publication Data available on request.

Library of Congress Control Number: 2024952261

ISBN (cloth) 9781503640542
ISBN (paper) 9781503641440
ISBN (ebook) 9781503641457

Cover design: Lindy Kasler
Cover art (top to bottom): Egypt in Chains, 1924, Special Collections, J. Willard Marriott Library, The University of Utah; Kamaladevi Chattopadhyay (1903–1988), Album/AlamyStock Photo; Great Britain Ordnance Survey, 1926, David Rumsey Map Collection, Stanford Libraries; Indian Muslim refugees at the Purana Qila Fort in New Delhi, August 1947. Illustrated London News Ltd. / Mary Evans.

Dedicated to the memory of

Tsunesaburo Makiguchi *Josei Toda* *Daisaku Ikeda*
1871–1944 *1900–1958* *1928–2023*

Eastern humanists who embraced the world as kin

CONTENTS

Acknowledgments   ix

Note on Translation and Transliteration   xv

Maps   xvi

Introduction   1

PART I   IMAGINING THE EAST

1. Morning in Cairo   13
2. Whose Caliphate?   40
3. The Poetic East   57

PART II   CAPITAL OF THE EAST

4. Abyssinia in the Headlines   83
5. Palestine HQ   105

PART III   AMBASSADORS OF THE EAST

6. The Diplomats   129
7. The Delegation   150
8. The Feminists   167

PART IV THE EAST AT WAR

9 Hearts and Minds — 181

10 No Way Back — 203

Epilogue Midnight in Delhi — 221

Dramatis Personae — 235

Notes — 243

Bibliography — 279

Index — 297

ACKNOWLEDGMENTS

The journey of this book began at St Antony's College, Oxford, where I was mentored by Margaret MacMillan and Eugene Rogan. Their wise counsel, warm encouragement, and unflinching support long ago exceeded even the most liberal interpretation of their duties. I can never thank them enough.

In its earliest incarnation, my project benefited from the careful reading and deft guidance of Avi Shlaim, John Darwin, and James Belich. Jim Jankowski was kind enough to meet me at a coffee shop in Colorado to discuss Egyptian politics and shared a bibliography of relevant material (as well as tips on local ski hills). Noor Khan had lunch with me at Kew, offering invaluable advice and heartfelt encouragement, which helped me to believe it was all possible. Wm. Roger Louis invited me to coffee at All Souls and asked wonderful questions that refined my own. Margot Badran shared sources, insights, and reminiscences from her years in Cairo. Faisal Devji graciously agreed to a one-off meeting to discuss Indian Muslim politics; I have been impinging on his time and benefiting from his professional generosity ever since.

Debbie Usher of the St Antony's Middle East Centre Archive helped to identify key resources early on and shared countless tea breaks at the archive over the course of many years. Paul Dalgleish, Susan Thomas, and Jacques Montagner, of Special Collections and the Academy Library, University of New South Wales, provided invaluable assistance in obtaining access and high-quality reproductions of a rare memoir, which I drew on extensively, particularly for what are now chapters 5 and 6. The same part of the book benefited from Laila Parsons's research into the Peel Commission, which she was kind enough to share with me ahead of publication; Arie Dubnov also sent over reems of sharp, canny feedback on a version of this work. During my Viva, Khaled Fahmy suggested I think more about King Fuad's caliphal bid and other 1920s precedents of the late 1930s themes I had addressed. The whole of part 1 ultimately sprang from this felicitous nudge.

While at Oxford, I had the pleasure of working on the teaching team for the undergraduate paper "The Middle East in the Age of Empires" for three years. I feel certain I learned more than I taught, thanks to brilliant colleagues including Eugene Rogan, James MacDougall, Hannah Louise-Clarke, Hussein Omar, and Peter Hill. It remains a badge of pride that our course became perhaps the first in Oxford's long history to have most of its tutors subjected to ad hominem attacks in the *Daily Mail*, following the "Ethics and Empire" letter spearheaded by James.

I arrived at Stanford in the final stage of writing up, where Joel Beinin, Ali Yaycioglu, and Priya Satia facilitated both my integration on campus and the evolution of my thinking about the entangled histories of Britain, India, and the Middle East. For this I can also thank the members of the British Studies Reading Group at Berkeley, especially hosts James Vernon and Tom and Barbara Metcalf. At Stanford University Press, Kate Wahl indulged me in numerous coffee chats and rounds of emails as I thought through the transition to a publishable manuscript.

I completed the first draft while a visiting fellow at the Bill Graham Centre for Contemporary International History at the University of Toronto, where I am grateful to Jack Cunningham and the late Greg Donaghey for welcoming me. There, I had the pleasure of working with Tim Sayle, Cindy Ewing, Amelie Tolvin, Sam Eberlee, and eighty brilliant second-years from the Trinity One Program. The lectures I wrote and, in particular, the astonishing questions and discussions prompted by the students helped me to discover and articulate my understanding of the global twentieth century and its connections to the present day. Teaching and getting to know that cohort was one of the great privileges of my life; they continue to inspire me and give me hope.

At various stages Hussein Omar, Madihah Akhter, Aaron Jakes, Faridah Zaman, Aditi Chandra, and Mattias Olesen shared work with me ahead of publication, for which I thank them sincerely. Anna Boghiguian created a magnificent drawing of a scene from chapter 8, destined to remain among my most cherished souvenirs from this time in my life. In the depths of lockdown, Chihab El Khachab used his access to a digitized archive to help me locate a poet's eulogy in the newspaper *al-Ahram*. Roy Bar Sadeh, John Chen, and Adrien Zakar shared sources, ideas, and advice and talked me through many half-formed thoughts. Liana Valerio, Sara Rahnama, Reem Bailony, Dylan Essertier, and Kristen Alff stood shoulder to shoulder with me in the authorial trenches. From Oxford and Stanford to North London, Arthur Asseraf, Liz Marcus, and Greg Hynes continue to triple-threat as dream neighbors, brilliant historians, and even better friends.

Everywhere this project has taken me, I have been put up, fed, and looked after by people I love. Thanks go especially to Mira Siblini, Jihene Ben Jazia and Hisham Siblini, Ali Issa, Lubna Fakhry and Jonny Hyams, Jehan Allam, Jo Lane and Tony Morris, Jim Johnson and Sarah Willet, Lea, Mari-Ann, Kurt and Marie Claude Larsen Volay, Phil Chambers, Kristen and Warren Brown, Jeanne Terrier, Isabelle De St Antoine, Steele Sternberg, Laurie Pascual, Jenine Abboushi, Sheza Abboushi-Dallal, Munir and Nadim Atalla, and Juliette Massot for their generous hospitality, which made so much of the research, writing, conferencing, and conceiving of *East of Empire* possible.

Over the years I have also received significant financial support from a variety of sources for training, travel, research, and writing related to the completion of this project. These include a T. E. Lawrence–All Souls scholarship in Middle Eastern history, a Mary Le Messurier award from the Canadian Centennial Scholarship Fund, multiple bursaries and awards from St Antony's College, a Beit Trust research scholarship in imperial history, a British Academy postdoctoral fellowship, and a Marie Skłodowska-Curie European research fellowship. I am grateful to every funding body that continues to invest in the humanities and every committee member who opted to invest in me.

My family has bent over backward to champion my work and sustain me in the midst of it. In addition to every conceivable support during and after grad school, the blazing certainty of my parents' belief propelled me through the darkest stretches. My father-in-law Paul tore through the first draft with his characteristic alacrity, grilling me for hours on every chapter. His exacting feedback made the manuscript tighter, clearer, and far more accessible to nonspecialists than I ever would have managed on my own. My mother-in-law, Diana, may have gone easier on my writing but has been no less ferocious in her love and support. During the bleak Canadian winters of the pandemic, my brother Donovan and sister-in-law Raquel were a lifeline, keeping my husband and I intellectually challenged, aching with laughter, and perpetually stuffed to the gills with fabulous food. My aunt Susan and cousin Kellie walked the length and breadth of the frozen west end with me on writing breaks. My magnificent friends called, wrote, cooked, showed up with coffee, sent encouraging cards and flowers, and when crisis struck even stayed overnight to help me keep writing. Similarly, the Soka Gakkai communities of Oxford, Palo Alto, Toronto, Cambridge, and North

London, and Shiva Lila in Beirut, have been the solid ground I could root into no matter what number relocation we were on.

I will not here enumerate the infinite ways in which my husband, Nick, has supported me and this project throughout the past decade—it would sound too much like bragging. It is enough to say that I frequently beam inwardly at having found and married him before anyone else could.

The final stages of this process were among the most intense. Rashid Khalidi emailed out of the blue asking where the book was, rousing me from months of stasis; Tony Morris, Zvi Ben-Dor Benite, and Nile Green all offered late-stage encouragement and assistance when it was sorely needed. Not for the first or last time, Faisal Devji pinch-hit on zero notice when I had to discuss a rash of new ideas very late in the game. My colleagues at the Cambridge Heritage Research Centre and the McDonald Institute for Archaeological Research have been nothing short of incredible; thanks go in particular to Dacia Viejo-Rose, Andreas Pantazatos, Cyprian Broodbank, and Matt Davies, who have unstintingly backed the modern historian in their midst. I could not feel luckier to work with them all.

My editors Kate Wahl and Margo Irvin are due particular thanks for their enthusiastic support as we navigated one unforeseen circumstance after another. Thane Hale guided me through the vagaries of copyright law with efficiency and tact, while Gigi Mark and Athena Lakri patiently combed my unruly intercultural text, standardizing spelling, grammar, and formatting. Both anonymous reviewers nominated by Stanford University Press provided wonderful criticism and thoughtful suggestions that helped to elevate the narrative and sharpen my arguments. Erin Greb created the beautiful map that has finally placed Egypt and India back on the same page, literally. In her role as series editor, Priya Satia went above and beyond, pushing me to think harder and dig deeper. As someone profoundly influenced and inspired by Priya's work over the course of many years, getting to work with her in this way has been a dream come true.

By now it is glaringly apparent that I have benefited from every possible advantage and assistance in the completion of my work, making any remaining faults or flaws utterly and inescapably mine. I look forward to hearing about them (though Paul will probably beat everyone else to it).

This book is dedicated to my mentors: a lineage of Buddhist humanists, educational reformers, and peace activists who all lived during the period documented in this book. From Japan, Tsunesaburo Makiguchi and Josei Toda went through similar processes and experiences to those of my Indian and Egyptian protagonists, fusing their global consciousness and progressive ideals with Eastern culture and Buddhist philosophy. Incarcerated by the Japanese regime for their beliefs, Makiguchi died in prison in 1944; Toda emerged awakened to a higher calling and determined to rebuild Japan as a just and peaceful society. By 1957 his movement, the Soka Gakkai, comprised over 750,000 households.

Shortly before his death, Toda told his disciple, Daisaku Ikeda, that he had dreamt he was in Mexico, where people were waiting eagerly to learn about Buddhism. His testament to the younger man was clear: Travel the world. Teach people everywhere to chant *Nam-myoho-renge-kyo* and become happy. And that is exactly what my Sensei did.

3 May 2024
London

NOTE ON TRANSLATION AND TRANSLITERATION

One of my best-loved memories of my Nana is watching her read my first scholarly publication on the porch at our family cottage in Muskoka, Canada. Halfway through the chapter, she looked up, pulled down her reading glasses, and asked me, "Now—how do you pronounce G-H-A-D-R?"

In her honor, when preparing this manuscript for publication, I attempted to make all nonstandard transliterations as accessible as possible for English readers—thus Saiza Nabarawi, not Céza Nabaraoui. Where relevant, I kept the spelling close to how a person would have pronounced their own name: Gomaa, not Jum'a for an Egyptian, but Jauhar, not Gohar, for an Indian. In those cases where a common English spelling exists, I went with that, despite the resulting internal discrepancies—thus Muhammad Ali Jinnah, but also Mehmet Ali, Mohamed Ali Jauhar, and Sultan Mahomed Shah.

I chose to remove the apostrophes normally used to denote 'ayns and hamzas as unnecessary for Arabic speakers and unintelligible to everyone else. In one case, although it is nonstandard, I added an apostrophe to the last name Fat'h to prevent the *t* and *h* from blending, as they otherwise would in English.

Experts will be relieved to know that the references and bibliography accord more closely with scholarly conventions for non-English citation and transliteration.

Unless otherwise stated, translations from Arabic, French, Italian, and Urdu are my own. Where citations refer to bilingual documents (as is often the case in UK archives), I have clarified if I retranslated the original.

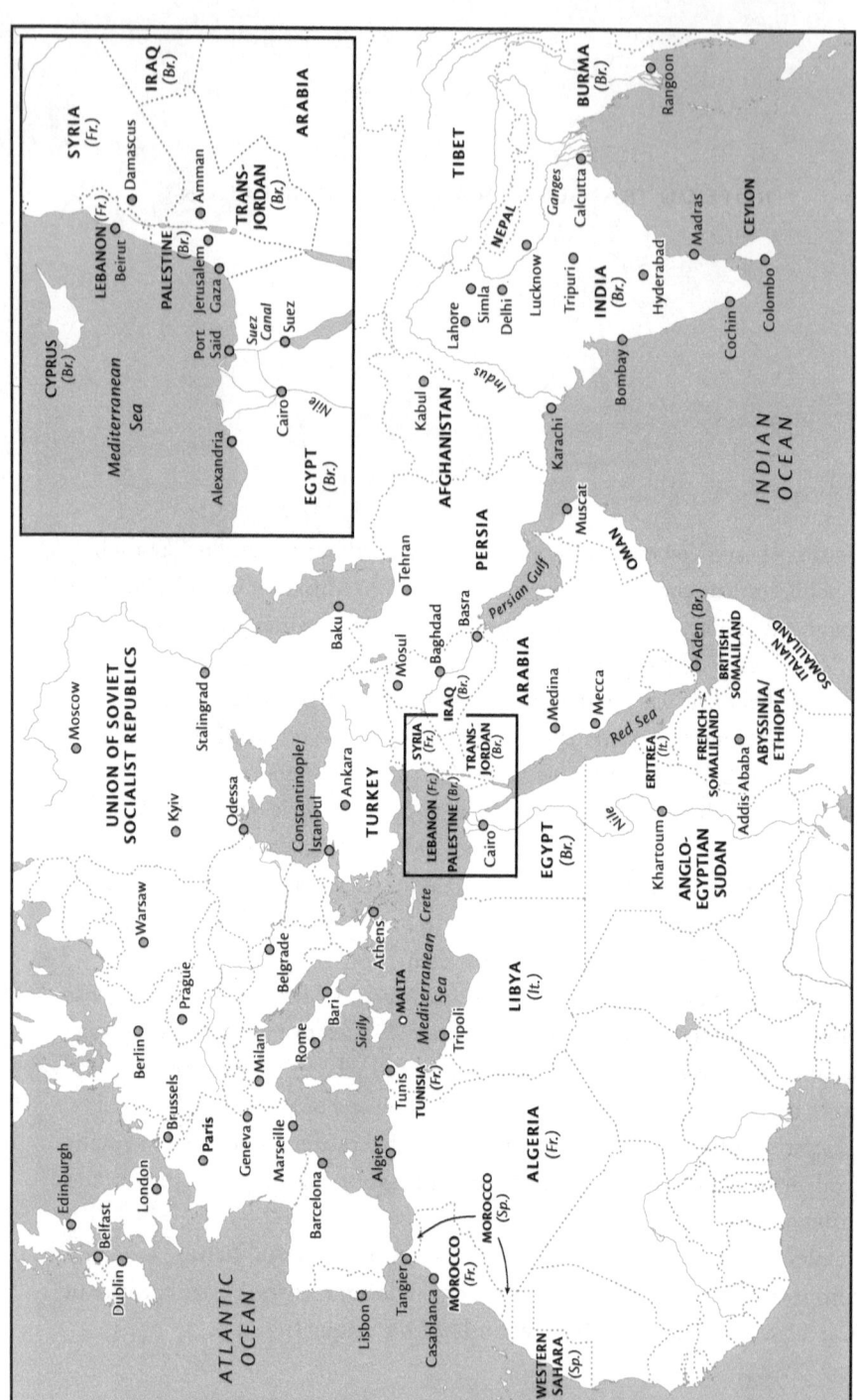

MAP I The World East of Empire, ca. 1930

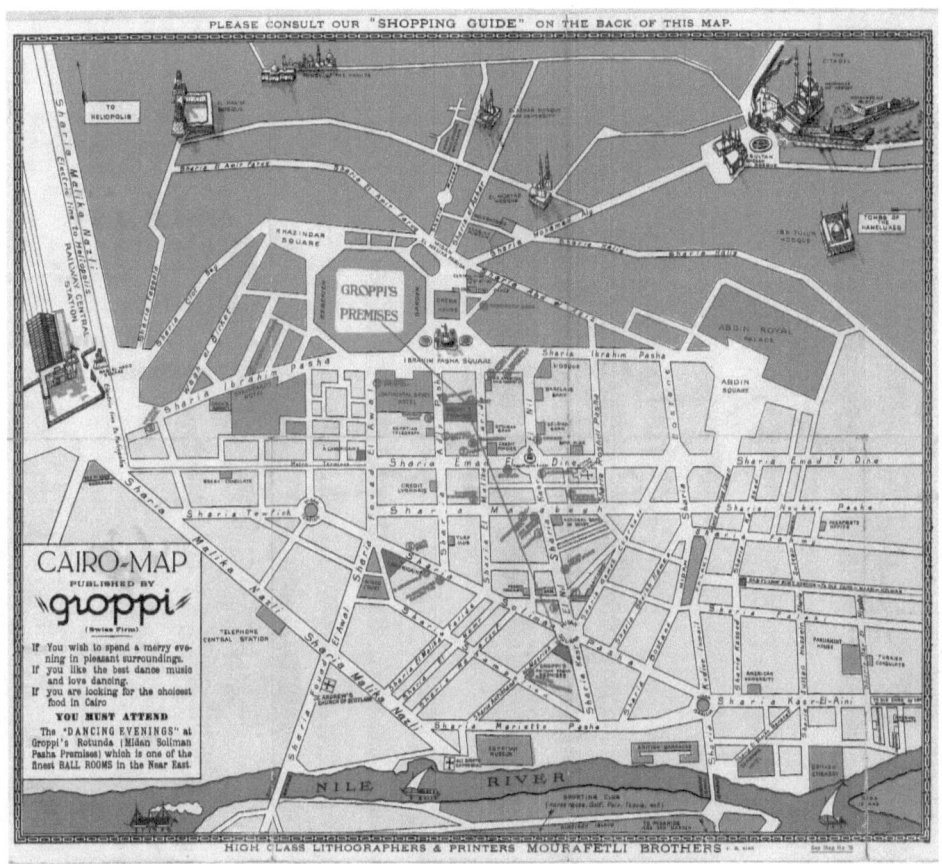

MAP 2 A tourist map of Cairo distributed by Groppi's, a popular cafe, ca. 1930. With its prime location in Ezbekiyeh Gardens, Groppi's was situated on the demarcation line between the new European arrondissements and the much larger, more ancient city that stood "behind" them. Map created by the Mourafetli Brothers, Cairo. Collection of the author.

EAST OF EMPIRE

Introduction

In the spring of 1939, as the wheels of European diplomacy began careening off the rails, the Indian National Congress (INC) played host to a delegation of Egyptian statesmen on a tour of the subcontinent. While these honored guests were being received by Gandhi in Delhi, two envoys of the All-India Muslim League were shuttling across the capitals of Europe in an increasingly desperate bid to drum up support for the embattled Arabs of Palestine. Within weeks, a leading Indian feminist had arrived in Cairo, where she stayed at the home of a legendary Egyptian activist for women's rights. The envoys of the Muslim League landed back in Egypt around the same time; there they worked alongside Arab ministers and heads of state in a last-ditch effort to convince the Palestinian leadership to accept a new British offer. While all of this was going on, the former (and future) Egyptian Prime Minister Mustafa al-Nahas received a letter from his friend and ally Jawaharlal Nehru in India. It proposed new strategies for bringing their political movements into closer alignment, toward the shared goals of democracy and independence from Britain.[1]

These events—crisscrossing the seaways, rail lines, and telegraph poles between Bombay, Cairo, London, Beirut, Milan, Geneva, Tripuri, and New Delhi—all took place within a span of about ten weeks, but they were decades in the making. *East of Empire* is about those decades: a brief but significant chapter in the much longer history of interaction and exchange between the peoples of the Arabic-speaking world and South Asia.[2] Our story takes place in the interval separating two world wars, during the twilight years of European empire, as alternative visions for the future gained traction and momentum. The men and women who populate these pages moved in the shadows of a gathering storm that would irrevocably transform their lives and the world around them. They also moved, wrote, and thought between what we now tend to think of as discrete regions: Egypt and the Middle East, India and South Asia, Britain and Europe.

In the immediate aftermath of World War I, the British Empire faced a rising tide of nationalist and anticolonial fervor across its empire, from the Caribbean to Southeast Asia;[3] but the epicenter of this upheaval lay in the geographic space connecting Egypt to India. These challenges from within the empire were coupled with an increasingly menacing international geostrategic environment, as authoritarian and expansionist powers emerged on the European continent and in the Pacific. Against this fraught international landscape, *East of Empire* explores the threads connecting Arabs to South Asians: artists, clerics, poets, and diplomats; journalists and activists; statesmen and spies.

Theses transregional relationships took place, as May Hawas has phrased it, "through the grids" of late empire.[4] They have long remained underreported and underappreciated, in part because they can be glimpsed in the historical record only in fragmentary ways, as if by the light of a flickering lamp. Taken together, however, they illuminate the rapid changes then underway across the British Empire and expand our understanding of the development, in the era immediately preceding decolonization, of complementary and competing visions for the future of the Middle East, South Asia, and the broader extra-European world.

The connections that existed between these places had much to do with the context and shared experience of British imperialism; yet by 1919, empire was only one in a multiplying set of axes tying Egypt to India, the Middle East to South Asia, and all of these places to Europe. At the very center of the map lay one city: Cairo. While the plot of this drama will whisk us from the grand hotels of Mayfair to Delhi's garden city, the Egyptian capital—the City Victorious, as its name translates into English—is in many ways the star of the show.

During the interwar years, Cairo emerged as a truly global metropolis. It was the center of a burgeoning Arab diplomatic bloc and the seat of a bid to revive the Islamic Caliphate,[5] the headquarters of a powerful feminist movement,[6] and the acknowledged "jugular vein" of British imperial defense planning. The Suez Canal (and increasingly, Egyptian airfields) served as the vital artery connecting Britain to its Asian and Pacific colonies[7]—a fact of which officials in Delhi and Simla were forever having to remind their less globally minded colleagues in London.[8] By the 1920s, Cairo also boasted the most developed free press and media sectors the Arabic-speaking world had ever seen. Its newspapers, publishing houses, radio, and recording industries catered to diverse readerships and listening audiences that spanned North Africa, the Middle East, and much of the Asian continent. The Muslim press in India, as in Singapore and Malaya, relied on Cairo for news and commentary. Musicians from throughout the Arab-Islamic world came there to record, while students from as far away as China and Japan were enrolled in its prestigious universities.[9] Partly for these reasons, the Egyptian capital became an epicenter of interwar anticolonialism and a host of related isms, among them pan-Islamism, Arab nationalism, feminism, and Easternism (on which, more in a minute). Thus what happened in Cairo mattered not only to Egyptians and Arabs but also to a whole host of actors in other parts of the world, from the English Channel to the Bay of Bengal and even further afield.

Beginning in the 1920s, Cairo, like many colonial cities, underwent a series of major societal, cultural, and political transformations, catalyzed by higher levels of education and literacy, shifting gender norms, increased trade and geopolitical interconnectivity, and the soaring popularity of press and new media—particularly the borderless, instantaneous, and visceral transmissions of broadcast radio.[10] As more and more Egyptians from diverse backgrounds and social classes were empowered to participate in the public life of their country, the discourse surrounding what it meant to be patriotic, modern, and right-thinking—a man or woman "of the times"—began to change.[11] Among the most prominent and well-documented results of this transition was a shift, between the 1920s and 1930s, toward a specifically Arab and Islamic identity;[12] but the expanding reach of media and education also contributed to the empowerment of women,[13] emerging class consciousness among workers,[14] radical new trends in art and literature,[15] and growing awareness of and identification with other Eastern countries: countries that were perceived as sharing an authentic cultural affinity with Egypt, though they were not necessarily Arab or Muslim. This included a strong identification, among a diverse cross section of Egyptian political thinkers and activists, with India and its anticolonial independence movement.[16] Simultaneously, Indian poets, anticolonial nationalists, women's rights activists, and pan-Islamists became increasingly interested and involved in the cultural, religious, and political developments taking place in the Middle East; and so they too found their way to Cairo. Among historians, a debate has emerged about how to explain this apparent cross-pollination and what to call it. In this book, the affinity that tied together a broad cross section of Indians, Egyptians, and other Arabs throughout the interwar period is described as *Easternism*.

Many historians writing about this period have picked up Easternism for closer inspection—only to place it swiftly back down again. They argue that it is too vague, amorphous, and internally contradictory to be of much use as an analytical category.[17] They are not wrong. Between the 1920s and 1940s, there were multiple (perhaps even countless) visions of the East in circulation. To sketch only some of the most prominent variations, there was the East of Orientalists—foreign, exotic, and "other";[18] the Anticolonial East—a geography of allies in the battle against foreign domination;[19] the Spiritual East—often juxtaposed against the Materialist West;[20] the Islamic East—a region populated largely (though never exclusively) by Muslims;[21] the Cosmopolitan East—a rich tapestry of cultures bound together by commerce and ideational exchange;[22] and the Strategic East—a geopolitical bloc or bulwark that might counter other constellations of power.[23]

It is important to underscore that none of these concepts were mutually exclusive; rather proponents of Easternism tended to connect several typologies together into a personally appealing hybrid. Thus in his memoirs, the Aga Khan revisited his long-cherished dream of an Eastern bloc of Muslim nations, serving as both a moral compass to the world and a healthy check on the power of Europe and the United States.[24] For the Egyptian feminist Huda Shaarawi, the East was unapologetically anticolonial; in the pages of her magazine, *l'Egyptienne*, it was frequently ancient and exotic; but it was also, crucially, a stage upon which women from many cultural, ethnic, and religious backgrounds would together forge the future in their image.

Given the dizzying array of potential Easts, it was never what academics would call a "coherent" political or intellectual project; this did not prevent it from being a highly prominent feature of both political discourse and political action in Egypt, India, and the broader Arab-Asian region throughout the interwar period. Easternism was, moreover, an intellectual, literary, artistic, and pop-culture phenomenon—employing what were at times stereotypical portrayals of "ancient" or "exotic" lands that excited Indian and Egyptian imaginations no less than European ones.[25] As we will find at a conference held in Jerusalem in 1931, pan-Islamic activities could be Easternist, for the East could be construed as a predominantly Muslim space, just as pan-Asianists in Japan imagined it as an essentially Buddhist one—and just as both looked to and embraced Hindu figures like Gandhi and Tagore as "authentically Eastern" regardless.[26]

Thus while conceding the obvious validity of intellectual critiques of Easternism, I have nevertheless found it an impossible term to part with, for the simple reason that an amazing cross section of Egyptians and Indians from radically different cultural and intellectual backgrounds have articulated their affinity as peoples of the Sharq, Orient, or East. In doing so, they claimed to belong to something larger than nation, language, religion, or ethnicity, while simultaneously embracing aspects of many of these identities. Acknowledging the broad sweep that Easternism sought to embrace, some authors have argued that when people spoke about the East, what they were actually gesturing toward was an ecumenical space of anticolonial solidarity that stood in opposition to Western imperialism.[27] Again there is a great deal of truth in this—Easternism certainly was anticolonial, if not all then at least most of the time—and yet this was still, as I have tried to elucidate, only one of its many registers. I have not felt justified in reducing Easternism to its anticolonial politics, given that "the East" clearly evoked both more and less than an alliance against empire for many of the people who wrote and spoke and moved about it over the course of many years.

There were Easts—a great many Easts—that were imagined, and then there was the East that was to some extent built. This book is not an intellectual history of Easternism (although fortunately for us all, rigorous scholarly work of this kind is underway).[28] Instead Easternism here serves as an admittedly untidy "way in" to the equally untidy web of real-world connections that bound together two culturally, linguistically, and geographically distinct countries—Egypt and India—between World Wars I and II. The many competing ideas and ideologies that swirled around these relations—British imperialism, nationalism and feminism, anticolonialism and pan-Islam, socialism and Easternism—frequently merged, overlapped, or clashed. They are all vital instruments for making sense of the action; but, I hasten to add, they are not, in and of themselves, the point.

In considering the influence, competition, and confluence of ideas like empire, nation, pan-Islam, feminism, socialism, anticolonialism, and the East over the course of two and a half decades, my aim is not to delineate the frontiers between these ideas or otherwise parse one from the other. As we will see (and as we no doubt know from our own experiences), complex worldviews were frequently recast in alternating registers and vocabularies, as circumstances or audiences might require (in some ways comparable to what we might now call code-switching). Thus the Abyssinian Crisis (subject of chapter 4) inspired widespread expressions of racialized anticolonial solidarity with the Christian African kingdom of Ethiopia; within a year, the outbreak of a revolt against the British administration in Palestine (subject of chapters 5 and 6) prompted many of the same people to discover the depths of their common bonds as Arabs or Muslims.

There were those—the poet Muhammad Iqbal, the feminists Huda Shaarawi and Kamaladevi Chattopadhyay, and of course the Hindu universalist Mohandas K. Gandhi—whose ideas and ideals were more fixed. They were, and are, exceptional instances of activist philosophers, informed more by the content of their principles than the vagaries of the world around them; yet as we will see, even Gandhi was forced to bend before the gale-force winds of change that engulfed the globe during World War II.

By contrast, the pragmatists—those willing to equivocate for the sake of political expediency, or indeed survival—were legion.[29] Trying to pin down the fixed content of their worldviews is, as one of my anonymous reviewers helpfully offered, "like nailing jelly to a wall." What is apparent is that in the highly charged context of the mid-1930s and early 1940s, almost any political stance or ideological commitment involved some level of internal contradiction. Thus prioritizing anticolonial or Arab nationalist commitments seems to have resulted not infrequently in collusion with Fascist Italy, whose own colonial exploits and oppression of Muslims were infamous. Similarly Indian and Arab nationalists who felt antifascism was paramount found themselves in the unlikely position of siding with the British Empire in its war against Hitler. On a handful of issues, notably the escalating crisis in British Mandate Palestine, the interests and priorities of many actors converged across a broad Easternist spectrum; on others, like the competing political currents of liberal empire and fascist totalitarianism, they parted like the Red Sea.

Throughout the 1920s and deep into the 1930s, a multiplicity of heterodox Eastern visions flowed in and out of alignment with one another as headlines changed, alliances evolved, and priorities shifted. With the onset of war in Europe in 1939, however, the stakes of these ideological differences began to spike. Subjected to the unrelenting pressure of war, the many strands of Easternism splintered, putting paid to the more fluid and open-ended possibilities that had animated preceding decades. In their stead emerged postwar ideologies with sharper edges, hardened national frontiers, and—following years of globally cataclysmic violence—little faith in the pacifist and humanist ideals of a bygone era. This almost chemical transformation is the background against which votes affirmed the partitions of India and Palestine in 1947, unleashing torrents of interpersonal violence and ethnic cleansing, which we have yet to staunch almost eighty years on. This, then, is the story I wish to tell: how a multiplicity of visions of a transnational, fluid, and heterodox East informed the interwar politics and diplomacy of India and Egypt—and under what conditions these visions gave way to militant nationalism, territorial partition, and large-scale ethnic cleansing across both the Middle East and South Asia.

Within this overarching narrative there are many smaller (but, I hope readers will agree, no less fascinating) stories: about the personal connections and ideational affinities forged between poets, feminists, artists, and politicians; the Khilafat crisis in India and its intra-Arab fallout; the anticolonial outrage and propaganda war that defined the Abyssinian Crisis (and presaged the dynamics of World War II); and how Indian Muslims and Eastern women fought to internationalize the Palestinian cause. I also revisit some of the more famous (and infamous) incidents from the national historiographies of Egypt, India-Pakistan, and Palestine-Israel, revealing transnational aspects and entanglements between them that have long remained obscure.[30]

The result is a political history, but one that takes a very broad view of the political—touching on art, poetry, religion, and the power of ideas as well as grassroots activism, interparty rivalries, military strategy, and conference diplomacy. I aim to give the reader something of the texture of the times and places we are moving through, and to trace not the deterministic influence of one factor over others but the constellation of mutually informing forces at work in complex colonial societies undergoing truly momentous, world-changing transition.[31]

LOCATING THE EAST

This is a book about India-Pakistan and the Middle East, sometimes also referred to as South and West Asia. Except that—whatever ancient Greeks or modern experts may claim to mean by *Asia*—Egyptians did not (and generally do not) think of themselves as Asians. More to the point and in marked contrast to their Indian counterparts, Egyptians of the interwar years forged vanishingly few concrete ties with East or Southeast Asia (this despite a rash of Japanophilia after 1905,[32] and the efforts of some Chinese Muslims to forge ties with Egypt).[33] Thus India still represented, in the period I am writing about, a frontier of Egypt's known East, which also embraced Turkey, Persia, the Levant, and the Arab Gulf.

This may seem like a quibble, but it is one of the key reasons why the hazy cultural and geographic boundaries of Easternism are so indispensable to making sense of Egyptian-Indian ties and why, by comparison, *Pan-Asianism* is a term of very limited utility for understanding what Egyptians thought they had in common with Indians. Reversing the question, Pan-Asianism holds more explanatory power for Indians, who tended to view Egypt as an appendage—albeit an important one—to India's natural Asian sphere of action and influence. In this conception, Egypt was a far western edge of Pan-Asia; especially for Nehru and Congress, the Egyptians were their chosen plus-ones to the continental party.[34] Turning to representatives of the All-India Muslim League working to forge ties with Egyptian and other Arab politicians, their perceived affinity was unambiguous: Muslims everywhere were conceived as part of the global *umma*, or community of believers. In this, the Muslim League's leadership placed a great deal of stock as not only a spiritual bond but a basis for common political action.[35] This was to be a source of much friction and misunderstanding, for on the whole, Egyptian and Arab nationalists did not share Indian Muslims' enthusiasm for pan-Islam; even Egyptian clerics motivated enough to send a delegation to the subcontinent managed to offend their hosts.[36] Hopefully this goes some way to illustrating that, as with many lovers, Egyptians and Indians engaged in shared admiration, cultural and political activities in the 1920s and 1930s did not necessarily see one another as they were but rather as they hoped to see themselves.[37]

In interrogating the kaleidoscopic element of this mutual gaze and its many implications for South Asian and Middle Eastern politics, this book breaks new ground, while also extending a line of inquiry initiated by Noor Khan's *Egyptian-Indian Nationalist Collaboration and the British Empire*, which appeared in 2011. Since then, it has remained the only book-length academic study on relations between Egyptians and Indians during the interwar years;[38] naturally it has profoundly influenced the present work.

Temporally, Khan begins her story in the late nineteenth century and concludes in 1939 (roughly twice the length of time dealt with here). Her book traces the links between secular nationalist currents and individuals who, by the 1920s, formed the core of the Indian National Congress and Egyptian Wafd parties. Khan's focus is exclusively on the Egyptian side of the narrative, in particular the influence of Gandhi, Nehru, and Congress on the nationalist politics of the Wafd.

Khan's study remains invaluable, and our ideas converge in many places; one where they part company is her use of the term *anti-imperial* to describe Congress-Wafd ties. Khan usefully distinguishes *anti-imperialism*, which she defines as a principled rejection of empire in all its guises, from *anticolonialism*, by which she means opposition to the domination of one's own country by a colonial power.[39] While readily accepting this distinction, I am less convinced this term can be uncritically applied to the Wafd, given its role in advancing a mainstream nationalist demand for Egyptian control over the Sudan throughout the interwar years. As Eve Troutt Powell and Rami Ginat have demonstrated, belief in Egypt's civilizational superiority and "natural right" to the Sudan was widespread, integral to Wafdist nationalism, and persisted into the 1950s.[40] Indeed, one of Mustafa al-Nahas's key breakthroughs in negotiations with the British, reflected in the 1936 Anglo-Egyptian Treaty (discussed in chapter 4), was the return of Egyptian soldiers and colonists to the Sudan. For these reasons Wafd leaders like Nahas and his predecessor, Saad Zaghlul, do not strike me as clearcut anti-imperialists; the term *anticolonial* as defined by Khan seems perfectly apt. In the case of the Wafd (and in almost all others), I prefer *anticolonial*, as leaving the question of consistency in principles conspicuously open.

More broadly and again in contrast to the framing of *Egyptian-Indian Nationalist Collaboration and the British Empire*, this book faithfully reflects my profound skepticism of the nation-state as the inevitable or even the best available receptacle for anticolonial aspirations post-1919.[41] In what follows I take seriously the "religious connections and vague assertions of Easternism" Khan passed over,[42] and the space they opened for alternative imaginaries of a more peaceful, prosperous, and equal world—a world depicted as lying somewhere east of existing systems of empire. These political imaginaries and projects were far more persistent than they are normally given credit for: it was not until the crises of the war years that the futures they projected were definitively foreclosed. For this reason my "interwar" narrative extends beyond 1939 and into the 1940s, to more fully account for their eclipse.

A final key distinction of the present volume is the extent to which it situates the discussion of interwar Egyptian-Indian relations within broader regional and transnational contexts (the "world" alluded to in the book's subtitle). The result is a study that, although ostensibly about Egypt and India, devotes significant attention to events elsewhere, from Paris and London to Ankara and Addis Ababa, and—in almost every chapter—the deepening crisis in Egypt's neighbor, Palestine. To me these events form the essential background (and in the case of Palestine, increasingly the foreground) of Egyptian-Indian relations; the more I read and thought and wrote, the more inextricably they seemed bound. It is perhaps fitting that in writing a book that engages with fluid, "borderless" imaginaries of the East, the narrative itself ultimately proved impossible to contain within national frontiers.

ITINERARY

The book is organized as four parts, comprising ten chapters and an epilogue, which proceed chronologically. Part 1, "Imagining the East," opens in the spring of 1919 at the Paris Peace Conference and concludes at the World Islamic Congress held in Jerusalem in December 1931. The first three chapters chart the rise of anticolonial nationalism, liberal cosmopolitanism, socialist internationalism, and pan-Islamism across Egypt and India throughout the 1920s. They draw on poetry, literature, posters, songs, conference proceedings, newspapers, monuments, sacred architecture, funerary rites, and places of burial as some of the myriad ways in which Indians and Egyptians articulated their national identities alongside and in dialogue with their perceived interconnection as Easterners.

Part 2, "Capital of the East," opens with the 1935 Abyssinian Crisis and closes in 1938, in the middle of the Arab Revolt in Palestine. During this brief period Cairo catapulted to greater prominence as both a strategic lynchpin of the British Empire and an Arab, Islamic, and anticolonial metropole. The chapters primarily draw on state and press archives, diaries, and correspondence to consider reactions to Mussolini's invasion of Ethiopia and the anti-British uprising in Palestine, and how each event gave rise to differing constellations, vocabularies, and fault lines of Eastern solidarity. These crises also spurred elaborate propaganda campaigns and debates over antifascism versus anticolonial solidarity in Egypt and India—both of which would later reemerge as decisive factors during World War II.

Part 3, "Ambassadors of the East," brings archives into conversation with personal histories and memoirs to present a series of interlocking stories about formal and informal Indian-Arab diplomacy in the years immediately preceding World War II. These chapters trace the engagement of Muslim Leaguers, Congressmen, and a Congress feminist with their Egyptian and Arab counterparts as they maneuvered between domestic agendas, the ongoing crisis in Palestine, and the looming war in Europe. Though they found causes for skepticism in their appraisals of Egyptian nationalists, Indians repeatedly overcame this reluctance, in part due to the symbolic significance they ascribed to an Eastern alliance with a prominent Arab-Muslim country. The potential depth of that alliance is glimpsed in the joint action of Egyptian and Indian feminists during an international conference in the fated summer of 1939.

Part 4, "The East at War," traces a crescendo of wartime shocks, and the multiplying cultural and political fault lines that they both exposed and exacerbated. Against the backdrop of the Nazi occupation of Europe, the Desert War, and Japan's lightning advance toward India, these chapters document the buckling and ultimately the fragmentation of interwar Easternism amid the immense heat and pressure of war. What ultimately emerged from the wreckage post-1945 was more militant, statist nationalisms—becoming the new political orthodoxy across much of the decolonizing world.

But let's not get too far ahead of ourselves. For now, it's still 1919. A world war has just ended, and there won't be another one for years.

PART I IMAGINING THE EAST

ONE

Morning in Cairo

> The East has risen from its deep slumber;
> destiny has given it fresh aspirations
> and loosened its ancient chains.[1]
> —MUHAMMAD IQBAL, 1936

On the morning of 9 March 1919, an Egyptian lady awoke, as she did most mornings, in the beautiful house at Number Two, Qasr al-Nil—one of Cairo's grandest boulevards. Huda Shaarawi was a self-possessed woman of forty, wealthy, elegant, and impeccably educated. It was early spring, the first since the armistice that had ended World War I. The first when one might dare to believe that the nightmare was finally over.

The Great War had wreaked havoc on the lives of ordinary people and proud empires alike. The Hapsburgs were ruined, the Hohenzollerns ousted, the Romanovs executed in cold blood. The Ottoman Empire, the last of Eurasia's great Muslim thrones, was being dismantled by the victorious Allies as Shaarawi stirred her coffee. Change was coming, was already at the door. The taut sense of anticipation, suspended somewhere between hope for the best and fear of the worst, must have been difficult to bear.

Would Britain now leave Egypt? Would the leaders amassed in Paris actually bow before their incessantly repeated maxim of self-determination? After decades (in some places, centuries) of foreign occupation and colonial rule, was liberation finally at hand?

Of course, in most of the extra-European world, the answer was to be No: Not really, not yet, not at all. In Egypt, India, and a great many other countries, the fragile optimism that had attended the armistice was about to give way to revolt.

As Shaarawi took her breakfast on that fateful morning and prepared for her day, she could not have known it, but Cairo would never be the same again—and neither, for that matter, would she.

EMPIRE AND REBELLION IN THE NINETEENTH CENTURY

To make sense of the momentous developments about to unfold, it is worth sketching the earlier history of British rule in Egypt and India. As the Indian story is older, and informed subsequent developments in Egypt, let us start there.

Initially, the British East India Company (EIC) was just one of several European commercial charters operating on the Indian subcontinent. In the early seventeenth century, however, it began to consolidate its position through a series of military exploits and predatory legal maneuvers. The Doctrine of Lapse, invented by the EIC's courts and wielded most infamously by Lord Dalhousie, allowed for EIC annexation of Indian princely states in cases where the sovereign was deemed (again, by the EIC itself) "manifestly unfit to rule," or if they had died without a male heir apparent.[2] At the Battle of Plassey in 1757, the defeat of the Nawab of Bengal and his French allies inaugurated a century of what became known as Company Rule. In time, the running of the state and in particular the voracious acquisition of territory would result in an inverse of the Company's priorities: whereas once it had been a commercial venture with a private army, it morphed gradually into a military regime with an exports division.[3]

By the end of the Napoleonic Wars in 1815, the EIC boasted one of the largest standing armies on the planet with 155,000 troops. The vast majority of these men were locally recruited "sepoys," an English corruption of the Urdu *sipahi* or *soldier*. In 1857, the centennial year of the victory at Plassey, Company Rule was brought to a dramatic close when these sepoys triggered a large-scale rebellion—or mutiny, to use the term that would burn itself indelibly into the British historical imagination.

The Rebellion of 1857 began in Meerut, a garrison town outside of Delhi, between 10 and 11 May. The ostensible spark was the newly issued service rifle, the Enfield, which required soldiers to bite the lids off of cartridges, rumored to be greased with cow and pig fat (offensive to both Hindu and Muslim sensibilities).[4] In reality, Indian sepoys could point to a host of economic and political grievances, from high rates of taxation to Christian evangelism to the Company's increasingly brazen land grabs—most recently the princely state of Oudh, a major center of recruitment for the Bengal Army. Much as the American Revolution was only tangentially about tea, the Indian Rebellion probably had more to do with this slow compounding of injustices and indignities than it did with gun cartridges.

At Meerut, eighty-five sepoys were arrested and court martialed for refusing to load the new Enfield rifle during firing drills. When most of these men were handed life sentences, the forces garrisoned at Meerut erupted. They killed their officers, broke their comrades out of prison, and marched on Delhi. The rebellion spread quickly, catching the Company off guard and galvanizing widespread popular resistance.[5] Rebels appointed the Mughal emperor in Delhi their figurehead and declared the revival of Hindustan. The dispossessed rulers of territories swallowed by the EIC also took up arms—including Lakshmibai, the Rani of Jhansi, robbed of her kingdom under the Doctrine of Lapse for having been born a woman. She died leading her troops into battle on horseback, in an episode that was to have long and powerful resonance for India's female freedom fighters down the ages.[6]

In both British and Indian accounts of the rebellion, it was remembered chiefly for the hideous violence it engendered. British newspapers were flooded with macabre accounts of murdered women and children, particularly during the infamous Siege of Cawnpore, when the brutalized cadavers of Company wives were found discarded in the town wells. Within months of the outbreak, British forces were diverted from other parts of the empire to help stamp out the rebellion. Once the tide had turned, these soldiers exacted vicious revenge. The deaths meted out to Indian rebels were specifically designed to inflict spiritual trauma: Hindus were sown into the bodies of cows, Muslims into pigs, rendering them ritually unclean. They were fired from the mouths of cannons, obliterating their bodies and preventing funerary rites or proper burial. Through such acts of calculated barbarism was the revolt put down in 1858.

Almost before the blood was dry, British rewriting and mythologizing of The Mutiny began. In the official memory, "religious fanaticism" would come to be blamed for the violence—thus eliding the social, economic, and political dimensions of the uprising, not to mention the cooperation between Hindus and Muslims that had characterized it.[7] Yet even as this element of intercommunal solidarity was broadly overlooked in formal recollection and analysis, the ghosts of 1857 proved difficult to dispel. Moving forward, Hindu-Muslim collaboration remained the nightmare scenario in official imaginations, even if, like a childhood trauma, the fear had been disconnected from its inciting event. Much official energy was spent in maintaining and deepening the social and political separation between Indian religious communities, while simultaneously insisting that this distinction was naturally occurring—for Hindus and Muslims were incapable of cooperating and had certainly never done so in the past.

For many Indians, meanwhile, 1857–58 marked the mutilated death of a dream that had briefly seemed within reach. In its wake Britain's hold on India was consolidated, as the EIC was disbanded and its territories came under direct rule by the Crown. But the suppression of the rebellion had shown beyond any shadow of doubt that, irrespective of the fine words and sentiments expressed by Queen Victoria (Empress of India, as she was henceforward styled), British rule was to be underwritten by violence of the most ferocious cruelty.

Let us turn westward to Egypt, then ruled by the descendants of Mehmed Ali, an Albanian Commander of the Ottoman Army who seized control of the country at the beginning of the nineteenth century. Though formally Egypt remained an Ottoman province, after 1805 Mehmed Ali was its ruler, a title retained by his heirs. Following his death they carried forward Ali's vision of a modern, centrally administered state, significantly expanding the functions of government and cementing Cairo's role at the heart of the new order.[8]

The cost of these ambitious state-building projects was monumentally increased by the predatory rates Egypt's rulers were offered by European creditors and compounded by the extravagance of Mehmed Ali's grandson, Khedive Ismail. The crowning achievements of Ismail's reign would prove ruinous to the country's economy, as Egypt paid (and Egyptian laborers died) to dig the Suez Canal—brainchild of the French engineer Ferdinand de Lesseps and cherished dream of European merchants and military strategists eager to connect the Mediterranean and Indian Oceans.[9] Completed in 1869, the opening of the canal was accompanied by celebrations attended by the luminaries and crowned heads of Europe. Preparations included the wholesale construction—at breakneck speed—of several new districts of Cairo, reimagined as a glittering, "Haussmannized" capital city.[10]

Combined with a failed expansionist military campaign in Ethiopia, the canal and the renovation of Cairo bankrupted the Egyptian economy. Ismail was forced to sell his shares in the Suez Canal Company to the British government and acquiesce in an Anglo-French takeover of the country's finances to oversee repayment of Egypt's debts. The Caisse de la Dette, as this committee was known, was established in 1876 and deposed Ismail three years later on the grounds of financial mismanagement—conveniently leaving European creditors in control of the country and its priceless new canal.[11]

Ismail's successor, his son Tewfik, was perceived by many as the plaything of these financial overseers. Egypt's pecuniary bondage left it vulnerable to Ottoman revanchism, as the Sultan sought to hem in the Egyptian army. A rebellion that began among disgruntled military officers under the leadership of Colonel Ahmad Bey Urabi quickly grew, tapping into popular resentment and pitting the upper echelons of society against the mass of the people. Urabi briefly succeeded in establishing himself and his allies in government, but the reforms they proposed to the constitution and the management of the Egyptian economy were too threatening to European interests. In 1882 British warships bombed Alexandria into submission. Unable to best Urabi's army in the field at Qassassin, British forces attacked them in their beds at Tel el-Kebir. What began that September as a "temporary" occupation would last, in one form or another, until the withdrawal of the last British troops from Suez in 1956.[12]

EARLY TWENTIETH-CENTURY CRISES AND THE RISE OF NATIONALIST PARTIES

For several decades after its suppression of the Urabi Revolt, Britain maintained the pretense that Egypt was an autonomous province of the Ottoman Empire; but everyone, from the diplomatic corps in Cairo to the peasants of the Delta, knew that Britain was actually in charge. The longer Britain held Egypt, the more essential it came to appear to imperial defense and communications. This was in large part due to the Suez Canal, which became the vital artery connecting Britain's fleet in the Mediterranean to its vast holdings in the East—especially India. From the beginning, then, Egypt was linked to India in the British imperial imagination, as it was in terms of strategy, defense, logistics, and communications. And for twenty-five years, from 1883 to 1907, British rule in Egypt was embodied in the person of a former servant of the British Raj: Evelyn Baring, the First Earl of Cromer. Cromer had served on the Caisse de la Dette for several years prior to the British invasion of Egypt, and he spent two significant stints in India, where he had worked at the side of the Viceroy. Historians Robert Tignor and Roger Owen have both argued that Cromer's time in India was crucial in shaping his subsequent term as Consul General in Egypt, which saw him draw heavily on administrative practices and personnel from the British Raj.[13] As part of this process, the system of local elections that had functioned in Egypt since the 1860s was abolished—on the grounds that Egyptians were too "fanatically" religious to participate in their own governance.[14] All of this stoked the development of anticolonial nationalism.

The first openly anti-British publications in Egypt, among them *al-Muayyad* and *al-Liwa*, were sponsored by the young Khedive Abbas Hilmi. Hilmi ascended the throne in 1892 at the age of eighteen and almost immediately came up against the limitations on his rule imposed by Cromer. The editor of *al-Liwa*, Mustafa Kamil, was a lawyer educated in France who sought to enlist French and international support for Egypt's nascent nationalist movement.[15] However none of Kamil's or Hilmi's advocacy was as effective as the British themselves in provoking popular opposition.

In June 1906, a group of officers on a hunting expedition near the village of Denshawai fell into an altercation with locals who objected to the shooting of their pigeons, an important source of food. In the midst of the scuffle, the officers wounded the wife of the village imam, and the conflict escalated. One of the party attempted to run back to the British camp but collapsed and later died, probably of heat exhaustion. A villager attempted to help but was set upon and killed by British soldiers arriving at the scene, who assumed him responsible for their comrade's death. The occupation authorities responded hysterically: fifty-two residents of Denshawai were tried for the murder of a man who had succumbed to the violence of the midday sun. Within a fortnight, four of these unfortunate souls had been hanged, with a further eight sentenced to public flogging and twelve to hard labor. News of the incident at Denshawai and the flagrant injustice of the trial provoked widespread outrage, and in the wake of the incident the cause of Egyptian nationalism as propounded by Mustafa Kamil and others—notably Ahmad Lutfi al-Sayyid, the attorney for the defense in the Denshawai trial—gained rapid and impassioned political momentum.[16]

The Denshawai controversy also inflamed liberal opinion in Britain, particularly among Irish, Scottish, and socialist politicians and activists, who were increasingly plugged into international anticolonial networks. The Irish Member of Parliament John Dillon dogged the Foreign Secretary, Sir Edward Grey, with questions about the incident while George Bernard Shaw, W.B. Yeats, and J. Ramsay MacDonald circulated a petition for the release and pardon of the Denshawai prisoners. Facing anger in Egypt and censure at home, Cromer retired; his successor, Eldon Gorst, sought to placate the Khedive and popular opinion through gestures toward eventual self-government. Chief among the new concessions, introduced in 1907, was the legalization of political parties, ushering in a "new national era" in Egypt.[17] Among the first and most important parties to be founded that year were Kamil's Hizb al-Watani, or Nationalist Party, and Hizb al-Umma, the People's Party, in which Lutfi al-Sayyid played a leading role. These two parties would represent the main currents of Egyptian nationalist politics up until the Revolution of 1919, and their influence would continue to be felt long after.

Mustafa Kamil died in 1908, mere months after founding the Watani Party. His funeral was the cause of intense public mourning. His political successor, Muhammad Farid, was a lawyer from a wealthy, land-owning family who had sacrificed his fortune in the service of the nationalist cause. The editorship of *al-Liwa* passed to Sheikh Abd al-Aziz Jawish, who became infamous for his attacks on Egypt's Coptic minority and anti-British vitriol. Under his direction, *al-Liwa* became increasingly affiliated with Islamist and pro-Ottoman sentiments, and it (along with the Watani Party) lost many of its more moderate supporters in the process.

By contrast the Hizb al-Umma (Party of the Nation) was drawn from Egypt's landed elite, and thus it rather predictably favored gradual, nonviolent reform. Its flagship publication, edited by Lutfi al-Sayyid, was *al-Jarida*, and from the beginning (in marked contrast to *al-Liwa*) it distinguished between Egypt, the Ottoman Empire, and the Islamic world: *al-Jarida*'s loyalty was exclusively to Egypt, making it an early proponent of territorial nationalism. Among the principal differences between the Umma Party and the Watanists proved to be their differing attitudes toward the Egyptian palace: whereas the Watanists viewed the Egyptian royal family as a legitimate Muslim source of authority in contrast to the outrage of foreign rule, the Umma Party emphasized the legitimacy of constitutional rule and were outspoken critics of the Khedive's authoritarian impulses and Ottoman loyalties.[18] In the coming years, Egyptian nationalists would continue to debate the comparative importance of Egyptian, Islamic, liberal democratic, and anticolonial priorities and return to the question of whether to focus their energies on the struggle against the British, or against monarchic rule.

The emergence of anticolonial nationalist parties in India followed a not dissimilar trajectory between the late nineteenth and early twentieth centuries. With the devastating consequences of the 1857 Rebellion still fresh in many memories, and British rule more entrenched than ever before, the Indian National Congress (INC) established in 1885 initially sought the moderate goal of expanded Indian participation in the governance of the British Raj. However, in 1905 the Government of India partitioned the province of Bengal into Muslim and Hindu "halves"—a cynical effort to break the power of anticolonial Hindu elites concentrated in Calcutta.[19] Predictably, the crisis prompted the emergence of more stridently nationalist politics, most prominently the launch of the Swadeshi ("of our own country") movement, which called for boycotts of British and other foreign imports and exclusive reliance on Indian-made goods. In 1907 Congress split, as moderates led by Gopal Krishna Gokhale called for Dominion status within the British Empire; they were opposed by supporters of Bal Gangadhar Tilak, who demanded complete independence from Britain—by force if necessary.[20]

Tilak's conflation of Indian nationalist and Hindu religious songs, symbols, and festivals alienated Bengali Muslims, a largely poor and rural population who, by the turn of the century, made up a clear majority in the province. Similarly, the nationalist movement's glorification of historical episodes like the struggles of Rajputs and Marathas against the Mughals presented Muslims as oppressors rather than countrymen. For these reasons nationalist activism against Bengal's partition exacerbated preexisting tensions between the province's largely disadvantaged Muslim community and its wealthier, more educated Hindus. It was within this context that, in 1906, a Muslim educational conference held in the Bengali city of Dhaka saw the emergence of a new organization, the All-India Muslim League, spearheaded by the Bengali Nawab Salimullah.[21] As with the INC, the League's initial manifesto was modest, professing loyalty to Britain and a desire to present the views and aspirations of Muslim Indians. However from its inception, the League was a reaction to the threat Indian Muslims perceived as emanating from Indian nationalism as a predominantly or even implicitly Hindu project.

By 1911 the strength of popular opposition to Bengal's partition forced Britain to backpedal, reuniting the province and proving in the process the potential power of organized resistance on nationalist lines. Yet Bengali Muslims were disillusioned; they saw the nationalists as determined to deny them a province of their own—resulting in greater anticommunal cleavages after reunification than had existed prior to partition.[22] Though Gokhale and Tilak did not live to see the evolution of the INC into the interwar years, their contrasting visions of Indian independence (and the methods by which it ought to be achieved) would continue to resonate throughout the decades that followed their deaths. So too would the legacy of profound misunderstanding between India's "mainstream" nationalist current and the subcontinent's 80 million Muslims.

THE GREAT WAR

With the outbreak of hostilities in Europe in 1914, the whole of the British Empire found itself at war. Following the entry of the Ottoman Empire on the side of Germany, Britain's "veiled protectorate" in Egypt was formalized. The British deposed the pro-Ottoman Khedive and introduced martial law. Nationalist and pro-Turkish elements were arrested and exiled, and heavy press censorship was imposed. Cairo became a crucial military and diplomatic headquarters for the British war effort in the Middle East and Mediterranean, and a new agency, the Arab Bureau, was established to coordinate intelligence gathering and outreach targeting Ottoman-Arab provinces. In addition to the enormous value placed on the Suez Canal, the emerging significance of airplanes in transport and warfare further underscored Egypt's vital role within the empire. Situated at the intersection of Europe, Asia, and Africa, the flat desert expanses surrounding Cairo swiftly became a global hub of military and commercial air traffic.[23] By the war's end, Egypt was more than a British strategic asset: it had become the "jugular vein" of imperial transport and communications.[24]

Yet just as the experience of war had intensified Britain's attachment to Egypt, it had driven the Egyptian people to a breaking point. The cost of staple goods such as wheat, rice, paper, cloth, and kerosene had skyrocketed, and Egyptians saw their equipment and livestock confiscated for the military's use. Approximately one million fellaheen, members of the rural peasantry, were recruited into army labor corps and sent to active combat theaters in Europe and the Levant. The Egyptian economy, too, was heavily manipulated, as Britain "borrowed" surreptitiously from the country's gold reserves and depressed the price of its most important cash crop, cotton, to almost half its market value in order to meet the needs of the British war machine at cut-rate prices.[25] By 1919, the fellaheen were starving, and many of Egypt's wealthiest families had been bankrupted. There was a strong sense, cutting across class and sectarian lines, that Egypt had been made to pay dearly for Britain's war—and in so doing, had surely purchased its freedom.

As in Egypt, the intense nationalist upheavals that came to characterize the 1920s in British India had their roots in World War I, and the painful tolls it took on the lives of ordinary people. The war inflicted heavy casualties—over sixty thousand Indian soldiers lost their lives[26]—and rampant inflation. Between 1914 and 1919, the cost of necessities like rent, kerosene, cloth, and basic foodstuffs more than doubled while wages stagnated.[27] India was also hit exceptionally hard by the outbreak of influenza in 1918: over the course of a single year, between 17 and 18 million Indians are thought to have lost their lives to the flu—one third of the pandemic's global death toll.[28] By war's end, the pressure on British authorities in India was palpable. In her memoirs, the prominent Indian sociologist and political activist, Kamaladevi Chattopadhyay, recalled her own optimism that change must finally be imminent: "India's contribution [to the war] had been tremendous. . . . The day it ended in victory for the Allies, fresh hope for the subject people had sprouted. In the victory celebration with sports and games, in which I won a prize, I took it as a good omen that the long-awaited freedom was at hand, little dreaming what was in store for us."[29]

Immediately following the armistice that November, a group of Egyptian politicians seized upon the announcement of a peace conference to be held in Paris where, United States President Woodrow Wilson proclaimed, the principle of "national self-determination" would inform deliberations.[30] The Egyptian Wafd, or "delegation," as it quickly became known, initially consisted of a handful of moderate nationalists led by former government minister Saad Zaghlul, who sought permission to travel to Paris and make the case for Egypt's independence before the assembled world leaders. The British High Commissioner, Reginald Wingate, refused their appeal, on the pretense that Zaghlul and his comrades could not claim to speak on behalf of the Egyptian people. This lit a fire under the men, who wrote out their proposal and distributed copies throughout the country. Despite British efforts at repression, hundreds of thousands of Egyptians signed the petition. Embarrassed, Wingate demanded Zaghlul cease his political agitation. Zaghlul refused, and on 8 March, he and his key allies were arrested and deported to Malta.

THE EGYPTIAN REVOLUTION

The following day, 9 March 1919, students in Cairo erupted in protest. They targeted British property and infrastructure that they associated with the regime, including trams and lampposts. Despite brutal suppression by the police that left many dead and wounded, the uprising spread rapidly to Alexandria and other Egyptian cities, and on to the villages of the Delta and Upper Egypt. Within a matter of days, the entire country was in a state of open revolt: telegraph lines were cut, railways and roads were blocked, and Egyptians from every sector of society were in the streets: Muslims, Jews, and Christians; fellaheen and pashas; sheikhs, priests, and street performers; students, men, and—for the first time—women.

Huda Shaarawi (of Number Two, Qasr al-Nil) was the wife of Ali Shaarawi, the treasurer of the nascent Wafd Party. When his colleagues were exiled, he assumed greater responsibilities for the nationalist movement, and his wife came out of the seclusion of the harem to support the revolution. She was among the organizers of the first women's demonstration in Cairo, on 16 March, which famously culminated in a three-hour standoff with the police.[31] In the subsequent weeks and months, as the revolution matured and entered new phases, Egypt's women came into their own as a political force to be reckoned with—and at their helm was Madame Shaarawi. The daughter of a wealthy family, she had been a naturally gifted child and benefited from a fine education. Photographs depict a handsome and well-dressed woman, whose elegant command of Arabic, French, and English made her a potent political communicator with foreign allies, as well as with her compatriots. Her impassioned speeches, delivered in a "deep, husky voice,"[32] clearly made an impression on those who heard them: in early 1920, at a meeting said to have attracted over a thousand women to the Cathedral of St Mark in central Cairo, Shaarawi was elected President of the Wafdist Women's Central Committee, officially launching what would become a storied political career.

The Egyptian Revolution of 1919 caught British authorities by surprise. They were forced to reverse course: Zaghlul and his colleagues were released and returned to Egypt as national heroes. The Wafd was permitted to travel to Paris, where they were stonewalled by Britain and its allies at the peace conference.

FIGURE 1   Huda Shaarawi, Founder of the Egyptian Feminist's Union. Undated.
HERITAGE IMAGE PARTNERSHIPS / ALAMY

Rather than the independence negotiations they had sought, the Egyptians found themselves on the receiving end of a unilateral British declaration. Egypt was now independent, it claimed, but the new constitution reserved Britain's right to control four vital spheres: imperial communications, defense, the protection of foreign interests, and the Sudan. Despite these caveats, the revolution ushered in a hopeful new era. In 1924 a Wafdist government was elected with a sweeping majority, and Zaghlul became Egypt's first Prime Minister.

PHARAONISM

At exactly the same moment that the Egyptian people were wresting control of (parts of) their government from the British and a new, nationalist party took office for the first time, a monumental discovery was made in the Valley of the Kings: British archaeologist Howard Carter and his patron, Lord Carnarvon, announced that they had located the tomb of the Amarna-era boy king, Tutankhamun. The discovery thrust Egypt even further into the international spotlight, sparking a global craze, "Egyptomania," and fueling a major tourism boom, as Europeans flocked to see the pyramids, cruise the Nile, and gawk at the artifacts in the Egyptian Museum.

In the wake of the discovery, Carter, Carnarvon, and the Wafd became embroiled in a dispute over concessionary rights, in the midst of which the Wafd forbade a tour of the tomb for the wives of European excavators. Enraged, Carter locked the site and filed a lawsuit against the Egyptian government. In response the government canceled Carter's concession, sawed off the locks, and orchestrated a pilgrimage of Wafd politicians to the tomb to mark the opening of Egypt's new parliament. The Wafd subsequently won the lawsuit, and the whole of the contents of the tomb were awarded to the Egyptian Museum.[33] A commemorative ode was penned by Ahmad Shawqi, the celebrated nationalist poet, titled "Tutankhamun and the Parliament." It included the following passages:

> [Tutankhamun] travelled forty centuries, considering them until he came home, and found there . . . England, and its army, and its lord, brandishing its Indian sword, protecting its India.
> [. . .] Pharaoh, the time of self rule is in effect, and the dynasty of arrogant lords has passed.
> Now the foreign tyrants in every land must relinquish their rule over their subjects.
> [. . .] Tutankhamun has returned his authority to our sons![34]

Books, newspapers, popular songs, and works of art all heralded the arrival of a new Egyptian golden age, comparable to the reign of the pharaohs. Mahmud Mokhtar's statue, *Nihdat Misr*, "the Awakening of Egypt," was unveiled in 1927, in the presence of Zaghlul and other members of the Wafd. The sculpture depicts a mighty sphinx rising on its haunches, as if stirring from a long nap. A fellah woman, her arm wrapped around the sphinx, lifts the veil from her face and gazes confidently toward the horizon. While evoking Egypt's glorious past, the statue depicts a country with its eyes on the horizon—looking toward an era when education and modern technology would uplift Egypt's peasantry and liberate its women. Both Egyptology and the Wafd were also disproportionately popular among Egyptian Coptic Christians, who made up approximately 6 percent of the population according to the 1917 British census. The connection had been encouraged by European archaeologists, who suggested that Copts were the true descendants of ancient Egyptians, while Muslims were supposedly descendants of later Arab invaders. Yet Christian and Muslim Egyptian nationalists embraced the pharaohs as their common ancestors, as illustrated by the lyrics of *Nem ya Khufu* (Sleep, Khufu), written by the celebrated composer Sayyid Darwish in 1919:

> Sleep, O Khufu, and rest in safety
> O glorious one, builder of the pyramids
> Christians and Muslims all volunteer to be in your service
> Their unity is an enduring one
> and tomorrow we will be the most civilised nation.[35]

In the Wafd's executive council of 1923, the ratio of Copts to Muslims was six to eight; in the election of 1924 and in subsequent elections that brought Wafd ministries to power, Coptic candidates for the party won seats even in Muslim majority ridings.[36] The interlinking of Pharaonism with the secular, territorial nationalism of the Wafd thus helped Christians to transcend their minority status and achieve a certain degree of political prominence in interwar Egypt.

GLOBAL CAIRO

Alongside the international popularity of ancient Egyptian art and motifs, and the tourists now flooding in from every corner of the globe, postrevolutionary Cairo was assuming an increasingly important role in the transnational culture of the Arabic-speaking world, thanks to its booming press, radio, and recording industries. As Ziad Fahmy notes, from 1919 to 1929, over 450 new print periodicals appeared in Cairo, dramatically enhancing its cultural influence.[37] The freedom of expression afforded Egyptian journalists under the new liberal parliamentary regime, the size and diversity of Egypt's cities, and the richness of its coffeehouse and theater cultures all combined to ensure that Egyptian newspapers, records, and radio broadcasts were among the most popular anywhere in the Middle East.

This "split screen" of interwar Egypt—perceived in the West as exotic and timeless, and in the Arab East as modern and sophisticated—was to some extent reproduced in the urban geography of its capital city, as described by a visitor: "European Cairo . . . is divided from Egyptian Cairo by the long street that goes from the railway station, past the big hotels to Abdin . . . and it is full of big shops and great houses and fine carriages and well-dressed people, and might be a western city. . . . The real Cairo is to the east of this . . . and . . . is practically what it always was."[38]

As Janet Abu-Lughod famously observed, this "physical duality was but a manifestation of the cultural cleavage"[39] between its native and foreign residents, its wealthy and its poor. Spread out along the bank of the Nile, extending inland perhaps a half-dozen city blocks, European Cairo was organized as a series of wide boulevards, *midans* or squares, and public gardens—adorned by large department stores, cinemas, cafes, supper clubs, and institutions like the Egyptian Museum, the Opera House, and the American University. In the middle of the river and connected to the mainland by two large bridges was the island of Zamalek, the south end of which was largely given over to the grounds of the Gezira Sports Club, whose swimming pools, tennis courts, and polo fields made it a favorite with British officers and administrators. From Zamalek, a short drive across Khedive Ismail Bridge would take one past the British Residency, the Egyptian parliament buildings, and several blocks further inland to Abdin Palace, the residence since 1917 of King Fuad and his family.

Old Cairo was located, in a sense, behind this European city, to the east of Abdin Palace, the Opera House, and Ezbekiyeh Gardens. Here the grand boulevards narrowed into alleyways and unpaved roads; the motor taxis and gleaming department stores of Midan Soliman Pasha gave way to public ovens, market stalls, and mule-drawn vegetable carts. Cairo's "native quarter," as it was often described in the early twentieth century, cannot be reduced to a backwater of crumbling hovels, despite being scandalously underserviced in terms of water, sanitation, gas, and electric power, compared to the European districts that stood mere blocks away. For Old Cairo was a thriving urban center in its own right, with grand architecture, thriving community fixtures, and public institutions. Among the most beautiful and important buildings in this part of the city were the hundreds of mosques, churches, tombs, synagogues, and shrines, many of which dated from the Fatimid period or even earlier. While tourists and pilgrims visited some of the more impressive complexes in Old Cairo (much as they would visit the pyramids or a museum), these centuries-old buildings also lay at the heart of residents' everyday life. Coffeehouses played a similarly vital role in the transmission of news, information, and culture. "For the price of a cup of tea or coffee," Ziad Fahmy explains, "readers had access to many newspapers and magazines. If the clientele happened to be illiterate, their mere presence in a crowded coffee shop exposed them to an unlimited amount of oral discourse, from the reading aloud of newspapers to conversations, songs, and theatrical performances."[40]

Whereas the European city boasted centers of higher education including Fuad I and the American University, Old Cairo had al-Azhar, the ancient and exalted seat of Islamic learning. Next to the mosque-university stood the entrance to one of the city's oldest and largest souks, Khan el-Khalili. Time itself operated somewhat differently in Old Cairo than it did in the European city, where clocks dominated business and social life and electricity was ubiquitous. In the alleyways and marketplaces east of Opera Square, clock time competed with the movement of the sun and moon and the connected five calls to prayer to set the rhythms of daily life.[41]

Old Cairo and European Cairo were distinct physical spaces, but far from insulated from one another. Many residents moved between them multiple times a day to go to work or attend classes, to pray, to do their shopping, to socialize, or simply for a change of scenery. There were points of overlap and intersection between the cities: cafés, theaters, markets, cinemas, and public squares. Many wealthier Egyptians lived in European Cairo, while many European Cairenes had been born there—or even belonged to families who had lived in Egypt for generations—and were established in Old Cairo. These communities, the *mutamassirun*, hailed primarily from southern Europe and the Levant and ran the gamut from lower-middle-class tradesmen, waiters, maids, and shopkeepers all the way up to the highest rungs of society. They tended to maintain distinct cultural identities, ways of life, and—until the mid-1930s—foreign legal status, which afforded them privileges and protections under the Capitulations. These were a hangover of Ottoman domination that, though abolished in Istanbul in 1914, persisted under the British in Egypt.

In addition to Italians, Greeks, Jews, Slavs, British, Armenians, Persians, Swedes, Chinese, Germans, French, Turks, Syrians, Cypriots, and Maghrebins, there were Indians living in Cairo throughout the interwar years, and many more lived in Port Said, although statistics are elusive. Most fell into one of two categories: students and scholars of Islam attached to a university or—the vast majority—merchants, many from the province of Sindh, involved in maritime trade. Until the late 1930s, Indian merchants in Egypt benefited from preferential legal status as British subjects under the Capitulations. There was even an Urdu newspaper published in Cairo, *Islami Dunya*, which emphasized the cultural, religious, and political affinities connecting South Asia to the broader geography of Islam. An issue of *Islami Dunya* printed in 1930 featured a large spread of photographs and flattering biographical sketches of Muslim rulers across India, Iran, and the Middle East.[42]

ANTIQUITY, NATIONALISM, AND "CIVILIZATION"

As we have seen, from the pyramid-imprinted pages of Cairo's *al-Ahram* newspaper to the ancient gods evoked in the poetry of Ahmad Shawqi, from the songs of Sayyid Darwish to the monumental neopharaonic sculptures of Mahmud Mokhtar, the symbols of Egypt post-1919 all heralded the arrival of a new Egyptian golden age, which, it was hoped, would once again empower the people of the Nile to play a leading role in the affairs of the world.

An early 1920s campaign poster shows Zaghlul and a woman in a pharaonic headdress, the embodiment of the Egyptian nation.[43] Zaghlul has one hand on the lion, symbolizing Great Britain, which holds Egypt's chains in its mouth. The leader of the Wafd urges patience to Egypt, then in the throes of drawn-out negotiations with the British, for "patience is the key to relief." In the background, two men stand sentinel for, respectively, Egypt and the Sudan. Egypt is imagined in a modern European suit of clothing and is racially white. He is depicted as a member of the *effendiyya*—the urban, educated class of Egyptians at the forefront of the Wafd.[44] The Sudan, meanwhile, is depicted in rural peasant's garb and is racially black. There are multiple depictions of this kind in contemporaneous political art, contrasting a white, civilized, and powerful Egypt with a black, "primitive," and sometimes diminutive Sudan.[45]

In this era, Zaghlul and the Wafd were locked in a political standoff with the British government to assert Egyptian sovereignty over the Sudan—the "Reserved Point" over which Anglo-Egyptian negotiations would break down again and again. During the 1920s it was still commonplace for wealthy Egyptians to have Sudanese servants in circumstances that amounted to indentured servitude; this reflected the pervasive attitude that Egyptian domination of the Sudan, both on the national and individual levels, represented "the natural order of things,"

FIGURE 2 "Have Patience, O Egypt—for patience is the key to relief!" Saad Zaghlul reassures Egypt that the British lion can be tamed. Wafd campaign poster, ca. 1924.
SPECIAL COLLECTIONS, J. WILLARD MARRIOTT LIBRARY, THE UNIVERSITY OF UTAH

dating back thousands of years. Egyptian nationalists utilized pharaonic imagery and symbolism to support their case: they evoked the ancient unification of Egypt and Nubia to bolster demands for the "Unity of the Nile Valley," a slogan whose origins Eve Troutt Powell dates to the Revolution of 1919.[46]

This dynamic had an Indian echo in Gokhale's final political testament, published posthumously in 1918, which suggested India should inherit the territory of German East Africa—a call supported by some British Indian officials and amplified by Gokhale's friend (and first President of the All-India Muslim League) Sultan Mahomed Shah, Aga Khan III.[47] According to the Aga Khan, the fact that Africa was "peopled by vast numbers of dark and aboriginal tribes" made it more appropriate that India, rather than Europe, colonize it: "Her immigrant sons must feel stronger sympathy and toleration for the Africans than the white settler, and will be singularly fitted to help to raise them in the scale of civilisation. The Indian cultivator and the Indian craftsman do some things as these children of the wilds do them, only they do them much better. Indians would teach the natives to plough, to weave, and to carpenter; the rough Indian tools are within the comprehension of the African mind, and even Indian housekeeping would be full of instructive lessons to the negro."[48]

Nor were such ideas narrowly limited to Muslim aristocrats, or men of a bygone era like Gokhale. Speaking in Mombasa in 1924, the feminist poet and Congress leader Sarojini Naidu told her audience of Indian residents, members of the East African Congress: "It does not take a very learned student to realize that naturally and inevitably East Africa is one of the earliest legitimate territories of the Indian nation. . . . East Africa is, therefore, the legitimate colony of the surplus of the Great Indian nation."[49]

While Egyptian and Indian nationalists contested British dominance of their own countries, this did not necessarily imply a wholesale rejection of colonialism, at least not as we currently understand it. Some nurtured imperialist impulses of their own, underpinned by historical claims as well as by concepts of racial difference, cultural essentialism, and civilizational hierarchy. These paradigms were heavily indebted to (if not wholesale replications of) European models that claimed to be empirical and even "scientific" categorizations of human difference.[50] Operating within the logic of racial and national hierarchies, some (including, infamously, a youthful Gandhi) argued that Indians or Arabs were more civilized than Africans or Aboriginals and thus more deserving of political rights.[51] Claims to the Sudan and East Africa took this logic further, endeavoring to demonstrate that not only were Egyptians and Indians "civilized enough" to govern themselves but also to possess and administer colonies of their own.[52]

THE MANDATES

The delusion of a civilizational pyramid—with Western Europe and America at the pinnacle, Asians two-thirds of the way down, and tribal peoples near the bottom—found its post-war legal embodiment in the mandatory regime devised by the peacemakers in Paris. This was an attempt to square the circle of President Wilson's insistence that the Peace Conference not descend into the sordid parceling out of new colonies for European powers. By 1919, the moral basis of empire was coming under sustained attack from many quarters; but the *reality* of empire, and the determination of the war's imperial victors to expand their holdings, remained intact. Thus came into being a multi-tiered classification system for the lands and peoples left exposed by the collapse of the German, Austro-Hungarian, and Ottoman Empires.

At the top of the pyramid, territories within Europe were granted sovereignty and independence. At its base, the small size, sparse population, and "remoteness from the centers of civilization" supposedly rendered Class C Mandates appropriate for annexation. Class B Mandates, mostly located in Central Africa, were deemed to be "at such a stage that the Mandatory must be responsible for the administration of the territory," without, however, prejudicing the trade and commercial opportunities of other powers.[53]

A separate category of mandate, Class A, was reserved for the former provinces of the Ottoman Empire, which had been sending elected representatives to the parliament in Istanbul off and on for decades (meaning they had significantly more experience of representative government than many European countries). Nevertheless, at Paris the British and French delegations ploughed ahead with the division of the Levant. The mandates were implemented against the strenuous objections of local inhabitants, who were polled,[54] and leaders including Prince Faisal. Faisal's father, Sharif Hussein of Mecca, had entered the war on the side of the Allies in 1916, in exchange for which Henry McMahon, the British High Commissioner in Egypt, had pledged official recognition of an independent Arab Kingdom to be ruled by Hussein's family, the Hashemites, after the war. Faisal had led the revolt in the Hijaz alongside a British agent, T.E. Lawrence. They both came to Paris in 1919 (Lawrence served as Faisal's translator); like so many others, they were to leave disappointed.

The most consequential of the mandates that the Allies awarded themselves in the wake of the Great War was the former Ottoman territory of Palestine. Under the terms of Britain and France's infamous wartime agreement, negotiators Mark Sykes and Georges Picot had designated Palestine as part of the French sphere of influence; in later years, Arab nationalists would brandish the Hussein-McMahon correspondence as proof that Palestine fell within the territory of the Arab Kingdom promised to the Hashemites. However in 1917, Arthur Balfour, the British Foreign Secretary, had also written to Lord Rothschild, a prominent leader of Britain's Jewish community, pledging government support for the creation of a "Jewish national home" in Palestine. There was much hope that this public endorsement might mobilize American Jews to help bring their country into the war. More concretely, the military campaign in the Middle East had alerted British strategic planners that the defense of their position in Egypt—and India, by way of the Suez Canal—required control of the coastal ports and desert advances from Palestine. For this reason, it had suddenly become a key British priority to secure the Holy Land for itself. At Paris, with the enthusiastic backing of the World Zionist Organization, that is exactly what they did.[55]

To be clear, there were and had always been Jews in Palestine—as there were in Aleppo, Cairo, and Baghdad, to name only some of the more prominent centers of Jewish life throughout the until-recently Ottoman world. But these were not the Jews, and certainly not the Jewish "nation," the men in Paris had in mind. The dilemmas of antisemitism and ethnic nationalism their program had evolved to address were European, and their solution was the establishment of a Jewish polity on European terms.[56] The pitch made by the British, Polish, and Russian representatives of the World Zionist Organization led by Chaim Weizmann had several prongs. These included playing on Western anxieties about mass migration. With the dissolution of the Russian and Austro-Hungarian empires, millions of Eastern European Jews were in need of a new home. Would the Great Powers absorb these "wandering aliens" into their own populations? Surely, it was more sensible to resettle them in Palestine.[57]

Next, they appealed to imperial self-interest. Jewish immigration to Palestine would give European powers a staunch ally in the heart of the strategically vital Middle East. As Leo Amery, the War Cabinet Secretary who helped to draft the Balfour Declaration saw it, "the Jews alone can build up a strong civilization in Palestine" that could counter German and Turkish designs on the region. Over time, Jewish influence would also help to spread Western modernity, civilization, and progress among the "backward" Arab inhabitants.[58]

Last but certainly not least, there was antiquity to be contended with. The Zionists came to Paris armed with maps of biblical Israel and historical accounts of Roman Palestine: "The country which is now very sparsely populated, in Roman times supported a great population. It could now serve admirably for colonization on a large scale."[59] The results of this presentation were suitably impressive: Lloyd George, the British Prime Minister, was inspired to proclaim that the new homeland for the Jews should run "from Dan to Beersheba" (a remark that caused, as Margaret MacMillan tells us, many headaches for his staff, who were tasked with determining where exactly these places might be).[60]

When Class A Mandates finally came into force in 1923, France had wrested Syria and Lebanon from Faisal's Arab government at gunpoint. As a sort of compensation prize, Faisal was parachuted into British Mandate Iraq, where, following a manufactured election, he was crowned King. His brother Abdallah was placed on the throne of Transjordan, another new British acquisition. Across the Jordan River, British Palestine boasted no new ruler or parliament; instead, inscribed into the preamble of the Mandate was the text of the 1917 Balfour Declaration. According to its terms, Britain took "responsibility for placing the country under such political, administrative and economic conditions as will secure the establishment of the Jewish national home."[61] This was to be accomplished without "prejudice" to "the civil and religious rights of existing non-Jewish communities in Palestine"—an unusual way of describing nine-tenths of the population, as historians have not tired of pointing out.[62]

Among those most dismayed by the pronouncement of the Balfour Declaration and its aftermath was the only elected official of the Jewish faith then serving in the British government: Secretary of State for India (and Liberal Member of Parliament for Cambridgeshire), Edwin Samuel Montagu. Shortly after his election in 1917, Montagu had submitted a memorandum to the British Cabinet on what he called the Balfour Declaration's inherent antisemitism:

> I assume that it means that Mahommedans and Christians are to make way for the Jews and that the Jews should be put in all positions of preference and should be peculiarly associated with Palestine in the same way that England is with the English or France with the French, that Turks and other Mahommedans in Palestine will be regarded as foreigners, just in the same way as Jews will hereafter be treated as foreigners in every country but Palestine. Perhaps also citizenship must be granted only as a result of a religious test.
>
> ... It is quite true that Palestine plays a large part in Jewish history, but so it does in modern Mohammedan history, and, after the time of the Jews, surely it plays a larger part than any other country in Christian history. The Temple may have been in Palestine, but so was the Sermon on the Mount and the Crucifixion.
>
> ... I would say to Lord Rothschild that the Government will be prepared to do everything in their power to obtain for Jews in Palestine complete liberty of settlement and life on an equality with the inhabitants of that country who profess other religious beliefs. I would ask that the Government should go no further.[63]

The profound ideological rifts within contemporary Jewish communities over the Zionist project are illustrated by the fact that Montagu's cousin Herbert Samuel very much disagreed with him and was soon to be appointed as the first British High Commissioner in Palestine.

Montagu did not have time to dwell on this policy defeat; there was too much to contend with at his actual job in the India Office. There he was attempting to press for reforms in line with postwar nationalist demands. In these efforts, he was up against stiff resistance from the Conservative members of the Rowlatt Commission, named for its President Justice Sidney Rowlatt. Lord Chelmsford, the Indian Viceroy, agreed to endorse Montagu's proposals for liberal reform on the condition that the restrictions on political freedoms proposed by Rowlatt were simultaneously brought into effect. The results were disastrous: even moderate Indian opinion was outraged by the draconian provisions of the Rowlatt Act, undermining any goodwill the Montagu-Chelmsford Reforms might otherwise have engendered. After years of quiet observation and local organizing, Mohandas Karamchand Gandhi chose this moment, in the spring of 1919, to step onto the national stage.

ENTER THE MAHATMA

Gandhi was already a familiar and popular figure in his home country, best known for his successful advocacy on behalf of the Indian community in South Africa in the decades prior to World War I. Though he had returned to India in 1915, he initially spent a year traveling the country and thereafter focused predominantly on the plight of peasants and farmers, especially in his home state of Gujarat. He also sought to win British support for a greater degree of Indian self-determination through active support of recruitment efforts during the final years of the war. Instead, 1919 saw His Majesty's Indian subjects stripped of further civil and political rights under the Rowlatt Act. Its passage in March spurred Gandhi in a different direction. Drawing on the techniques of nonviolent resistance, which he had first deployed in South Africa, he announced a nationwide campaign of satyagraha (literally "truth force"), calling for a series of *hartals* (strikes) and other acts of civil disobedience to protest Rowlatt's "Black Act."

His call was immediately taken up in several cities including Delhi, but it was not until several weeks had elapsed that the movement began to assume historic proportions. The catalyst was the massacre of unarmed satyagrahis and bystanders by British soldiers, under the orders of General Reginald Dyer, inside a walled public garden in the city of Amritsar on 13 April. At least four hundred people were killed, and well over one thousand more wounded, within a span of ten minutes. In the wake of this obscene tragedy, Gandhi doubled down, calling for full Indian independence through a national campaign of "Non-Cooperation," meaning the wholesale boycott of British institutions, goods, and services.

Kamaladevi Chattopadhyay was a sixteen-year-old student when the satyagraha campaign was announced; she recalls taking to her bedroom to pray for the success of Gandhi and his movement.[64] Her sister-in-law, Sarojini Naidu, was forty, the same age as Huda Shaarawi. By 1919 Naidu was already a prominent poet and campaigner, and she now became a devoted lieutenant in Gandhi's movement, alongside her ongoing feminist activism. In time, Chattopadhyay would follow in her elder sister's footsteps, and, as we will see, both women would forge enduring ties with their counterparts in the Egyptian nationalist movement.

CONNECTED MOVEMENTS

From the beginning, Egyptian and Indian nationalist leaders were inspired by one another's campaigns for self-determination. Noor Khan has traced contacts between these movements to the turn of the century, when students, journalists, and political activists from across the colonized East began encountering one another in European capitals.[65] Mutual admiration between the Wafd and Congress dates from the spring of 1919, as international press coverage of the Egyptian Revolution and the Indian satyagraha campaign ensured that Zaghlul and Gandhi were made aware of one another. In 1922, a book-length translation of the writings of Indian Muslim nationalist Abul Kalam Azad on the anticolonial movement in India was published in Cairo by *al-Manar*, the Islamic reformist magazine edited by Rashid Rida. *Thawrat al-Hind al-Siyasiyya* (India's Political Revolution) detailed Gandhi's strategy of nonviolent civil disobedience, as well as collaboration between his satyagraha movement and the Indian Muslim campaign that had emerged to protest the division of Ottoman territories (the subject of chapter 2).[66]

The following year, a popular book edited by Mohi al-Din Rida, *Abtal al-Wataniyya*, also published in Cairo, celebrated nationalist heroes. It has chapters on Egyptians, including Zaghlul and the late Mustafa Kamil (editor of *al-Liwa* and founder of the Watani Party); it also devotes a chapter to Gandhi, describing him as a prophet.[67] This sentiment would later be echoed by Ahmad Shawqi in a poem celebrating Gandhi's passage through the Suez Canal.[68] Depictions of the devout Hindu in Arabic nomenclature, normally reserved for Muslim saints, go some way to illustrating the recognition and respect many Egyptians afforded Gandhi. A later (1934) biography of al-Ruh al-Azeem (the Arabic translation of Mahatma, or "Great Soul"), written by Fathi Radwan, the cofounder of the Islamist Misr al-Fatah, or Young Egypt Party, praised Gandhi as worthy of emulation by every Egyptian: "He fasted and gave up eating, his wife, clothing and a peaceful life to free his soul from his body."[69] For Radwan, the perceived sincerity of this spiritual commitment, and the way it informed Gandhi's struggle against the British, seemed more salient than the theological differences between Hinduism and Islam. As in Shawqi's poem, Gandhi's Hindu piety served to render him legible to Muslims. If this was the case for Islamists such as Radwan, Gandhi was equally (if not yet more) popular among secular and Coptic Egyptian nationalists, by offering a model of a non-Muslim leader who nevertheless exuded Eastern authenticity, and whose anti-imperial credentials were unassailable. In Noor Khan's words, "no Indian excited the Egyptian imagination more than Gandhi."[70]

The admiration went both ways. In April 1919, Gandhi printed and distributed a list of books and other publications for satyagrahis, including a biography of Mustafa Kamil.[71] Later, he would tell an Egyptian diplomat that he considered Saad Zaghlul to have been "the father of all Nationalist movements in the East, including India."[72] His exhortations that Indian nationalists learn from the example of Egypt paid dividends. In October 1928, a series of posters went up all over Bombay in response to the arrival of the much-maligned Simon Commission, a British parliamentary committee sent to report on Indian constitutional reform (absent any input from Indians themselves). The posters evoked the Milner Commission, which had been sent to Egypt on a similar errand at the height of the 1919 Revolution. The posters read:

WHAT EGYPT DID
INDIA CAN DO
In Egypt the hated Milner Commission was avoided everywhere
Like the plague.
When some of the members entered the Law Court,
the Judge walked out to show his contempt.
If they went to a restaurant,
the waiter refused to serve them.
If they wanted a taxi,
the chauffeur refused to carry them.
Everywhere the mark of the people's
DISPLEASURE
pursued them
Baffled, humiliated, their machinations frustrated,
they beat an inglorious retreat to their
own country.
Youths of Bombay!
Who brought about
THIS WONDERFUL AWAKENING?
None but the
BRAVE EGYPTIAN YOUTHS
Therefore
Youths of Bombay
BE UP AND DOING
To Break the Simonites[73]

By 1923, Indian and Egyptian feminist activists had also begun to seek out one another's company. A photograph from the Ninth Congress of the International Alliance of Women, held in Rome that May, shows Huda Shaarawi, Sarojini Naidu, and the national delegations they led—ten women in all—standing in an Italian courtyard arm in arm, intermingled and smiling.[74] As the only two delegations from Eastern, colonized countries to have attended the conference, the affinity between the women was quite natural. Upon her return to Egypt, Shaarawi drew inspiration from Gandhi's Non-Cooperation movement, which she learned about from her Indian colleagues, in organizing a successful Egyptian boycott of British goods and services in 1924.[75]

Sarojini Naidu's older brother, Virendranath Chattopadhyaya ("Chatto"), was one of several nationalist revolutionaries to forge ties with Egyptians and other anticolonial activists in Europe during the war years.[76] After the armistice he stayed on in Berlin and became instrumental in connecting his sisters and others—including a youthful Jawaharlal Nehru—to socialists and anti-imperialists, including Egyptian and Arab nationalists.[77]

Yet even at this early stage in their relations, there were important differences between the mainstream nationalist movements of Egypt and India. While both Zaghlul's Wafd and the Gandhian satyagrahis looked to their countries' ancient forebears for inspiration, the nationalist visions that emerged out of these idealized pasts were radically different from one another. As we have seen, the neo-Pharaonism promoted by the Wafd celebrated a worldly empire ruled by powerful kings. The Wafd also embraced many aspects of Western modernity—notably expanded access to education, parliamentary democracy, and modern technology—in their bid to restore Egypt to its former glory and ensure it a central role on the world's stage.

By contrast, the idealized ancient India evoked by Gandhi was a land of simplicity and spiritual purity, unsullied by the corruption and materialism of the West. His political vision was inspired by the Hindu epic *Ramayana*, which emphasizes religious virtue and devotion, as well as the traditional way of life of India's peasants, whose modesty and simplicity—their very unworldliness—he held up as an example for the nation. Whereas in Egypt the nationalists coopted the regal sphinx and pyramids as symbols of their movement, Gandhi chose the equally ancient *charkha*, or spinning wheel, and urged his disciples to use it to make their own clothes. The differing nationalist attitudes toward materialism and modernity are even visible in the photograph of the Indian and Egyptian women's delegations at the IAW Congress in 1923. Almost all the Indian dele-

FIGURE 3   Gandhi and his charka: Swadeshi movement poster. 1930.
HISTORIC COLLECTION / ALAMY

gates are modestly dressed in traditional sarees. By contrast, in their enthusiasm for the current European trends in women's fashion—heeled shoes and stockings, jaunty caps, and tailored ensembles—the Egyptian delegates mirror the art deco movement's corresponding embrace of ancient Egyptian motifs.

Another important distinction between the two nationalist movements, already apparent in the early 1920s, was their attitudes toward the question of religious plurality. Of course, both Egypt and India were home to multiple faith communities—though India's size and demographic complexity dwarfed Egypt's. Nevertheless, their contrasting approaches to uniting religious minorities is instructive.

Drawing on the territorial nationalism and liberal heritage of the Umma Party, the Wafd promoted ideals of equal citizenship and a secular, democratic state, which resolved the question of communal diversity by seeking, in effect, to blind the state to them, in favor of a universal criteria of Egyptian citizenship. The outsized presence of Coptic Christians within the leadership of the Wafd helps to underscore that membership of the national movement was perceived as a way for minorities to claim national belonging and equality, overcoming other barriers to Egyptianness.

Like Gokhale before him, Gandhi was deeply committed to the ideal of intercommunal harmony, but he believed this could only be achieved through the full embrace of religion. His political vision was steeped in Hindu teachings and culture: the principles of nonviolent resistance, the utopian kingdom of Ram Raja which he held up as a model for India, and the very word *satyagraha*—all had their origins in the Vedas. Gandhi's call for unity between India's religious communities was, in contrast to the Egyptian Wafd, rooted in a rejection of secularism. He saw religion as the irreplaceable pillar at the center of Indians' individual and collective lives, thus it was natural for politics to be informed by religious belief and shaped by communal identities. Of course, others within the Congress fold held differing views, and as we will see in the decades to come, communalism would prove to be among the most important and complex hurdles confronting the party. In the early 1920s, however, Gandhi was unassailable, and it was on the basis of a sympathetic alliance between religious communities that he would make his most ambitious bid, between 1919 and 1924, to win India's Muslims over to the cause of national independence.

TWO

Whose Caliphate?

> India is grief-stricken and Egypt mournful,
> crying over you with streaming tears.[1]
> —AHMAD SHAWQI ON THE DISSOLUTION
> OF THE CALIPHATE, 1924

> Even if I'd had seven sons,
> I'd sacrifice them all for the Khilafat.[2]
> —ATTRIBUTED TO ABADI BEGUM, CA. 1920

> Free yourselves first; then choose a Caliph.[3]
> —A WAFDIST RETORT, 1925

NEW LIGHTS

Choudhry Khaliquzzaman was thirty years old in 1919, a youthful lawyer and passionate political activist at the center of a movement whose time, it seemed, had come. Khaliquzzaman was a native of Lucknow—the large, wealthy, and cosmopolitan capital of the United Provinces in northern India, which had played a major role in the Rebellion of 1857. Since his teens he had been engaged in nationalist and pro-Muslim activism, attending sit-ins and rallies to protest the Italian invasion of Libya in 1907. While a student at the elite Muslim university of Aligarh in 1913, he volunteered for an Indian medical mission to the Ottoman Empire. In India during World War I, he quietly abetted a cousin and several college friends who were funneling money and information to the Germans, in the hopes that a victory for the Central Powers would result in India's liberation from British rule.[4] The ultimate triumph of the Allies was thus a significant disappointment to him, but it was nothing compared to the calamity of the peace that was to follow.

Internally divided by sect, class, language, and geography, Indian Muslims were always far from a homogenous bloc. Yet by the early twentieth century, political loyalty to the British Crown and service in the army had to a certain extent become hallmarks of some north Indian communities, due in no small measure to the influence of the nineteenth-century educational reformer Sir Syed Ahmad Khan. Not only had Khan rebuffed attempts by the Ottoman Sultan to exercise sway over India's Muslims,[5] he also refrained from involvement in the Rebellion of 1857, believing British patronage essential to the long-term goal of Muslim advancement. Toward the same end, in 1875 he founded the Muhammadan Anglo-Oriental College, better known, after its locality, as Aligarh. In many ways, Aligarh was intended as a Muslim Oxford: an elite institution referential of Islam's glorious past, while grooming its pupils for leadership in an increasingly modern, secular, Western-dominated world.[6] Late in life, Choudhry Khaliquzzaman still recalled with pride the school robes he and his fellows had donned: a black cloak paired with a fez cap. He praised the university as the site of a "Muslim Renaissance" that "conjured up visions of Cordova and Baghdad."[7] Yet despite this deep affection for his alma mater, Khaliquzzaman was part of a generation of Aligarh students who took issue with its founder's maxims of detachment from the Ottoman throne and strategic loyalty to the British Empire.[8]

With the outbreak of war between Russia and the Ottoman Empire in the Balkans in 1912, a group of Aligarh students—including Khaliquzzaman and his close friend Abdurrahman Siddiqi—joined a Red Crescent medical mission to provide humanitarian assistance to the Ottoman Empire. The mission was led by Dr. Mukhtar Ahmed Ansari, another Aligarh alumnus who had become involved in nationalist politics while completing his training as a surgeon in Britain.[9] The medical mission was one indication of the growing identification many Indian Muslims felt with a broadly defined Islamic East. This worldview owed much to the itinerant political firebrand Jamal al-Din al-Afghani, a contemporary of Sir Syed Ahmad Khan's, and among his fiercest critics and rivals.[10] A Persian Shia who claimed to be a Sunni from Afghanistan, al-Afghani spent considerable time living in Cairo, Alexandria, and Paris; he also resided in India for several tumultuous years, during and after the 1857 Rebellion. These experiences in India, later recounted by Afghani to his friends and students in Cairo, may have helped to inspire the 1879–82 Urabi Revolt.[11] Afghani was virulently opposed to British imperialism and saw in the peoples of the East—their languages, histories, and spiritual and cultural traditions—the means to challenge foreign domination. In India he preached Muslim-Hindu unity, exhorting his listeners to dig deep within their own traditions to throw off the British yoke. To audiences in Cairo, he preached Islamic solidarity toward the same end; writing in the Arabic press, he called for unity and common purpose among "Easterners in general and Muslims in particular."[12] These sentiments would echo and reverberate throughout the early twentieth century.

As World War I broke out in 1914, popular identification with the new regime of the Young Turks in Istanbul was rife among younger Indian Muslims like Khaliquzzaman and Siddiqi, whose education had encouraged them to think in global ways. The British also bore some responsibility for this development because, for decades, the Ottomans had been perceived in London as a useful bulwark against Russian expansion, which threatened both the balance of power in the Mediterranean and the approaches to India itself. These geostrategic considerations had tempted officials in Simla and Westminster to support the Sultan's claim to be the Caliph, implying spiritual leadership of the global Muslim *umma* (community, or nation). It was a title many Europeans interpreted, erroneously, as a kind of Sunni pope.[13] Thus, a generation of Indian Muslims who came of age in the early twentieth century were encouraged by British authorities, among other influences, to think of themselves as something approaching dual citizens: temporal subjects of King George V and spiritual allies of Sultan Mehmed V.[14]

Pro-Ottoman sentiments were front and center in a press advertisement that ran in nearly every issue of the Delhi newspaper *The Comrade* throughout the autumn of 1914. The ad promoted Calpack hats sold by S.F. Chishti & Co. for four rupees apiece. These "Genuine Turkish Military Caps" were said to be made using "the same pattern as worn by Turk high officials like Enver Pasha" and allowed a young man "to make himself appear more respectable, and to attract attention."[15] Prospective customers for such an item made up much of *The Comrade*'s readership: modern, cosmopolitan young Muslims—the Nai Raushani, or "new light,"[16] looking to carve out space for themselves within India's rapidly evolving sociopolitical landscape. For these men, sporting a Calpack could signal both their communal identity as Muslims and their worldly sophistication in adopting the politically charged fashions of Istanbul. Their somewhat romantic self-image as "honorary Ottomans" fueled increasing interest and concern for the plight of their coreligionists abroad, as evidenced by undertakings such as Dr. Ansari's medical mission. This expanded political consciousness also prompted renewed

FIGURE 4 Enver Pasha, Commander of the Ottoman Army, in his signature Calpack hat. 1911. Portrait by Nicola Perscheid.
WIKIMEDIA COMMONS

soul-searching over Britain's role in the invasion of historically Islamic lands, and the subjugation of Muslim peoples.

World War I was to bring all of these issues to a head. In the aftermath of the war, a movement would emerge from within the Muslim cosmopolitan circles in which Khaliquzzaman and Siddiqi moved. Tapping into widespread attachment to the sacred geography and holy places of Islam, the Khilafat campaign would briefly unite many Muslims behind Gandhi's satyagrahis in a campaign against the British Empire. The collapse of that alliance, the dissolution of the Ottoman Caliphate, and protracted infighting between the Egyptian and Saudi pretend-

FIGURE 5   Mohamed Ali Jauhar in a Calpack of his own, 1920. Portrait by Auguste Léon.
MUSÉE ALBERT KAHN, BOULOGNE

ers to a new caliphal throne left India's spiritual rebels in search of a new cause. Like so many before them, they were to find it on the southeastern shore of the Mediterranean.

CALAMITY

In November 1914, the Ottomans entered World War I on the side of the Central Powers. From Delhi, *The Comrade* lamented this "calamity," which forced Indian Muslims to choose between their political loyalty to the Crown and spiritual affinity with the Sultan:

> We are using no conventional language when we say that war between Turkey and England is a calamity that the Indian Mussalmans would have given

anything in the world to avert. [. . .] It would be a hypocrisy to disguise the fact that love of Turkey is to the Indian Mussalmans a deep and abiding sentiment and that millions of them reverence [sic] the Sultan as their Caliph. [. . .] It would not, therefore, be supposed that Indian Mussalmans would be indifferent to the fate of Turkey even though she might herself bring it upon her head. [. . .] Through a cruel conjunction of circumstances their feeling of Islamic fraternity and their reverence for their Caliph have been brought into direct conflict with their sense of plain secular duty.[17]

Taking into account these eloquent anxieties (but perhaps more moved by the disproportionately high representation of Muslims within the Army of India), Raj officials pressed London to make certain pledges to their 80 million Muslim subjects, guaranteeing the inviolability of their holy places in the Middle East—which were soon to become active theaters of war. On 2 November, the Viceroy was permitted to issue a statement to this effect, quickly echoed in remarks by Prime Minister Herbert Asquith, speaking at the Guildhall in London on 9 November: "Our Sovereign claims among his most loyal subjects millions of men of Moslem faith, and nothing is further from our thoughts than to encourage a crusade against their creed and their holy places. We are prepared to defend them, should need arise, against all invaders, and to maintain them inviolate."[18]

Yet despite these promises, deployments to Middle Eastern theaters left many Muslims deeply disillusioned.[19] Indian sepoys witnessed and were subject to unspeakable brutalities during the war, notably during ill-conceived and ultimately catastrophic campaigns at Gallipoli and Kut. For Muslims, these horrors were compounded by the inescapable reality that they were fighting on behalf of a Christian alliance against Ottoman coreligionists in Arabia, Mesopotamia, and Palestine—the sacred heartlands of Islam.[20]

With the opening of the Paris Peace Conference, India's staggering contributions to the Allied war effort was recognized by the inclusion of an Indian delegation alongside those of the United Kingdom and the Dominions. But the hope and good feeling that initially accompanied the armistice in India was soon replaced by growing alarm, as it became apparent that the victorious Allies intended to dissolve the Ottoman Empire and divide its territories among themselves. Many war veterans found themselves overcome with remorse at having unwittingly participated in the dismantling of the last great Muslim Empire. Their grief was mingled with a profound sense of betrayal: Britain, they charged, had broken its pledge to protect the sanctity of Islam's sacred geography and holy sites in the Middle East. Mushirul Hasan underscores how important this was in mobilizing the Khilafat (Caliphate) movement: "The protection of the Holy

Places rather than the preservation of the tottering Turkish Empire provided the rallying point for virtually all sections of the Muslim community. Money and ornaments poured into the Khilafat fund and thousands of enthusiasts flocked to the Khilafat meetings to voice their deep concern and uneasiness over the safety and preservation of the Holy Places."[21]

As *The Comrade*'s founder, Mohamed Ali Jauhar bellowed into a crowd of protesters in 1919: "The Indian Musalmans fought for the English and shed the blood of their own co-religionists, even against their Khalifa [Caliph], and it was with their assistance that Baghdad, Jerusalem, Mesopotamia, and Arabia were run over and taken."[22]

During the crisis, Mohamed, his brother Shawkat, and other Khilafat leaders played important roles in founding the Anjuman-i Khuddam-i Kaaba, or "Society of the Servants of the Kaaba," whose goal was "protecting Muslim holy places from non-Muslim aggression."[23] The Ali brothers were both Aligarh alumni and college friends of Choudhry Khaliquzzaman. Like him, they were passionate, educated, and idealistic cosmopolitans from the United Provinces; unlike him, they spent much of the war in prison, on charges of sedition. The Ali brothers' ancestors had played a major role in the 1857 Revolt, a source of immense family pride.[24] Upon Gandhi's return from South Africa in 1915, he took an interest in the incarcerated siblings on account of their anti-British politics and their apparent willingness to face the wrath of the state for the sake of their cause. Gandhi perceived that for these pan-Islamists as much as for himself, religious piety stiffened their resolve, providing the sort of moral courage necessary to risk life and limb. He became an outspoken advocate of their release, winning the trust of many in their circles—including their mother, the formidable Abadi Begum.

ALLIES

Abadi Begum (or Bi Amman, as she was affectionately known) lost her husband while her children were still young. She was determined to give them a fine education, as a method of girding them for a lifetime of confrontation with the British. In one anecdote, while her son Mohamed was imprisoned, she was made aware that a bargain had been offered to him: in exchange for a retraction of his anti-British statements, he would be released to visit his daughters, who were gravely ill. The Begum wrote immediately to her son, warning that, were he to accept this bribe, she "still had enough life left in these old hands to choke you."[25] A pious lady, the Begum, like Gandhi, viewed her engagement in nationalist politics as a sacred undertaking: "In the glorious days of our great Prophet . . .

we the women of Islam also used to shoulder our share of the burden and march along with our men, even to the Holy Wars. . . . I do not think that we women are at all inclined to shirk today such duties as the changing times may once more require us to perform."[26]

Through his friendship with the Ali family, Gandhi was able to seize on the outrage animating the burgeoning Khilafat protests in the Muslim community and yoke them to his own campaign for Indian *swaraj*. For their part, the Alis saw in Gandhi a fiercely capable and courageous ally who could understand and embrace their cause on its own terms—namely, as a religious crusade. In Khaliquzzaman's recollection, "the incident which impressed them [the Ali brothers] very greatly about Gandhiji's views was his address to Calcutta students, in March 1915, in which he had said, 'Politics cannot be divorced from religion.'"[27] As with Gandhi's Egyptian admirers, for the Ali brothers, the fact that he was a Hindu was less salient than the fact that he understood the world—and the anticolonial struggle—through a religious lens. It was the fervency, rather than the content, of his faith that inspired their trust and admiration.

With some difficulty, Gandhi persuaded the leadership of the Khilafat movement (made up largely of Aligarh alumni) to embrace the nonviolent methods of satyagraha. With their support, he secured the leadership of the Congress Party in 1920. The resulting coalition between Congress and Indian Muslim politicians is often described as the high-water mark of Hindu-Muslim nationalist cooperation in India.[28] Between 1920 and 1922, it galvanized a veritable tidal wave of mass strikes, civil disobedience, and boycotts of British goods and institutions throughout the subcontinent. And as was occurring simultaneously in Egypt, the urgent necessities of the popular movement created new spaces for women to step onto the national stage.[29]

Among the newcomers were Bi Amman and her daughter-in-law, Amjadi Begum, the wife of Mohamed Ali Jauhar. Much like Huda Shaarawi, Amjadi Begum had been involved in ladies' charitable organizations in the years before the war. It was the imprisonment of her husband and his brother Shawkat in 1915 that served as the catalyst for her increasingly prominent role in the nationalist movement. She began speaking in his place at meetings and events, winning the praise of Gandhi, who felt she was a better public speaker than her husband and could "touch the hearts of the listener very movingly in very few words."[30] But it was Bi Amman, already seventy years old in 1920, who emerged during the Khilafat years as a true force to be reckoned with. According to the Ali brothers' biographer, Shan Muhammad, their mother "would not be tired of touring the country from one end to the other, delivering speeches and exhorting the people to do or die for the attainment of Swaraj. In her speeches she said that 'the exploiting traders' had devastated India and would continue to exploit it unless the people came forward and offered stout resistance to the imperialists. For herself she was prepared to go to gaol or be shot dead"[31]—and she urged other women not to be deterred by the threat of imprisonment; if India's jails beckoned, she instructed her listeners, they were to go in.[32] The most famous poem of the Khilafat years was an ode to Bi Amman. As Gail Minault found, even fifty years after the movement's demise, its lines were still being recited by Indian Muslims:

> Thus spake the mother of Muhammad Ali,
> Son, give your life for the Khilafat
> ... Even had I had seven sons,
> I'd sacrifice them all for the Khilafat
> This is the way of faith in the Prophet,
> Son, give your life for the Khilafat.[33]

The movement also had the ears of some British officials, notably the Viceroy, Lord Reading, and Edwin Montagu, the Secretary of State for India, whom we met protesting the Balfour Declaration in chapter 1. Montagu was ultimately forced to resign over his advocacy on behalf of Turkey's territorial integrity, a position he adopted in deference to Indian Muslim opinion. The publication of a leaked telegram in March 1922 laid bare to the British public the deep rift that had developed between officials in India and London. In it, Montagu and Reading repeated the Khilafatists' claim that, owing to their service during World War I, Indian Muslims were entitled to a special role in defining British policy in the Middle East. This would become a hallmark of petitions advanced by both Raj officials and Indian politicians and activists throughout the 1920s and 1930s: "India's service in the war, in which Indian Muslim soldiers so largely participated, and the support which the Indian Muslim cause is receiving throughout India, entitle her to claim the utmost fulfilment of her just and equitable aspirations. The Government of India particularly urge ... (1) the evacuation of Constantinople; (2) the Suzerainty of the Sultan over the Holy places; (3) the restoration of Ottoman Thrace, including Adrianople and Smyrna. The fulfilment of these three points is of the greatest importance to India."[34]

As we shall see in chapters 5 and 6, Britain's wartime pledge to maintain Islam's holy places inviolate held no less weight for Indian Muslims than the Hussein-McMahon correspondence did for Arabs, or the Balfour Declaration for Zionists. Indeed, just as proponents of Arab nationalism or a Jewish national home found frequent cause to relitigate Britain's wartime commitments over the course of subsequent decades, Indian Muslims, too, would brandish London's pledge to them as evidence of their privileged right to participate in the formation of British policy in the Middle East.

Yet even as the Khilafat movement won the support of high-ranking Raj officials and Gandhi's satyagrahis, it alienated some leading figures within Muslim nationalist circles—notably the prominent lawyer and political activist Muhammad Ali Jinnah. Only three years prior, Jinnah, as President of the Muslim League, had partnered with Congress to forge the first formal alliance between the two nationalist movements. Yet in 1920, as that alliance apparently deepened, Jinnah exited the Congress-League fold in disgust. To his mind, Gandhi's endorsement of the Khilafat campaign amounted to little more than craven political pandering to Muslim religious sentiment. It offered them emotional support—which was cheap—in exchange for swelling the ranks of the Non-Cooperation movement. Yet this bargain, charged Jinnah, conceded nothing of substance to Muslim demands for equitable political representation.[35] The poet Iqbal, too, scorned Khilafat as "an act of foolishness on the part of the Indian Muslims" and "a surrender to the Hindus"[36]—statements that echoed Jinnah's views. Nor were these critiques easily dismissed, for the Congress-League honeymoon was to be short-lived. In February 1922 in the town of Chauri Chaura, protesters retaliated against police who fired into the crowd; the police station was burned down, killing everyone inside. In response to this breach of satyagraha's strictly nonviolent code, Gandhi called off Non-Cooperation and receded from public life, entering a period of fasting.[37] Many among the Khilafatists were left feeling abandoned by Congress and disillusioned about the prospects for Hindu-Muslim unity. However, the more devastating betrayal, in some senses, was to come from an unexpected quarter: Ankara.

KHILAFAT, INTERRUPTED

In his memoir, Sultan Mahomed Shah, Aga Khan III—leader of the worldwide Ismaili community, founding member and first President of the Muslim League, and deep-pocketed patron of Aligarh—concluded his narration of the postwar Ottoman Empire on a summer's day in the Swiss resort town of Lausanne. There, on 24 July 1923, he witnessed the signature of the agreement that superseded the reviled Treaty of Sèvres, conceding to a new Turkish Republic de jure recognition of the frontiers it had prised from the Greeks in the course of a bitter war. Reflecting approvingly on the Treaty of Lausanne, which could be construed as a victory for Indian Khilafatists, the author took the opportunity to write himself off into the sunset: "For myself an eventful period of close association with the politics and diplomacy of the Middle East in general and Turkey in particular drew to a close," he sighed. "Of all that [subsequently] happened . . . I was a spectator—occasionally in the columns of *The Times* a critic—but thenceforward I ceased to be, as I had so long been, an active participant."[38] This, somewhat uncharacteristically, was the Aga selling himself short; for there remained a climactic scene to the Ottoman drama, in which the illustrious imam was to play a rather vital role.

Just four months after the ceremony in Lausanne, on 24 November 1923, three Turkish newspapers published the text of a letter addressed to the country's Prime Minister, Ismet Pasha. The letter, written by the Aga Khan and another prominent Indian Muslim, Amir Ali, claimed to speak on behalf of the Khilafat movement. It cited the profound investment of Muslims throughout the world in the institution of the Caliphate, which, they suggested, had been amplified by Ankara's recent move to dissolve the Ottoman Empire and concentrate political power in the republican government of Mustafa Kemal. The knock-on effect was to render the Caliph a purely spiritual authority. While reluctantly accepting this curtailment of the office, the authors of the letter cautioned Ismet Pasha that "any diminution in the prestige of the Caliph as a religious factor from the Turkish body politic would mean the disintegration of Islam"[39] and urged that the Caliphate itself be safeguarded "on a basis which would command the confidence and esteem of the Muslim nations and thus impart to the Turkish State unique strength and dignity."[40] It was suggested, though never firmly established, that the authors of the letter deliberately leaked it to the press, in the hopes of rallying public opinion.[41]

Whatever their intentions, the move backfired spectacularly. Mustafa Kemal's vision of a modern, secular Turkey rooted in the Anatolian heartland was already straining against the divine vestiges of a cosmopolitan empire. Perhaps more damningly, the incumbent, Abdulmecid II, had proven dangerously popular; from his ornate perch in Istanbul, the Caliph (a rather celebrated painter and patron of the arts) risked emerging as an alternative national figurehead. Kemal seized on the Khilafatists' letter as a smoking gun, proof that the continuance of the Caliphate invited foreign meddling in the affairs of the new Republic. That the Aga Khan and Amir Ali were not even Sunni was underscored in the regime's indignant public rebukes—for what could their true interests in the Caliphate be, when Ismailis and Shias did not even recognize the legitimacy of the institution? In his own remarks to the press following the letter's publication, Mustafa Kemal took pains to explicitly reject the Muslim cosmopolitanism that underpinned the

Indian Khilafat movement: "The idea of a single caliph, exercising supreme religious authority over all the peoples of Islam, is an idea drawn from books, not reality. . . . The criticism provoked by our recent reform [i.e., the dissolution of the empire] is inspired by an abstract, unrealistic idea: the pan-Islamic idea. This idea has never found expression in facts."[42]

Building on this momentum, the Turkish parliament pushed through legislation dissolving the Caliphate early in the new year. A hastily issued passport for a "M. Abdulmejid, fils d'Abdalaziz," facilitated the journey into exile of the last Ottoman Caliph and his family, aboard the *Orient Express*. For legislators in Ankara, the entire ordeal was put to bed in a matter of days. For Khilafatists in India, five years of public advocacy were just as swiftly robbed of their animating principle. But across the Arabic-speaking world, the Caliphate was only just beginning to come into focus, as people awoke to the stunning news that—seemingly overnight—it had ceased to exist.

A CALIPHATE FOR EGYPT

In Cairo, there were widespread expressions of shock and dismay at the reports from Ankara, on political as well as religious grounds. In the press, Liberal Constitutionalists no less than conservative ulema regretted the Kemalists' "hasty" decision, which threatened to weaken the bonds between Muslim countries.[43] Yet there was grudging acknowledgement that, however unfortunate the circumstances might be, the writ of Turkey's new regime had to be respected. In the newspaper *al-Siyasa*, the liberal journalist, Muhammad Hussein Haykal, conceded that any other response would be hypocritical: "We Egyptians who demand self-rule on our own terms, and insist that no outsiders should interfere in our affairs, cannot [justify], either logically or politically, interfering in the affairs of others."[44]

Though many lamented the impiety of Turkey's new regime, others sensed a unique opportunity to advance Egypt's interests. After all, the announcement of the Caliphate's dissolution coincided with the inauguration of Egypt's first parliament controlled by the Wafd and led by Zaghlul. Surely it might also be time for it to assume a more central role in the Islamic polity. Some argued for the reinstatement of the Caliphate—and even the deposed Sultan himself—in Cairo. Aside from Abdulmecid II, three new caliphal contenders also emerged: in Arabia, Ibn Saud and Sherif Hussein of Mecca would ultimately go to war over control of the Hijaz and the right to style themselves "Guardian of the Two Holy Places." From Cairo, King Fuad also threw his crown into the ring.

Hussein, who proclaimed himself Caliph a mere two days after Abdulmecid was sent into exile, was easily the least popular of the three candidates, owing to his alliance with the British during World War I. Despite the limited appeal of Wahhabi Islam, Ibn Saud was for a time considered a more serious contender, and he courted Indian Muslim opinion with some success; initially the Ali brothers, among others, favored his candidacy.[45] Fuad was no doubt tempted by the power and prestige afforded a caliph, but he was also motivated by the desire to prevent the title from falling into his rivals' hands. Rather than enter the fray directly, as Hussein had done, he delegated his public relations to allies of the palace within Egypt's clerical establishment. Sheikh Mustafa al-Maraghi, then serving as President of Egypt's supreme religious court, was appointed by the King to act as a sort of goodwill ambassador—the public face of Egypt's caliphal bid.[46] In the early phase of the post-dissolution crisis, supporters of an Egyptian caliphate existed not only among the ulema but within liberal nationalist circles as well. Saad Zaghlul even met with the King to discuss the prospect of Cairo serving as the seat of a new caliphate.[47] The pro-British paper, *al-Muqattam*, got in on the act, declaring "we do not see a land more suitable for the Caliphate and more fitting as its centre than Egypt." In a lengthy editorial near the end of March, *al-Ahram* agreed; for what could be more natural than to reestablish the Caliphate in "the largest and most advanced Muslim state"?[48]

Thus preparations got underway for an Islamic Caliphate Congress in Cairo. The Sheikh of al-Azhar sent out hundreds of invitations, addressed to organizations and prominent individuals across the Muslim world. Yet just as the Egyptian bid for the caliphate was picking up steam, it began to encounter serious resistance both at home and abroad. Alerted to the potential risks of investing King Fuad—not exactly a champion of constitutional democracy—with new titles and supranational prestige, Zaghlul and the Wafd reconsidered their support. Indians and other Muslims beyond Egypt's frontiers also expressed skepticism. Then in September 1924, Ibn Saud launched his invasion of the Hijaz, further complicating the prospects of a negotiated settlement. And so the Caliphate Congress in Cairo was postponed, but Fuad was not so easily dissuaded. As war raged in the Hijaz through 1925, he sent Maraghi to negotiate with the Hashemites and Ibn Saud, in the hopes that military aid might win their consent to Egyptian control of the pilgrimage to Mecca. When it became apparent that Ibn Saud would win the war outright, Maraghi appealed to the British for support, proposing a scheme for international Muslim trusteeship of the Hijaz—thus keeping the door ajar for Egyptian suzerainty.[49]

COMPETING ASSEMBLIES

Ibn Saud's announcement that he would host a "Congress of the Muslim World" in Mecca may well have prompted the resumption of preparations for a Caliphate Congress in Cairo—scheduled for May 1926, just edging the Saudi event. However, the popular discourse on the caliphate had evolved significantly since the spring of 1924, becoming increasingly fractious and divisive. Some Egyptian commentators cautioned that being the seat of such a global institution would invite foreign intervention in Egypt's affairs, much as international ownership of the Suez Canal already did (certainly Ankara had pointed to the perceived "meddling" of Indian Muslims in opting to dissolve the institution in the first place).[50]

Some liberals and Islamic modernists saw the potential to renovate the institution along more democratic lines. In his 1926 treatise, *Le Califat: Son évolution vers une société des nations orientales*, Egyptian jurist Abd al-Razzaq Ahmad al-Sanhuri imagined the office of caliph as a rotating post equivalent to a chairman or secretary general, within a representative body of Muslim Member States. This, he posited, could form one branch of a broader League of Oriental Nations with separate councils for Hindu and Buddhist majority countries.[51] The exiled former Khedive, Abbas Hilmi II, had floated a proposal not dissimilar to Sanhuri's for an Alliance Musulmane Internationale during the Lausanne Conference in 1923.[52] Tellingly, these formulations left unanswered the question of where and how India's Muslims might be represented; though a "minority" in India, their numbers dwarfed the populations of all the Arab countries combined.

Notwithstanding these technicalities, many prominent Muslims (including Indian Muslims) who remained invested in the spiritual dimensions of the Caliphate—from the Aga Khan,[53] to the Ali brothers,[54] Abul Kalam Azad, and Rashid Rida[55]—were seduced by the idea of a League of Eastern Nations, connecting Muslim, and in some iterations non-Muslim, Asian countries through representative international institutions. For more secular liberals, a caliphate-by-committee could, as an "authentically Eastern" institution, further the political projects of anticolonial solidarity and independence from the West, while wriggling free of the traditional fetters of religious authority. In the lead-up to the 1926 Cairo Congress, even the pro-British *al-Muqattam* expressed its hope that the gathering could serve as the forerunner to a "society of Islamic or Eastern nations."[56]

Following two years of heated debate and breathless speculation, it was perhaps inevitable that the event itself would fail to live up to expectations. Cairo's Islamic Caliphate Congress was predictably boycotted by nationalists, including the Wafd and Liberal Constitutionalists, who viewed it as an attempt to consolidate power in the hands of the palace and its religious allies. Only thirty-nine foreign delegates attended, most from neighboring Palestine.[57] Despite their best efforts, the organizers failed to attract any participants from India—something they had regarded as crucial to the success of their endeavor.[58] In fact, the Khilafat Committee had sent Dr. Ansari and another leader, Ajmal Khan, to Cairo in 1925 on a fact-finding mission ahead of the congress, but the trip apparently confirmed their suspicions that the meeting would be used to promote Fuad as a new caliph. The Khilafat leaders viewed Britain's continued presence in the country as disqualifying Egypt and its monarch; they, alongside many other would-be foreign delegates, chose to stay away.[59] Ultimately, attendance at the congress was so paltry that the subject of the caliphate was barely mooted. It was, by all accounts, a very public failure for both the palace and the ulema of al-Azhar who had organized the event. If anything, as Basheer Nafi observes, the congress signaled the eclipse of conservative religious authority in Egypt and its replacement by the new cult of the nation.[60]

Though enjoying significantly better attendance than its direct competitor in Cairo, the Congress of the Muslim World in Mecca a few short weeks later was just as disappointing for proponents of a revived caliphate. As victor of the war in the Hijaz and newly recognized sovereign of the Two Holy Cities, Ibn Saud was enjoying the benefit of the doubt in many circles (both within and beyond the Muslim world). Notwithstanding widespread reservations about the Wahhabi interpretation of Islam, the King had worked hard to cultivate good communication with the Indian Khilafat Committee and Indonesian leaders, as well as influential political and religious figures from across the Arab region. Thus in the midst of the 1926 hajj—and the relentless heat of the Arabian midsummer—illustrious personages descended on Mecca from as far afield as North Africa, the Russian Caucasus, and the island of Java.[61] Among them were three delegations from India, including four representatives of the Khilafat Committee. However, the Mecca Congress was destined to snuff out their burgeoning alliance with the Saudis. Sheikh Muhammad al-Ahmadi al-Zawahiri, who led the Egyptian delegation to Mecca, related Mohamed Ali's attitude in his memoirs: "He said that all their hopes were riding on the Turks, but that the Turks had frustrated them. When Ibn Saud's movement had arisen, they turned their hopes toward him but when they came to Mecca and saw what they saw, he let them down also."[62]

What they "saw," as John Willis has documented in detail, was Ibn Saud's profound apathy toward the Khilafatists' liberal cosmopolitan aspirations for his newly conquered realm.[63] The Ali brothers had been hopeful that an international board of trustees could be established to oversee Islam's holiest cities, along lines not dissimilar to the "League of Eastern Nations" concept then pinging its way around more progressive Muslim intellectual milieux. They were aghast at Saud's unilateral assumption of the title King of the Hijaz and his desecration, in line with stringent Wahhabi beliefs, of the tombs attributed to relatives and companions of Muhammad—long-standing sites of devotion for millions of Muslim pilgrims. As their disillusionment grew, the Khilafatists made common cause with Zawahiri's Egyptian delegation to oppose the Arabians.[64] The Mecca Congress also brought the Ali brothers into the orbit of Hajj Amin al-Husseini, the Mufti of Jerusalem and Palestinian nationalist leader. As we will see, this alliance was to survive long after they had departed the Hijaz, proving consequential for the evolution of Palestinian and Indian Muslim politics for decades to come.

Returning from Mecca, the Ali brothers launched a campaign to discourage Indian Muslims from completing the hajj, essentially calling for a boycott of Ibn Saud. Turning definitively away from both Istanbul and the Hijaz, they now looked toward a new site as a focal point for their activism in defense of Islam's holy places.

It is worth underscoring that the Caliphate issue gained traction in Egypt at the exact moment at which it began to fall off the agenda in India (even if key players like the Ali brothers were to remain invested). For Egypt, the question presented by the crisis was how to fill the power vacuum created by Turkey's abdication of spiritual leadership—specifically, whether Egypt should step in to fill the void. This sparked a regional power competition, with long-term repercussions for Egyptian-Saudi relations in particular. It also served as the catalyst for broader disagreements within the umma, between supporters of the Wahhabists and their detractors. With Egyptians hopelessly divided on the issue, Fuad eventually dropped his bid to replace Abdulmecid II. The key takeaway from the Caliphate Crisis in Egypt was that there was little to be gained politically from "pan-Islamic" causes, given the fractious debates they engendered between the conservative religious establishment and more liberal, secular forces (among other axes of dissent). As if to underscore this point, the Cairo Caliphate Congress of 1926 was a near total failure, reflecting poorly on Egypt's regional and international prestige. Egyptian critics of Fuad's caliphal aspirations were focused on the still-fragile national project. It was precisely Egypt's centrality to the Arab-Islamic world that both gave rise to the caliphal bid and provided the basis for its rejection; for Egypt did not need to host a caliphate in order to claim its importance, or perhaps even its primacy, among Muslim and Eastern nations.

Muslims in India were naturally less sanguine. The interests of the community had for many years been conceived of as linked to imperial formations, whether British, Ottoman, or both. Despite their imposing numbers, Indian Muslims were conscious of being peripheral to the Islamic centers of Istanbul, Mecca, and Cairo. Nevertheless, they perceived the existence of such a center as crucial to their position both within India and facing the British. In a sense, what the community lacked as a domestic political force could possibly be made up for through alliance or even integration with an Eastern-Islamic bloc. Thus the lessons of the Khilafat years in India were almost the complete inverse of what they were in Egypt: between 1919 and 1924, both the INC and the Muslim League witnessed the potential of pan-Islam to serve as a lightning rod for mass political mobilization. Crucially, the aspect that resonated most deeply with ordinary Indian Muslims—and brought in the most donation rupees—was the need to defend Islam's holy places. For this reason, the Middle East could serve as a useful land bridge between pan-Islam and anticolonial politics, with the potential to yoke Muslims to the mainstream Indian nationalist movement.

Whether in Egypt or in India, the lessons of the Caliphate Crisis would not soon be forgotten. Indeed, from Egypt's nationalist quest for regional leadership to the mobilization of Indian Muslim concern over protection of the holy places to the Congress Party's efforts to win Muslim support via the Middle East, the dynamics of these years would be reproduced with striking uniformity in relation to a new crisis, already brewing in Mandate Palestine.

THREE

The Poetic East

Where the world has not been broken up into fragments by
    narrow domestic walls
... Into that heaven of freedom, my Father, let my country
    awake[1]
        —RABINDRANATH TAGORE, *GITANJALI*, 1912

O Sons of Egypt! Raise up your laurels
to greet the hero of India
and pay due homage
to this rightful luminary.
He is your brother, struggling alongside you
in your bitter adversity
... and in his words and deeds, he resembles the long-
    awaited Mahdi[2]
        —AHMAD SHAWQI, "GANDHI," 1931

Not like to like, but like in difference;
Self-reverent each and reverencing each;
Distinct in individualities,
But like each other, e'en as those who love[3]
        —MOHAMED ALI JAUHAR, "THE UNITED
        FAITHS OF INDIA," 1930

INDIA'S LAUREATE

It was nearing six o'clock on a late November evening, and the Alhambra Theatre in Alexandria was heaving. Denizens of the city's culture scene and heterodox communities, resplendent beneath the glittering chandeliers, greeted each other as they made their way to their seats, exchanging pleasantries in half a dozen languages. Gradually the lights dimmed, and as the clock struck six, a figure emerged onstage—his flowing beard and brown robes a stark contrast to the bow-tied and bejeweled throats assembled in the audience before him. A hush momentarily enveloped the crowd. Then, "spontaneously," the theater erupted into thunderous applause, "in greeting to the man who is hailed and revered as a prophet in his own country."[4]

It was Rabindranath Tagore's second visit to Egypt. He had first set foot in the country as a teenager, in the company of his father. Now, however, he was a globally renowned poet—a celebrated mystic-philosopher, and the first non-European recipient of the Nobel Prize in Literature. Arriving in Egypt on the last leg of a major tour, he was given an ecstatic welcome in Alexandria and Cairo. "AUDIENCE SPELLBOUND," read one rapturous headline in *The Egyptian Gazette* "—AN AMAZING PERSONALITY." Onstage, Tagore preferred to sit behind a desk and deliver unscripted remarks on Indian philosophy, steering clear, for the most part, of politics and current events. His lecture would be followed by a recitation of several of his poems, first in English for the sake of comprehension "and then in his liquid sounding Bengali tongue," so that his listeners might appreciate the musicality of his compositions ("the second reading in each case was enthusiastically applauded"). In Alexandria, Tagore was met onstage by Mrs. Dayaldas and Mrs. Tilokchand Gopaldas, representatives of the significant Indian merchant community in Port Said, who wreathed him in garlands. He was hosted and feted by the European community, and the introduction to his lecture was given by Henry Barker, Alexandria's leading British citizen.[5]

But in Cairo a few days later, Tagore was claimed by Egypt's nationalists. At the Ezbekiyeh Theatre, the introductory remarks were delivered in Arabic by Lutfi Bey Said of the Egyptian University; and in taking the stage, Tagore addressed himself to "the people of Egypt," thanking them "for the warm welcome and hospitality he had received." In particular, he thanked Ahmad Shawqi for his collegial "poet's welcome" and remarked on the friendship that had blossomed between them.[6] Shawqi arranged a tea reception for Tagore at his home, which Saad Zaghlul was so eager to attend that he insisted on rescheduling a session of the Egyptian parliament. Taha Hussein, the literary giant, recalled that it was the last time he spoke to the Prime Minister before Zaghlul's death the following August: "It was when Shawqi was giving a reception for the great Indian poet, Tagore. A good many figures in cultural life and in government circles were invited. I was among them, in the middle of a group of friends."[7] May Ziadeh, a Lebanese poet resident in Cairo, hosted a second reception for the visiting luminary before he left—clearly there was no shortage of guests for these events.[8]

Tagore's appeal in Egypt was in some senses not dissimilar to Gandhi's (although the poet's general avoidance of politics, and specific rejection of nationalism, may have made him more palatable to British colonial audiences). Like Gandhi, he eschewed Western habits of dress, though unlike Gandhi, he kept his hair and beard long and flowing, as well as his robes. These aesthetic choices were appealing to British and Egyptian audiences alike, as "authentically" Eastern . . . and undeniably exotic.[9] Like many of his European and Asian contemporaries, Tagore posited the East as a spiritual civilization, which he contrasted with the materialism of the West. It was a distinction that many people of different backgrounds and ideological persuasions were then willing to entertain, and which the capitalist Englishman Barker applauded during his opening remarks in Alexandria: "We have with us to-night one of India's greatest sons, a man who is venerated as a prophet by millions of his own countrymen and who is making his influence felt throughout the materialistic West, in spite of and in the teeth of its materialism. . . . We call him a mystic and a visionary."[10]

EASTERN BONDS

Tagore was part of a broader, highly idealistic postwar wave of artists, authors, poets, and creatives whose work fused elements of spirituality, Eastern culture, internationalism, and anticolonialism in the decade after World War I. Combined with the national mass movements of 1919–24 and the multiplication of Islamic imaginaries that attended the dissolution of the Caliphate, this cultural milieu nurtured a new level of popular awareness, elite interaction, and intellectual exchange between Egyptians and Indians. The men and women who animated the "poetic" East not only perceived multiple levels of connection between their countries; they also worked to enhance these bonds, forging relationships across a space that they called *Sharq*, *Orient*, or *East*. Amorphous, vast, and frequently contradictory, the East of the 1920s was a romantic, aspirational, cultural construct as much as it was a political, anticolonial one. In this era as in the years ahead, the sense of affinity and admiration that existed between political leaders drew on mutual perceptions of civilizational grandeur and heroic projections of Eastern unity as well as the bond of a common anticolonial cause. In this context, symbolic gestures, sacred sites, poetry and rhetoric, and rites and rituals all became invested with heightened power and meaning.

Tagore's lecture in Cairo was sponsored by Jamiyyat al-Rabita al-Sharqiyya (Society of the Eastern Bond). Founded in 1921, it brought together prominent figures from a wide variety of backgrounds, including Islamist modernists, religious conservatives, Christians, liberals, and secularists. They founded a clubhouse in central Cairo and sponsored a series of lectures and events throughout the 1920s. Tellingly, their first major undertaking was a symposium dedicated to the life of Jamal al-Din al-Afghani, the anticolonial Islamist who had spent much of his life crisscrossing the Mediterranean and the Asian continent, exhorting colonized peoples to mine their own cultures for inspiration and band together in the face of European encroachment.

Lecturing in India, Afghani had encouraged his audiences to turn not only to the subcontinent's rich Islamic tradition but also to its Hindu and Vedic past, as sources of inspiration for their anticolonial struggle. Similarly he saw the pre-Islamic history of ancient Egypt as a potential unifying and mobilizing axis for the country's resistance to the West.[11] For the membership of al-Rabita al-Sharqiyya, as for Afghani in an earlier era, the unity of the East was not perceived as an alternative to Islamic or Arab unity; rather, it was their natural extension and corollary. In the words of one of the Society's foremost proponents, "anything which advances a nation or a religion or a language of the East, advances the East as a whole."[12] In this sense, the membership of al-Rabita al-Sharqiyya shared with other nationalists the belief that Egypt was central to—and arguably even *the* center of—overlapping Arab, Islamic, and anticolonial constellations. This created a common basis for enthusiasm about the East among Christians, Islamists, modernists, and conservatives as an arena within which Egypt could play a leading role. The Society's journal, *Majallat al-Rabita al-Sharqiyya*, began publishing in 1928 and had a distribution network that extended to Baghdad, Damascus, and Bombay.[13]

It is notable that al-Rabita al-Sharqiyya did not attract membership from within Zaghlul's Wafd due to the predominance of Liberal Constitutionalists (their parliamentary rivals) within the Society's ranks. This has sometimes been put forward as evidence that the leading personalities of the Wafd were unenthusiastic about forging connections with other Eastern countries;[14] in fact, foreign dignitaries and personalities visiting Cairo from other parts of the Middle East and Asia—including many Indians—simply met separately with representatives of the Wafd and the Society of the Eastern Bond.[15] Tagore's visit to Cairo, where his lecture was sponsored by the Society, while Zaghlul's Cabinet attended the reception hosted by Shawqi, is a case in point.

There have also been suggestions that the word *Sharq*, or East, was in practice used to define an Islamic or Arab geography, rather than something more expansive.[16] Yet Easternists in Cairo appear to have worked hard to broaden the scope of their interests and events, in a self-conscious effort to create the intercultural context they imagined themselves acting within. A case in point is the proudly

Eastern-cosmopolitan women's magazine, *L'Egyptienne*, edited by Huda Shaarawi. The first page of each issue featured a photographic portrait, accompanied by a biographical sketch; one series of articles was titled "Les grandes figures féminines de l'Orient." Essays spanned modern political and legislative developments, cultural and literary events, history, archaeology, and philosophy—from the Mediterranean to East Asia. Issues of *L'Egyptienne* from the year of Tagore's visit featured the portrait and biography of Soumé Tcheng, a Chinese Supreme Court Justice; a report on reforms to the legal status of women in Algeria; an extract from the recently published memoirs of the Turkish feminist Halide Edib; the review of a novel based on the life of Confucius; an essay on the status of women within Judaism; and an article describing the imperial interests of New Kingdom pharaohs on the Asian continent[17]—this last perhaps exceptionally telling.

During the same era that the Society of the Eastern Bond was active in Cairo (and as the ladies of the city explored the intellectual riches of the Orient from the comfort of their chaise longues), a young Indian nationalist was also beginning to think in new and transcendent ways about his country's relationship with other parts of an expansive East.

In 1927, Jawaharlal Nehru attended the founding conference of the League Against Imperialism (LAI) in Brussels. Drawing together socialists, communists, and anticolonial activists from across Europe, America, Asia and other parts of the colonized world, the conference was responsible for shaping Nehru's political consciousness on several levels.[18] Nehru's biographers have emphasized the role played by the Brussels Conference in his socialist education,[19] but it was also where he became oriented toward a broadly defined East as the natural zone of engagement and outreach for the INC. In his report on the conference for his colleagues back home, Nehru argued that the key advantage of Indian affiliation with the LAI would be "opportunities to keep in touch with many Asiatic and other countries with problems not dissimilar to ours," while identifying the principal disadvantage as "the socialist character of the League and the possibility that Russian foreign policy might influence it."[20] Michele Louro accurately describes Nehru's orientation as Asianism, yet even Nehru alternated between the words *Asia* and *East* to define this political geography, which he envisioned as including Egypt, Turkey, Persia, and Syria, as well as countries like China and Indonesia—mapping closely onto the sharq of al-Rabita al-Sharqiyya and other Egyptian Easternists. Within this geography, Nehru identified Egypt as among the most important partners for India in the struggle against imperialism.[21] In a document he prepared shortly after his return from Brussels, Nehru laid out a rose-colored vision for the foreign policy of a future independent Indian state:

> In developing our foreign policy we shall naturally first cultivate friendly relations with the countries of the East which have so much in common with us. Nepal will be our neighbour and friend; with China and Japan, Indonesia, Annam, and Central Asia we shall have the closest contact. So also with Afghanistan, Persia, Turkey and Egypt. Some people, living in a world of their own creation, imagine that there is a pan-Islamic bloc which may threaten India. This is pure fancy. Every one of the Islamic countries is developing on intensely national lines and there is absolutely no room in them for an external policy based on religion. Indeed even their domestic policy has little to do with religious dogmas. The interests of these countries are and will continue to be our interests.[22]

Thus Nehru's initial contact with socialist anti-imperialism seems to have provided him with an opening onto a borderless vista of the East as a space of engagement—the internationalist extension of the nationalism he was committed to pursuing at home. His contemporaries in Egypt, and in many other places besides, arrived at similar visions of the East during the mid-1920s through various ports of entry—whether pan-Islamic, socialist, or communist, anticolonial nationalist, feminist, or creative. Inevitably, they differed in their views on what defined it and where exactly to draw its frontiers, but they all agreed that it was something broader than the categories of religion, ethnicity, geography, or language could fully contain. In positing an expansive East, its enthusiasts articulated a self containing multitudes, at the intersection of identities and loyalties that, though seeming incompatible in the abstract, were in practice metabolized both within individual lives and shared imaginaries. Mohamed Ali Jauhar, another poet, articulated his experience of multiple identities as belonging "to two circles . . . which are not concentric. One is India, and the other is the Muslim world. . . . We belong to these two circles, each of more than 300 millions, and we can leave neither. We are not nationalists but supernationalists."[23]

Going further, to think of oneself as an Easterner could express a claim, however tangential, to a shared heritage far beyond one's own lived experiences—an affinity with distant lands, where people spoke in foreign languages and prayed to other Gods. This was the claim extended by Tagore who, in his 1888 poem, "Duranta Asha," imagined himself as an "Arab Bedouin":

> Vast desert under the feet . . .
> Flame within my heart . . .
> Marching on, spear in hand
> Only on courage to stand.[24]

As documented extensively elsewhere, Tagore was part of a transnational generation of anticolonial thinkers who felt a profound sense of Eastern affinity with Japan.[25] His family had hosted Japanese authors and intellectuals at their home in Calcutta, beginning with the philosopher of pan-Asian unity, Okakura Tenshin. While residing with the Tagores between 1901–2, Okakura completed the manuscript of his first book, *The Ideals of the East*, in which he laid out his vision of a unified Asia, bound by a spiritual and universalist "common thought inheritance" that connected "every Asiatic race, enabling them to produce all the religions of the world." For Okakura, the East was "a united living organism, each part dependent on all the others, the whole breathing a single complex life." Tagore's Japanophilia was sparked initially by his intimate friendship with Okakura, and later it was encouraged by the rising profile of Japan as a challenger to Western

FIGURE 6   Rabindranath Tagore, poet and Nobel laureate, ca. 1920.
WIKIMEDIA COMMONS

hegemony, following its naval victory over Russia in 1905.[26] Short years after he had imagined himself a Bedouin, Tagore wrote a series of haikus, including a reflection on a reversal of roles: whereas once his country had mentored Japan in the wisdom of Buddhism, now India sought "the teachings of action" from its former disciple. Following Okakura's death, Tagore traveled to Tokyo in 1916, where he expressed his profound hope that Japan would serve as a guiding light for the rest of the East: "Of all countries in Asia, here in Japan you have the freedom to use the materials you have gathered from the West according to your genius and your need. Therefore your responsibility is all the greater, for in your voice Asia shall answer the questions that Europe has submitted to the conference of Man."[27]

Back in Cairo, the no-less-Japanophile Rashid Rida was prone to musing that the Land of the Rising Sun might one day be persuaded to embrace Islam.[28] The retort came (unwittingly) from Okakura, for whom Buddhism was not just a bridge but the "great ocean of idealism" connecting all of Asia; the coming of Islam, by way of the Mongols, had signaled the end of the continent's last golden age and resulted in its fragmentation.[29]

The poetic license of the Easternists is apparent in Okakura's florid prose and Rida's overactive imagination, as too in Tagore's and Nehru's condescending admiration of the "typical fighting men" of the Arab East ("wholly untainted," as Nehru had it, "with the slave mentality of more intellectual races").[30] Yet whether we consider Arabic-language films about Indian maharajas,[31] or essays about Hinduism and Confucius in the pages of *L'Egyptienne*, Egypt's urbanites appear to have been no less enamored with a rather exotic vision of the world East of Suez. There is no question that Western metropoles—Hollywood as much as Paris or London—had a great deal to answer for in the emergence of this Orientalist fun-house mirror, which reflected to Eastern audiences fancifully distorted images of themselves.[32] Whoever the culprits, Easternism was a romantic cultural phenomenon of the 1920s, as much as it was a political one; and this is crucial to understanding the immense popular enthusiasm for "Arabia" and "all things Egyptian" across both Europe and Asia, as well as the outpouring of goodwill and even reverence accorded to figures like Gandhi and Tagore. The mutual enthusiasm that resulted would have important ramifications for relations between Indian and Egyptian nationalists throughout the following decades.

ROOF OF THE ISLAMIC WORLD

The poetic impulses of Easternism could, of course, be pressed into service for more prosaic ends. In the early 1920s, British authorities in Mandate Palestine encouraged the recently appointed Mufti of Jerusalem, Hajj Amin al-Husseini, to spearhead a fundraising campaign for badly needed repairs to the Haram al-Sharif mosque complex,[33] considered among the holiest sites in Islam.[34] Palestinian delegations were dispatched to solicit donations in Mecca, Egypt, Syria, Iraq, Bahrain, and Kuwait, as well as India. Whereas a Zionist fundraising effort on the subcontinent had been studiously ignored by the Raj in 1921 (out of concern for Muslim opinion in the midst of the Khilafat crisis), the government gave official recognition and support to the Dome of the Rock Fundraising Committee, headed by the Mufti's cousin Jamal al-Husseini, between 1923 and 1924.[35] The Palestinians were received by the Viceroy upon their arrival in November, before traveling throughout the country. The British High Commissioner to Palestine, Herbert Samuel, also sent letters to Egypt and India in support of the fundraising efforts.[36]

The Palestinian delegation to India succeeded in raising £22,000, including a £7,000 donation from the Nizam of Hyderabad. In Egypt, King Fuad donated £10,000, contributing significantly to the total sum of £84,000. Thanks to these funds, al-Aqsa and the Dome of the Rock were duly renovated under the direction of the Turkish architect Kamal al-Din, and works were carried out throughout the Haram al-Sharif. Famously, the roof of the Dome of the Rock was plated in gold.[37] It was the resumption of renovation works around al-Buraq—the interior portion of the Western Wall, whose exterior is regarded as the holiest site of the Jewish faith—that served as the immediate catalyst for a series of Zionist protest actions and marches in the summer of 1929. These in turn resulted in the worst intercommunal violence yet seen between Jews and Arabs in Mandate Palestine.

While a comprehensive discussion of the Buraq Revolt lies beyond the scope of the present work, there are several crucial points worth highlighting. The first is the centrality of the "sacred geography" of the Temple Mount and the built environment—the actual wall—to the conflict. In the months preceding the eruption of violence, Zionist fundraisers circulated retouched photographs to overseas donors, showing a "Third Temple" erected on the site of the Haram al-Sharif.[38] Fears of a Zionist "takeover" of the site stoked Muslim animosity in turn. Jewish and Muslim committees were formed—the Western Wall Defense Committee and Committee for the Defense of al-Buraq, respectively. When the youth of the militant Zionist Beitar movement took to the streets in August, their rallying cry was "The Wall Is Ours."³⁹

The second point is the internationalization of the crisis. The Mufti was alarmed by Jewish appeals to a broad international public—both overseas Jewish communities and gentile Zionists—in support of their claims to ownership of the Temple Mount. He concluded that Palestinians, too, would need to mobilize a network of support beyond their borders in order to counter the influence of the Jewish Agency in places like London, New York, and Geneva. During the fundraising campaign for the Haram al-Sharif, the Mufti had promoted a self-consciously universalist image of a what, as Roberts notes, we might today call a Muslim world heritage site, to be visited by "Easterners and Westerners, Moslems as well as non-Moslems."⁴⁰ In the midst of the Buraq Revolt, he turned to the network of contacts first established during that fundraiser, but now he tweaked the framing, calling on Muslim countries to help defend the Haram al-Sharif from a Zionist takeover.⁴¹ This rallying cry resonated with Indian Khilafatists' earlier efforts to defend Muslim holy places from Western encroachment. The Ali brothers, who had been instrumental in facilitating the efforts of the fundraising committee in India and had befriended the Mufti during the Mecca Congress in 1926, now proclaimed Palestine to be "the best center for our work"⁴² and embraced the cause of the Haram al-Sharif as their own.

To this end, they hosted a conference on Palestine in Bombay in April 1930, hailed at the time as "the largest Muslim gathering that was ever held in India." While this was certainly an exaggeration, there were over four thousand delegates in attendance. One of the conference's more intriguing attendees was Muhammad Ali Jinnah, then working as a barrister in London. Jinnah even cosponsored a resolution with the Ali brothers—a dramatic volte-face after their falling out ten years prior. Notwithstanding their profound disagreement over the Khilafat issue, Palestine apparently created new grounds for the erstwhile enemies to unite around a shared vision of Indian Muslim engagement abroad. A few weeks later, and responding to the Mufti's call, 16 May was observed as Palestine Day in over twenty towns and cities throughout India; in Bombay, thirty thousand people joined a procession, including Muslims and Hindus.⁴³

That autumn, as the Ali brothers traveled by steamer to the First Round Table Conference on Indian self-governance being held in London, they disembarked at Suez and traveled inland to Cairo to meet with the Mufti, who had come by train from Jerusalem for the express purpose of conferring with them. Hajj Amin hoped that the Ali brothers would raise the issue of Palestine during the Round Table, as a matter of utmost importance to India's Muslims. He even sent his cousin, Jamal al-Husseini, to London to keep in touch with the brothers and follow developments at the conference. Hopes were running high that the Round Table could lead to a breakthrough on the subject of India's independence.

RITES OF PASSAGE

These hopes were, of course, to be dashed. Among the crucial shortcomings of the First Round Table was the absence of Gandhi, who had fallen out with the Muslim League and an important faction of his own party in the lead-up to the conference. In his remarks to the assembled, Mohamed Ali Jauhar regretted the absence of his former comrade. He was gravely ill that November and requested the "privilege of the invalid" to remain seated while delivering his speech:

> I say no sane man with all these ailments would have travelled seven miles. And yet I have come seven thousand miles of land and sea because where Islam and India are concerned, I am mad . . . the fact is that today the one purpose for which I came is this: that I want to go back to my country, if I can go back, with the substance of freedom in my hand. Otherwise I will not go back to a slave country. I would even prefer to die in a foreign country, so long as it is a free country; and if you do not give us freedom in India you will have to give me a grave here.
>
> [. . .] It is for the sake of peace, friendship, and freedom that we have come here, and I hope we shall go back with all that; if we do not, we go back into the ranks of fighters where we were ten years before.
>
> [. . .] As I said two or three days ago, India has put on fiftyleague boots. We are making forced marches which will astonish the world, and we will not go back to India unless a new Dominion is born. If we go back to India without the birth of a new Dominion we shall go back, believe me, to a lost Dominion. We shall go back to an America.[44]

Only a few weeks later, on 4 January 1931, Jauhar died suddenly in London. The shock on the subcontinent was immense; his dramatic call for a grave abroad took on a prophetic quality. Within days, a flurry of telegrams between Shawkat Ali in London and Amin al-Husseini in Jerusalem had resulted in a momentous proposal: that the deceased Muslim nationalist, erstwhile hero of the Khilafat movement and more recent champion of Palestine, be buried on the grounds of the Haram al-Sharif.

After some deliberation, the British authorities in London decided to give these arrangements their blessing. It was felt that whatever the impact of burying Jauhar in Palestine, it would be far less explosive than the symbolism of his returning to British India literally in a casket. And so officials in London leaned on the High Commissioner in Jerusalem to make the necessary arrangements for what amounted to a quasi state funeral. Every courtesy was extended to the mourning family of the deceased; when they arrived by steamer at Port Said, the High Commissioner's train carriage was waiting to transport them into Palestine.[45]

Telegrams poured in, including a carefully worded message of condolence to Jauhar's family from the Jewish Agency "on behalf of the Jews of Palestine" (Jewish leaders had explained to the High Commissioner that no member of their community would accept an invitation to attend the event, as setting foot on the Temple Mount risked treading on the Holy of Holies and was thus forbidden to Jews). From the Arabs of Haifa came a message honoring the departed's "activity to expand Islamic solidarity in India regarding the holy places in Palestine."[46] This tribute was particularly apt, for the activism of the Ali brothers—from the Khilafat years onward—had indeed focused on Muslim holy sites, both within Palestine and across the Middle East. The initial connection between Jauhar and the Mufti had come via his solicitation of a caretaker for the Indian Lodge in 1922.[47] Thus Indian Muslim internationalism in general, and its engagement with Palestine in particular, was rooted in the "sacred geography" of Muslim holy sites and material culture, a framing that was to become, if anything, more emphatic through their alliance with the Mufti. As Muslims from a country they could not claim to possess, the sacred geography of Islam as a universal trust (or *waqf*) concerned the Ali brothers deeply—more than the anticolonial struggle against the British and certainly more than political control of Palestine. For this reason, the Ali brothers (much like the Mufti himself in this era) were willing to work with the British authorities to secure Muslim interests, both in India and elsewhere. Unlike the Mufti, they were also open-minded about cooperation with the Zionists, on the premise that peace in Palestine was an essential requisite for the protection of Muslim holy sites, and in the long-term interest of the Muslim community there (once Shawkat actually arrived in Palestine and witnessed the situation on the ground, he apparently began to change his mind).[48]

The funeral took place on Friday, 23 January. The Mufti issued five thousand invitations to his religious and political allies, as well as Christian faith leaders and foreign dignitaries. Close coordination between the Mufti and the British authorities ensured the procession went off without a hitch. There were claims in the Arabic press that one hundred thousand turned out along the parade route—but even assuming these figures were exaggerated, the crowd was certainly impressive. Jauhar's widow, Amjadi Begum, was accompanied throughout the day by Palestinian feminists.[49] These were, in all likelihood, women affiliated with

FIGURE 7   Shawkat Ali (fourth from left), Amjadi Begum (fourth from right), and their companions receive a Palestinian flag from Hajj Amin Al-Husseini (center). Jerusalem, January 1931.
PALESTINIAN MUSEUM DIGITAL ARCHIVE, SA'EED AL-HUSSEINI COLLECTION

the Arab Women's Association or one of its precursors.[50] It is unclear whether she had previously corresponded with some of these women, but the funeral would have been her first time meeting them in person. They were certainly fitting companions for the grieving widow, given her own role in the mobilization of women during the Khilafat and Non-Cooperation movements.

At the chosen gravesite—located just on the inner edge of the hotly contested Western Wall—eulogies were read by the Mufti and Shawkat Ali, as well as by Ahmad Shawqi, the Egyptian "Prince of Poets," and the Lebanese-Palestinian nationalist poet Wadih al-Bustani.[51] According to Esmat Elhalaby, Bustani later claimed to be the first Christian to have delivered a eulogy on the grounds of the Haram al-Sharif; he thought that Jauhar had died while in London "with the Hindu leader Mahatma Gandhi, in the service of the Indian nation."[52] Although this was not quite true—Gandhi and Congress were not represented at the First Round Table—Bustani clearly wished to emphasize the ethic of interfaith cooperation that he saw Jauhar as championing.

The presence of Christian faith leaders and foreign dignitaries, the readings by al-Bustani and Shawqi, and above all the interment of an Indian Muslim in Jerusalem—all of these choices were intended by the organizer to demonstrate the broad international coalition in support of the Palestinians, and against the similarly international Zionist movement, in the ongoing contest over Jerusalem's physical and spiritual geography. Even news outlets opposed to the Mufti conceded: "Many Muslim leaders will ask to be buried close to the Haram al-Sharif. In this manner the connection between the Muslim world and Palestine will be enhanced and the strength and resistance to the Zionist movement will be augmented."[53]

Somewhat ironically, however, there would be only one other high-profile burial on the Haram al-Sharif, mere months after Jauhar was laid to rest. Perhaps seeking to capitalize on the momentum generated by the first funeral (which was, by all accounts, an unqualified success for the Mufti), that summer Sharif Hussein of Mecca was buried in state next to al-Aqsa mosque. Hussein was, of course, the wartime ally of the British, whose rebellion against the Ottoman Empire had utterly horrified Khilafatists—none more so than the Ali brothers. Though it is difficult to prove, the fallout between Shawkat Ali and the Mufti, which would be readily apparent by December of that year, may have had something to do with the close quarters Shawkat's late brother was abruptly forced to share, for all eternity, with a man he had utterly reviled in life.

As it transpired, Jauhar was not the only famous corpse to have new bedfellows foisted upon him in 1931. Though Saad Zaghlul had died in Cairo mere months after Tagore's visit, in August 1927, arrangements for his interment dragged on for nearly a decade. There were ambitious plans for his tomb, designed in a neopharaonic style reflective of the Wafd's golden era. It was intended by his widow to be an ecumenical choice, on the premise that ancient Egyptian themes and symbols "belonged" equally to the country's Muslims and Copts.[54] Works got underway in 1928 but stalled repeatedly, with progress pegged closely to the political fortunes of the Wafd. As a result, the mausoleum was not finished until the winter of 1931—but even its completion proved ill-timed and controversial.

The failure of Anglo-Egyptian Treaty negotiations in 1930 and the Wafd's subsequent resignation from government precipitated a very dark period in Egypt's history. The King appointed in its stead an administration led by Ismail Sidqi, who repealed the 1923 Constitution, dismissed hundreds of pro-Wafd officials, imprisoned the party's leaders, violently suppressed popular demonstrations, and muzzled the country's vibrant free press. In the midst of this orgy of executive authority, Zaghlul's tomb was finally completed, but the Prime Minister was loath to preside over the inauguration of a monument to his late political opponent. In a bizarre countermove, he ordered the transfer of royal mummies from the

Egyptian Museum to the newly completed mausoleum, ostensibly mocking the neo-Pharaonism of the Wafd leader. When Madame Zaghlul heard of the plan, she was aghast and blocked the interment of her husband's remains alongside the mummies.[55] The late Prime Minister would have to wait until the Wafd returned to power in 1936 before finally being laid to rest—alone—in the mausoleum built for him.

Returning to the winter of 1931, as Jauhar found his eternal resting place in Jerusalem and Zaghlul was temporarily denied his in Cairo, they were joined beyond the veil by Motilal Nehru, Jawaharlal's father, a giant of the Congress Party who died relatively suddenly on 6 February in Lucknow. Word of his passing stole headlines, rather fittingly, from the imperial pageantry of the Delhi Durbar, which had been planned to celebrate the formal inauguration of British India's new capital city.[56] The festivities had been years in the making, but the nation and its newspapers were instead captivated by the spectacle of Motilal's son, Jawaharlal, and Gandhi carrying the body of the elder statesman draped in the Indian tricolor to the banks of the Ganges for cremation.[57]

The deaths of both Jauhar and Zaghlul had presented opportunities to concretize nationalist claims through the planting of human remains like flags in the earth. In the case of Jauhar, it was precisely his identity as a foreigner, that is, a non-Palestinian Muslim, that had rendered his interment within the sacred geography of the Haram al-Sharif so valuable to the Mufti, who sought to internationalize the defense of Palestine. Meanwhile Zaghlul's tomb evoked the ancient civilization of the Nile Valley as a means of engaging Egyptian Christians and Muslims in a common nationalist commemoration.[58]

On the banks of the Ganges, Gandhi no less powerfully asserted the claim of India's nationalists to the sacred geography of their land—embodied by the river goddess Ganga—and the ancient heritage of the Indus Valley, which gave rise to the practice of cremation and the funerary rites that surround it. Nor were the proceedings any less ecumenical for their distinctly Hindu character. Speaking before the smoking funeral pyre, Gandhi paid tribute to the late statesman as a martyr of the nationalist cause, who joined the ranks of other fallen heroes like Mohamed Ali Jauhar, whose sacrifice, Gandhi emphasized, was equally worthy of honor:

> One by one, many eminent leaders and great sons of the Motherland have passed away when the country needed them most. We should not weep for them. Do not think that we are to-night offering the body of clay that enshrined that beautiful soul to fire. In fact you are all witness to the fact that the high soul has sacrificed itself for the country.

> It is not the first sacrifice in freedom's cause.... The Lokmanya [Tilak]'s martyrdom had crowned his life. Similar was the case of Pandit Motilal. So had done Deshbandhu Das, Lajpat Rai, Hakim Ajmalkhan, [and] Maulana Mohammad Ali [Jauhar] who died for the cause of the country. His sacrifice was a matter of joy and pride.
>
> ... If you regard it as national *yajna* [Sanskrit: sacrificial offering] and feel it your duty to take part in it, then one and all, take the sacred vow on the holy Ganges bank to-night that you shall make all the necessary sacrifice required for the attainment of complete independence and for the good of the country. If you take this vow tonight we will achieve our object.[59]

Despite Gandhi's intentions, no doubt sincere, to embrace Muslims as full partners in the achievement of national liberation, he was to find the practical implementation of this ideal increasingly elusive in the months and years ahead. This was already apparent to those following Indian politics by the late 1920s, but the Second Round Table would reveal to the world the extent of the rift that had opened up between Gandhi and his former allies in the Muslim League.

AL-RUH AL-AZIM

The steamship *Rajputana* departed Bombay in late August 1931, bound for London and carrying on its second-class deck an exceedingly famous passenger who by all accounts insisted on sleeping under the stars.[60] Traveling on the same ship were Mohamed Ali Jauhar's daughter Gulnar and her husband, Shuaib Qureshi. Gandhi was of course an intimate friend of the family and fond of Gulnar's infant daughter, Aziz Fatima, born only a month after her grandfather's passing, and said to have been named according to his wishes.[61] It was rumored that Gandhi was in such a foul mood over the prospect of the London talks that the press photographers, in desperation, asked the Qureshis to borrow their daughter—the only being on board he seemed incapable of scowling at.[62] Their ploy worked. Images of the old man and the baby laughing in mutual delight (dubbed by photographers "the toothless grins") were reprinted across the globe, contributing to the fanfare surrounding Gandhi's first voyage to London in many years. Disembarking at Aden, he delivered a speech in front of a large audience at a "citizen's meeting." There he appealed to the Arabs to help bridge the growing divide between Hindus and Muslims in India for the sake of their common nationalist cause.[63] This was to become a common Congress refrain in its relations with the Middle East.

Possibly alarmed by the tenor of the Aden publicity stunt, British officials

FIGURE 8   The Toothless Grins: Gandhi and Aziz Fatima bound for London aboard the SS *Rajputana*, August 1931.
DINODIA PHOTOS / ALAMY.

ensured that the SS *Rajputana* spent as little time as possible in Egyptian waters and discouraged the ship's famous passenger from disembarking. Nevertheless, Gandhi's short journey up the Suez Canal was met with front-page headlines in every major Egyptian daily. The widowed Madame Zaghlul ensured her greetings were conveyed as soon as the ship passed into Egyptian territorial waters. Zaghlul's successor as leader of the Wafd, Mustafa al-Nahas, issued an invitation for Gandhi to visit the country, which was delivered to him onboard and subsequently reprinted in the press. Among the flurry of articles that appeared the next day was an exclusive interview with al-Ruh al-Azim (literally "Great Soul," the Arabic translation of *Mahatma*), conducted by Mahmud Abul Fat'h of *al-Ahram*, who had boarded the SS *Rajputana* at Suez. Asked to impart some wisdom to the Egyptian nation, "Gandhi replied that true freedom did not come just from imitating the West. Noting that the Egyptians were also an ancient race, he said that he expected India's freedom to lead to Egypt's as well, and that achieving this through nonviolence would have a great effect on all "Eastern nations."[64]

Once in London, Gandhi encountered another Egyptian admirer. The diplomat Amine Youssef had just received a summons from his government in Cairo, but he was determined that on no account would he miss the opportunity to meet the Indian leader:

> After I had received the telegram recalling me [to Egypt] . . . I ventured so far to disobey orders as to stay a few days for what I regarded as a very important purpose. Gandhi and the Indian Nationalist leaders were in London and I was anxious for many reasons to establish contacts with them. I saw Gandhi and had a very interesting talk with him for two hours. . . . He spoke very highly of the late Zaghloul Pasha whom he considered the father of all Nationalist movements in the East, including India.[65]

Youssef also invited Gandhi to a reception at which he was to give a speech. Although the elderly statesman did not personally attend, he sent his son as an envoy. According to Youssef, the reception was attended by "a number of influential members of both the Indian and the Egyptian Nationalist Movements."[66]

Despite his popularity with Middle Easterners and East Enders alike, Gandhi's gloomy premonitions on board the SS *Rajputana* were borne out—the Second Roundtable ended in disappointment and frustration. The Muslim delegates to the talks, including many of his former allies, banded with the Dalits, Christians, and other minority representatives to block Gandhi's proposals. Their argument was that Congress, with its principally Hindu base, could not claim to speak for the majority of Indians—that, in fact, in their very diversity, the minority communities outnumbered the Hindus. For this reason, they argued it would be unjust to subject them to majority rule—what Jauhar had earlier described, during the First Roundtable, as the "domination" of one community by another. Thus the conference wound up inconclusively in December.

The excitement generated by media attention during Gandhi's outward journey, as well as ongoing press coverage of the Second Roundtable, likely had something to do with the much larger Egyptian reception that awaited him during his return journey through the Suez Canal. While Nahas was forbidden by the Sidqi government to host a welcome tea at the home of Saad Zaghlul, a convoy of Wafd supporters and officials, accompanied by members of the Egyptian Feminist's Union, traveled to Port Said to greet Gandhi on board his ship.[67] One such fortunate young feminist was Saiza Nabarawi, editor of *L'Egyptienne*. In the report she published on her interview with Gandhi on board the *HMS Pilsna*, Nabarawi waxed poetic about everything from the barren tent into which she was ushered on the third-class deck ("thus evoking the image of a temple of Peace realised by the purity of the Spirit and the Heart!") to the near-silence that met her ("With an exquisite courtesy and modesty he responds to our fraternal messages with an amiable nod of the head, from time to time joining his hands in a sign of thanks. He doesn't speak much but listens attentively"). The true prize from her interview was a handwritten note from Gandhi addressed to the women of Egypt, reproduced in the pages of *L'Egyptienne*: "I hope that the Egyptian sisters will play the same part that their Indian sisters are playing in the liberation movement of their respective lands. For I believe that non-violence is the special prerogative of women."[68]

Gandhi's "visit" to Egypt in 1931 inspired a host of Egyptian journalists, politicians, and activists. Ahmed Shawqi, Egypt's most celebrated poet, wrote a long tribute in his honor. Three biographies, all lavish in their admiration, appeared in Egypt in the year 1934 alone.[69] Several Egyptian authors, including Mohi al-Din Rida, drew parallels between Gandhi and Zaghlul.[70] The Wafd naturally sought to promote this perceived connection between their movement and the famed father figure of Indian nationalism—a much more prominent figure globally than any of their own local heroes. And, as Nabarawi remarked shrewdly, Gandhi was useful to Egyptian nationalists for another reason: as an "eye-witness of that solidarity in misfortune which unites Eastern nations," he could "destroy, once and for all, that absurd myth which our enemies have endlessly spread: our religious fanaticism."[71]

But Gandhi was not the only Indian politician visiting the Middle East that week; for as he met with his Egyptian admirers on board the *Pilsna*, several of the delegates he had recently been sparring with in London disembarked in Port Said and took the train north into Palestine. They were headed to the World Islamic Congress in Jerusalem, organized by Hajj Amin al-Husseini and Shawkat Ali.

RECONVENING ISLAM

Plans for the World Islamic Congress in Jerusalem had taken shape during Jauhar's funeral the previous winter and benefited from the extensive list of international contacts they had assembled at that time.[72] So it was that in December 1931, a host of outsized personalities—from the Islamist modernist Rashid Rida to the great Urdu poet Muhammad Iqbal—descended on Jerusalem, the guests of Hajj Amin. Though the question of the caliphate was definitively off the table (as the Mufti had promised a deeply skeptical King Fuad),[73] it was impossible for the event to avoid comparison with the two earlier Islamic conferences in Cairo and Mecca. However, both the tone and objectives of the Jerusalem Congress were quite different.

To begin with, the choice to frame the event as Islamic had a great deal to do with the Mufti's desire to avoid British interference. Partially through watching his neighbors in the Zionist community, and partially thanks to a colonial policy with its origins in India, he had learned that the British authorities were loath to intervene in the sphere of religious ritual and belief. Framing the congress as an Islamic event thus neatly sidestepped British objections. In practice, however, the event could have been more accurately described as Easternist, for its participants gave voice to the colonial grievances and national aspirations of Palestinians and Arabs, while affirming in a resolution the congress's explicit solidarity with Arab Christians, and implying their alignment with Gandhi and his secular movement in India.[74] The Mufti, who had long cultivated close ties with the Egyptian Wafd and the Cairo-based Society of the Eastern Bond,[75] believed that this sort of broad international coalition, embracing both pan-Islamic and secular anticolonial networks, was the most effective way to counter European and American support for the Zionist movement.

As previously alluded, the Jerusalem Congress also served as the backdrop for a significant falling out between Hajj Amin and Shawkat Ali, its organizers. Though greatly outnumbered, delegates hostile to the Mufti coalesced around Shawkat Ali, including a large delegation from the Young Men's Muslim Association in Egypt. They sat together throughout the congress's sessions and voted as a bloc.[76] The sticking points between Hajj Amin and Shawkat were telling: while both had agreed in principle to establish an Islamic university in Jerusalem, their visions for the institution were sharply at odds. The Mufti explicitly intended for the new university to rival the recently established Hebrew University in Jerusalem, but Shawkat Ali viewed this framing as unnecessarily antagonistic. He imagined a more modern and "globalized" institution that could hold its own—and ultimately join the ranks—of the great centers of learning in the West, much as his alma mater, Aligarh, had positioned itself as a Muslim Oxford. To this end he posited that the main language of instruction should be English. Hajj Amin and many other delegates found these proposals almost offensive—the only possible language of instruction for a great Islamic university could be Arabic.[77]

Above and beyond these disagreements over the hypothetical university, the question of how to defend Jerusalem and its holy places was also the subject of profound disagreement. When delegates called for the congress to reject the authority of the Mandate administration, Shawkat Ali objected on the ground that "discussion of the Mandate was extraneous" and risked embroiling the proceedings in "avoidable problems" with the British authorities. This went down poorly; the future Prime Minister of Lebanon, Riad el-Solh, publicly reprimanded him for his lack of support for Arab independence.[78] The discord marked a veritable sea change from World War I—when Shawkat and his brother had spent considerable time in prison for their opposition to the Raj—or the years of the Khilafat movement, when the Ali family rallied the masses in favor of Home Rule. The immediate cause was Gandhi's refusal to support Muslim federalism, which had lately brought Ali and many of his fellow Muslim Leaguers into closer alignment and cooperation with the British government and against the INC. In Jerusalem, Ali was called out for his break with Gandhi; delegates expressed suspicion of a man who would sell out India's nationalist cause over communal issues.[79] These "Islamic" conference attendees apparently sided with an absent Hindu over the event's coorganizer, precisely because he was seen to have prioritized the interests of Muslims over the common anticolonial struggle in India. Whatever they claimed to be doing in Jerusalem, the political solidarity of at least some delegates was clearly more expansive than either pan-Islam or Arab nationalism alone could account for; their statements and actions were both broadly Eastern in their orientation, and pointedly anticolonial in their priorities and goals.

This was also, incidentally, the analysis offered by Saiza Nabarawi, in an astute aside to her report on Gandhi's passage through the Suez Canal that month. What greater proof could there be, asked Nabarawi rhetorically, "of our tolerance and our love of liberty than Muslim Egypt supporting the nationalist claims of the Hindus against the adversaries of full independence—even if they were coreligionists! Religious Crusades are in effect no longer of our era. This was clear during the latest Muslim Congress held in Palestine. What ensured its success was not intolerance in religious matters, but the solidarity of all of its members against the foreign imperialism which enslaves oriental countries."[80]

THE POETS' FAREWELL

Ahmad Shawqi, Egypt's "Prince of Poets," was the next nationalist giant to journey across the great divide; he died in Cairo in October 1932. A committee was assembled to plan the commemorative ceremony for his *arbayn*, which marks the fortieth day after a person's death. The committee reached out to at least two Indian poets who had known Shawqi, with invitations to attend the ceremony in Cairo. The first was Tagore, whom Shawqi had hosted in Cairo in 1926; the second was Iqbal, with whom he attended the Jerusalem Congress the previous winter.

On a superficial level, it might have been anticipated that Shawqi's closer bond would have been with Iqbal, who shared with him both his Muslim faith and his beloved Arabic language. Iqbal did send his dutiful, if brief, regrets to the organizers in Cairo, expressing his hope "that Shawqi's immortal spirit will lead Egypt to life, light and glory."[81] But by far the lengthier and more personal tribute came from Shawqi's Hindu friend Tagore, who wrote of his "esteem and admiration for that immortal spirit who, in his greatness, was able to raise the banner of glory and illuminate—not Egypt alone—but the countries of the East as a whole":

> It was my great good fortune and privilege to have had the pleasure of meeting the honorable departed [Shawqi] during my brief stay in Cairo, years ago. I still carry the most beautiful memories of that time. What I witnessed of him—from the charm of his personality, to his sense of mission in pursuit of the ideal—left a profound impression on me. On behalf of my country, and speaking from my soul, I mix my voice with those emanating from across the world, voices paying tribute to a poet, and such a patriot. Since his death, he has taken up his eternal place in the hearts of mankind.[82]

The deaths of Ahmad Shawqi, Mohamed Ali Jauhar, Saad Zaghlul, and Motilal Nehru marked the symbolic end of an era: the first, idealistic wave of interwar nationalism, internationalism, and anticolonialism in the East, which forged a new level of popular awareness, elite interaction, and intellectual exchange between Egypt and India. Similarly the focus, dating from at least the time of the Khilafat crisis, of Indian Muslim activists on the sacred geography of Islam formed part of a broader Muslim cosmopolitan discourse in which religion could serve as a bridge into global citizenship. In contrast to Mustafa Kemal in Turkey or Ibn Saud in the Hijaz—who each for different reasons rebuffed Indian Muslim "meddling" in their internal affairs—Hajj Amin al-Husseini welcomed Indian involvement in Palestine with open arms. The particular focus of Zionism on the holy land resulted in competing claims to specific sites, such as al-Buraq / the Western Wall. For this reason Hajj Amin embraced and encouraged the Khilafatists' existing preoccupation with the protection, or defense, of Islam's sacred geography, as creating a valuable transnational counterweight to the equally global Zionist movement. Despite the clear ideological continuity between their previous activism and present endeavors, Palestine also apparently became the site of a rapprochement between the Muslim League and its estranged leader, Jinnah, from at least 1930 onward. Precisely how and why this happened remain somewhat mysterious; nevertheless it is apparent that in Palestine both Jinnah and Iqbal, the anti-Khilafatists, perceived a worthier cause for Indian Muslim activism, and even leadership.

Of course many of the figures at the forefront of this "first wave" of interwar Easternism, including Gandhi, Tagore, Shawkat Ali, and Huda Shaarawi, would carry on energetically into the coming decade. But by the time of Ahmad Shawqi's death in 1932, the tone of international engagement had shifted definitively. The Great Depression and the rise of fascism in Europe had supplanted the delirious optimism of the postwar years. Egypt's brief dalliance with liberal nationalism was under attack from the authoritarian Sidqi regime (as Shawqi was laid to rest, the earthly vestiges of Zaghlul, hero of 1919, remained trapped in administrative purgatory). In India, the nationalist alliance between Congress and the Muslim League, which had shaken the very foundations of British rule in the early 1920s, was already giving way to communal infighting, mutual suspicion, and recriminations, which the Raj proved only too willing to exploit. The romantic idealism of the immediate postwar years that had created space for poetic visions of the East had all but evaporated; in its place, harder edged political "realism" and authoritarian ideologies began coming into vogue—antidotes, so they claimed to be, to the crises and disappointments that liberal cosmopolitanism had failed to prevent.

Still, many of the political and cultural impulses of the poetic East proved difficult to snuff out. In the chapters that follow, we will continue to find meaningful echoes and allusions to this romantic register embedded within the increasingly earthbound deliberations, diplomacy, and decision-making of the 1930s and 1940s.

PART II CAPITAL OF THE EAST

FOUR

Abyssinia in the Headlines

> The vultures of Europe yet ignore
> the poison lurking in Abyssinia's corpse
> That rotting carcass is no more
> the zenith of man, virtue's downfall
> In our age pillage is what nations are for
> every wolf would some hapless lamb devour[1]
> —"ABYSSINIA," MUHAMMAD IQBAL, AUGUST 1935

AN ABRUPT CHANGE OF PLANS

On 1 October 1935, the Egyptian press reported the arrival at Port Said of the British High Commissioner, Sir Miles Lampson, and his wife Lady Lampson (Jacqueline to her friends), aboard the RMS *Viceroy* of India. The Lampsons' return to Cairo from their annual holiday in England was almost a month ahead of schedule, a detail not lost on *al-Ahram*, Egypt's leading daily newspaper: "Sir Miles' sudden return is surrounded by intrigue and inference, particularly as it came on the heels of a meeting at the Foreign Office last Monday. In other words, it was the British Government that decided on the High Commissioner's return, and not he who had requested the remainder of his holiday be cancelled. Nor did anyone anticipate that Sir Miles would so suggest; for he was known to have been eager to enjoy his holiday to the fullest."[2] So, indeed, he had been. In his diary he recorded on 18 September: "Was actually on the point of leaving for our round of visits . . . when letter came from Vansittart saying S. of S. would like me to get back to Egypt prontissimo! . . . It's extraordinary how no plan of mine ever works out as arranged. There is a fate about it."³

The reason behind the untimely (and unwelcome) end to Lampson's vacation was alluded to with a single word: *prontissimo*. The High Commissioner was sent back to Cairo in light of Italy's looming invasion of Ethiopia, then often called Abyssinia in Europe. On 1 October the Egyptian press reported, in articles running alongside reports of the High Commissioner's return, that Ethiopian Emperor Haile Selassie had ordered the general mobilization of his troops, said to number over a million men. Selassie had appealed to the League of Nations for help in repelling the Italian advance; both Italy and Ethiopia were League members, which meant the invasion was expressly forbidden under Article X of its constitution. All eyes were on Britain, a champion of the League and regarded by many as the logical enforcer of its will. Popular opinion was strongly in favor of some intercession on Ethiopia's behalf; the British public was staunchly internationalist, and the Baldwin government was then campaigning for reelection on a platform that placed support for the League at the heart of British foreign policy.⁴

As Lampson settled back into his Cairo rhythms that autumn—golf at the club, luncheons at the residency, shooting at the weekend—the simultaneous dramas of the Italian advance in East Africa and the diplomatic wrangling at the League of Nations in Geneva unfolded in the city's papers, followed closely by Egyptians and foreigners alike. How long would the war last, and who would emerge victorious? What sanctions, if any, would the League impose on Mussolini? Would Britain—champion of international law and liberal empire—defend the rights of an independent African nation against a blatantly aggressive European power? At a time when political polarization on the continent was increasing and military rearmament had ramped up from Germany to Japan, the answers to these questions seemed of vital importance to the fate of international society.

In Egypt the reverberations of the Abyssinian Crisis would prove hugely consequential. The war "two doors down" in East Africa would transform the nature of the country's relationship with Great Britain, reenforce its military dependence on India, and usher in an era of high-stakes Arabic media warfare, which would ultimately give birth to the BBC World Service. Simultaneously the crisis became, for a time, the focal point of nationalist and anticolonial discourses across the globe as journalists reported on Italy's flagrant violations of the laws of war, including the aerial bombardment of Red Cross ambulances and field hospitals, proscribed chemical weapons attacks, and massacres against civilians.⁵ As the world followed reports out of Addis Ababa, London, and Geneva, the question on everyone's mind was how the international legal regime enshrined by the League of Nations would hold up against the realities of a world dominated by and for Western power. As this question was met with mounting evidence of liberal internationalism's naked hypocrisy, the ideological frontiers between different shades of anticolonial thinkers and activists were also brought into sharp relief. To be sure, the Abyssinian Crisis prompted many Egyptians and Indians to embrace the Ethiopians as Eastern brothers. There were also, however, small yet ambitious minorities in both countries who saw in Mussolini's fascist regime a model for their future independence—or at least a natural ally in their struggle against Great Britain. In this sense, the crisis of 1935 was a vivid harbinger of things to come.

DEBATING BRITISH INTERVENTION

Public opinion across the Middle East (as elsewhere) viewed the Abyssinian Crisis as a pivotal moment in determining the Mediterranean balance of power, as well as a litmus test for Britain's ability to defend its interests in the region. A British intelligence report from September 1935 described the Arab view as follows: "The League, which curiously enough is believed to be Great Britain, and no-one else, is on its supreme trial, says the popular voice, and will come to an end if it does not take . . . [its] courage between two hands and do something definite."[6]

Notwithstanding the tone of this report, many British officials shared the Arab take—for Britain was widely acknowledged to play a singularly important leadership role in Geneva. In a letter to Prime Minister Stanley Baldwin on 8 September 1935, William Ormsby-Gore, the Colonial Secretary, offered his own analysis of the Abyssinian Crisis in which he, too, treated British and League interests as basically synonymous:

> I take the long view that the coexistence of the British Empire and militarist dictatorships on the make are irreconcilable. . . . Any weakening in the face of Mussolini's derision and threats against us will only make the role of Britain more difficult in the years of struggle which lie ahead of us. Because we try to stand up for international right, order, justice, treaties and our imperial interests, we are daily insulted by this Dago dictator. We can't go on eating humble pie indefinitely and a victory in the field by Italy against our wishes makes it certain that our turn will come next.[7]

British military officials stationed in Egypt were similarly convinced that a stand should, and could, be taken (this was an opinion echoed in the Indian

Legislative Assembly, where some members called for the deployment of the Indian Army to defend Ethiopia against its Italian invaders).[8] Yet as tensions between Italy and the League mounted over the summer of 1935, Britain's mission to Geneva remained tight-lipped, and the Mediterranean Fleet was moved from Malta to Alexandria to keep it out of Italy's firing range. Such precautions grated on servicemen like Admiral Fisher, Commander in Chief of the Mediterranean Fleet, who saw his force as perfectly capable of standing up to the Italian menace (he later told his brother that he could have "blow[n] the Italians out of the water").[9] Docked in Alexandria, Andrew Cunningham, then Rear Admiral (Destroyers), held a similar view: "It seemed a very simple task to stop him [Mussolini]. The mere closing of the Suez Canal to his transports . . . would have cut off his armies. . . . Such a drastic measure might have led to war with Italy; but the Mediterranean Fleet was in a state of high morale and efficiency, and had no fear whatsoever of the result of an encounter with the Italian Navy."[10]

Yet while the British and international public, civil servants, Indian politicians, and military men on the spot all called for intervention, the Joint Chiefs of Staff in London pleaded for restraint. British defense strategy was then focused on Imperial Japan in the Pacific and Nazi Germany in Europe. In March 1935, Hitler had boasted to the British Foreign Secretary that the Luftwaffe—whose establishment, in open defiance of the Treaty of Versailles, had only recently been announced—had supposedly achieved parity with the Royal Air Force. Key figures in defense policy, such as the First Sea Lord Admiral Chatfield, felt that as a result of these looming threats, and given that numerous ships and airplanes were to be taken out of commission for refurbishment as part of Britain's rearmament program, it was imperative that Britain refrain from an avoidable confrontation in the Mediterranean. There was a sense that ships and aircraft should not be "wasted" on an engagement with Italy when they might later be needed against Germany or Japan.[11]

British policymakers were moreover hesitant to commit to an engagement in the Mediterranean because naval defense was premised on what was called the Main Fleet to Singapore strategy, perceived as a necessary guarantee to the Pacific Dominions in exchange for their increased contribution to the imperial defense budget. It was also intended to deter Australia and New Zealand from seeking alternative defense arrangements with the United States.[12] However, it required Britain to avoid any military engagement that could tie up ships in the Mediterranean, or otherwise threaten their passage from Gibraltar to Suez—the key artery connecting Britain to its empire in the East. "The net moral result," as the American journalist Constantine Brown noted in December 1935, was that "pacifists are becoming militarists and vice versa, hard-boiled soldiers and admirals are becoming pacifists."[13]

There was another factor influencing British calculus at the highest levels. In a letter sent from Rome several months after hostilities had broken out, the British Ambassador to Italy (and formerly the founding Secretary of the League of Nations), Eric Drummond, explained to the Foreign Secretary Anthony Eden why Britain could not lodge material objections against the Italians at the League of Nations: Italy, he pointed out, was merely following the British playbook. From the aerial bombardment of civilians to chemical weapons attacks, Italy was replicating tactics that Britain had been using for years to "manage" colonial uprisings in India, the Middle East, and the Caribbean. "With these facts before them the British must be silent at Geneva. Here again Italy is only following England's example," he signed off.[14]

EGYPT IN THE CROSSHAIRS

The official preference for avoiding conflict with Italy was complicated by the threat Mussolini's invasion obviously posed to Britain's vital strategic interests in Egypt. Though it was assumed that Britain would triumph in any actual war, it was also agreed that Mussolini could not be counted on to avoid such a confrontation. After all, as British politicians and military planners kept reminding each other, Mussolini was unpredictable, and even "a madman" or "rabid dog"—an impression that the Duce was well aware of and only too happy to encourage, as it made British officials skittish about confronting him.[15]

"In his present mood and apparently enthusiastically backed by Italian people Mussolini appears capable of attempting anything," wrote the Chief of the Imperial General Staff, Archibald Montgomery-Massingberd, in an October telegram inquiring as to the feasibility of reinforcing Egypt with two additional brigades of Indian Army troops. "Although Egypt as a whole appears anti-Italian in present crisis," the telegram noted, drawing on a political assessment provided by Lampson,[16] "Italian propaganda is active and Italian population is large. Moreover Wafd not above using present crisis for their own ends. So long as Egyptian Army can be depended upon to assist in maintaining internal security we need have little anxiety. But if any doubt regarding dependability of Egyptian Army arises in near future reinforcements will be required."[17]

Montgomery's telegram succinctly laid out a set of complex and interlocking concerns, beginning with the question of Mussolini's designs on Egypt. Fascist Italy's appetite for territorial conquest was no secret; the Duce spoke regularly of Italy's claims to territories on both shores of the Mediterranean. He openly dreamed of adding Egypt to his North African holdings—part of a broader fantasy to reconstitute the ancient Roman Empire, granting Italy unfettered access to the Atlantic and Indian Oceans in the process.[18] Still, in 1935 the British position in Egypt was militarily unassailable; there was little risk of an actual attack or invasion. Instead, as the telegram underlined, propaganda and subterfuge were the principal sources of concern. In the mid-1930s there were seventy thousand Italians living in Egypt, concentrated primarily in Cairo, Alexandria, and Port Said. Italian schools, newspapers, social clubs, and charitable organizations formed the scaffolding on which had been built, by 1935, a sophisticated and far-reaching fascist propaganda campaign targeting both European and Arab communities.[19] When Montgomery's telegram was dispatched in early October, Egyptians were watching Italian military vessels packed with soldiers make their way down the Suez Canal, cheered by crowds of local Italians who gathered on shore to wave at the passing troops.[20] Montgomery suggested that both the Wafd and the Egyptian Army were also potential sources of threat, should either attempt to take advantage of Mussolini's belligerent posturing in North Africa. While Montgomery was wrong to suspect the Wafd of fascist leanings, subsequent events would prove that he was right to suggest that the party and its leader, Mustafa al-Nahas, were "not above" taking advantage of the situation to further their own political agendas.

TENNIS WITH SIMLA

Montgomery's telegram was the opening salvo in what became a somewhat convoluted negotiation for Indian Army reinforcements for Egypt, which Lampson requested as the crisis escalated in early fall. After the initial troop estimates and time frames were cabled to him, the High Commissioner proceeded to quibble:

> Paragraph 1 does not indicate whether two infantry brigades from India would include any native Indian troops. Before I had received your telegram King Fuad had expressed to me the earnest hope that no Indian troops would be employed in Egypt and this view was independently expressed to General Spinks by the [Egyptian] Minister of War to-day. I am convinced and General Officer Commanding and General Spinks agree that from political point of view the effect would be very unfortunate apart from any question of relative value as fighting units of Indian and British troops. I would therefore strongly recommend that two infantry brigades which I still regard as absolute minimum should be British. If any Indian troops must be included they should be Moslems not Hindus.[21]

There are several reasons why Lampson himself may have been inclined to view British soldiers as preferable for the reinforcement of Egypt. Given that they were being sought in the context of Italy's nearby colonial conquest, British reliance on Indian soldiers could easily have been criticized as either a lack of serious commitment to Egypt's defense or cowardly, colonial hypocrisy, or both. Such impressions were to be avoided particularly at a time when Britain's prestige was already under scrutiny—in Egypt as elsewhere. That said, the reservation was clearly not that Indian soldiers were likely to defect or join in an Egyptian mutiny; otherwise, Hindus and Sikhs, rather than Muslim co-religionists, would have been the obvious choice.

Regarding what Lampson characterized as King Fuad's strongly held opinion on the subject, it is worth underscoring that one of the recurring themes in the Arabic press of the day was frustration over Egypt's inability to defend itself, and its reliance on Britain for protection. In this context, the arrival of foreign troops (from a colonized country, no less) would have reflected especially poorly on the Egyptian monarch as formal head of state. Perhaps Fuad felt his embarrassment would be lessened if the troops could be presented as Muslim brethren rallying to Egypt's defense. But then, why the stated preference for British troops over Indian Muslims? It seems that the King—who was famously quite snobbish about his own Circassian ancestry—is likely to have expressed stereotyped views of Indians or Hindus during his audience with Lampson. Though it remains unclear what exactly Fuad said, what is clear is that he made an impression. Lampson was to become increasingly convinced that Egyptians saw India as "a country of black men, to be regarded with condescension or even contempt."[22]

Placing to one side the irony of a British imperial administrator leveling charges of racism at Egyptians—and acknowledging that royals are not necessarily reliable barometers of popular sentiment—it is undeniable that perceptions of ethnic and racial difference existed between Eastern peoples. In part 1, we saw this illustrated by Gandhi's South African sojourn and the Aga Khan's "pitch" for East African colonization, Egyptian nationalist claims to the Sudan and racialized depictions of Sudanese, and Nehru's romantically racialized depictions of Arab and African delegates attending the League Against Imperialism. And while details are scarce, the topic of perceived Egyptian prejudice against Indian soldiers would not go away—cropping up multiple times in British dispatches between London, Cairo, and Simla in the years after 1935, and eventually serving as the catalyst for a unique propaganda initiative in the midst of World War II (which we will return to in chapter 9).

So much for Fuad and Lampson's request. The reply from the Indian Army was at least thorough, if not exactly sympathetic: "1. Despite possible political reactions in India the Viceroy and the Commander-in-Chief are prepared to send reinforcements to Egypt . . . but there is a limit to the size of these reinforcements, and this is the point I wish to draw attention to. 2. If all were peaceful in India, I think the reinforcements asked for . . . could be spared without any great anxiety, but India has her own preoccupations at present, and these must be adjusted before reinforcements can be spared."

The reference to "possible political reactions" was an oblique acknowledgment of the level of popular vitriol that Italy's invasion had aroused in India across class and religious lines. Outrage was further stoked by the revelation that Indian troops were being sent to Ethiopia without local consultation—not to help defend the country but merely to shield British citizens and interests there. In a Legislative Assembly debate on the deployment in September, Sardar Mandal Singh, a Sikh leader from the Punjab, insisted that the Indian Army should instead be used "to defend poor Abyssinia against European capitalism." It was a sentiment echoed by many of his colleagues,[23] and in particular by members of the Muslim League's Khilafatist old guard like Choudhry Khaliquzzaman and Maulana Shawkat Ali, who had spent their college days protesting Italy's earlier colonial war in Libya. It did not matter that Ethiopia was not Muslim (a point that Italy was at pains to emphasize, at least in its Arabic propaganda); the sheer colonial hypocrisy, or perhaps even the plain moral injustice of the situation, was sufficient to rally the Khilafatists' support. In the same legislative debate, Shaukat Ali rose to call on the army to send more troops, not fewer, to the African continent: "If the people of Abyssinia, who are under-dogs, are being treated disgracefully, and are to be trampled down, then it is the duty of India to send out, not one hundred soldiers, but ten divisions, if necessary; and if the Government ask for money, I hope I will be one who will persuade all of my friends and the whole of India to sanction all the money and men needed to serve this noble country [Ethiopia]."

In conclusion, he claimed, though an old man, to be "very glad to offer to be a soldier and work in that army that goes to defend the weak and the oppressed and fight unjust people out to rob others of liberty, hearth and house."[24]

The commanding officers of the Indian Army did not feel similarly inspired. The note sent to Lampson listed five ongoing "internal security operations" in India that mitigated the Army's ability to spare troops for overseas deployments, including the suppression of the Mohmand rebellion on the Northwest Frontier, the need to respond to "signs of Afridi trouble," and confronting "Bengal Terrorism." It outlined in some detail exactly how many British battalions there were in

India, where they were stationed, and why the government could not spare two brigades—equivalent to six battalions, upward of three thousand men:

> Egypt can only have mixed Brigades (1 British and 3 Indian Battalions per Brigade) from India and nothing else, to substitute 6 more British Battalions in place of the 6 Indian ones would reduce the British element in India to, in my opinion, a dangerous extent. . . . Should a further 6 be asked for only 19 would remain in India, which is insufficient. . . . There are a few Hindu class Battalions in India, but no Mohammedan class Battalions . . . hence Indian reinforcements from India <u>must</u> include Hindus.[25]

The tone of the entire document is palpably exasperated: India, it sighs, is not an inexhaustible storehouse of men and munitions, to be raided at will; nor are beggars usually quite so choosy.

No acknowledgement from Cairo of the receipt of this letter—or the appreciation of its contents—is preserved. Instead, by way of compromise, it was determined in London that the First Royal Dragoons, a British regiment then returning home from a tour of duty in India, would be disembarked at Port Said and remain in Egypt until further notice.[26] One is left to speculate as to the effect of this announcement on the Dragoons themselves.

PROPAGANDA

The threat posed by Italy's invasion of Ethiopia was heightened exponentially by the extent of the information warfare that accompanied it. The literature on Mussolini's use of propaganda in the Middle East is well developed,[27] but in Egypt, compared to other Arab countries, fascist information warfare was exceptionally multifaceted and expensive. Beginning in mid-1935, Italian spending on propaganda in Egypt was 70,000 lire (or, one lire for every Italian resident of Egypt) per month. In comparison, the budget spent in Syria at the same time was roughly 5,000 lire, issued on a sporadic basis.[28] This was in addition to fascist intelligence and espionage activities that targeted Egyptian political groups, as well as formal Italian diplomatic efforts to strengthen ties with Egypt and disrupt Anglo-Egyptian and Egyptian-Ethiopian bilateral relations.

Egypt was home to a number of Italian language newspapers and publications, in particular the *Giornale d'Oriente*, whose bureaus in Cairo and Alexandria doubled as headquarters for Italian state propaganda and intelligence.[29] Ugo Dadone, a personal friend of Mussolini, slid easily out of his chair at the *Giornale*, where he had served as Editor in Chief, into a new post as head of the Agence de l'Egypte et de l'Orient, or AEO—Italy's official press office in Cairo. According to a 1935 British intelligence summary, "this office issues two bulletins a day in French and Arabic . . . full of pro Italian and anti British propaganda. Its other function consists in buying up newspapers and journalists with a view to their making pro Italian propaganda."[30] The AEO also produced political pamphlets in French and Arabic, which were distributed throughout Cairo and Alexandria by youths on bicycles. One example, preserved in the records of the Foreign Office, was entitled *L'Abyssinie et l'esclavage* and sought to highlight the Ethiopian regime's persecution of Muslims, among its other supposed sins.[31]

In the spring of 1935, Radio Bari, another outlet for Italian state propaganda, launched a daily forty-five-minute broadcast program in Arabic—a significant expansion over the fifteen-minute bulletins it had been broadcasting three times a week since 1934. It included the latest Arab music records and popular entertainment, news bulletins from Italy and the Arab region, and a talk show component, rapidly gaining a significant following in parts of North Africa and the Middle East. In villages and rural areas, café owners would acquire a shortwave radio to attract customers; often this one set would become the focal point of a community's evenings, and Radio Bari's mix of popular music and anti-British sentiment went down well, particularly in British-controlled areas of the Levant.[32] A contemporary report from Palestine remarked that Arab café patrons "sipped their coffee and swallowed Italian propaganda with every mouthful."[33]

In Egypt, as elsewhere, part of Radio Bari's appeal was down to high rates of illiteracy, especially in rural areas. One indication that the Italians were fully cognizant of this fact was Bari's decision to publish an illustrated weekly digest, also called *Radio Bari*, to capitalize on their program's success. The captions were written in colloquial Egyptian dialect, easier to read or sound out for those unfamiliar with classical Arabic.

Another key component of Bari's popularity was its hostility to Britain and criticism of British colonial policies; to this end it often sought to draw listeners' attention to the plight of Palestinians and Indian Muslims. On 15 June 1935, the Bari broadcast included a report about Bengal:

> CAIRO. *El Hilal* newspaper published in Cairo has stated that a bloody fighting took place in Calcutta between the British troops and Moslems of that town. It is said that this fighting was agitated when the British troops decided to demolish the Moslems Mosque which was alleged to be built upon a land which is not a Moslem property, so the religious excitement persisted upon them until they attacked the British troops and bloody fighting took place in

which about 16 Moslems killed and 400 injured. Many people were arrested and the troops had overcome the rioters when a re-enforcement was supplied, and rioters dispersed. We are sorry to hear of such aggression from the British troops, who have not respected the religious inviolability. So the day in which the oppressors will understand what is the result of oppression is coming.[34]

Italian agents in India likewise worked to influence press and public opinion there, pointing to Mussolini's supposedly pro-Muslim and anti-British policies in the countries of the Middle East. A series of pamphlets were distributed by Italian consular officials in Calcutta describing Italy's positive contributions to the situation of Arabs in Egypt and Palestine "and how Mussolini was causing considerable embarrassment to the British Empire" in those places.[35] Again as in Egypt, there were efforts made to "purchase" favorable coverage from local journalists and editors.[36] The Italian Consul in Kabul even paid a visit to Muhammad Iqbal, the celebrated poet we last encountered at the 1931 Islamic Congress in Jerusalem. According to agents from the Raj's notorious Criminal Investigation Department (CID), "The Consul in his conversation impressed upon Sir Mohammad Iqbal that Italy's first purpose was to champion Islamic countries, and mentioned that he (the Consul) saw the vision of the ascendancy of Italian naval power in the East Mediterranean which would relieve the Palestinian Arabs of their troubles and would help the export trade in Egypt. The Consul depicted the uncivilized condition of Afghanistan and how much Italy could help her in her industrial progress and culture."[37]

The intended message—of Italian solidarity with Muslims and colonized peoples against British imperialism—is transparent (Iqbal wasn't taken in).[38] A Radio Bari transcript from 17 October, when tensions between Italy and Britain were near their apex, was similarly unnuanced: "We shall open the eyes of all the Moslems throughout the world to this false, egotistical, cowardly and imperialistic policy, the British policy which holds more than three quarters of the Moslem world under its thrall."[39]

The success of Radio Bari's Arabic broadcasts (particularly in Palestine and Iraq) prompted the establishment of a similar service for India, under the leadership of the former Ghadar operative and a close confidant of the Italian fascist leadership, Muhammad Iqbal Shedai. Daily shortwave broadcasts in both Urdu and Hindi were launched from Naples and Rome in 1938 and expanded following the outbreak of war. These efforts predated and, to some extent, inspired Subhas Chandra Bose's exploits on Azad Hind Radio, which would begin broadcasting from Nazi Germany in 1941.[40]

AN EASTERN CONSENSUS

For the most part, however, Egyptians and Indians weren't buying what Italy was trying to sell. Across the board and in both countries, the scholarly literature is quite clear: the vast majority of recorded opinion, cutting across religious and class lines, rejected Italian propaganda and embraced the Ethiopian cause as an extension of their own.[41] Most Egyptians and Indians loudly condemned what they accurately diagnosed as the racist and imperialist impulses behind the Italian invasion.

Egyptian Copts and Levantine Christians expressed their horror at the attack on a fellow Eastern Christian community; among Egyptian Muslims, too, there was an instinctive sense of solidarity with Ethiopia, the last independent kingdom in Africa, as it faced a European onslaught. Committed Easternists like Muhammad Lutfi Gomaa highlighted what they saw as Ethiopia's embodiment of ecumenical solidarity, as its rich history embraced Christian, Jewish, and Muslim stories of migration, shelter, and coexistence.[42] In the words of Nir Arielli, "The majority of the leading intellectuals in Egypt and practically all the major newspapers in the country denounced Italy's venture in Ethiopia as colonialist, expansionist and an unwarranted attack on the last independent African state.... The invasion of Ethiopia created a consensus between people as far apart politically as Hasan al-Banna, the leader of the religious Muslim Brotherhood, and the radical socialist intellectual, Salama Musa, who was appalled by the way the Italians had bombed civilians."[43]

Egyptians moreover perceived that what was happening in Ethiopia was a threat not only to their country but to less powerful countries generally; the impotence of the League of Nations in the face of such flagrant violations of its charter dispelled any lingering illusion that they might rely on Geneva to defend their interests or protect them from aggression.[44] In the British imperial historiography, it has often been suggested that these developments sent Egyptian nationalists scuttling for cover under Britannia's mighty wings.[45] Instead, confronted by the reality of fascist colonial aggression and Britain's patent unwillingness to intervene, Egyptian newspapers reflected popular frustration that British suzerainty had prevented Egypt from developing its own defensive capacities or participating in international diplomacy as a sovereign state. The mood was captured by a former Egyptian Minister Plenipotentiary, Dr. Hafez al-Afifi, in an early October interview with *al-Jihad*: "Egypt, small state that it is, wishes the Covenant of the League of Nations to be respected and also wishes that the rights of small states should be respected equally with those of the big powers.

Why then should Egypt be prevented from becoming a member of the League of Nations? And why should Egypt be prevented from starting to raise an army fit to defend it?"[46]

The desire to defend Egypt encompassed both weapons and words. Throughout the summer and autumn of 1935, many stakeholders from Lampson to the India Office to private Egyptian citizens lobbied the British government to step up their ripostes to Italian propaganda in the country. One such petitioner was E.D. Saleh, an Egyptian from Alexandria, who in September 1935 urged Britain to open a propaganda bureau in his city to counter Italian efforts.[47] However, the Foreign Office and its likely accomplice, the BBC, struggled to reconcile their positions on a propaganda outfit: What would it do, who should steer it, and who would foot the bill? A scribbled comment by Oriental Secretary Walter Smart summed up official avoidance: "We cannot begin anti-Italian propaganda as suggested: we would have to wait until we were nearer war with Italy than now. We can only try to counter Italian propaganda against us."[48]

Such "counters" to Italian propaganda mainly consisted of complaints to Italian consular officials. The response was invariably a flat denial of any wrongdoing—or even claims that local press outlets were in fact the hostile party. Italian representatives in India went so far as to lodge formal complaints of their own against the "violent anti-Italian campaign" being waged by Indian journalists. They moreover called on British authorities to censor (factual) press reports of Italian atrocities in Ethiopia. Consular officials protested that their country "had never done anything wrong to the Indians"[49]—so what right did Indians have to criticize Italy's behavior elsewhere?

In an interview with *L'Écho de Paris*, Mussolini went several steps further. Was the League of Nations, he inquired, "to become the court before which the negroes, the backward and savage peoples of the world, drag the great nations"?[50] Crass as his language undoubtedly was, Mussolini knew he was touching a raw nerve. The prospect of an actual reckoning with colonialism conducted by its victims was as outrageous and inconceivable to officials in London and Paris as it was in Rome or Berlin.

IN BRITAIN'S MISFORTUNE...

As Montgomery had worried aloud in his telegram to the Indian Army High Command, Egyptian nationalists were as alive as any other anticolonial movement to the possibilities created by the Abyssinian Crisis to press new concessions from London. Fortunately for the British, the Wafd's leader, Mustafa al-Nahas, deemed it politically expedient to soften public attitudes toward Great Britain as he and his colleagues worked the screws behind the scenes.

The concessions at the top of the Wafd's list of priorities included, first, the restoration of the Egyptian constitution, suspended since 1924. This would trigger new elections, which the Wafd was certain to win. Next, the Wafd wanted the reopening of treaty negotiations between Britain and Egypt, on ice since 1930. If successful, these negotiations would enable Nahas to take credit for several major national milestones: formal Egyptian independence along the lines already achieved by the former British Mandate in Iraq, a rolling back of the British military presence, an end to the hated Capitulations, and membership of the League of Nations. Five years since the Wafd had been muscled out of Egyptian politics by Sidqi and the palace, these were victories that the party desperately needed, especially given the emergence of new movements like Young Egypt and the Muslim Brotherhood, which also claimed to be fighting for Egypt's liberation from imperial rule. If the Wafd wished to keep its place at the center of the nationalist mainstream, it had to deliver the goods—or risk being overtaken by a younger, more hardline movement. In practice, however, this required negotiation, rather than confrontation, with the British; for confrontation would only result in further suppression of the Wafd, strengthening the hands of its many rivals.

Throughout the summer and autumn of 1935, as the Abyssinian Crisis was at its apex, newspapers and periodicals affiliated with the Wafd, including *al-Jihad*, *Kawkab al-Sharq*, and *al-Musawwar* began to publish increasingly alarmist accounts of Italy's designs on Egypt. There were maps illustrating the proximity of Egypt to Ethiopia and the threat that Italy's invasion posed to the Blue Nile, a major source of Egypt's fresh water supply. British intelligence reports suggest that, during the same period, Nahas himself intervened in newspapers not affiliated with the Wafd to prevent them from publishing pro-Italian articles.[51] As Hassan Ahmad Ibrahim argues, Nahas and his party were eager to convince Egyptians of the grave danger posed by Italy—and that alliance with Britain was preferable by comparison.[52] Efforts to vilify Italy and moderate public opinion on Great Britain were likely intended to create latitude for the Wafd to reenter treaty negotiations with the British government. As Gershoni and Jankowski note, articles in the major Egyptian dailies repeatedly warned their readers that "Fascist Italy, once victorious in Ethiopia, could use its territories in East Africa as a springboard for further expansion.... Yet if war in East Africa posed danger, it also presented opportunity; *al-Ahram* argued that Egypt should attempt to take advantage of the tense international situation to persuade Great Britain to conclude a treaty of alliance with an independent Egypt, thereby establishing an effective defensive front against possible fascist aggression."[53]

This stands in contrast to Indian nationalist responses to the Abyssinian Crisis, where commentary focused more on the hypocrisy of Britain and other European countries. Nehru, for example, pointed out that Western leaders who feigned outrage over Mussolini's actions continued to promote their own brands of imperialism, using the same lexicon of "civilization" and "social uplift" employed by the Italian fascists:

> I repudiate utterly the suggestion that imperialism has gone to Abyssinia, or come to India, for humanitarian motives or the spread of civilization. Imperialism goes to exploit and remains to exploit and the people under its heel sink materially and spiritually. Its true messengers in Abyssinia have been poison gas and liquid fire and they reveal its nature more than any argument. That is the foretaste of the civilization that it brings, and we in India, who suffer humiliation enough in our land, cannot permit the additional spiritual degradation of remaining silent when imperialism spreads its cruel wings and crushes other people.[54]

Similarly, in a poem authored by Iqbal, the Italian dictator offers a scathing challenge to the liberal empires of Europe:

> Why does pot feel offence, if kettle has a blot?
> Our culture [is the] same: I kettle and you pot
> My craze for Empire makes you sneer and frown,
> But walls of weak states, you too have brought down.[55]

These critiques were no less available to the politicians and media outlets of the Wafd than they were to their Indian counterparts, yet the Egyptians chose a different tack. By using the invasion of Ethiopia to ratchet up popular fears of Italy in the press and create a denouement with the British, the Wafd was able to score several long-overdue political victories against their domestic adversaries between the autumn of 1935 and the spring of 1936. During that period the 1923 Constitution was reinstated, new elections were called (and won by the Wafd), and the long-stalled negotiations over a new Anglo-Egyptian Treaty finally resumed—with Nahas at the helm of the Egyptian delegation.

ENEMIES IN COMMON

Britain did monitor, and in several cases expel,[56] Italian diplomats and journalists working in India and the Middle East, and it kept tabs on local reporters suspected of collusion with Italy. One such individual was Anis Daoud Effendi, a translator for the Egyptian *Kawkab al-Sharq* newspaper and an agent for Misr el-Fatah, or Young Egypt, a nationalist party with authoritarian leanings. According to his intelligence profile, Daoud saw the Abyssinian Crisis as "a golden opportunity to seize independence with Italian support, both at the League of Nations, and on the ground in a national uprising against the British." To this end he was in contact with Ugo Dadone at the AEO and other "hardline Egyptian nationalists." At the time, however, British officials in Cairo felt confident that their network of intelligence agents and informants could effectively neutralize the threat posed by figures like Daoud and the leadership of Young Egypt.[57]

Much higher profile was Shakib Arslan, a celebrated Islamist and Arab nationalist author. Born a Druze prince in the Chouf region of Mount Lebanon, Arslan spent most of the 1920s and 1930s living in exile in Geneva, from where he cultivated a strong following across Muslim and Arabic speaking audiences as a poet and syndicated editorialist—"arguably the most widely read Arab writer of the interwar period"[58]—also called Amir al-Bayan, the "Prince of Eloquence." During the Abyssinian Crisis (and not for the first or last time), Arslan courted serious controversy by lending his illustrious pen to the defense of Mussolini. He claimed that his support for the Duce long predated the war in Ethiopia and expressed his belief that Italian victory would liberate the country's Muslim minority from the yoke of Christian rule.[59] Arslan's editorials were followed meticulously at the Italian Foreign Ministry, where they may have helped to shape the government's evolving pro-Muslim policy. His talking points were amplified by Radio Bari and other propaganda channels, and there was some (fanciful) talk among Italian officials of bringing him to India to address the country's Muslims.[60]

Daoud and Arslan were not alone in their views; in Egypt, other parts of the Middle East, and South Asia, a small but consequential minority of nationalist writers and activists viewed the conflict in Ethiopia as an opportunity. In India, Subhas Chandra Bose openly embraced Mussolini as an enemy of Great Britain and thus a natural ally in the struggle for national liberation.[61] In Palestine, the Mufti of Jerusalem, Hajj Amin al-Husseini, became embroiled in a public scandal when the newspaper *al-Jama'a al-Islamiyya* reproduced a letter that it claimed proved his and Arslan's involvement in orchestrating pro-Italian propaganda.

While both men vehemently denied the veracity of the correspondence, they each became increasingly aligned with Italy in subsequent months.[62] Mussolini's campaign in Ethiopia also won him some admirers within the Jewish Yishuv, in particular the Revisionists led by Ze'ev Jabotinsky. At the height of the war in late October and early November, the right-wing movement's official newspaper, *HaYarden*, published multiple editorials celebrating the prospect of "an Ethiopia conquered by Italy, which would thrive and prosper like any other European colony," and warning that reversals in policy would amount to "a failure for the white race."[63] Back in Cairo (and presumably unbeknownst to his Islamist and "hardline Egyptian nationalist" supporters), Ugo Dadone also courted local representatives of the Jewish Agency, telling them the British would never deliver on a Jewish state—but Italy could.[64]

Such maneuvering was anathema to the Eastern humanism of the Egyptian author Muhammad Lutfi Gomaa, who saw in the intercommunal history of Ethiopia, no less than in its current oppression, an emblem and a rallying cry for Eastern solidarity. In his influential writings on the war in Ethiopia, Gomaa took issue with those like Arslan who prioritized communalism over solidarity with the Ethiopians. Recalling the story of the *najashi*, Ethiopian Christians who had sheltered and protected early Muslim emigrants, Gomaa admonished Arslan that true anti-imperialism meant solidarity with any people "oppressed and downtrodden," irrespective of their religious beliefs.[65] On this, he and the Indian Khilafatists calling for intervention to defend Ethiopia were in resonant agreement.

As the intellectual historian and biographer of Gomaa, Mattias Olesen, has observed, the Abyssinian Crisis became the "quilting point" at which national and transnational debates over liberalism and fascism, nationalism and pluralism, and the ongoing struggle against colonialism converged. Whereas the West was perceived as "regressing and losing their liberal heritage" under the combined weight of fascism, totalitarianism, and capitalist materialism, "countries across the awakened, spiritual East were progressing towards democracy, liberty and equality."[66] For Gomaa and a wide range of other thinkers across the Middle East and South Asia, from Muslim cosmopolitans to socialists and liberal nationalists, Abyssinia created a common front—whether expressed in the language of anticolonialism, antifascism, antiracism, or universal ethics. Mobilized in defense of Christian Africans, this was the East at something approaching its most expansive, universal-humanist frontiers. It was equally telling who fell beyond the Eastern consensus: a minority of Islamists, anticolonial nationalists, and militant Zionists all perceived in the Italian invasion a classically Machiavellian opening for advancement of narrower agendas. These were the ideological fault lines along which not only the Eastern imaginary but the human geography of the Middle East and South Asia would ultimately break apart during and after World War II.

THE EMPIRE HOLDS BACK

Seeming to prove Gomaa's point (at least concerning the fate of Western liberalism) was the revelation of the Hoare-Laval Pact in December 1935. The details of a meeting between British Foreign Secretary Samuel Hoare and his French counterpart, Pierre Laval, were leaked to the press: Ethiopia, the two men had agreed, would have to be partitioned, with Italy annexing two thirds of the country (more than it had by then conquered).[67] The newspapers reported that provisions were to be made for the settlement in this territory of up to 1.5 million Italian colonists.[68] The whole of the country was, moreover, to be placed "under the aegis" of the League of Nations—demoting it from the status of a Member State to something like a Class B or C Mandate.[69]

The sellout implied by these terms was transparent; in Britain, where the news broke hot on the heels of the Conservative reelection victory, it outraged voters who took seriously the government's campaign pledge to support the League of Nations. Secretary of State for War Duff Cooper later remarked, "During my experience of politics I have never witnessed so devastating a wave of public opinion. . . . The post-bag was full and the letters I received were not written by ignorant or emotional people but by responsible citizens who had given sober thought to the matter."[70]

The wave of opprobrium extended far beyond British shores. As Susan Pedersen notes, "Demonstrations of support and solidarity campaigns sprang up among anti-colonial intellectuals and diasporic populations from Harlem to Jamaica, Cairo to Natal. . . . Selassi's under-supplied armies and the credibility of the 'civilizing' project alike reeled under the onslaught of Italian planes and poison gas, and then the revelation that the British and French were willing to buy a settlement by granting Italy substantial territorial concessions."[71]

The pact was quickly dead in the water and both Hoare and Laval were forced to step down, scapegoated for an initiative that almost certainly had the backing of their colleagues. In the days prior to the leak, Hoare had publicly threatened the imposition of oil sanctions against Italy, but these were never implemented. In the absence of an oil embargo, the sanctions cobbled together by the League of Nations were toothless, beyond adding to Mussolini's sense of personal aggrievement. As Nicholas Mulder points out, this stood in stark contrast to the way sanctions had previously been applied by the League to conflicts in China and the Balkans, underscoring the "double standard" at work when the offending party was also a European power.[72]

Neither Britain nor any other country ultimately intervened in the Abyssinian Crisis, even as Italy bombed the Red Cross and resorted to poison gas attacks to overcome the determined resistance of outgunned Ethiopian troops. This willful failure to act created a series of devastating knock-on effects, both for Europe and the world. As shown by Steven Morewood, British reticence emboldened Mussolini, who from 1937 began planning for the invasion of Egypt on the grounds that British power was in decline. It also drew Hitler and Mussolini closer together. Hitler was impressed by the Duce's victory in East Africa, which he had initially dismissed as a reckless provocation of Great Britain. The crisis moreover influenced Nazi military strategy in Europe—from the remilitarization of the Rhineland to support for Franco in the Spanish Civil War—because Hitler calculated, correctly, that these maneuvers would be met with the same British reticence as had the invasion of Ethiopia.[73]

RENEGOTIATING EMPIRE

The spring of 1936 was tumultuous and fast-moving in Cairo. In April, King Fuad passed away, and his teenage son Faruq was recalled from England, where he had been at school. The new King of Egypt—young, handsome, and immaculately unknown—ascended the throne in May. That same month, Nahas and the Wafd swept back into office in a landslide electoral victory.

Within days of these heady developments, news hawkers were announcing Italy's formal annexation of Ethiopia. On the broader international stage, the recent signature of the Anti-Comintern Pact between Germany and Japan heightened concerns about a potential threat to British interests in the Pacific. In Europe, too, the clouds were gathering. Seizing on the strategic opportunity presented by the Abyssinian Crisis, Hitler reoccupied the Rhineland in March 1936. Soon Spain would be plunged into a brutal civil war, which Italy and Germany did not hesitate to exploit for their own ends. For the first time, British planners were faced with the unthinkable scenario of a war on three fronts: against Italy in the Mediterranean, Germany in Europe, and Japan in the Pacific. By August, Britain's First Sea Lord, Admiral Chatfield, was confiding in a memorandum that it was "open to debate" whether the British Empire was "in reality strategically defensible."[74]

For all of these reasons, British negotiators grew determined to finally hammer out a new treaty with the Wafd, even if it required significant concessions to Egypt. The extent of Lampson's disquiet is particularly telling, given his habitual confidence and optimism. By late May, he was warning his government that the consequences of failure could be dire: "With Italy on our shoulders, Palestine in an uproar next door, and general unrest in the Arab world I should personally have thought that a genuinely friendly Egypt should have been worth a good deal."[75] With some difficulty, he was able to convince the British Cabinet that it was.

When the treaty was concluded that summer, it was based, as the Egyptian delegation had initially sought, on the military clauses of the 1930 draft treaty.[76] The British committed to withdrawing their troops from Cairo and Alexandria, Egyptian forces were permitted to return to the Sudan for the first time since 1924, and Egyptian citizens were granted unrestricted immigration rights. However, the two most important concessions from the Wafd's perspective were Britain's commitment to ending the detested Capitulations and to facilitation of Egypt's entry into the League of Nations as a full Member State. These breakthroughs were interpreted by the Wafd as heralding, at long last, the advent of a sovereign Egypt, through the unchallenged primacy of its laws and institutions domestically and the assertion of an independent foreign policy abroad. During the formal debate over the treaty's ratification in the Egyptian parliament, Muhammad Hussein Haykal declared that Egypt was now finally free to chart her own course in the world and develop a new "Arab or Eastern or Islamic policy" all her own.[77] A declaration of independence, the Anglo-Egyptian Treaty was not; but it was more than successive British governments had previously dreamed of conceding, and it was welcomed by many in Egypt as the dawn of a new era.[78]

A COLLABORATIVE MOMENT

Exactly one year prior, in August 1935, the Government of India Act had been passed on the floor of the House of Commons. The product of years of agonized debate and deliberation, the reforms it introduced included the devolution of considerable power to the provinces; the introduction of direct elections (thus expanding the electorate from 7 million to 35 million voters); the extension of provincial assembly membership to include more Indians, who would now be able to form a majority government; and the establishment of a federal court system.[79]

The India Act, said to be the longest in the history of the British parliament, pleased no one. Conservative "diehards," lead by Winston Churchill, viewed it as nothing short of a capitulation to native demands—the beginning of the end for the British Empire. The drawn-out parliamentary debate had nearly cleaved the Conservative government in two. In India itself, Jawaharlal Nehru and many of his fellow Congressmen rejected the new legislation as no more than the latest imperialist attempt to refuse Indians *swaraj* through delay, distraction, and limited reform.[80] This closely resembled contemporary debates in Egypt, where critics of the Anglo-Egyptian Treaty, including Huda Shaarawi, denounced it for falling so far short of true independence.[81]

Debate within the Congress Party was essentially focused on how far it was acceptable to negotiate or compromise with the British. A split emerged within the party between an older generation—centered on Gandhi—which saw parliamentary politics and a process of gradual reform as the best means available to realize lasting change, and a youthful, more radical element rallied behind Nehru, which viewed compromise with the enemy as potentially lethal to their party's ultimate goals. The division over the India Act threatened to split Congress, just as it had done with the Conservatives. Ultimately it was Gandhi who brokered a deal between the competing factions of his own party and the British government.[82] Despite his personal opposition to the India Act, Nehru was reluctantly obliged to confirm, as Congress President, that the party would contest the first provincial elections to be held under its terms.

Thus in the spring of 1936, as election campaigns got underway across the length and breadth of India, Congress—much like the Egyptian Wafd—found itself drawn into participation in a "renegotiated" imperial framework: an experiment in joint administration. Over the next few years, Egyptian and Indian nationalists would increasingly collaborate with one another on shared projects, while in both countries they also entered into an unprecedented level of participation and investment in British-backed government institutions—at the risk, articulated by John Darwin, of becoming "trapped in the constitutional labyrinth the British had constructed around [them]."[83]

Throughout the late 1930s, the various organs of the British imperial state would also struggle to reconcile competing priorities and policy objectives among themselves, as had been on display throughout the negotiations over the India Act and Anglo-Egyptian Treaty. These priorities were broadly shaped along departmental and geographic lines, which in turn gave rise to dramatically different visions of the empire, its core interests, and the policies it ought to pursue. This lack of consensus created space, flexibility, and opportunities for individuals to significantly influence the direction of British policy in a given region; it also drastically complicated the ongoing processes of negotiation with nationalist movements—increasingly resembling a hybrid between "interior" colonial relations and "exterior" foreign diplomacy. For Congress and the Wafd, as for other parties, the key motive for participation in collaborative government was domestic: leaders of movements that had once cut across class, sectarian, and other lines to challenge British rule now faced multiple internal challengers determined to shape the nationalist project in their own image. For leaders focused on holding their political coalitions together, protecting their leadership, and preventing the empowerment of rival movements, participation in the "halfway house" of reformed imperial structures loaned them extensive state power, authority, and legal legitimacy that could be wielded against their domestic competitors. As we shall see, this domestic political calculus would continue to comingle with transnational visions of Eastern affinity and solidarity throughout the late 1930s and early 1940s, as Egyptians and Indians negotiated, then renegotiated, their relations with the British.

———

In September 1937, Egypt's Foreign Minister, Wasif Butrus Ghali, rose to deliver Egypt's maiden address to the annual meeting of the League of Nations General Assembly. This event was one of the prizes negotiators had sought to obtain through the Anglo-Egyptian Treaty: formal membership in the prestigious club of sovereign states (battered and embattled as it by then was). In his speech, Ghali devoted a significant portion of his remarks to the ongoing conflict in Egypt's neighbor, the British Mandate of Palestine. Distancing his government from its former master, Great Britain, Ghali used Egypt's debut as a formally independent nation to call for a resolution to the crisis on the basis of "right and justice," insisting that Palestine must "remain for the Palestinians" within a unified state (thus rejecting the partition plan recently unveiled by the British government).[84] The address signaled a turning point in Egypt's relations not only with Britain but also with the Middle East and the broader Islamic world. Beginning that fall, Egyptian political activists, organizations, government ministers, and even the palace would seek to play an increasingly central role in the unfolding crisis in Palestine—prompting a new cycle of engagement with Indian politicians and activists in turn.

FIVE

Palestine HQ

> O neighbor of the Holy Land, have you heard what has happened to your siblings [in Palestine]? . . . Will you abandon us, though you have a tongue that speaks and a heart which beats?[1]
>
> —TELEGRAM FROM THE WOMEN'S COMMITTEE OF ACRE TO HUDA SHAARAWI, 1937

TUNING IN

On New Year's Day, 1938, the celebrated Urdu poet Muhammad Iqbal took to the airwaves from the All-India Radio station in Lahore. He had already been suffering with an illness for some time, which affected his throat and thus his intonation. But if his voice was strained, it suited his subject. The poet's address surveyed the state of global affairs with bitter acuity:

> The modern age prides itself on its progress in knowledge and its matchless scientific developments. No doubt, the pride is justified. Today space and time are being annihilated and man is achieving amazing successes in unveiling the secrets of nature and harnessing its forces to his own service. But in spite of all these developments, the tyranny of imperialism struts abroad, covering its face under the masks of Democracy, Nationalism, Communism, Fascism and heaven knows what else besides. Under these masks, in every corner of the earth, the spirit of freedom and the dignity of man are being trampled underfoot in a way to which not even the darkest period of human history presents a parallel. . . . As I look back on the year that has passed and as I look at the

world in the midst of the New Year's rejoicing, it may be Abyssinia or Palestine, Spain or China, the same misery prevails in every corner of man's earthly home, and hundreds of thousands of men are being butchered mercilessly. Engines of destruction created by science are wiping out the great landmarks of man's cultural achievements. . . . The world's thinkers are stricken dumb. Is this going to be the end of all the progress and evolution of civilization, they ask, that men should destroy one another in mutual hatred and make human habitation impossible on this earth? . . . Only one unity is dependable, and that unity is the brotherhood of man, which is above race, nationality, colour or language. So long as this so-called democracy, this accursed nationalism and this degraded imperialism are not shattered, so long as men do not demonstrate by their actions that they believe that the whole world is the family of God, so long as distinctions of race, colour and geographical nationalities are not wiped out completely, they will never be able to lead a happy and contented life and the beautiful ideals of liberty, equality and fraternity will never materialise.[2]

FIGURE 9   "The Poet of the East": Muhammad Iqbal in Calcutta, 1935. Portrait by Ottoline Morrell.
NATIONAL PORTRAIT GALLERY

Iqbal concluded with an appeal to the divine: "Let us therefore begin the New Year with the prayer that God Almighty may grant humanity to those who are in places of power and government and teach them to cherish mankind." It was to be one of his final public utterances. Shair-e-Mashreq, the "poet of the East," passed away that April in Lahore. He was sixty years old.

THE NEWS FROM PALESTINE

While Egypt and India had been the twin epicenters of anticolonial uprisings in the early 1920s, by the mid-1930s politicians and activists in both countries had begun to respond to external crises in Ethiopia, Spain, China, and Palestine—the victims of what many, including Iqbal, perceived as connected forms of fascist, totalitarian, and colonial violence. Between 1937 and 1939, Palestine was to emerge as the key point of convergence between Egyptian and Indian activism, and one the most contentious policy issues facing the British Empire—resulting in heated debates, schizophrenic decision-making, and barely contained hostility among the officials and branches of government involved.[3]

The Arab Revolt in Palestine had broken out in April 1936 with a countrywide general strike. Organizers called for a halt to Jewish immigration, the prohibition of further land sales to Jews, and the formation of a democratic government to replace the British Mandate administration. That as late as 1936 Palestine lacked even the semblance of a national legislative assembly was a telling anomaly; British authorities had almost immediately determined that representative institutions were incompatible with the privileged position the Mandate envisaged for Jewish settlers, who in 1920 made up only 10 percent of the population. Thus the Yishuv developed its own separate Knesset and other protonational institutions under the aegis of the colonial administration, simultaneously benefiting from the philanthropic support of the overseas Zionist movement.[4] Transnational fundraising for organizations including the Jewish Colonial Association and the Jewish National Fund also played a major role in the purchase of large tracts of Palestinian land, which were then held "in trust" for the Jewish people as a whole.[5] That Zionists called for Jewish-only labor across the Yishuv (and organized pickets and boycotts against those who employed Palestinians) further exacerbated communal tensions and intensified the segregation between a minority of European settlers and an impoverished (and increasingly enraged) local population, two-thirds of whom were peasants. According to the estimates of the Colonial Office itself, by 1935 one-fifth of Arab villagers were landless, and the problem was understood to be getting worse.[6]

From 1927 to 1931, Jewish immigration to Palestine had averaged 3,896 people per year; then came the rise of Hitler's National Socialist Party in Germany, and with it the intensification of antisemitic sentiments and policies across the West. Discriminatory quotas heavily restricted Jewish immigration in Europe and the Americas, meaning refugees from Germany and other prospective Jewish migrants had very few places to go.[7] In this context of rising threat, the Zionist movement negotiated the Haavara Agreement with the Nazi government, which from 1933 to 1939 permitted German Jews to transfer a portion of their assets to Palestine through a banking and export exchange plan, thus enabling Jewish emigration and creating a large influx of private capital to the Mandate.[8] Between the Nazis' first major election victory in 1932 and the outbreak of the Arab Revolt five years later, the average number of new arrivals to Palestine surged to 38,245 per year, almost ten times the average of the previous five-year period. In 1935 alone, 66,472 Jews moved to Palestine—more than the estimated combined total of the First and Second Aliyas, or waves of Zionist immigration between 1882 and 1913. By the end of the decade, the Yishuv had more than doubled in size.[9]

This sudden and dramatic spike added fuel to longer-term Palestinian grievances against the imposition of the British Mandate, its privileging of Jewish political aspirations, and the corresponding rapid expansion of economic stratification. To this tinderbox of resentments, the death at the hands of British police of the celebrated Palestinian resistance leader Sheikh Izzedine al-Qassam lit a match.[10] A coordinated general strike and mass demonstrations across Palestine were accompanied by the outbreak of armed insurrection in the countryside, which swiftly attracted British repression (and brutal reprisals) in close coordination with local Jewish militias. Alongside the systematic torture of prisoners, the aerial bombardment of villages, and other forms of collective punishment, British tactics included the outdoor caging and starvation of villagers, sending busloads of the condemned over buried landmines, and killing women and children in their sleep. These "unconventional" methods owed much to the ruthless leadership of men like Charles Tegart, the former Calcutta Commissioner of Police, and David Petrie, former Director of the Indian Intelligence Bureau, as well as the importation of the infamous "Black and Tan" British military police from Ireland to serve as Palestine's police force.[11]

The 1936–39 Arab Revolt made front-page headlines across the Middle East and beyond, attracting instinctive sympathy from Arabs and Muslims and winning supporters further afield on anticolonial grounds. The public outcry only intensified following the publication, in mid-1937, of the Report of the Peel Commission, which had been sent to Palestine to determine the causes of the revolt and advise the government on how to respond.[12] The Peel Commission recommended the partition of Palestine into Arab and Jewish states. This marked a new and yet more explosive chapter of the revolt as armed insurrection resumed, now fueled by apparent proof positive that British rule and Jewish settlement would together tear the country apart. The renewal in violence was accompanied by a mounting transnational diplomatic and protest movement whose slogan was the defense of Palestine from partition.

The Arab Revolt was, firstly, a crisis of the colonial state, placing British policy in a part of the Middle East that it controlled outright at odds with its interests in other parts of the Middle East that it did not. It raised uncomfortable ethical questions and seemingly unanswerable practical ones about the legitimacy, correct policy, and material cost of the British Mandate. The initial failure to contain the revolt made Britain look weak in the eyes of its enemies, while the escalation of violence—and the oppressive measures used to contain that violence—provided easy headlines for Italian and German propaganda targeting Muslim audiences in the Middle East and Asia. The stakes of the crisis were thus intensified by the gathering clouds in Europe, as the prospect of a new war between Britain, France, and the fascist powers loomed ever more ominously into view.

The revolt was, secondly, a regional Arab crisis—in many ways the defining event of Arab politics in the interwar years. It drew much of the Arabic-speaking world, from North Africa to the Gulf, together around a shared political concern and provided enormous momentum to a wave of grassroots political movements, ranging from conservative Islamist to militant nationalist to progressive feminist. Among the most important of these was the emergence of a pan-Arab bloc centered on Cairo, incorporating the leading politicians and heads of state of much of the Arabic-speaking world, and defined by its commitment to the defense of Palestine. It was these prominent figures who would participate in a series of conferences in 1939 that sought, unsuccessfully, to negotiate a settlement to the Palestine crisis on Arab terms—in collaboration, as we will see, with politicians from British India.

For the crisis in Palestine was also, thirdly, perceived as a crisis of the entire Muslim *umma*. In Egypt this was reflected in the leadership of the Muslim Brotherhood and the Young Men's Muslim Association in pro-Palestinian protests and fundraising campaigns. In India, the reaction to the Arab Revolt constituted the most significant Muslim political campaign focused on an external issue since the Khilafat movement of the early 1920s. And, especially in its early years, pro-Palestinian activism in India featured many of the same prominent Muslim individuals: men like Hasrat Mohani, Ahmed Ansari, Mohamed Ali Jauhar, and, following his death, his brother Shawkat Ali—now joined by Muhammad Ali Jinnah, who returned to India and assumed leadership of the All-India Muslim League in 1935. Following the announcement of the British government's new policy of partition in 1937, the Muslim League began passing resolution after resolution concerning the situation in Palestine. It convened regional and national conferences on the issue, and petitioned the Viceroy, the Indian Secretary, the Colonial Secretary, and the British Prime Minister on behalf of their Arab brethren. Dissatisfied with the limited impact of these efforts, they resolved to send a delegation on a tour of the Middle East and Europe to make their case in person. But influencing policy on Palestine was an excessively complicated task, given that the British government was itself almost paralyzed by internal divisions on the issue.

THE BIRTH OF BBC ARABIC

Two days after Iqbal's poignant New Year's address, the British Broadcasting Corporation inaugurated its first radio service in a foreign language. BBC Arabic launched with a one-hour transmission from Daventry to audiences across the Levant and the Arab Gulf, marking the beginning of what would swiftly become the World Service. Within three years of that initial broadcast, the BBC would offer programming in thirty-four different languages, including Hindi, Urdu, Bengali, Farsi, Gujarati, and Marathi.

The need for British-sponsored programming in Arabic resulted directly from the anti-British propaganda of Radio Bari during the Abyssinian Crisis, and yet it took until mid-1937 for the Cabinet to sanction the creation of the Arabic service. By then, the revolt underway in Mandate Palestine was providing Italian propagandists with plenty of fresh material. "The ferocity of British tactics in suppressing the revolt," notes Peter Partner, "had consequences all over the Muslim world: not only the Foreign Office but the India Office were interested in some kind of shield against the exploitation of these events by Bari."[13]

Alongside technical and logistical considerations, the Committee on Arabic Broadcasting was determined that the language used by the BBC should be superior to that of the Italian-sponsored radio programming, having received reports that its announcer was the subject of ridicule for his ungrammatical and heavily accented Arabic. The opinions of British diplomats and Arabists working in the region were solicited, and it was ultimately the advice of Robert Furness, then a press censor in Mandate Palestine, that carried the day. Furness had worked for decades in the Egyptian Civil Service and had lately served as Deputy Director of the Egyptian Broadcasting Corporation. He recommended that the new BBC broadcaster speak what he termed "Egyptian *nahwy*," a compromise between classical Arabic and Egyptian dialect, which would be respectable to the educated ear and readily comprehensible to the average café patron. Furness argued for the Egyptian accent on the grounds that Egypt was "the largest and most advanced of the countries affected, and the centre of Islamic education. A broadcaster will be best understood by the most of the listeners, and least criticized, if he uses Egyptian *nahwy*. . . . It is the nearest approach to a common language."[14] The BBC promptly hired Ahmad Kamal Surour, a former Egyptian Radio presenter, for its new program, further contributing to the growing preeminence of Egyptian personalities and the Egyptian accent in Arabic broadcast media.

BBC Arabic went on the air on 3 January 1938. Its maiden transmission was feted in parliament by both benches, and British embassies and outposts throughout the Arab East received congratulatory messages from local rulers and elites. The broadcast was scheduled for 17:15 Greenwich Mean Time, or 19:15 in Egypt and the Levant, an hour later in the countries of the Arab Gulf. Across the region, listening parties assembled. In Saudi Arabia, British diplomats were invited to join King Ibn Saud in his tent, alongside members of his coterie.

> An introductory announcement in Arabic was followed by a brief recital by a group of Cairo musicians led by a zither player. There were messages from one of the sons of the Imam of Yemen, and from the Egyptian Chargé d'Affaires and from the Saudi and Iraqi Legations [in London]. At six o'clock Big Ben sounded, and [BBC Director General] Sir John Reith spoke in English.

Then came Surour with the news bulletin:

> Another Arab from Palestine was executed by hanging at Acre this morning by order of a military court. He was arrested during recent riots in the Hebron mountains and was found to possess a rifle and some ammunition. . . . A small battle took place yesterday between a police force and an armed band at Safad. . . . A train travelling in the hills near Jerusalem was fired at, but there were no casualties.[15]

The announcer moved on to other subjects, but the same could not be said for many of the listeners. Sir Reader Bullard, British Minister to King Ibn Saud, later recounted the event in his memoirs:

> There was silence in the tent and our party broke up without any talk. When I saw Ibn Saud the next day he spoke of the broadcast. For months, he said, he had refused to listen to the Arabic broadcasts from Jerusalem, because he

found them so painful, but he had looked forward to the inaugural Arabic broadcast from London, and had filled his tent with his followers so that they might listen too. 'When the announcer spoke of the execution of that Arab in Palestine', he said, 'I wept and I wept', and as he spoke a tear rolled down his cheek and he scrubbed it off with his kerchief.[16]

GRUMBLING IN THE RANKS

At the Colonial Office and within the Government of Palestine, what had heretofore been a quiet resentment of the BBC project—on the grounds that it amounted to "poaching on the part of the Foreign Office in respect of Palestine"—now boiled over into something like mutiny. The entire point of these broadcasts had supposedly been to counter Italian propaganda; now it appeared that the BBC was intent on doing Bari's job for it. Mocking the Foreign Office's desire to promote "friendly relations" using the Arabic Service, one Palestine government official wrote acidly that Arab opinion could be summarized as "Let England settle the Palestine problem satisfactorily if they want Arab friendship, and until they do that, England can go to hell!"[17]

The BBC hit back at its critics. J.B. Clark, then head of the Empire Service (and soon to become the Director of the Overseas Service), insisted that in keeping with the BBC's tradition of journalistic credibility and independence, the news in Arabic would be kept as close as possible to the English language bulletins transmitted daily across the globe. His minute to this effect became legendary within BBC circles, articulating the lofty self-image of generations of World Service reporters and journalists: "The omission of unwelcome facts of news and the consequent suppression of truth runs counter to the Corporation's policy laid down by appropriate authority."[18]

Yet recent research by Simon Potter indicates that Clark's statement reflected the minority view within BBC leadership, at least insofar as the Middle East was concerned. While he was out of the country on official business, Clark's superiors, BBC Director General John Reith and his deputy, Cecil Graves, in fact came to a "gentleman's agreement" with the Foreign Office to allow for a high degree of government oversight on the new Arabic broadcasts.[19] In the midst of the fallout from that first Palestine news bulletin, the head of the Foreign Office's News Department, Rex Leeper, interceded to remind the BBC of their "understanding":

> (1) That these foreign language broadcasts should be regarded as a special service distinct in character from the Home and Empire services and that while the news and talks should be straight in the sense of being

strictly truthful and accurate, the idea of giving a favourable impression of ourselves to the countries to which they are addressed should be the guiding motive of the whole service.

(2) That news items of special interest to these countries should be included ...

(3) That it should be regarded as permissible to omit items of news which might have a harmful effect and that when it is found necessary to include any such item care should be taken to add an explanatory comment.

(4) That any item dealing with foreign affairs should be referred to the Foreign Office for their advice where the editor may have any doubt as to the effect it may produce.[20]

On the subject of Palestine in particular, BBC News Editor A.S. Calvert was required to visit the Foreign Office daily to receive "authoritative guidance" on how not to just report the events but also place them within what the government deemed their appropriate context. Within two months, the Foreign Office appears to have overcome whatever initial resistance they encountered from Clark and his staff and felt that "the gentleman's agreement with the BBC was working pretty well."[21] From the outset, then, the Arab Middle East in general and Palestine in particular were deemed special exceptions to the BBC's policy of editorial neutrality.

In British outposts throughout the Arab region, however, many diplomats—including Bullard in Arabia and Lampson in Egypt—tended to blame the Colonial Office's policy in Palestine, rather than the BBC's reporting of it, for the bitterness of local feelings on the subject. In the wake of that first Arabic broadcast, Lampson wrote to the Foreign Office from his desk in Cairo: "As long ... as our policy in Palestine remains unacceptable to the Arab world, the Italians must continue to have a very great advantage over us in propaganda. Palestine will remain a thorn in the flesh until our line is changed: it is in fact a veritable millstone round our neck."[22] Events were to prove the veracity of Lampson's grim prophecy.

TROUBLE NEXT DOOR

As previously alluded, the Arab Revolt was of immense significance in Egypt. Until 1936, successive Egyptian governments had tended to remain aloof of regional politics, preferring to focus on domestic concerns and avoid foreign entanglements. All of this changed with the outbreak of the revolt. As the strife consuming it neighbor deepened, the Wafd government that swept to power in May 1936 felt increasingly obliged to wade into the fray.

One reason for this was the death of King Fuad in April, just as the revolt got underway. The popularity of his heir, Faruq, created an opening for the palace to shift the balance of power in its favor. This opportunity was seized on by several of the King's advisors, notably Ali Maher, as well as Sheikh Maraghi, now rector of the mosque-university of al-Azhar. Faruq's regular attendance at Friday prayers and close relationship with Maraghi helped to earn him sobriquets like al-Malek al-Salih, the Pious King. Maraghi, who had been so intimately implicated in Fuad's diplomatic wranglings with the British and Saudis during the Caliphate Crisis in the mid-1920s, sought to capitalize on the youthful new monarch's reputation for religiosity to revive the campaign for an Egyptian caliphate, with Faruq at the helm. The emergence of this potent new alignment between the palace and al-Azhar signaled a shift in Egypt's center of political gravity away from the Wafd, at precisely the moment when the party's electoral victory and successful conclusion of a treaty with Britain were meant to have bolstered the nationalists' position.

Another consequence of Fuad's death was the mending of Egypt's relations with Saudi Arabia, which had been suspended in 1926 and resisted earlier resolution largely due to the personal animosity between the Egyptian and Saudi monarchs. This rapprochement between two of the largest and most powerful Arab countries lifted an important barrier to regional cooperation of particular significance within the context of the mounting crisis in Palestine.

The domestic political scene in Egypt had evolved considerably by 1936, with several new parties, including Young Egypt, the Saadists, and the Muslim Brotherhood gaining traction at the Wafd's expense—especially among the country's urban and educated youth. The Arab Revolt was seized on by the Muslim Brotherhood and the Young Men's Muslim Association (YMMA) as a cause célèbre, and their leadership in protests, strikes, and fundraising campaigns contributed to the expansion of their membership throughout 1936–39.[23] The Egyptian Feminist's Union (EFU), led by Huda Shaarawi, also threw itself headlong into campaigning and fundraising on behalf of the Palestinians, after Shaarawi received formal appeals for help from the Palestinian Arab Women's Committee. Among them was a poignant telegram from the Women's Committee at Acre begging Shaarawi and other Egyptian women to prevent their looming "erasure":[24] "O neighbor of the Holy Land, have you heard what has happened to your siblings? It is as terrible as a flood, and about to sweep over you as well. . . . Will you abandon us, though you have a tongue that speaks and a heart which beats? Ask your ally

[Great Britain] what is to become of the 400,000 Muslims and the 500 Mosques [of Palestine]? ... O God, awaken Egypt to the severity of this calamity!"[25]

As a result of the EFU's membership in several international bodies focused on feminism and world peace, it became the first and probably the most consequential Egyptian organization to advocate on behalf of the Palestinian cause in international fora, including at the 1936 Universal Peace Congress held in Brussels.[26] The activism of the EFU, the Muslim Brotherhood, the YMMA, and other local organizations in some ways forced the hand of the Wafd, which in the spring and summer of 1936 was still in the midst of negotiating the Anglo-Egyptian Treaty (and thus wary of upsetting relations with the British government). Yet despite this and their landslide electoral victory in May, the Wafd could not afford to ignore a cause with such passionate and widespread support among the Egyptian people.[27] Moreover, and as we saw in the last chapter, the conclusion of the treaty in August cleared the way for an "independent" Egyptian foreign policy and membership at the League of Nations, providing the government with a new lease to express its views on foreign affairs and a platform for those views on the world stage.

The other major factor that drove Nahas and the Wafd toward involvement in the Palestinian cause was the regional political landscape, as Arab leaders began jockeying for influence over the crisis and its resolution. Iraqi Foreign Minister Nuri al-Said contacted the British government to offer his assistance, as did Ibn Saud; meanwhile, King Abdallah of Transjordan saw the crisis in neighboring Palestine as an opportunity to expand his own kingdom to the shores of the Mediterranean. The treaty with Britain may have given Nahas and the Egyptian government the opportunity to pursue, for the first time, an independent Egyptian foreign policy, but it was this unsubtle maneuvering on the part of Egypt's brother Arab states that created much of the impetus.

To avoid scuttling months of painstaking diplomacy with Britain, Nahas took a cautious and calculated approach to his ministry's early involvement in the Palestine crisis, while the Anglo-Egyptian Treaty was still under negotiation. The public statements he and other Wafd deputies made in 1936 were sympathetic to the Palestinians, but measured in tone. A joint declaration by the lower and upper houses of the Egyptian parliament in July hoped that the "crisis will be resolved in accordance with principles of justice and fairness"—and left it at that.[28] Similarly, on a regional level, Egypt held back from formal diplomacy and did not affiliate itself with a joint declaration issued in October by the leaders of Iraq, Saudi Arabia, Syria, and Transjordan, calling for a ceasefire. In conversation with a British diplomat, Nahas explained his sense that it would be "better in the circumstances for the King of Egypt not to join in declaration to Arab rulers. This will leave Egypt as a card to be played later in case that declaration proves fruitless."[29] It was a deft move. While the declaration of the Arab heads of state did result in the temporary halting of the revolt, the Palestinian people felt betrayed by their leaders' acquiescence to the declaration, which had asked the Palestinians to place their faith "in the good intentions of your friend Great Britain, who has declared that she will do justice."[30] The fact that Egypt avoided association with the joint declaration no doubt helped its credibility when it entered the diplomatic fray in earnest the following year.

Meanwhile, throughout the spring and summer of 1936, Nahas worked behind the scenes in Cairo to crack down on violent public demonstrations, temper the vitriol of Arabic newspaper editors, and keep the subject of Palestine out of Friday prayer sermons. This won him praise from Lampson, who wrote approvingly that he and the Wafd had "definitely tried—and with considerable success—to control manifestations of Egyptian feeling against British policy in Palestine."[31] But while working to maintain public order for the sake of the negotiations, Nahas brought his own private protests repeatedly before British officials. According to Israel Gershoni and James Jankowski, in June 1936 alone, he spoke "at length" with Lampson on at least four separate occasions about "the situation in the Mandate and its potential repercussions in Egypt": "The substance of [Nahas's] remarks consisted of several interrelated points: admonitions that the unrest in Palestine was due to solid Arab grievances; recommendations that the British temporarily suspend Jewish immigration in order to ease the tension; warnings that his own government was sitting on an 'oven' because of the situation in Palestine, with violent agitation and anti-Jewish violence inside Egypt being distinct possibilities; and pointed reminders that 'we [Egyptians] also are Arabs' and thus should not be expected to remain aloof from the problem."[32]

The joint Arab declaration in October was accompanied by an announcement that a Royal Commission would be sent to assess the situation in Palestine and advise on the best course of government action. The uneasy truce that resulted held until the publication of the commission's report the following July, which recommended that the territory of the Palestine Mandate be partitioned into separate Arab and Jewish states. With the adoption of this recommendation as official British policy, the violence resumed—as did Arab, Muslim, and anticolonial solidarity movements, now inflected with an even greater sense of urgency and outrage.

THE 1938 CAIRO CONFERENCES

As soon as its details became known, Muhammad Ali Jinnah announced that the Muslim League would send a delegation to the World Interparliamentary Congress of Arab and Muslim Countries for the Defense of Palestine, to be held in Cairo in October 1938. Its origins lay in a pan-Arab conference on Palestine that was held in Bludan, Syria, in September 1937, shortly after the announcement of the policy of partition. At that time, the conference had invited official Egyptian government participation; Nahas had refused, still apparently holding out in the belief that Egypt could play its hand separately from the other Arab states. He told the conference organizers that "he preferred to work independently and in his own way towards a solution of the Palestine problem."[33] The same month that the Bludan Conference took place, the Wafdist Foreign Minister, Wassif Butrus Ghali, made his own forceful plea on behalf of the Palestinians during Egypt's inaugural address to the League of Nations General Assembly in Geneva. There is certainly the sense, as Gershoni and Jankowski argue, that Nahas sought Egyptian control over the crisis on its Eastern border, rather than a solution founded on Arab unity. His strategy was cut short by King Faruq, who dismissed Nahas from the premiership in December 1937, under the influence of his most trusted advisors, Sheikh Mustafa al-Maraghi and the politician Ali Maher.

Grooming Faruq to lead a bid for a new Egyptian caliphate, Maraghi had sought to arrange a religious coronation ceremony for the new monarch in the summer of 1937. This was an almost unheard-of innovation for a Muslim ruler, one calculated to garner international attention and boost Faruq's prestige as well as his Islamic credentials. Nahas's Wafd government shot down Maraghi's coronation proposal, on the grounds that it would undermine the secular and democratic character of the Egyptian state. Maraghi and his allies labeled this Coptism, and the rift between the Wafd and al-Azhar grew wider. Then in the fall, Faruq sought to appoint his ally Ali Maher, Chief of the Royal Cabinet. The Wafd resisted Faruq's nominee, on the grounds that the government had the right to appoint a candidate of its own choosing to the post. The result was Nahas's summary dismissal; in his place, Faruq appointed Muhammad Mahmud to form a new government.

Meanwhile, however, the Bludan Conference took place. Among the Egyptians who attended the conference as private citizens was Muhammad Ali Alluba. A lawyer by training and until 1934 a leading figure of the Liberal Constitutionalist Party, Alluba was a passionate supporter of the Palestinian cause. He had previously been elected Vice President of the World Islamic Congress in

Jerusalem in 1931 and traveled as part of its delegation to India in 1933 to discuss the conflict in Palestine.³⁴ In Bludan, Alluba was again elected a Vice President of the proceedings. His experience at Bludan and the contacts he made there pushed him to further activism once back in Egypt; the following May, he headed the group of parliamentarians who began to organize an international conference on Palestine, to be held in Cairo. That August, invitations were sent to Iraq, Morocco, Iran, Transjordan, Palestine, Yugoslavia, Syria, the United States, Yemen, and, yes, India.

Alluba was not the only Egyptian inspired by the meeting in Bludan. Huda Shaarawi had initially planned to hold a women's congress on Palestine in parallel with the Bludan Conference. According to Margot Badran, "the British intercepted a letter from Shaarawi to [a leader of the Women's Committee for the Defense of Palestine, Bahirah] al-Azmah suggesting that representatives be invited from women's associations throughout the East, especially from Iran and India."³⁵ Most intriguingly, while the men's pan-Arab conference in Bludan went ahead, the British prevailed upon the authorities in Syria to put a stop to the women's conference, possibly in response to the prospect of Indian participation.³⁶ In July, the British Consul in Damascus reported with evident satisfaction that "the Syrian Prime Minister has forbidden the holding of a Women's Congress in Syria to discuss Palestine and has taken steps to ensure that negotiations for it cease."³⁷

Never easily dissuaded, Shaarawi changed tack, and began planning instead for a women's conference on Palestine in Cairo. Alluba, who had initially encouraged her plans for a meeting in Bludan, now coordinated with her for the holding of a women's conference in parallel with his own World Interparliamentary Congress. Granted "power of attorney" by women's organizations in Palestine, Lebanon, Iraq, and Syria, Huda rejected the suggestion from a male organizer that her conference be called the Arab Women's Conference; the cause, she felt, was broader than that. Instead, the invitations sent from Cairo to prominent feminists and women's organizations requested their participation in an Eastern Women's Conference.³⁸

So it was that in the first half of October 1938, roughly two hundred male and female delegates from over a dozen countries descended on the Egyptian capital to discuss the crisis in Palestine. They were not official representatives of their governments, although many were parliamentarians or prominent political figures in their own right. In addition to representatives of the Arab countries, there were delegations from Iran, China, Spanish Morocco, Yugoslavia, Turkey, the United States, and India. Among the Indian delegation was Choudhry

Khaliquzzaman, by now a leading Muslim League politician from the United Provinces. He recounted the journey from Allahabad to Cairo to attend the congress in his autobiography, *Pathway to Pakistan*: "[My family] all arrived in time to see me off, this being my first experience of an airplane flight. With night stops at Jodhpur and Baghdad we reached Alexandria and travelled from there to Cairo by train. . . . The main question before the Arab world at the time was to save Palestine from partition, in which we all agreed."[39]

The British-owned *Egyptian Gazette* reported on the opening of the conference in much the same tone as it might have covered the colonial pavilions at a World Expo: "Variegated dress and headgear, from the turbans of the Azharites to the Tarbooshes of the Egyptian Senators and Deputies to the Kafia and Agal of the Palestinians, the queer black Iraqui caps and their even queerer grey glengarries, and a salmon coloured shapeless tarboosh of an Indian Moslem delegate, gave a colourful air to the scene inside the somewhat ornate but dilapidated Casino."[40]

An editorial from the same day, headlined "Sabean Odours," remarked, "There has been so much speculation as to the political results of this gathering of the clans that it is pleasant for a little at least to see these Arab visitors—or rather these Moslems from other lands—as picturesque strangers borne upon some Sabean breeze, rather than as participants in the international hurly-burly."[41]

And yet consequential players in an international political process was indeed how these delegates saw themselves—the women as much as the men. During the Women's Conference proceedings, a Palestinian activist, Sadhij Nassar, exhorted her sisters to prove that "Arab women are just as capable as men and can accomplish great acts."[42] Delegates were, moreover, acutely conscious of the crisis brewing in Europe and of their own strategic importance as an Arab-Muslim bloc in any coming international conflict. In his opening remarks to the Interparliamentary Congress, a Muslim League delegate and member of the Bengal Legislative Assembly, Abdurrahman Siddiqi, claimed to speak "on behalf of the eighty million Indian Mulims" and "exhorted Great Britain to learn the lesson of the recent meeting in Munich, to revise its policy in Palestine accordingly, and choose between the Arabs and the Jews. He warned that, if the Palestine question was not resolved in conformity with the decisions of the present Congress, the Muslims of the entire world would refuse their support to British imperialism."[43]

A telegram sent to Neville Chamberlain by Huda Shaarawi on behalf of the "Eastern Womens' Committees" also made the connection between developments in Palestine and Munich, albeit in an entirely more optimistic tone: "Hearty congratulations extended from Oriental Women Societies on success of your magnanimous efforts to save Europe from war devastations. Confident this same humane spirit will urge you to do justice to Palestine Arabs to safeguard peace in Orient also."⁴⁴

CALIPHAL AMBITIONS

The vast majority of the Egyptian delegates at the Interparliamentary Congress were drawn from the Saadist and Ittihad parties, which then formed the government; their opposition rivals in the Wafd were pointedly excluded. At the opening session, the ranks of the Egyptian delegates were swelled by many hundreds of attendees from the Muslim Brotherhood and the YMMA; in total, the *Egyptian Gazette* estimated there were 2,500 participants.⁴⁵ The palace, al-Azhar, and their youthful supporters sought to take advantage of the presence of so many foreign Muslim delegates in Egypt to promote King Faruq's bid to revive the caliphate. Khaliquzzaman recalled that "some young Egyptians actually asked us what would be the reaction of Muslims in India if Egypt agreed to make him the Khalifa [Caliph]."⁴⁶ Through subsequent inquiries with friends in Cairo, the Indian delegates discovered that Sheikh al-Maraghi had already approached the Aga Khan in an attempt to win Indian support for Faruq's elevation to caliph. The previous year a group of sheikhs from al-Azhar had also been sent on a fact-finding mission to India, ostensibly to assess the state of Muslim religious sentiment and education there. Lampson observed that this and similar Azharite missions planned for Kenya, Nigeria, Somalia, and Zanzibar were "part of the general attempt made by the more conservative elements here to give Egypt Turkey's old preponderant position in the Muslim world."⁴⁷ According to Khaliquzzaman,

> We were greatly disillusioned. Next day we met Sheikh Maraghi to talk over the matter with him. I had my own views on this question and told the Sheikh that King Farooq did not enjoy the confidence of the Muslim world and would not therefore, so far as I could see, be acceptable to the Muslims of India. The Sheikh then asked me whether he might have the title *Amirul Mominin* [Commander of the Faithful] in the Muslim world. I replied that this word had invariably been associated with the Khilafat and as such it would create great confusion in the Muslim mind if this title were given to him. Our talk thus ended.⁴⁸

Prime Minister Mahmud was apparently less than enthusiastic about the Interparliamentary Congress, in part because of what he saw as this "increasingly religious aspect" to pro-Palestinian activism.[49] It was a concern shared by Nahas, whatever his other political differences with Mahmud, because of the opportunity it provided for precisely the sort of overtures to foreign Muslims described by Khaliquzzaman. Yet despite their qualms and the glaring absence of the Wafd from the proceedings, both Mahmud and Nahas found it politically impossible to oppose the congress, given the immensity of popular Egyptian support for the Palestinian cause. Indeed, they each felt obliged to host receptions for the delegates, Nahas presiding over his event in a traditional Palestinian keffiyeh.[50] There, he found himself in a somewhat heated confrontation with Khaliquzzaman, who later remarked, "I found that Nahas Pasha was singularly ill-informed about the history of the Muslims in India or their differences with the [Indian National] Congress and applied his experience of life in Egypt to India so literally as to make the Muslim problem of India exactly as the Jewish or Christian problem which Saad Zaghlol Pasha had to face in Egypt, thus completely ignoring the difference in the size of the two countries. . . . I implored him to leave us to our fate if he found himself unable to sympathize with us."[51]

As observed by Faisal Devji, Khaliquzzaman and his colleagues were to remain implacably opposed to the partition of Palestine while becoming increasingly wed to demands for a separate polity for India's Muslims.[52] This will be explored further in chapters 6 and 9.

The resolutions that the Interparliamentary Congress passed at its closing session on 11 October reiterated what had by then become familiar Arab refrains: there was an unequivocal rejection of the partition plan, and there were calls for a halt to Jewish immigration in Palestine, an end to the British Mandate, and the establishment of a sovereign Arab state in its place. Despite the aspirations of participants, however, the Interparliamentary Congress had a negligible impact on British (or Arab) policy. The Palestinian participants were said to be disappointed, while the British were relieved, deeming the proceedings "less venomous and anglophobe" than anticipated.[53] The congress was, in any event, swiftly eclipsed by the high-level Arab leaders' meeting arranged by Prime Minister Mahmud in Cairo in January 1939, itself a prelude to the St James's Conference scheduled to be held in London the following month.

The Eastern Women's Conference had somewhat more of a lasting political impact than its male counterpart. In its wake, new women's committees "for the defense of Palestine" were established in Palestine, Egypt, Iraq, and Lebanon; within two months, a Cairo-based subcommittee focused on charitable contributions had raised 2,000 Egyptian pounds for Palestine relief.[54] Huda Shaarawi's EFU headquarters in Cairo became a veritable clearinghouse for information and communications on the situation in Palestine, and not only among women. In the months after the Women's Conference, the Arab Society of Damascus and a group of Jerusalem ulema also wrote to Shaarawi repeatedly to ask for her help in promoting awareness of the Palestinians' plight.[55] As Lampson observed ruefully in a telegram to the Foreign Office, shortly after the close of the conferences in Cairo, "the power of the women in the East, as in France, is far greater than their legal disabilities indicate."[56]

Despite its muted impact, however, the Interparliamentary Congress as well as the Women's Conference were indicative of Cairo's new place at the heart of inter-Arab mobilization in defense of Palestine. The claim of the Egyptian capital to regional preeminence would be further strengthened by the conference of Arab leaders held there in January 1939, when, in the words of Gershoni and Jankowski, "Cairo became the diplomatic center of the Arab world."[57] The Interparliamentary Congress had another important outcome, in that it served to strengthen the connections between several of the Muslim League delegates and their Egyptian and Arab counterparts. Following the completion of the

FIGURE 10   From left to right: Abdurrahman Siddiqi, Choudhry Khaliquzzaman, and Muhammad Ali Alluba, Cairo, 1938. In C. Khaliquzzaman, *Only If They Knew It* (Karachi, 1965).
SPECIAL COLLECTIONS, UNIVERSITY OF NEW SOUTH WALES, CANBERRA

congress's work, Choudhry Khaliquzzaman and Abdurrahman Siddiqi were nominated to travel to London with the Egyptian organizer, Alluba, to make representations to the British government on their colleagues' behalf. This was likely due to their uncommon fluency, as trained barristers, in English rhetoric and legal terminology, as well as the possible perception that as British subjects they enjoyed greater access to official channels of government. Certainly, once in London, these Indian Members of the Legislative Assembly (MLAs) sought to press their advantages into service on behalf of the Palestinians.

CONFRONTING FASCISM IN CAIRO

As the conferences broke up and delegates departed the capital toward the end of 1938, a political manifesto began making the rounds among Cairo's intellectual and artistic cadres. Opposite a large print of Picasso's *Guernica* (unveiled the previous summer at the World Expo in Paris), a slogan was emblazoned in Arabic and French: Yahya al-Fann al-Munhatt / VIVE L'ART DEGENERE. Beneath this bold headline was an impassioned condemnation of totalitarian restrictions on artistic expression, which the authors saw epitomized in the Nazi regime's 1937 *Entartete Kunst* (degenerate art) exhibition in Munich—an elaborately curated effort to ostracize Jewish artists and other works the regime deemed subversive. The Cairo artist's manifesto read in part:

> We consider absurd and worthy of the most perfect contempt the religious, racist and nationalist prejudices, under the tyranny of which certain individuals, drunk on their provisional omnipotence, claim to enslave the fate of works of art.
>
> In these regressive myths we cannot make out anything besides veritable concentration camps of the mind.
>
> . . . In Vienna, delivered to the barbarians, Renoir's paintings are lacerated; Freud's works are burned in public squares. . . . In Rome a so-called Commission of "Literary Improvement" has just completed its own dark work, deeming it necessary to remove from circulation "everything that is anti-Italian, anti-racist, immoral, and depressing."
>
> Intellectuals—writers—artists! Let us take up this challenge together. With this degenerate art, we are in absolute solidarity. In it resides all our hopes for the future. Let us work for its victory over this new Medieval Era, rising in the very heart of the West.[58]

Art and Liberty—*al-Fann wa al-Hurriya* in Arabic—was no regular political organization, and this was no standard call to arms. Centered on an intimate group of surrealist artists, writers, and intellectuals who gathered frequently in Cairo's Nawras Café, the collective sought to contest fascism and imperialism, both at home and abroad. Their 1938 manifesto has sometimes been interpreted as an Egyptian response to the call issued by Frida Kahlo, Leon Trotsky, and Diego Rivera "For an Independent Revolutionary Art" and their proposal for a Fédération Internationale de l'Art Révolutionnaire Indépendant (FIARI).[59] Yet while Art and Liberty was committed by its charter "to maintaining a close contact between the youth of Egypt and the current literary, artistic and social developments in the world,"[60] it was, as Sam Bardaouil argues, far more than the branch office of a foreign movement.[61]

The leaders of the Cairo collective believed that surrealism was, at its core, a universal call for social and moral revolution as well as an artistic movement, firmly rooted in the unique cultural and political milieu of urban Egypt and radiating its message outward toward both East and West. Writing in 1939, Kamel el-Telmissany opined that "surrealism is nothing but a contemporary scientific term for what we call imagination, freedom of expression, and freedom of style, all of which can be found in the East." He was writing in response to accusations, lodged by Egyptian nationalists, that the cosmopolitanism of his movement amounted to an embrace of European values, hence cultural imperialism—a charge he vehemently denied. "Have you been to the Egyptian Museum?" he challenged his critics. "Many of the Pharaonic sculptures from ancient Egypt are surrealist. Have you been to the Coptic Museum? Much Coptic art is surrealist. Far from aping a foreign artistic movement, we are creating art that has its origins in the brown soil of our country and which runs in our blood."[62]

Yet el-Telmissany simultaneously rejected the nationalism of artists like Mahmud Mokhtar, whose sculptures had in so many ways defined the 1920s mix of anticolonial nationalism and pharaonic imagery.[63] In his seminal 1940 essay "al-Insaniyya wa al-Fann al-Hadith" (Humanity and modern art), he condemned these works as a "regression [into] the shackles of land and regionalism," insisting there was no greater crime for an artist than "to limit his art within a specific piece of land." Instead, el-Telmissany maintained that "to feel for humanity and all that it is suffering from in our present age is one of the main problems that modern art is concerned with."[64] In line with this thesis, Art and Liberty championed an ethic of radical antinationalism and human solidarity. The 1938 manifesto was signed by thirty-seven artists, including Egyptians and foreigners living in Egypt—Christians, Muslims, Jews, Arabs, and Europeans, men and women, communists and liberals.

Through the activism of its members, including prominent women artists like

Amy Nimr, Inji Efflatoun, Ida Kar, and the writer Iqbal el-Alaily (daughter of Ahmed Shawqi), Art and Liberty was plugged into a transnational network of artists and intellectuals spanning San Francisco, Santiago, Moscow, Paris, Buenos Aires, Tunis, Copenhagen, Beirut, Tokyo, Mexico City, and Martinique (where the Négritude movement was similarly harnessing surrealism to contest European hegemony).[65] The movement's political convictions were hardly abstract: the fascism, nationalism, religious conservativism, and imperialism its members sought to combat were all manifest forces in late-1930s Egypt. A crucial turning point came with Italy's promulgation of the Manifesto della Razza in July 1938, which stripped Italian Jews of their citizenship. Given the size of the Italian community in Egypt, the law had profound repercussions there. According to Bardaouil, Art and Liberty's manifesto, published mere months after the race law's passage in Italy, "was meant as a denunciation of local fascist sentiment" as much as a protest of events taking place in Europe.[66] Underscoring the link between the two, in May 1939 members of Art and Liberty protested a lecture in Cairo by Filippo Tommaso Marinetti, a prominent Italian Futurist and close ally of Mussolini. Georges Henein, one of the leaders of Art and Liberty, rose from his seat to confront Marinetti, attacking "the political endorsement that the Futurists gave to Fascism": "Henein declared that such a position was not welcome in Egypt, especially just a few years after the Ethiopian invasion in 1935. . . . Henein criticized the nationalist, imperialist nature of Futurism, while celebrating the freedom of Surrealism and its status as an independent cultural movement."[67] The altercation reportedly devolved into a street brawl between antifascist and Futurist artists.[68]

The next year, Art and Liberty held its first group show at Il Nilo, a venue formerly known as the Risotto Club, which had served as a bastion of Cairo's Italian social scene prior to 1938. In the wake of the Manifesto della Razza, much of the club's membership had withdrawn en masse. Il Nilo sprung up in its place, embracing a defiantly cosmopolitan identity—as we can surmise in part from the prominent participation of Jewish and anti-Fascist Italian artists in Art and Liberty's exhibition. "As the world prepared for the worst," notes Bardaouil, "Art and Liberty understood all too well that they had their own war to wage."[69]

1938 opened and closed with very similar manifestos: one delivered on the radio by an ailing Muslim poet in Lahore, the other printed as a pamphlet by secular, avant-garde artists in Cairo. Yet both understood the precipice on which the world then stood as something far more existential than a clash of political ideologies, or East versus West. Instead, nationalism, fascism, imperialism, capitalist

FIGURE 11 Members of Art and Liberty in Cairo at their second exhibition, March 1941. Kamel el-Telmissany is third from left; Ramses Younane is third from right; Georges Henein is fifth from right in tinted glasses.
THE YOUNANE FAMILY ARCHIVE / WIKIMEDIA COMMONS

democracy, and Soviet totalitarianism were all fronts behind which the human fabric of the world was being hollowed out and stripped for parts—transformed by materialism and militarism into a "thing-oriented society,"[70] in which people themselves held no intrinsic value.

In this sense, Iqbal's New Year's message and Art and Liberty's manifesto were both eloquent rejections of the false dichotomies that lay at the heart of many contemporary debates among Eastern artists, intellectuals, and activists.[71] Iqbal did not live to witness the dark years that lay ahead, but in their journals, public events, and exhibitions, the members of Art and Liberty's surrealist vanguard fought against the cynical realpolitik and tribalism gaining ground around them. They worked instead to promote social and economic justice, creative freedom, borderless humanism, and other increasingly unpopular ideals.

PART III AMBASSADORS OF THE EAST

SIX

The Diplomats

> Let [the Palestinians] take advantage of [Britain's] weakness as the Congress in India was doing successfully.[1]
> —CHOUDHRY KHALIQUZZAMAN'S ADVICE TO THE PALESTINIANS AT THE ST JAMES'S CONFERENCE, 1939

> Jamal Eff. Husseini took exception to the use of India as an analogy [for Palestine]. Its international status was quite different. Palestine had never been a colony; its people had been partners in the Ottoman Empire.[2]
> —MINUTES OF THE ST JAMES'S CONFERENCE, 1939

WARNING SHOTS FROM BENGAL

In the immediate wake of the Munich Crisis and the Palestine conferences in Cairo, the Viceroy of India forwarded to London the text of a letter he had just received from the Government of Bengal. This was the first provincial ministry formed under the new India Act, which had devolved significant power to the provinces and expanded the electoral franchise by many millions. The government was a coalition between the populist (Muslim-led) Krishak Praja Party and the All-India Muslim League. Their letter expressed grave concerns over Britain's handling of the ongoing Arab Revolt in Palestine. It noted, too, that given the success of the anticolonial Congress Party in the last election, the British government would be well-advised to keep Indian Muslims onside, particularly in light of the volatility of European politics. Though insisting that the loyalty of Indian Muslims to the Crown was "beyond question," the letter writers hinted that events in Palestine had the power to dramatically alter that fact. The warning was straightforward: "Should the issue in the Palestine question be decided in such a manner which the Arabs and the Muslim world might consider to be inconsistent with the principles of international justice and contrary to Great Britain's own pledges to the Arabs, the repercussions on Muslim feelings in India would be serious and it is not unlikely that they might tell upon the Muslim sense of loyalty and devotion to the British power affecting the prospects of assistance from that community in case of a future war."[3]

Letters such as this one go some way in illustrating the pro-Palestinian pressure that was then mounting on the British Government of India, as well as British Ambassadors and Foreign Office staff stationed in Arab and Muslim countries.

Particularly following the release of the Peel Commission Report in September 1937, many of these officials attempted to effect a change in policy in London on the grounds that the revolt and proposed partition ran against British interests in those parts of the world where they were stationed. These efforts were met with varying degrees of hostility by the Colonial Office, which regarded Palestine as falling exclusively within its jurisdiction. The upshot was that, by the late 1930s, the British line on Palestine tended to vary drastically depending on which official or branch of government was consulted. As we will see, this bedeviled the task of the Arab and Indian negotiators who now attempted to insert themselves between the British government and Palestinians and engineer a diplomatic settlement to the ongoing revolt.

Prominent among them were the Indian MLAs and former Khilafatists Choudhry Khaliquzzam and Abdurrahman Siddiqi. Tasked by Jinnah (and elected by the delegates of the Cairo Interparliamentary Congress) to defend Palestine at the St James's Conference in London, the MLAs proved willing to go to great lengths in support of their mission. Crucially, however, there was a novel domestic angle to their diplomacy: for Jinnah was anxious to prevent the hybridized Muslim-anticolonial politics of Palestine from creating too powerful a bridge between Indian Muslim voters and the Congress Party—what he and his deputies termed the prospect of a "second Khilafat."

THE WHITEHALL WALTZ

In the middle of September 1938, Victor Hope, Second Marquess of Linlithgow and Viceroy of India, telegraphed Lawrence Dundas, Second Marquess of Zetland and Secretary of State for India, to sound him out on an idea he hoped might kill two birds with one stone: "In view of growing concern with which Moslems viewed developments in Palestine, it might be useful if H.M.G. would agree to receive a deputation of Indian Moslems. . . . It occurs to me that, in the present position of things in Palestine and in view of the European situation, it is going to be impossible to implement policy of partition within any reasonable lapse of time. A representation from Indian Moslems might provide H.M.G. with an opportunity to make a declaration modifying present policy."[4]

Zetland's private secretary dutifully wrote to his opposite number at the Colonial Office, Gerald Creasy. The message elicited a rather chilly response: "Mr. MacDonald has asked me to say in reply that . . . there can be no question of any modification of the policy of His Majesty's Government as regards Palestine, and that in any case he does not feel that it would be appropriate to make the first announcement of any change of policy to a deputation of Indian Moslems. If he were to receive such a deputation, he could only defend the policy of partition and emphasize the advantages which that solution offers to the Arabs of Palestine."[5]

Within weeks, however, government policy on Palestine *was* on the verge of a reversal. As Britain faced the growing possibility of war on the continent, an alarming number of its troops remained tied up in Palestine. Moreover, the policy of partition continued to sour relations with Arab governments, whose cooperation would be vital to any future war effort.[6] In the wake of the Munich Crisis, the Cabinet thus determined that political concessions to the Arabs were necessary. In anticipation of the official announcement of the Woodhead Report on 9 November, Zetland summarized its contents for Linlithgow as follows:

i. Partition is impracticable;

ii. H.M.G. will continue their responsibility for government of whole of Palestine;

iii. Understanding between Arabs and Jews is fundamental to permanent peace and progress in Palestine. H.M.G. therefore propose to hold conference in London to which would be invited representatives (a) of Jewish Agency (b) of Arabs of Palestine, other than active rebel leaders or deportees* (c) of Egypt, Saudi Arabia, Iraq, Syria, Lebanon and Transjordan.

iv. If conference in London is unable to reach conclusions within reasonable period, H.M.G. will make own announcement of policy.

... * Balance of opinion is against inviting Mufti to conference.[7]

Linlithgow replied to Zetland, expressing his satisfaction and relief. He could not, however, resist suggesting, "though it is none of my business," that the government ought to reconsider its exclusion of the Mufti, "on the basis of his proving much more of a nuisance outside than in." The experience of India, where attempts to shut Gandhi and his disciples out of the political process had backfired spectacularly, was likely in his thoughts. He continued:

> I recognise that basis at present contemplated for round table conference is essentially the representation of Arab or Arab-speaking countries adjacent to Palestine, but given the great imperial importance of Moslem reactions here to this question and very marked growth of Indian interest in it in these last few months, I would like to suggest ... that case for adding a representative of India is a very strong one. ... I am sure that the inclusion of a representative of India would give keen satisfaction here and would much ease my difficulties and those of the Governors, and I rather apprehend that we may apart from that anticipate criticism and difficulty if India in fact goes unrepresented.[8]

The man the Viceroy had in mind was the Aga Khan, who we last encountered as the coauthor of an ill-fated op-ed in the Turkish press. The Aga was a reliably monarchist sort of Muslim, the kind who bred champion racehorses and vacationed in the south of France. His correspondence with government officials in London was often punctuated by fresh mangoes, which he took evident pleasure in shipping off to damp, gray corners of the Earth. Linlithgow proposed that, even if it was deemed inappropriate for an Indian to actually participate in the Palestine conference, the Aga Khan might arrange to be in London during its proceedings with a "listening brief."[9]

Zetland agreed and wrote to MacDonald at the Colonial Office. Their correspondence indicates that they also spoke about the matter in person several times. Following these discussions, the Indian Secretary explained MacDonald's reservations to the Viceroy: "One can draw a logical line at the rulers of the adjacent Arab countries, but if you were once to go beyond such a line, it would be difficult to know where to stop. Moreover, the Jews would undoubtedly complain that the dice were being loaded heavily against them, and would almost certainly demand increased representation for themselves."[10]

Nevertheless, a direct line of communication between the Indian and Colonial Secretaries had been opened, and, in late November, the Aga Khan flew to London to attend a meeting with Zetland and MacDonald to discuss the upcoming conference on Palestine. Having been briefed, the Aga Khan strongly endorsed the Viceroy's stance that India be represented, and he pressed for Jinnah, in particular, to be invited. The Colonial Secretary explained, in keeping with his prior statements to Zetland, why he felt this was impossible. At the conclusion of their meeting, the Aga Khan agreed to return to London during the conference, if Zetland and MacDonald thought it useful.[11]

AMBASSADORS OF MUSLIM SENTIMENT

On the same day, in a different part of London, MacDonald's Secretary, Creasy, received a letter from Abdurrahman Siddiqi. Having just arrived from Cairo, the MLA introduced himself and Khaliquzzaman and requested a meeting with the Colonial Secretary "to acquaint him with the state of Muslim feeling in India on the question of Palestine and its repercussions on the situation in India."[12]

Creasy was immediately suspicious. He wrote to a colleague in the Colonial Office, Mr. Downie, attaching the letter and suggesting that the supplicants were "two professional agitators who are in this country with a view to making trouble over Palestine and the forthcoming discussions." Downie responded, "I don't see why the S of S's time should be wasted in discussing Palestine with Indian Moslems. The Palestine problem is only secondarily a matter of Moslem, and in no respect a matter of Indian, concern." Predictably, John Shuckburgh chimed in: "I should like to record my strong view (1) that the S. of S., with all his other preoccupations, ought not to be troubled with these tiresome people; and (2) that it is altogether wrong that Indian politicians should obtain direct access to the Colonial Office on matters of Colonial policy that do not affect Indian interests. They have their own S. of S., and ought to go to him if they want to make representations to H.M.G."[13]

But MacDonald was now alive to India's interest in Palestine, thanks to his discussions with Zetland and the Aga Khan. He proved to be more open than his staff to Siddiqi's request, especially after ascertaining that the two Indian gentlemen were prominent leaders of the Muslim League—with Khaliquzzaman "being possibly second in importance to Mr. Jinnah himself"—and that Zetland was in favor of the meeting.[14] In December, MacDonald wrote to Zetland detailing the first of several private audiences he held with Siddiqi and Khaliquzzaman. Of course, they too were keen for India to be represented at the upcoming conference and put themselves forward as potential candidates. "One argument which my visitors used, which impressed me," recounted MacDonald, "was that the Congress Party in India are ready to exploit the Palestine situation not only to the disadvantage of Britain but also to the disadvantage of the Moslem League in India. This was put forward as an additional reason why we should make a point of bringing Indian Moslems into the London discussions, so that their followers in India would realise that Great Britain was heeding Indian Moslem opinion and not be taken in by the Congress propaganda."[15]

The argument is markedly similar to the one put forward by the Government of Bengal in its letter to the Viceroy. Other contemporaneous Muslim League petitions warned pointedly of a second Khilafat—raising the specter of a movement that, of course, many of them had been intimately involved with. The Muslim League argued that because Gandhi and Nehru were also critics of Britain's policy in Palestine on anticolonial grounds, the conditions existed for a potential recurrence of the Khilafat phenomenon. If the Muslim League was seen to be ineffective in its pro-Palestinian advocacy, Muslims might look instead to the INC, easily the strongest political bloc in India, for leadership on the issue.[16] The prospective consolidation of Indian Muslims and Hindus opposed to British rule was not only a threat to the Raj; it was also a deeply worrisome prospect for the Muslim League, which would sink into political irrelevance if its base aligned with Congress. Thus in the petitions sent to provincial governors, the Viceroy, and the British government, and in the interviews held by Khaliquzzaman and Siddiqi with ministers in London, the Muslim League stressed that its efforts to defend Palestine were intended to *avert* the disaster of mass Muslim identification with the INC.

MacDonald appears to have appreciated the "second Khilafat" argument, made particularly forceful given the growing threat of war, both in Europe and the Pacific.[17] Thus he proposed a compromise to Zetland: if Siddiqi and Khaliquzzaman were to remain in London during the conference, they could be kept abreast of the progress of discussions and be seen to meet with the Colonial Secretary and the Indian Secretary, for the sake of public opinion in India. "Needless to say," he signed off, "I would do anything I could to help, short of complicating the discussions themselves."[18]

But for Siddiqi and Khaliquzzaman, unaware of MacDonald's proposal to Zetland, there now seemed little hope that their bid for representation would succeed. They thought of returning to India, but their Egyptian colleague Ali Alluba convinced them to stay on, to encourage the Palestinian delegates who would soon arrive. They agreed, becoming frequent visitors at Izzat Tannous's Arab Centre in Trafalgar Square. "It was a great trial on our nerves," recalled

Khaliquzzaman, "to stay for months together doing nothing but walking on the streets of London."[19]

The antidote emerged in the form of a "tall, graceful, well-cut figure" who invited the MLAs to tea in early December 1938 and met with them frequently over the course of subsequent months. The gentleman in question was Choudhry Rahmat Ali, already well known in India for his promulgation of "Pakistan"—an acrostic poem of a political program comprising the Muslim regions of South Asia (Punjab, Afghania, Kashmir, and Baluchistan) and translating to "land of the spiritually pure" in Urdu. Khaliquzzaman was profoundly impressed: "When we started talking about the scheme of Pakistan I found that not only had he thought deeply over the question but was earnest about its realization.... After some discussion I informed him that I was already a convert to the idea."[20]

(ANOTHER) CAIRO CONFERENCE

While the MLAs were roaming the West End and contemplating the upsides of partition, Arab delegates invited to participate in the upcoming St James's Conference gathered in Cairo to devise a joint strategy for their negotiations with the British. The governments of Egypt, Iraq, Yemen, Saudi Arabia, and Transjordan were represented, alongside representatives of the Palestinians. The Mufti of Jerusalem was conspicuously absent from the list of invitees, despite the Viceroy's advice, and despite the warnings of Arab and Indian politicians that, in the phrasing of yet another Muslim League petition to the British government, "the Grand Mufti, who alone is in a position to deliver the goods, should be invited to the conference."[21] His views, however, were represented by other members of the Arab Higher Committee, who had been released from their exile in the Seychelles to attend the conference. Upon their arrival in Cairo, these delegates even flew to Beirut to consult with Hajj Amin.[22] The Mufti's closest ally (and to prove among the strongest advocates of the Palestinian position in London) was his cousin Jamal al-Husseini, who had earlier fundraised in India for the Haram el-Sharif refurbishment and who subsequently met with prominent Khilafatists. Nine years prior, Husseini had traveled to London as an observer of the First Round Table Conference on India; now he would be the one participating in direct negotiations with the British government. For a time following his initial trip to India, Husseini had called for a "Gandhian" approach to the struggle against Britain in Palestine, by which he meant nonviolent boycott and noncooperation.[23] By 1939, however, his position had changed. At the St James's Conference he would maintain that no comparison was possible between the situation in India—an outright colony of the British Empire—and Palestine, which had enjoyed elected representation under the Ottomans and whose right to independence was admitted by the wording of the League of Nations Mandate.[24]

In Cairo, the Arab delegates agreed to the proposal of Iraqi Prime Minister Nuri al-Sa'id, to focus on the international status of Palestine, rather than contesting any one grievance such as Jewish immigration or British violence. They adopted this strategy on the assumption that movement toward Palestinian independence, along the same lines as Iraq (another former mandate), would axiomatically resolve the other outstanding issues. Arabs still made up over two-thirds of the population of Palestine in 1938; were the country to become independent and hold elections, they reasoned, its government could then legislate its own controls on immigration. The "normal protections" afforded minorities were to be granted Palestine's Jewish community, again modeled on the constitution of Iraq, which included guarantees for numerous minority communities. Independence would lead to the withdrawal of British troops and police—putting an end, it was presumed, to the violence of the Revolt. Having arrived at this formula, the Arab leaders agreed to press Britain for Palestinian independence at the earliest possible date.[25]

From the minutes kept by the Arab Delegation's Secretary, George Antonius, we know that they pursued this policy in earnest throughout the conference.[26] Their faith in their formula goes some way to indicating how very recent was their arrival on the scene. By contrast, as Laila Parsons has observed, by the late 1930s the Palestinians themselves had lost confidence in the British government's broken cycle of commissions and reports, which raised Arab hopes only to dash them.[27] But the representatives of Iraq, Egypt, and Transjordan—and perhaps to a lesser extent, Yemen and Saudi Arabia—still saw the British as honest brokers and believed that negotiations could result in a Palestinian state. After all, Egypt and Iraq had both recently won independence (of a kind) through similar processes of negotiation.[28] It was, in many ways, an understandable mistake, based on the flawed assumption that the British government could be persuaded to publicly abandon its commitment to the Zionists.

With a perhaps undue sense of optimism, then, the Arab delegates embarked for London. There they were greeted by Khaliquzzaman and Siddiqi, who had by now been awaiting their arrival for a full two months.

INDIANS AND ARABS IN LONDON

As the opening day of the St James's Conference approached, the Muslim League rallied in a final bid to win Indian representation. On 25 January, the two MLAs had a second interview with the Colonial Secretary, who now informed them definitively that they would not be able to participate in the conference—not even as observers. MacDonald reasoned that the conflict was "political" rather than "religious" in nature: "the admission of Indian Moslem representatives to the discussions might have the effect of introducing the religious factor, and was open to serious objection on that ground."[29] MacDonald suggested that, in lieu of participating in the talks, Siddiqi and Khaliquzzaman could submit a memorandum on Indian Muslim views; he promised that he would study it carefully. Several days later, a telegram arrived for MacDonald from India. Its tone was urgent and beseeching: "The All-India Muslim League urges upon His Majesty's Government give representation Muslim League Palestine Conference and concede Palestine National Arab Demands. Muslim India awaiting most anxiously results. I cannot by means telegram express adequately and impress intensity feeling throughout India. Failure Conference will be most disastrous throughout Muslim world, resulting grave consequences. Trusting this earnest appeal will receive your serious consideration. Jinnah."[30]

Jinnah received a cordial reply, not from MacDonald but Linlithgow, explaining the delicacy of the situation, expressing regret, and offering assurances that Indian Muslim opinion would be taken into account by the government.[31] Zetland also made a final, unsuccessful bid to impress upon his colleagues in Cabinet the stakes of the conference, from his perspective: "We have been warned by the Secretary of State for India that the Palestine problem is not merely an Arabian problem but is fast becoming a Pan-Islamic problem and that if the London Conference fail to reach any agreement or end in what is regarded as a substantial victory for the Jews, serious trouble in India must be apprehended."[32] In early February, Jinnah wrote again: "Deeply disappointed His Majesty's Government not inclined extend representation Muslim India at Palestine Conference. No analogy comparison Muslim India other parties in view of solemn promises assurances given to the Mussalmans India during war. Palestine their first Qibla[33] Muslims deeply and vitally concerned their Holy Places. Earnestly urge His Majesty's Government meet request."[34]

In this exchange we find Jinnah, the famously secular and rather unobservant Muslim, pressing the emotional dimension of Muslim attachment to their holy sites and evoking Britain's wartime pledges. This is the grammar and vocabulary of the Khilafat movement, over which Jinnah had once abandoned his party in disgust.[35] Still, Muslim religious sentiment was a tried and tested bargaining chip in communications with the Raj; Zetland's somewhat dramatic warning to his colleagues makes clear the extent to which he and his office still took such considerations seriously, much as Montagu had done in an earlier era. As Siddiqi and Khaliquzzaman were discovering to their dismay, however, the Muslim card did not carry much clout in London; it was downright unattractive to the Colonial Office, which was determined to avoid acknowledging that the conflict in Palestine even had a religious dimension.

As requested, Siddiqi submitted a memorandum to the British government at the end of January on behalf of the All-India Muslim League Palestine Delegation, as he and Khaliquzzaman now styled themselves. In his covering letter, he echoed Jinnah's disappointment:

> We are constrained to remark that the intensity of the feeling in India is, perhaps, not yet realised fully in London, for the reasons that public opinion had not found expression in any violence of language or in unconstitutional activities, due mainly to the influence of moderate opinion which has been holding out hopes of a satisfactory settlement in consonance with the promises made to Indian Muslims.[36] . . . We may also be permitted to question the wisdom, or even the efficacy, of circumscribing the international character of the problem so vitally touching the deep rooted sentiments of the Muslim World and restricting it to almost parochial dimensions, especially when no such restrictions are likely to be applied to the representatives of the Zionists.[37]

This was a bitter allusion to the comparatively global composition of the Jewish Agency's delegation to the conference, which sought to bolster its claim to represent "all Jews" by including delegates from the United States, Britain, South Africa, and various European countries, alongside those from Palestine. To Siddiqi and Khaliquzzaman, this participation by "international Jewry" stood in bold-faced contradiction to the stated rationale behind their own exclusion: that the conflict in Palestine was local and political, not global and religious.

The memorandum itself was a long and detailed treatise, printed as an attractive pamphlet by the Arab Centre in central London. Entitled *Statement of Indian Muslim Views on Palestine*, it began with a detailed exposition of Britain's entry into the war against the Ottoman Empire in 1914, and the promises then made to Indian Muslims regarding the inviolability of the Muslim Holy Places. In this sense, it mirrored the Arabs' insistence on the Hussein-McMahon correspondence, by rooting its claim to legitimacy in Britain's wartime pledges. The peti-

From left to right:
 Nuri Said Pasha, Prime Minister of Iraq, Prince Faisal, now H.M. King Faisal of Soudi Abrabia, Ali Mohd Pasha, Prime Minister of Egypt, Prince Saiful Islam of Yeman and Ch. Khaliquzzaman

FIGURE 12   Dinner hosted by the All-India Muslim League for the Arab delegates to the St James's Conference, February 1939. In C. Khaliquzzaman, *Only If They Knew It* (Karachi, 1965).
SPECIAL COLLECTIONS, UNIVERSITY OF NEW SOUTH WALES, CANBERRA

tion did not fail to allude to the specter of a second Khilafat movement uniting Hindu and Muslim nationalists across India, and it emphasized the traditional importance of Indian Muslim opinion in British policy formation in the Middle East. Drawing on this heritage, the pamphlet argued forcefully in favor of the Palestinian cause on political, economic, legal, and moral grounds. It warned that the failure to achieve a just settlement in Palestine would result in a perpetual state of conflict involving the entire Muslim world—including India.[38] The memorandum was, it seems, read with interest at the India Office and the Colonial Office, as evidenced by the marked copies preserved by the National Archives. But their warnings ultimately went unheeded.

INDIAN MUSLIM OPINIONS

As they had promised Alluba Pasha, and despite their failure to win seats at the conference, Siddiqi and Khaliquzzaman stuck it out in wintry London throughout the proceedings at the St James's Conference. They even hosted a well-attended dinner for the Arab delegations at Claridge's hotel on 3 February. Khaliquzzaman recalled feeling encouraged by the initial stages of negotiations, only to be disappointed by Britain's eventual offer to the Arabs, which limited immigration but set no fixed date for the transfer of power to an independent Palestinian government. His account, published in Karachi when he was in his mid-eighties, appears in an Urdu-English volume titled *Only If They Knew It*. The book recounts the author's involvement in political activism for Muslim causes around the world and contains several important revelations regarding the Muslim League's involvement in the Palestine cause. It may hopefully be forgiven its idiosyncrasies:

> When this new proposal came to light we ran up to Dorchester Hotel where the Palestine delegates were staying. All of them were furious and every one of them was shouting reject! reject! we shall never accept it and to my great surprise Mr. Abdul Rahman Siddiqi also joined them in their demand. The writer, however, took courage in both of his hands due to such a serious situation and said to his Palestine friends. "My friends, I am just as much shocked as you are but I would not advise you to reject the offer outright. The British people are strange creatures. They first create an institution and then they begin to worship their own creation. I have the experience of British people in India before me. They have created provincial governments in most areas dominated by Hindus and having created them they are now slavishly following their unjust and unfair policies toward muslims due to majority rule. Let them create a Palestine Government in which you will be in majority and they will slavishly follow you not caring for the minorities view as we find it in India. If you are a government, the Clandestine immigration of Jews from all the world over will at once stop and your majority will be secured. Therefore, for God's sake do not throw it over and do not take any hasty step. If I had the least hope that our Mujahids in Palestine will be able to throw over the British Forces in the Mediterranean, I would agree to your views." But no one was prepared to accept the writer's views. I knew that Egyptian, Iraqi and Saudi delegations were also not in favor of rejection but due to the unanimous opinion of the Palestine delegate they all agreed [to reject the British proposal] so as not to give embrace [*embarrassment?*] to the Palestine delegates.[39]

This was far from being the only instance that spring when the Indians and Arabs would attempt, without success, to encourage the Palestinians to accept the British offer, which became known as the 1939 White Paper on Palestine. Also among the chorus was the Aga Khan. Near the end of the conference, he had been summoned to London by Zetland and MacDonald, where he met with the representatives of the Arab delegations:

> On 23rd [March] morning had a long conference with the Egyptian Minister, the Iraqi representative, the Foreign Minister of Saudi Arabia and Mr.

George Antonius. . . . With great difficulty, and after much argument, they agreed to approach the position taken by His Majesty's Government on the two most important points, namely they agreed to the British emigration [*sic*] figures and also to the fact that after the period of ten years (when Palestine is to be made an independent country) Great Britain will reserve the right, if she finds it necessary, to retard this declaration. . . . The final draft seemed practically to meet the British position.

. . . I have submitted to the Foreign Office, the Colonial Office and the Secretary of State for India a plan which, if immediately accepted and carried out, will lead to the present agitation being called off, finally bringing peace to Palestine. This, however, will not be possible till May or June because the essential part of it will be to get the Egyptian Government to send their Prime Minister (or one of their most important statesmen) to see the Mufti and other leaders to call off the rebellion.[40]

Like Khaliquzzaman, the Aga Khan counseled acceptance of the British offer and was apparently able to bring the representatives of the Arab states on board. However, and in keeping with the objections raised by the Muslim League and the Viceroy prior to the conference, the acquiescence of the Mufti of Jerusalem was seen as "essential" to any accord; the revolt could not be ended without his agreement. The Aga Khan made plans to travel to Cairo later that month to hold further discussions with the Egyptian and Arab delegates.

Thus at the end of the British government's keystone conference on Palestine, it was left to an Indian Muslim to negotiate with the Arab representatives, in a bid to secure the willingness of the Egyptian Prime Minister to intervene with the Mufti of Jerusalem, who had himself been deliberately sidelined from the proceedings. With so many proxies involved in the negotiations, it was perhaps inevitable that the resulting agreement would be fraught with misunderstanding, and ineffective at achieving its stated purposes: namely an end to the violence in Palestine and a devolution of powers toward self-government.

PORTS OF LAST RESORT

Although they were disappointed by the outcome at St James's, Siddiqi and Khaliquzzaman made the most of their time in London. Prior to their departure, they met with Colonel Muirhead, the Undersecretary of State for India, and subsequently with Zetland. The point of these interviews was to propose to the British government the partition of India into Muslim and Hindu majority areas. They did so, apparently, without consulting Jinnah or anyone else.

The tone of these meetings was circumspect, yet hopeful. Years later, Khaliquzzaman was able to confirm (and I have verified) that Zetland had written to Linlithgow after their interview, alerting the Viceroy to this new departure in the Muslim League's thinking.⁴¹ It was thus precisely in the midst of working to *prevent* Palestine's partition that the League's demand *for* the partition of India took concrete form—not in a speech by Jinnah, but in private meetings between his emissaries and the British government in London, on the sidelines of the St James's Conference.

Following these interviews, and still unwilling to give up on their stated mission, the MLAs decided to travel to Geneva, in the hopes of convincing the League of Nations to take official action on the Palestinians' behalf. As Khaliquzzaman recounted, "The Secretary General of the League of Nations looked sympathetic but expressed his inability to interfere in the Palestine affairs. From his talk we could see the League of Nations was a dwindling organization and was completely effete to save any nation from the clutches of powerful governments."⁴²

Frustrated, the two men decided that the time had come for drastic action. "Taking a very great risk to our lives," they resolved

> to go to Italy to meet Mussolini to request him to send arms to the Mujahids of Palestine to fight the British. We did suspect that we were being followed by British C.I.D. but we did take the risk. We first went to Milan where through Mr. Shedai,⁴³ an Indian Muslim from Punjab, who somehow had great influence with the Italian big bosses, got a date for an interview with Count Ciano.⁴⁴ Entertaining great hopes we went to Rome but as ill-luck would have it, Italy attacked Albania a Muslim state and our interview did not come off.⁴⁵

According to Renzo De Felice, the first meeting took place in Geneva with R. Bova Scoppa, then serving as Italian observer to the League of Nations (Italy having withdrawn from the League in 1938). The Italian archives indicate that Siddiqi was also in touch with Arnaldo Mussolini, the brother of the Italian dictator, at this time.⁴⁶

With their Italian adventure cut short, the MLAs moved on to Beirut, where they held multiple interviews with the exiled Hajj Amin al-Husseini. "On one occasion when I was alone with him," recalled Khaliquzzaman, "I expressed my disagreement with the policy that brought about the failure of the London Conference. He caught hold of my hands and asked me to come with him to the lawn outside to explain to the young enthusiasts who were sitting there, but my pleading there also did not succeed."⁴⁷ It is easy to interpret this scene as the Mufti sparing himself the inelegance of disagreeing with his guest. Yet Rashid Khalidi has pointed to evidence that as late as that April the Mufti was still open to negotiating with the British,[48] lending some credence to Khaliquzzaman's depiction of a man willing to being convinced. If that were true, however, the window of opportunity was swiftly closing.

All of Siddiqi and Khaliquzzaman's efforts—to lobby on behalf of the Palestinians with the British government, to represent Indian Muslims at St James's, to persuade the League of Nations to intervene, to procure arms from Italy to support the Palestinians militarily, and to reason with Hajj Amin to accept the

FIGURE 13   Left to right: Abdurrahman Siddiqi, Hajj Amin al-Husseini, and Choudhry Khaliquzzaman, Beirut, April 1939. In C. Khaliquzzaman, *Only If They Knew It* (Karachi, 1965).
SPECIAL COLLECTIONS, UNIVERSITY OF NEW SOUTH WALES, CANBERRA

British offer—ultimately proved abortive. Yet the extent of their tour, their political and tactical flexibility, and the obvious sincerity of their commitment to "the protection of Palestine from partition" illuminate the broader significance of the many pro-Palestinian telegrams, letters, personal petitions, and resolutions produced by Muslim Leaguers throughout the late 1930s.[49] Moreover their painful failure to impact policy—or to even be considered deserving of a seat at the table in London—may well have driven home that, in the emerging configuration of global politics, even the impassioned pleas of a large and wealthy religious minority were no match for the claims of nationalism. After all, Jews were a religious community even more dispersed than India's Muslims, but Zionism was something entirely more compelling—or so it appeared at St James's. At a famous speech in Lahore in the spring of 1940, Jinnah would remark wryly that "the word 'nationalist' has now become the play of conjurers in politics."[50] As we will see in chapter 9, the failure to defend Palestine continued to haunt the Muslim League as Jinnah took the fateful decision to conjure up a nation of his own.

THE RETURN TO CAIRO

From Beirut, the MLAs returned to Cairo in late April, where the Arab and Palestinian leaderships now reconvened.[51] A report of the meeting by the *Daily Telegraph*'s Cairo correspondent described "a conference of Palestinian Arabs and representatives of the Arab States, joined for the first time by Indian Moslems"[52]— but of course, it was far from being the first time; the Arab and Indian Muslim delegates were by now quite used to one another's company. Among the fullest accounts of the talks, which began on 29 April, are the minutes provided by Ali Maher, now serving as Chief of the Egyptian Royal Cabinet, to the British Embassy's Oriental Secretary, Walter Smart. This was unquestionably an attempt by Maher to ingratiate himself with the Embassy; nevertheless, the minutes make fascinating reading. They indicate that—consistent with Khaliquzzaman's account—the Egyptians and Iraqis sought to convince the Palestinians to accept the terms of the White Paper but were met with deep skepticism by Jamal al-Husseini and the rest of the Palestinian delegation:

> The Palestinian Arab delegates represented that the proposed scheme does not carry independence to Palestine, which is what they have been fighting for.
>
> Maher Pasha [Ali Maher] . . . advised them to accept what is now offered. . . . Independence does not consist only in signing an independence agreement; it requires moral power, training in administration and readiness

for defence. The present scheme will relieve Palestine from extermination and ruin; will revive it morally and financially; and will give the Arabs chances to be trained in administration. When the time for complete independence comes, they would be more fit and adapted to it. They are not called upon to sign any document, but simply to accept it—some of them would become Ministers. . . .

Palestinian Arab delegates: If we accept, the Revolution will end.

Maher Pasha: Do you believe that Great Britain is unable to crush your revolution, with all modern satanic war implements and inventions?—Is it not better for you to come nearer the British authorities and get them to forsake the Jews? You would be in a position to carefully control immigration.

Mohammed Mahmoud Pasha [Prime Minister of Egypt] said that the British Government has promised to limit the new immigrants to 75,000, and at any rate to keep the ratio of Jews to Arabs at one third.

Palestinian Arab delegates: The scheme proves the evil intentions of the British Government.

Aly Maher Pasha: If you believe so, you have to convince us, Arab Governments, of your statement. The scheme is a declaration by one party and as such it is not expected that all the Palestinian demands are acceded to. However, it provides for Arab Ministers to join Government, for a constitution to be laid down in due course, and then the Ministry will become responsible to Parliament—all that is required of you now is to co-operate.

Suedi Bey [Tawfiq al-Suwaydi, Foreign Minister of Iraq]: As soon as peace and order are re-established, a Palestinian front would be formed; and in a number of years all the Ministers would be Palestinian—and there will be Parliament. All these are privileges which should not be ignored.

Mohammed Mahmoud Pasha: The decision is now left to the Palestinians—but they should remember that in case of war (which is coming), and if the present scheme is not accepted by them, the situation in Palestine will be deplorable. The country will be at the mercy of military men who know of no mercy or clemency, whilst the Arab fronts will be too busy in their own internal affairs.[53]

In the context of these talks, the Egyptian and Iraqi officials Ali Maher, Muhammad Mahmud, and Tawfiq al-Suwaydi appear at first glance as brutal pragmatists, in contrast to the revolutionary idealism of the Palestinians. They call on the Palestinians to place their faith in the gradual transition of power through democratic institutions, and to welcome the opportunity to gain "training in administration" under British tutelage. They suggest that, in this way, the scales will gradually be tilted in the Palestinians' favor. All of these arguments resonate with the earlier speech of Khaliquzzaman at the Dorchester Hotel, hinting at something approaching a consensus in their assessment of Britain's habits and tendencies of colonial government. Based on their experiences of British governance—mitigated by the Foreign Office and the India Office—the Arabs and Indians apparently believed that, having established an institution, the British "then begin to worship their own creation."[54] But the Palestinians, whose experience of British governance was of bitter disappointment and reversals in policy year on year, could not share in this assessment. For Palestine was not, and had never been, administered as India or Egypt or Iraq were.

THE POLITICS OF DISAPPOINTMENT

Indeed, the Arabs and Indians were to be surprised and dismayed by the unhelpful position taken by the Colonial Office. That May, in keeping with what the Aga Khan had underscored as the "essential" element of a deal, the Egyptian leaders Maher and Mahmud petitioned the British government to pardon the Mufti and allow his return from exile, as a gesture of goodwill. This effort was apparently in coordination with the Arab Higher Committee, as Jamal al-Husseini and Musa al-Alami traveled to Geneva to make the same case to another British diplomat, Eric Phipps, around the same time.[55] Miles Lampson, Britain's Ambassador to Egypt, may have signaled his approval of the scheme, but the Colonial Office rejected the proposal out of hand and instead announced that the Mufti was to be banished from Palestine in perpetuity. The Egyptians were aghast; the Arab Higher Committee protested that neither Gandhi in India nor Éamon de Valera in Ireland had been so poorly treated as the Mufti.[56]

On 1 June, an interview with Mahmud was published in *al-Jezireh*, a Syrian newspaper, in which the Egyptian Prime Minister poured scorn on what he saw as the Colonial Office's incompetence and intransigence:

> He complained bitterly against the mentality of the British Colonial Office and said that its atmosphere differs greatly from that of the Foreign Office. He added that had matters depended on Lord Halifax the problem [of Palestine] would have been settled.
>
> Two weeks ago Mohamed Mahmoud Pasha was certain that the problem was on the way to being settled. His meetings with Sir Miles Lampson had made him very optimistic.
>
> ... Thus the Prime Minister has received with amazement and disgust the British Government's decision to follow the advice of the Secretary of State for the Colonies in preventing the Mufti from returning to Palestine. What

> has surprised him most is that the Foreign Office had promised him to permit the immediate return of the Mufti to Palestine.
>
> ... He [Mahmud] summoned journalists to his office and asked them to report on his behalf that he will not be able to advise the Arab governments or the Palestinian leaders to accept the British plan.
>
> ... He said that the policy of the Colonial Office will certainly be met with antagonism on the part of the Arabs.[57]

Lampson denied that he had made such a promise to Mahmud, but he may have "winked." His diary entries from April and May record multiple occasions when his own telegrams, transmitting Arab proposals to break the impasse, "crossed" instructions from London that he viewed as unhelpful, and even "singularly stupid":[58]

> Take, for example, their telegram on which I acted yesterday with the Prime Minister [Mahmud]. Just when the poor man was doing his hardest to win the Palestinians round to tacit acquiescence in our policy, in comes a huge hammer-blow from London saying that that is not at all what we want; that the British Government is determined to have no truck with the Palestinian Arabs and that they do not care a damn whether they agree to our policy or not. My immediate reaction on reading our telegram was: God help the British people if they are run in that way. For, what have we been working for over Palestine during the last years and months? Surely to get a settlement of an amicable kind and to get this festering sore healed up and disposed of once and for all? Whereas at the Colonial Office at home what preoccupies them is that they should have a "case" with which to go to Parliament to show that they have not taken sides against the Jews. It strikes me as all too puerile and foolish.[59]

Reactions in the Indian Muslim press were also vehement in their condemnation. The Muslim-owned *Eastern Times*, for example, zeroed in on the exclusion of the Mufti as a principal grievance in its editorial of 26 May:

> Has it not struck anybody as strange that the [Palestinian] Arabs—after all, it is their country whose fate is being decided—have not only had no hand in the framing of the scheme, but have even been not allowed to express an opinion on it? Moreover, whose accredited leader is to remain for ever in exile from his beloved country under that scheme? The Palestinian attitude to the British scheme may, however, be judged by its categorical and emphatic rejection on the part of Arabs of other countries like Egypt, Iraq, and Saudi Arabia, whose Governments were naturally and rightly expected to be on the side of moderation, and by the Indian Muslims, whose two representatives at the

Cairo Palestine Conference on behalf of the All-India Muslim League have expressed their condemnation [of the White Paper] in no uncertain terms.[60]

In the months preceding the conference—in meetings, letters, telegrams, and petitions—the Viceroy, the Indian Secretary, and representatives of the Muslim League all sought to warn the Colonial Office that the exclusion of the Mufti was inadvisable, on the grounds that his acceptance of the terms of any settlement would be vital to its implementation. In the immediate aftermath of the conference, the same rationale was echoed by the Aga Khan, who emphasized that his plan—to which the Arab delegations apparently agreed—hinged on the Egyptian leadership being able to bring the Mufti onside. In May, following the Cairo Conference, representatives of the Arab Higher Committee and leading Egyptian statesmen also reached out to British officials, proposing a compromise: the return of the Mufti in exchange for Palestinian acquiescence to the terms of the White Paper. That they chose to make their case to diplomats from the Foreign Office (Lampson in Cairo and Phipps in Geneva) may reflect their perception that the Foreign Office was more sympathetic to their case than the Colonial Office—a view Mahmud subsequently made public in his interview with *al-Jezireh*. Certainly Lampson perceived his Colonial Office colleagues as having gravely mismanaged the negotiations out of intransigence toward the Palestinians. His attitude was archetypal; the conciliation of the Arabs was a policy chiefly promoted by the Foreign and Indian Offices, which the Colonial Office had always tended to oppose.

While the Colonial Office decision to exclude the Mufti of Jerusalem from the St James's process was only one factor among many in the failure of negotiations, it was certainly a policy *choice*—not an inevitability. Khalidi has attributed his exclusion to a sense of personal betrayal and animosity on the part of the British government, as well as their "embarrassment" at his hands during the tumultuous years of the Arab Revolt.[61] Emotions are certainly powerful forces, in politics as in all other human endeavors. Yet as it stood, there was no real way of excluding Hajj Amin from a decisive vote on the matter. Instead, Arab Higher Committee delegates and Egyptian, Indian, and Iraqi politicians were all obliged to shuttle back and forth to Beirut, for (as even one of his fiercest detractors was forced to concede), the Mufti's "magic influence on the Palestinian masses" made his blessing essential. [62]

Despite the disappointment of St James's, it seems just possible that the efforts of Arab and Indian Muslim leaders to salvage the proceedings might still have succeeded if not for the Colonial Office's refusal to consider their proposals for compromise—among them, the Mufti's return from exile. Given that his rejection of the White Paper is frequently cited as the final nail in the coffin of Arab acceptance,[63] the Colonial Office's decision to double down on the Mufti's perpetual exile was significant. As the Arab Higher Committee pointed out at the time, many interned anticolonial leaders had been returned home over the years, notably in Egypt and India, as well as Ireland. Had the Mufti been similarly permitted to return, the Arab Higher Committee—and with it the Arab states—may have found their way to accepting the White Paper. What remains unclear, and perhaps impossible to know, is in what ways that might have altered the course of events in Palestine, given the devastating and transformative nature of the war already hurtling inexorably into view.

Siddiqi and Khaliquzzaman made landfall in Bombay on 12 May 1939, having been absent from their homes for over eight months. They were met on the pier by Abdullah Brelvi, the editor of the *Bombay Chronicle* and a close friend of Khaliquzzaman's. The newspaperman was jubilant to share the news that Congress leaders were eager to negotiate with the Muslim League and "prepared to go all out to satisfy" the Muslim League's demands. Khaliquzzaman replied, "'My dear Brelvi, events have travelled much faster than expected and now partition of India appears to be the only solution.' He was horrified and said, 'Are you in your senses?' I replied, 'With all the sense that I possess.' He started arguing with me but I assured him that it was our destiny rather than our choice."[64]

That evening the two Muslim League emissaries met with their President to debrief. In his memoirs, Khaliquzzaman described Jinnah as listening carefully to his and Siddiqi's account of their meetings and travels, asking for occasional clarifications. Khaliquzzaman emphasized their final interview with Zetland, and his personal conviction that the British would ultimately acquiesce in India's partition. As he spoke, Jinnah would stop him and make him go back to repeat certain words. Finally, the President of the Muslim League asked, "Have you weighed the consequences?"

Khaliquzzaman's response was telling: "We cannot go on *talking on the old basis* without any result." The problem as he framed it was one of vocabulary: Muslim India's barristers required new words. "He [Jinnah] assured us that he was not opposed to it but it had to be examined in all its bearings. I said, 'There is ample time for you to form your opinion.'"[65]

And with that, the world-weary traveler took leave of his colleagues. He caught a train bound for his beloved Lucknow that very night.

SEVEN

The Delegation

> Other causes led to the defeat of the Wafd. But the real reason is the inherent weakness of the party.... The whole outlook of the Wafd has been moderate and somewhat primitive.[1]
> —JAWAHARLAL NEHRU IN A LETTER TO THE CONGRESS WORKING COMMITTEE, JUNE 1938

> We have the example before us of what you have been able to achieve in Egypt.... I have no doubt that with the example of Egypt before us and your goodwill to help us, we can deal with this problem [of sectarianism] with success.[2]
> —JAWAHARLAL NEHRU IN A LETTER TO MUSTAFA AL-NAHAS, OCTOBER 1938

WELCOME(S) TO BOMBAY

On 8 March 1939, just as the St James's Conference was winding down in London, the RMS *Strathnaver* put into port at Bombay, en route from Tilbury to Brisbane.[3] Among the passengers who disembarked were several members of the Egyptian Wafd leadership, who had boarded the ship at Suez: Mahmoud al-Bassiouni, Ahmad Hamza, Ahmad Qasim Gouda, and Mahmud Abul Fat'h. Awaiting them on the pier was quite the welcome committee—two committees, to be exact.

The Congress Party, who had issued a formal invitation to the Wafd the previous autumn to attend its session in Tripuri, had erected a large marquee and assembled a crowd of party notables and volunteers to greet their honored guests. Nearby, a smaller party of Muslim League representatives had also gathered to welcome the Egyptians. They were invited, and declined, to join the Congress members in their tent.[4] For the Egyptians, it was the beginning of what would be, at times, an awkward month-long tour of the subcontinent, being as they were the official guests of Nehru and the Congress Party's and co-religionists of the rival Muslim League. During their time in India, the Wafd envoys met with Nehru, Gandhi, Jinnah, and many other national and regional Indian politicians from both parties. Throughout, they were also trailed by Indian intelligence agents and officers of the Cairo City Police.

The story of the Wafd's engagement with the INC and its official visit to India on the cusp of World War II has been recounted a handful of times;[5] what follows is the most thorough effort to date to piece together all available sources across multiple languages and national perspectives. Doing so reveals sharp differences in emphasis and interpretation between the various Indian and Egyptian participants, as well as the British agencies that documented and dissected their interactions. In particular, the account presented here forces a reassessment of Noor Khan's presentation in *Egyptian-Indian Nationalist Collaboration and the British Empire*, which emphasizes anticolonial solidarity and personal friendship as the causal factors behind the embassy, while depicting sectarian politics as the unfortunate but incidental backdrop against which it took place.[6]

However the sources presented here as well as the broader Indian political context of 1938–39 suggest that both the visit and the Congress-Wafd alliance were shaped to a considerable degree by Congress leaders' efforts to shore up the party's prestige and electoral credibility, given the rising popularity of the Muslim League. Khan is clear, and we agree, that the Congress Party's alliance with the Wafd hinged on their shared rejection of sectarian politics; yet crucial to understanding what this meant in practice is the fact, missing from her account, that Jawaharlal Nehru asked Mustafa al-Nahas for the Wafd's help in countering the sectarian appeal of the Muslim League. This, I argue, became the leitmotif of the 1939 tour—inevitably stoking tensions with the League and its supporters in the process. Overcoming "the communal issue" was undoubtedly perceived by Congress as a vital component of the longer-term goal of Indian independence, and not divorced from its anticolonial commitments; yet in the specific context of 1938–39, this domestic battle for Muslim hearts and minds took precedence over any standoff with Britain, and led Nehru to embrace allies whose other political credentials he found less than wholly inspiring.

THE FIRST MEETING: ALEXANDRIA, 1938

Following the signature of the Anglo-Egyptian Treaty, the Wafd's political star began to fade. Efforts to revamp the party's image and shore up its base in urban constituencies were no match for King Faruq and the coalition surrounding the palace. As we have seen, Nahas and the Wafd were banished by Faruq into the "political wilderness" at the end of 1937; yet in opposition, as is so often the case, its options and horizons expanded. Freed from the constraints of the institutions of government it had until recently represented, the Wafd now became more vocal in its support for the Palestinians, inter-Arab cooperation, and alliances with other anticolonial movements—especially the INC. The Congress Party had sometimes been compared to the Wafd and perceived, in both Egypt and India, as an allied movement since the days of Zaghlul; it had also seen its stock rise just as that of its Egyptian counterpart nose-dived in the latter half of 1937. Congress had won a landslide victory in the first elections held under the expanded franchise of the new India Act, and its members now controlled ministries in a majority of British India's provincial governments. Moreover, the party's central leadership—especially Gandhi and Nehru—were celebrated international figures on a scale Nahas and his colleagues could only dream of.

It is therefore hardly surprising that, when news reached the Wafd of Nehru's impending arrival in Egyptian waters in June 1938, they leapt at the opportunity to host him. A private airplane was chartered on short notice to transport him to Alexandria, where the political class had by then migrated for the summer months.

From Nehru's own description—which appears in a report he wrote to the Congress Working Committee while still traveling—it is apparent that the meeting was unforeseen and hastily arranged; he had actually decided against disembarking from his ship at Suez (as was common) and had intended to remain on board during the passage through the canal: "But three hours before reaching Suez, I received a marconigram from Cairo conveying to me the welcome of the Wafd Party and requesting me to get off at Suez and proceed from there by private aeroplane . . . to Alexandria, to meet Nahas Pasha. I decided to accept this invitation and cabled accordingly. But the time was short and my cable reached too late. So when I disembarked at Suez there was no one to meet me."[7]

Nehru managed to arrange for a car to take him to Cairo, where, late at night, he was finally tracked down by a representative of the Wafd, who booked him on a plane to Alexandria departing the following morning. There he would meet Nahas and several other party leaders, before flying on to Port Said to rejoin his ship. In the brief hours between midnight and dawn, Nehru managed to pay a moonlit visit to the pyramids, before catching his flight.

His meeting with the Wafd the following morning was held at the San Stefano, a luxury hotel. Nahas opened their encounter by describing how he had sought in vain to meet the Congress President's mentor years earlier:

> [Nahas] reminded me of the attempts he had made in 1931 to meet and do honour to Gandhiji as the great leader of the fight for Indian independence. He had arranged a great party in his honour at Heliopolis, near Cairo, and issued invitations for five hundred guests to it, but the then government would not permit it. He had then tried to meet him at Port Said. Again, the government would not allow him to go on board or Gandhiji to set foot on Egyptian soil. In this way all his attempts to meet Gandhiji had been frustrated and he could not convey personally, as he desired, the greetings and the admiration of the Egyptian people to the people of India, through their great leader.[8]

Alongside Nahas, the welcome committee included Makram Ebeid, party Secretary-General and former Minister of Finance; Mahmoud Bassiouni, former President of the Senate; Naguib Hilali, former Minister of Education; and Abdul Fat'h Tawil, the former Minister of Health. As Nehru recounted, the formal meeting lasted for two hours, following which—in grand Egyptian tradition (and in rather marked departure from the ascetic habits of Gandhi and his disciples)—they "had to consume an enormous and magnificent lunch for another hour." While it is nowhere indicated in Nehru's description, the conversation almost certainly took place in French, the language of Nehru and Nahas's subsequent correspondence. Nehru did not speak Arabic, and Nahas, like many of his contemporaries among Egypt's elite, was far more comfortable in French than English. "I began," recalled Nehru,

> by conveying the greetings of the Congress and of the Indian people to Nahas Pasha and to the Wafd Party which had carried on for many years the struggle for Egyptian freedom. I told them how deeply we were interested in this and how we had followed it, as far as we could, for we looked upon it as part of the great world struggle for freedom. Between Egypt and us there were many other bonds also and our opponent was the same imperialism. Nahas Pasha reciprocated these sentiments and said that they had looked upon the Indian struggle and its leaders with admiration.[9]

In his letter, Nehru recorded Nahas's description of the Egyptian political scene at the time, which was estimated as "very bad" for the Wafd, citing the palace's dominance, supported by the British. The former Egyptian Prime Minister insisted that the Wafd maintained its overwhelming popularity among the fellaheen but had been foiled at the polls by voter intimidation and the falsification of results (claims that Nehru took the time to verify with British and French sources). At the same moment in India, developments were more promising for the Congress Party, given their sweeping success in the 1937 elections. Nehru was thus in a position to compare his movement favorably to the Wafd. His analysis of his Egyptian counterparts' weaknesses and the causes of their present crisis are deeply perceptive and worth quoting at length:

> I put it to Nahas that such tactics [as electoral fraud] had always to be faced by a nationalist or socialist movement struggling for freedom. Every device and method of oppression was employed by imperialism and reactionary cliques and vested interests. Unless the movement itself had sufficient strength, it could not cope with such tactics. Strength only could come from organised mass support. It therefore seemed to me that the Wafd did not have this organised mass support, for otherwise it would not weaken so rapidly because of Palace intrigues. He admitted that there was some truth in this although the Wafd was still very popular with the masses.[10]

Nahas proceeded to explain to his guest the Wafd's predicament, vis-à-vis the British. There has been much speculation, both at the time and subsequently, over the nature of Nahas's perception of and relationship with the British in the post-treaty period. The fact that Nahas's private papers have not been made available, nor did he ever publish a memoir, means that Nehru's account of his conversation with the Egyptian Prime Minister stands out. Rarely, if ever, cited by historians of Egypt, it is among the few credible sources we have of Nahas's own perceptions of the Wafd's relationship with Britain at this time. His remarks are paraphrased by Nehru:

> The Wafd leaders had thought that with their treaty with Britain, the independence struggle had practically ended in their success, and they had thrown themselves enthusiastically into the task of preaching Anglo-Egyptian friendship. As a government, they became absorbed in the work of the government and neglected their organisation and agitational work. This ultimately weakened the Wafd and when the time for a trial of strength came, they were unable to rise to the occasion. They had been over-confident, too full of faith in the bona fides of the British Government, not in sufficient touch with the masses.[11]

These were important lessons for Nehru to convey to the Congress Working Committee back in India, as he worried about the impact governing India's provinces would have on his party's ability to continue the struggle for independence.

Two years on from the Anglo-Egyptian Treaty, Nahas appeared conscious of his mistake (though not enough to avoid making it again, as we will see in chapter 10); being "too full of faith in the bona fides of the British Government" was, moreover, a regret soon to be shared by the Arab and Indian negotiators involved in diplomacy on Palestine. Nehru, meanwhile, was more interested in the second aspect of the Wafd's miscalculation. Focused on the potential of India's workers and rural peasantry, which he believed had the power to overcome India's "communal issue," Nehru interpreted the Wafd's alignment with Egyptian landowners and merchant classes as perhaps its fatal flaw:

> As a matter of fact it is quite clear that the Wafd Party, while it was in power, did little or nothing for the peasantry. They were afraid of alienating the big landlords as well as the palace . . . These big landlords put a brake on the Wafd's activities and at the same time organised themselves under the shelter of the palace, to oppose the Wafd. The palace succeeded in creating a split in the Wafd. One group started criticising the main party on the ground that it was not advanced enough and was too friendly to the British. As a matter of fact this was a ruse, for this dissentient group consisted chiefly of the big landlord elements and it has subsequently cooperated fully with the palace group and even, to some extent, with the British.
>
> The Wafd would not have been much affected by this if it had a powerful organisation behind it. But it had neglected this and thought of itself more as a government . . . other causes led to the defeat of the Wafd. But the real reason is the inherent weakness of the party. It is definitely an upper middle class party with a certain mass support but with no roots among the masses. Even the middle classes in Egypt have not grown sufficiently (less than in India); and such as exist are largely tied up with foreign interests. There is no real agrarian movement, no labour movement at all (trade unions are not permitted by law), and the whole outlook of the Wafd has been moderate and somewhat primitive.[12]

Nehru's assessment was largely accurate: the Wafd was, essentially, a liberal capitalist movement in terms of its leadership, outlook, and principal loyalties. Within Congress, Nehru—despite his bourgeois background and education—had been much more connected to and influenced by socialist movements and ideology. Thanks in part to his engagement with the League Against Imperialism, Nehru also perceived a deep interdependence between the Congress movement and struggles for independence occurring elsewhere.[13] In his autobiography,

FIGURE 14 Jawaharlal Nehru's first meeting with the Wafd, Alexandria, 1938. Mustafa al-Nahas sits to Nehru's left.
UNIVERSITY OF CONNECTICUT COLLECTION / ALAMY

he described the outbreak of the Spanish Civil War in 1936 as a turning point in his consciousness: "In my mind, the problem of India was tied up with other world problems. More and more I came to think that these separate problems, political or economic, in China, Abyssinia, Spain, Central Europe, India, or elsewhere, were facets of one and the same world problem."[14]

SUMMER OF INTERNATIONALISM

This internationalism was reflected in Nehru's 1938 travel itinerary. From Egypt he went to Italy (where he politely turned down an audience with Mussolini) and on to Spain, then still in the throes of civil war. There, he met with Republican leaders and volunteers, and he bore witness to the bombardment of Barcelona, expressing deep admiration and respect for the courage of the residents of that city and their resolute resistance to fascist terror.[15] Following a brief stop in Paris to record a radio broadcast, he then proceeded to London, where he remained for a month, taking meetings with—among others—a delegation of Palestinians.

For Nehru, and in the 1930s increasingly for his party, the struggle between the

British, Jews, and Arabs in Palestine was important because it was an anti-imperial struggle; but it was only as important as all the other similar struggles then underway. This stood in contrast to the view of the Muslim League, which, as we have seen, considered Palestine as secondary in importance, perhaps, only to the cause of India's Muslims themselves. But Nehru's comments on Palestine from this time make clear that, whatever the extent of his commitment to Palestine, talking about the crisis in the British Mandate was, for him—as indeed it was for Siddiqi and Khaliquzzaman—another way of talking about domestic politics in India. Thus, while the Muslim League had insisted in its treatise submitted to the Colonial Secretary that Palestine was a matter of Muslim as well as Jewish concern, Nehru was adamant that the matter at stake was not religion but the universal struggle against imperialism. To this end, his speeches and letters from this period called for Jews and Arabs in Palestine to come together to oust the British.[16] In this way, both parties reproduced their position on the political struggle for India by interpreting the violence in Palestine as, in one way or another, its extension.

Throughout the summer of 1938, Nehru and Nahas wrote letters to one another. In this correspondence, we see Nehru's influence on the older man and on the shifting political orientation of the Wafd movement. Thus the Wafd annual meeting, scheduled for November 1938, was envisioned by Nahas, in his description to Nehru, as having "a wider Oriental stamp over and above its local character," with invitations issued to representatives from India, Palestine, and other "oppressed people of the Near East."[17] This was a clear break with the almost isolationist Egyptian territorial nationalism that had characterized the movement from the late 1920s until the mid-1930s.[18] Evidently, and in tandem with the changes taking place in Egyptian domestic and international politics, Nehru's frank criticism during their meeting in Alexandria, and his friendly advice since, had made some impression.

A second meeting took place in France that September, at which time they drafted an agreement for increased communication and collaboration between their political movements. Nehru subsequently wrote to Nahas that "there was so much in common between us and our respective national movements that it would be to the great advantage of both of us to cooperate with each other as much as we can." In practical terms, this cooperation was articulated as a variety of exchanges from press and publications to formal delegations, participation in the same international organizations, and cooperation between their affiliated youth wings. Nehru requested that the Wafd keep the Congress Party informed of developments in Palestine, as the Congress Party did not have its own contacts there—nevertheless, he permitted himself to add his two cents:

> We have looked upon the struggle in Palestine as a struggle for national freedom and not as a religious or racial struggle.... The essential thing is that Palestine is an Arab country and should achieve freedom as such, with Jewish rights protected. We feel that the only way out of the present difficulty is by means of an agreement between the Arabs and the Jews on the above basis and without any interference by British imperialism. I understand that there are many Arabs and some Jews who accept this basis and who would gladly cooperate together. I have no doubt that you can exercise a powerful influence in this direction.

This rather lofty compliment served as a segue to Nehru's next, and final, request: "In India, unfortunately, some difficulties occasionally arise between certain groups of Mussulmans and others." By late 1938, this was putting the matter delicately. A "Mass Contact" campaign devised and enthusiastically spearheaded by Nehru the previous spring had failed to make the promised inroads with Muslim peasants. Nehru's strategy of treating them "as non-Muslims," focusing instead on "the economic issue," was sound socialist doctrine—and was just as soundly defeated in the villages of rural India.[19] Just prior to Nehru's letter to Nahas in September 1938, Congress had lost another by-election to the Muslim League, which took 75 percent of the vote—following which Mass Contact was called off, and the office running it abolished. In this climate, Congress scrambled to identify a new strategy toward the "communal issue."[20] "It is our earnest desire to remove every grievance and build up a unified nation," wrote Nehru to Nahas that fall. "Still some elements in the community, for political or other reasons, have opposed the national movement"; "We have the example before us of what you have been able to achieve in Egypt.... I have no doubt that with the example of Egypt before us and your goodwill to help us, we can deal with this problem with success."

"Of course," Nehru hastened to add, "it would be improper for you or your party to associate yourselves with any particular group in this matter.... Nevertheless your influence in favour of unity will be helpful."[21] Gracious, discrete, and almost subconsciously persuasive, Nehru was a master of his chosen art. Whether the Wafd could actually serve as a model of Muslim antisectarianism for Indian consumption was to be put to the test the following spring.

Shortly after their meeting in France, Nehru received word of the 1938 Interparliamentary Congress on Palestine, which was then about to open in Cairo. Concerned that the event appeared to be anti-Wafdist and pan-Islamic, Nehru wrote to his party's leading Muslim figure, Abul Kalam Azad, warning him of the danger posed by the conference to the Wafd—a movement now firmly allied with their own. He also predicted, correctly, that the Congress Party's domestic rival, the Muslim League, would seize the opportunity to send a delegation of their own to Egypt. However, Nehru drew too direct a parallel between his experience of Indian politics and the situation in Egypt, presuming that as a result of its Islamic character and exclusion of the Wafd, the Interparliamentary Congress must ipso facto be promoted by the British. This was an exaggeration of the embassy's wary tolerance of the event (though Lampson later wrote, with legible relief, that it had proved less vitriolic in its criticism of Britain than he had been braced to expect).[22]

At the same time, Nehru began making arrangements for a Congress delegation to visit Egypt that November, to attend the Wafd's annual meeting. When it became clear that this event would be banned by the Egyptian government, Nehru determined to visit Egypt of his own accord. He and his daughter Indira arrived in Cairo in early November and remained there for about a week. By this point, and as Noor Khan notes, Nehru and Nahas were certainly becoming personal friends: When Indira made the journey from England to India alone, her father worried that war might break out in Europe while she was en route and advised her that in case of such an emergency, she was to disembark in Egypt and seek out Nahas.[23]

WAFD TO INDIA

Back in India, the recently elected Congress President, Subhas Chandra Bose, followed up on Nehru and Nahas's correspondence with a telegram formally inviting Nahas to send a delegation to the Congress Party's session scheduled for 10 March 1939 in Tripuri: "As leader of Egyptian people your visit will serve to strengthen solidarity between our two nations and will also be an inspiration to our countrymen. India will give you warmest welcome."[24]

Reporting on the telegram to the Director of the Indian Intelligence Bureau, the Oriental Secretary in Cairo, Walter Smart, noted that "this invitation expressed the hope that Nahas himself would proceed to India." "Incidentally," Smart continued—with, one senses, an eyebrow creeping northward—"Nahas considers that his prestige has received a 'fillip' by reason of the invitation being addressed to him as 'Leader of the Egyptian people.'"[25]

Fillip or no, Nahas did not ultimately travel to India. The Wafd representatives sent in his place were not particularly high-profile figures, a fact that did not escape the notice of either British officials or the Egyptian press. Bassiouni was President of the Senate at the time, but a relatively modest figure within the

Wafd when compared to Nahas or Makram Ebeid, both of whom had originally been slated to attend. The official reason given for the change in schedule was "ill health"; the Wafd's detractors in Cairo speculated that it was in fact an effort to avoid upsetting the British. And indeed, officials at the Foreign Office were not displeased with the amended guest list, noting it was "perhaps fortunate" that Ebeid's name in particular had been "dropped."[26]

By contrast there was no denying that Bose was true to his word in promising that India would afford the Wafd its "warmest welcome": the Foreign Office was forced to concede that "in spite of their personal insignificance the Wafd delegation seem to have been given a magnificent reception."[27] Congress rolled out the red carpet for their Egyptian guests. As they set foot on the pier in Bombay on 8 March, they were greeted by the secretaries of the Congress Party and Congress volunteers, by pro-Congress Muslim notables, and by the wife of Bombay's Minister of the Interior. There was a large marquee erected near the port to receive these honored guests, who, the government suspected, had been invited in the hopes of bolstering Congress's appeal among Muslim voters—a suspicion that Nehru's earlier letter to Nahas tends to support.

Because of the coincidence in timing, and being somewhat out of both the Indian and Colonial Office loops, the Foreign Office interpreted the Wafd visit to India and the Palestine Conference in Cairo as linked events. When word reached London of the departure of the Egyptian delegates aboard the *Strathnaver*, Vansittart commented, rather naively, that "if a settlement of the Palestine problem, satisfactory to the Arabs, is reached before this Congress opens, these Egyptians will not have much material for speeches."[28] He overestimated the importance of Palestine in relations between Congress and the Wafd, perhaps extrapolating from what he knew or had heard of Indian Muslim activists in London. Nevertheless, Vansittart was to be disappointed on both counts: the Palestine problem was not resolved to the satisfaction of the Arabs, and the Egyptians had no trouble filling their allotted speaking time in India—though Palestine was relatively low on their agenda.

The tour first proceeded from the port in Bombay to Tripuri, where the delegation was met at the station by Nehru and billeted in the Government Rest House. In the evening, the Wafd members were the guests of honor at the first sitting of the Congress session, presided over by Jawaharlal Nehru. In his presidential address, Subhas Chandra Bose introduced Congress's Egyptian guests: "We are extremely happy that they found it possible to accept our invitation and make the voyage to India. We are only sorry that political exigencies in Egypt" —and not poor health—"did not permit the President of the Wafd, Mustapha

El Nahas Pasha, to personally lead this Delegation. Having had the privilege of knowing the President and leading members of the Wafdist Party, my joy today is all the greater. Once again, I offer them on behalf of my countrymen a most hearty and cordial welcome."[29]

The Cairo City Police detectives assigned to shadow the delegation described their reception at Tripuri in a dispatch to the Foreign Office: "They were received with clapping and cheers for Egypt, the Wafd, Nahas Pasha and the Mission. . . . [Nehru] explained the significance of sending this Mission, which is the beginning of a close and continual cooperation between the two countries in the future, saying that the chief of the ties between the two countries was that they fight one enemy, Great Britain."[30]

In this connection, one particular irony of the tour was not lost on British observers: on the covering sheet of the police report, Foreign Undersecretary P.L. Rose noted with amusement "that in order to make themselves understood to each other Indians and Egyptians should have to speak the language of their common enemy and oppressor—English."[31]

Reports on the Congress session vary widely between three contemporary sources: one from the Indian Intelligence Bureau, one (previously cited) from the Cairo City Police, and one by the Wafdist delegate Mahmud Abul Fat'h (who had interviewed Gandhi for *al-Ahram*, back in the heady days of 1931). For example, Indian Intelligence claimed that at Tripuri the Wafd witnessed Congress "rent by internal dissensions and, on occasion, in a state of uncontrolled uproar."[32] By this, they referred to the division at Tripuri between Bose, then serving as Congress President, who delivered the welcome address, and loyalists of Gandhi (including Nehru), who viewed Bose's preferred strategy toward the British as unnecessarily confrontational. Tripuri was rather famously the scene of a showdown between these factions. Still, it may be closer to the truth to say that Indian Intelligence agents, well versed in the acrimonious character of Indian politics and always quick to give importance to divisions between local communities, *themselves* saw Congress "rent by dissension" and presumed that the effect on their Egyptian guests would be unfavorable. Quite the opposite would appear to have been the case, judging by Abul Fat'h's own account of the meeting. He waxed poetic about the "two currents" of political thinking within Congress, and the ultimate victory of Gandhi's moderates over Bose's extremists. This outcome, which Abul Fat'h undoubtedly considered as positive and hopeful, was of much greater interest to him than the existence of these "internal divisions"—a reality of political life that the Wafd was only too familiar with and that Fat'h appears to have taken somewhat for granted: "Gandhi's great popularity and influence delivered his victory over Subhas Bose, who had to step down and cede his place to another president. [This new president], designated by Gandhi, is at the same time his great friend and disciple: Babu Rajendra Prasad, who has contributed to the creation and strengthening of the soul of Gandhi's movement in Bihar."[33]

As for the Cairo City Police, their own description of the Congress session dwelled on the sheer scale of the event, which clearly made an impression on law enforcement officials from a country with only a fraction of India's population: "The number attending the Congress was estimated at 150,000. They covered the plain and the neighbouring hills and were all of the Congress Party. Loud speakers were used.... The audience did not sit on chairs but on mats, etc., laid down on the ground, as it was impossible to provide chairs for such a number."[34]

In a telegram to Lord Halifax, Lampson noted that he had been informed that "a secret meeting took place at Tripuri between the Egyptian delegates and some Congress leaders ... it was decided that the All-India Congress Committee should henceforth be linked up with the Wafd Party of Egypt in connection with their political movements."[35] In the context of the letter sent by Nehru to Nahas the previous September, this meeting may have represented a formal adoption of the steps Nehru had earlier discussed with the Wafd leader for closer coordination between the two parties.

The Egyptian delegation next moved from Tripuri to Allahabad and then on to Lucknow, Delhi, Lahore, and Peshawar—all northern Indian cities with large Muslim populations. Calcutta and Benares were also included in the original itinerary but were eventually cut, apparently due to the "ill health of the members."[36] The stops on the tour all followed a similar format: large rallies or meetings consisting of tens of thousands of Congress supporters included speeches by leading politicians and the Wafd delegates, whose contributions were translated from Arabic or English into local languages. Inevitably, one or several teas or banquets were given in honor of the Egyptian guests, attended by large numbers of local notables and party officials. Throughout, the Wafd members were housed in palatial settings, where possible at a governor's or notable's private residence. Letters between Nehru, Bose, and provincial party officials reveal that all the expenses related to the fortnight-long tour—from first-class train fares to luxury hotels—were covered by the Congress Party, out of both provincial and national party budgets.[37] In a letter from Bose to the party's General Secretary, he clarified that, when conveying news of the impending visit to provincial committees, "you will have to ask them to provide for their maximum comfort."[38] While this reflects conventions of diplomatic hospitality, it is also indicative of the great importance placed by the Indian nationalists on this visit from their allies; this, and the fact that the itinerary focused on areas of the country that were predominantly Muslim, gives further credence to Indian Intelligence's claim that the tour was an effort to shore up Congress's support among Muslims.

MEETING GANDHI, JINNAH, AND CHATTOPADHYAY

In Delhi, the Wafd was gratified by an hour-long audience with Gandhi, who was eager to introduce his Egyptian guests to a lieutenant on the frontlines of the Indian nationalist movement. Her name was Kamaladevi Chattopadhyay—the young woman introduced in chapter 1 who had prayed for Gandhi's success from her childhood bedroom during Non-Cooperation in 1919. Since then she had proved her mettle in years of dedicated service to the satyagraha campaign. Just prior to the Wafd's tour, she published a series of articles in the press on anticolonial movements abroad, "particularly highlighting the Egyptian Saga." It is for this reason that Gandhi was eager to introduce her to his visitors.[39] The Wafd leaders were gracious in their meeting with Chattopadhyay and invited her to visit Egypt as their guest. However, everyone was clearly more focused on Gandhi, the anti-imperial superstar—for none of the men, whether Egyptian nationalists or Anglo-Indian intelligence agents, bothered to mention Chattopadhyay in their reports.[40] According to Indian intelligence agents, the Wafd and Congress leaders once again "spoke about their visit and the necessity of cooperation between Egypt and India, to fight their adversary and obtain independence." On the whole, however, even these agents of Indian Intelligence judged the tone of the tour to be not all that anti-British—beyond a few references to a common "enemy," for the benefit of the Congress masses: "There is no reason to believe that the members of the Delegation indulged in any anti-British talk while in India, indeed it is on record that on one occasion at least they said that Egypt was on very good terms with England, and depended on England for military protection until she had built up her own defence forces."[41]

It was not only the visitors who spoke this way: Abul Fat'h later revealed that Gandhi had told him and his Wafd colleagues that in the event of war, Congress would remain loyal to the British Crown, in the expectation that Britain would reciprocate by granting India greater autonomy after the war: "They do not ask for a very large measure of independence immediately; rather for the moment they aspire to a larger role [in governance], with promises that as soon as the global crisis has dissipated, they will be granted a greater independence."[42]

Nehru may well have disagreed with his aging mentor on this point of strategy; nevertheless, it did not fail to impress his Egyptian guests.[43] The exchange of

FIGURE 15   Members of the Wafd meet with Gandhi and his retinue in Delhi, 18 March 1939. Gandhi reclines in the center of the circle; Mahmud Abul Fat'h is facing toward the camera.
MAHATMA GANDHI PHOTO GALLERY / INTERNET ARCHIVE

views is also significant, for in it we see clearly that both the Wafd and the Gandhian current within Congress, in the spring of 1939, regarded their relationship with Great Britain in similar terms, as they contemplated the near inevitability of a second global conflict. Neither party felt the relationship to be hostile or zero-sum; rather, these nationalist leaders viewed London as a partner in ongoing negotiations. The slow devolution of powers from Britain to Cairo and Delhi was perceived as tolerable, and perhaps about to accelerate—once the international situation had stabilized. There was potential, too, in the coming war for Egyptian defenses to thus be "built up," and for India, with its vast army, to purchase its freedom through service to the empire.[44]

While in the Indian capital, the delegates also met with Muhammad Ali Jinnah, leader of the Muslim League. The meeting did not take place behind their host's back: on the contrary, Nehru wrote during the tour that "we are trying to give them full opportunities of meeting the non-Congress elements like the Muslim League."[45] Jinnah, apparently, was less than enthusiastic: Indian Intelligence reported that he took the meeting "against his will . . . and did not mince matters in the expression of his opinion" regarding the Wafd's acceptance of an invitation from Congress.[46] Jinnah was far from alone in his "opinion," according to the same report: "Generally Muslims recognized the Delegation for what it was, an instrument of Congress, and ignored it, or noticed only to sneer."[47]

While the Wafd was apparently unfazed by political infighting within Congress, the evident sectarian rift between Hindus and Muslims was clearly a point of negative focus—unsurprisingly, given the tenor of Nehru's prior communications with Nahas. Notwithstanding Nehru's insistence that he wouldn't dream of asking them to pick sides, upon their arrival the Wafd almost immediately determined that, as guests of Congress, they would not accept any Muslim League invitations until all their official engagements had taken place. Much like Nehru himself, Ahmad Qasim Gouda placed the blame on British imperialism—which, as Nehru had earlier observed during his meeting with the Wafd in Alexandria, had had more time to settle in India than in Egypt.[48] In Gouda's memoir, *Marid min al-Sharq* (Giant from the East), published in 1950, he compared his two voyages to India: the Wafd tour in 1939 and a second trip in 1949, shortly after India achieved its independence, at the cost of the country's partition and the shocking violence that accompanied it.[49] Possibly as a result of this context, Gouda describes the communalism he witnessed in 1939 with particular scorn. He remembers the two separate tents awaiting his party in Bombay—one Congress and one Muslim—and the dilemma faced by the Wafd, as the guests of one party to this internal struggle, which "benefited the British in everything." "As a result," lamented Gouda, "Indians were delayed in realizing that most cherished and sought by all nations, namely freedom and independence."[50] While his antisectarianism was no doubt sincere, Gouda failed to acknowledge that his own country, supposedly absent this communal discord, had still failed to dislodge the British Army from its bases on the Suez Canal as his book went to print.

Meanwhile, back in 1939 Lahore, the Indian Intelligence Bureau reported that Wafd members met with the Muslim Premier of the Punjab and his ministers. It surmised that "what was said [by the Indian politicians] was not to the benefit of Congress": "One cannot help but wonder if the effect of Northern India was really responsible for the pruning of the further programme, and if the rather lame excuse [of illness] put forward was adopted because none better was available."[51]

It is difficult to speculate on the merit of this supposition. However, the Egyptians do appear to have been faithful to their hosts, and evidently they took their duty as model antisectarian nationalists quite seriously: "Press publicity, for which the delegation was responsible, was cautiously worded. Praise for Congress was constant and stress was usually laid on the claim that in Egypt there neither was, nor is, any minority problem, and that there, religion was not allowed to make National politics difficult."[52] Phrased almost as a direct retort to the Muslim League, this passage seems a fitting place to return to Khaliquzzaman, who was still bitter decades later about the Wafd's tour of India—despite having been, himself, in Beirut and Cairo at the time. In his autobiography published in 1961, he claimed that when they had met in Cairo during the Interparliamentary Congress in October 1938, Nahas had promised to consult with him again before deciding whether or not to accept the Congress invitation. Then, in his 1965 memoir, the Pakistani statesman complained that the next he heard of it, Nahas had gone back on his word and agreed to the visit: "After some more discussion [Nahas] Pasha promised me not to send any delegation before my return to Egypt on my way back home. Inspite of it he sent a delegation [. . .] to advise the Muslims of India to surrender to the Congress. This unfortunate attempt on the part of Nahas Pasha gave the muslims a great shock and muslim India felt that they were let down by a prominent Egyptian Ex-Prime Minister."[53]

One may well imagine the elderly statesman's disillusionment, had he realized the full extent of the planned cooperation between his rivals in Congress and the Egyptian Wafd. At the end of their time in India, and despite the slight curtailing of their itinerary, the delegation sailed home, carrying a personal letter from Nehru to his friend Nahas. Meanwhile, the Congress Party made preparations to send a delegation to Egypt for a reciprocal visit, slated for 1940.

EIGHT

The Feminists

> To the Union of Women of Europe, to that of the Pan-Pacific, we would answer with a League of Eastern Women.[1]
> —SAIZA NABARAWI IN *L'EGYPTIENNE*, 1929

PORT SAID AT NIGHT

Hot on the heels of the returning Wafd embassy was Kamaladevi Chattopadhyay, who had found an early opportunity to take them up on their invitation to visit Egypt. She was asked to attend an upcoming conference of the International Alliance of Women (IAW) in Denmark, and needed to enroll her son at a British university; Egypt was conveniently en route.

Unlike the higher profile tour that preceded (and prompted) it, the fact that a "reciprocal" visit to Egypt was undertaken almost immediately by an Indian Congress activist has been overlooked by even the small subset of historians writing about interwar anticolonial internationalism and Indian-Egyptian ties.[2] Yet if claims from the Congress-Wafd podium of undying commitment to a shared struggle against the British "enemy" may provoke our skepticism, the slim but poignant collection of documents that attest to Chattopadhyay's time in Cairo and her blossoming friendship with Huda Shaarawi provide a compelling counternarrative of Eastern solidarity during the same moment in time. For, as we will see, Chattopadhyay and Shaarawi proved themselves to be deeply committed to the intersectional pursuit of emancipation for their gender, their respective countries, and the East as a whole.

By 1939 Chattopadhyay was a senior women's leader of the Seva Dal, which trained Indian volunteers in the physically and mentally exacting methods of nonviolent resistance. During the 1931 Salt March, she led the procession to the beach in Bombay on 6 April (a date chosen to mark the anniversary of the Amritsar Massacre) and lit one of the first copper pans in the nationwide campaign to illegally evaporate sea water. Her description of the scene on the beach that morning is breathtaking:

> Great sky-rending cries of 'Jai' filled the air. Heavy-scented flower-garlands almost smothered us. From the balconies and roofs unseen hands showered rose-petals until the road became a carpet of flowers.
> [. . .] The long narrow strip of sand that borders the city like a white ribbon was transformed this morning into another sea—a sea of human faces that swayed and danced and bobbed about even as did the deep azure waves that rimmed the shore. The city seemed to have disgorged of almost its entire population into the sands . . . and still they kept coming, thousands of women amongst them, striding like proud warriors. . . . Even as I lit my little fire to boil the salt water, I saw thousands of fires aflame dancing in the wind.
> [. . .] The police found it hard to break through the circle so deep was it, that they charged with their batons. The human wall was still unyielding. In the meantime police on horseback charged at the general crowd, but they sat silent and immovable. I could hear the dull thud as the blows fell, faint moans as the wounded struck the ground. Still not a cry, not an angry snarl. Men and women, young and old, were all facing the attack . . . their faces alight with a strange composure.[3]

For her defiance, Chattopadhyay was beaten unconscious by British police, and later arrested and imprisoned. At her sentencing, she recalled that the judge told her he was "obliged" to deal with her case severely, "for you have been responsible in making more people break the law than any other single individual." When she then learned that she was to spend one year in jail, she remarked that it "sounded rather light after the ominous pronouncement that preceded it."[4] In total she would serve four separate jail terms for the sake of the national cause, including a year in solitary confinement between 1933 and 1934. The teenager who spent 1919 praying for Gandhi and his movement from her bedroom had matured, by the 1930s, into one of Congress's fiercest and most capable lieutenants.

She had also honed her credentials as a leading feminist; indeed, it was Chattopadhyay's intercession that persuaded Gandhi to allow women to participate in direct action, from which he was initially inclined to shelter them.[5] In 1927 she helped found the All-India Women's Conference (AIWC) alongside her friend and mentor Margaret Cousins ("Gretta"). In 1929, at age 26, Chattopadhyay attended her first IAW Congress in Berlin. She recalled that on the eve of its opening, she and her colleagues had discovered that India was the only delegation whose flag was not hanging in the main hall; in its place, a Union Jack had been erected. Chattopadhyay complained to the organizers, who confessed they had not realized India had its own flag, but they would of course be happy to raise it if one were provided to them. Upon hearing this news, the women returned to their accommodations, opened their suitcases, and tore up their sarees to fashion a makeshift Indian tricolor. "No one grudged tearing up their fineries," she recalled. "In fact, we felt free and liberated at the gala opening function watching our flag fluttering proudly amidst the others."[6]

In Berlin, Chattopadhyay was stunned to realize that the "international" feminist meeting boasted only two major Eastern delegations—from Egypt and India (she noted, with obvious contempt, that other colonized countries were represented only by their rulers; Egyptian accounts of the Berlin congress note the presence of a delegate from Japan). Nevertheless, she found herself deeply impressed by Huda Shaarawi who, as leader of the Egyptians, was by that point an IAW veteran and close colleague of Chattopadhyay's sister-in-law Sarojini Naidu, head of the Indian delegation. Between them, these two "dominant leaders . . . with their personality and golden eloquence," were able to make "a pretty good and spirited showing" on behalf of the East.[7]

The impression seems to have been shared by Saiza Nabarawi, whose report on the Berlin congress for *L'Egyptienne* ended with a call for Eastern women to establish their own union or regional organization: "Already, North and South Americans have formed a united front for the defense of their common interests. Why don't we Eastern peoples follow their example? . . . To the Union of Women of Europe, to that of the Pan-Pacific, we would answer with a League of Eastern Women."[8]

In addition to the congress's formal proceedings, Sarojini Naidu's brother Virendranath was once again able to use his connections to international socialist networks to set up other opportunities for the women to speak on the subject of India's struggle for freedom. They gave lectures in labor union halls where Chattopadhyay was gratified to have the opportunity to meet with ordinary German workers and learn more about their lives. During the same trip, she accompanied "Viren," as she called him, to a conference of the League Against Imperialism in Frankfurt, where she met delegates from across Asia and North Africa and leading European leftists, including the French philosopher Henri Bergson. "As we were the only two Indians fresh from India which was reportedly in revolt under

Gandhiji, we were much sought after," she remarked. "It was a novel experience for me to be received as a mature political personality whereas in India I had been treated as a youth with condescension by elders."[9] These encounters with anticolonial socialists in Europe helped to inform Chattopadhyay's own growing interest in socialism—mirroring to some extent the political evolution of Nehru.

Returning home, she remained inspired by the transnational anticolonial context she had experienced in Germany, and in particular by her meeting with Huda Shaarawi, which had aroused in her "a special interest" in the case of Egypt. She thus took it upon herself to learn more about the ongoing struggle for national and women's rights in that country and to share her findings with other Indian nationalists. This is what had spurred the series of articles she published on anticolonial movements, highlighting the case of Egypt, in the lead-up to the Wafd's tour of India in 1939. Although she came to Egypt as the guest of the Wafd, Chattopadhyay arranged to stay in Huda Shaarawi's Cairo home.

It was late at night as the boat made its way into harbor at Port Said. Kamaladevi Chattopadhyay stood gazing out at the dark shoreline, exhausted by

FIGURE 16   Kamaladevi Chattopadhyay, feminist sociologist and satyagrahi. Undated.
ALBUM / ALAMY

the long voyage. Suddenly she noticed "a number of small boats with sparkling lights" making their way steadily toward her much larger ferry. The glittering fleet of fishing boats were, it transpired, her official welcome committee. "Our Arab hosts got us off within minutes and I found myself right in the midst of the twinkling boats, the air shaken by vibrant slogans from young throats." These were the youth of the Wafd, chanting themselves hoarse in a rousing display of anticolonial hospitality. They were "very excited," her hosts explained, "over a fraternal visit from a freedom fighter from India."[10]

CHEZ MADAME SHAARAWI

The next morning, Chattopadhyay awoke in Shaarawi's famously beautiful home at Number Two, Qasr el-Nil street. She describes the scene in unusually luscious detail:

> Bright sun was pouring in when I got out of bed. No I was not dreaming, I was wide awake but in an Arabian Nights Palace, so it seemed to me. An exquisite breakfast of sweet melon, russet red grapes, crisp melting toast, fresh dates that put me in mind of palm jaggery at home, was spread out before me. The only object that seemed real and not part of the hazy dream was my hostess sitting opposite me, solid, down to earth, inspite of her exquisitely chiselled face and statuesque figure, Madame Charaoui Pasha. With her keen sensitive nature she had modelled her house on the traditional Arab architecture. The furniture was Syrian, with the fine lacy carved patterns. The tiniest, the most innocuous item was delicately chosen.

Over her sumptuous breakfast table, Shaarawi caught up her guest on the recent trials and tribulations of Egypt's nationalist movement. She shared her view that "the Wafd had lost its teeth for lack of dynamic leadership" in the years since Zaghlul's passing. Over the course of the following days, as Chattopadhyay became more acquainted with Nahas and his colleagues, she found herself largely agreeing with Shaarawi's analysis. The Wafd, she concluded (much as Nehru had done the previous year), was a party of "typical bourgeois politicians—patriotic no doubt, but too firmly set in a smooth life of ease"; "there was very little fight about them." Again like Nehru, she found herself taken aback by the Egyptian habit of extravagant meals and late-night parties, which took up "far too much time" in her estimation.

Where politically she found Egypt somewhat lacking, emotionally it pulled her in. The dream sequence of Shaarawi's "Arabian Nights Palace" was only the beginning: "The most enticing adventures were around the Museums, with their panorama of exotic scenes of ancient Egypt, like the fabulous Tutenkhamun treasures." Chattopadhyay also appreciated the opportunities she was afforded to connect with Egyptian women, who, she wrote with unconscious sensuality, "generously parted the curtain of formality and revealed deeper scenes."[11] While Shaarawi's journal *L'Egyptienne* and other Cairene media outlets captivated their readers with descriptions of a Hindu and Buddhist East, Chattopadhyay was no less enamored by the charms of an Arab Orient she had only previously heard tell of, or glimpsed on the printed page.

The Cairo meeting that seems to have left the deepest impression on her was with Abdel Krim, the storied hero of the Rif War against the Spanish in northern Morocco, now living in exile.[12] The two had a long interview, which Chattopadhyay recorded in detail. During their interview, she asked if he knew of the Indian struggle for freedom, to which he replied, "Yes. You have the advantage of the inspiration and guidance of the greatest leader in the world today. I know of his sympathy and support for all the freedom fighters everywhere and we are grateful." He also told her that "the days of colonialism are numbered. The coming war will end it, I have no doubt."

Here, far more than with the men of the Wafd, was a comrade Chattopadhyay felt she could identify with, even if the battle she was waging was nonviolent. This once more mirrored the political experiences of Nehru during the same period. His time in Barcelona the previous summer had left him longing to join the leftists in their doomed defense of the Spanish Republic: "Reluctantly I came away from these gallant men of the International Brigade, for something in me wanted to stay on this inhospitable looking hillside which sheltered so much human courage, so much of what was worthwhile in life."[13] After World War II, Nehru would confide in Chattopadhyay his overwhelming admiration for Subhas Chandra Bose's own "resistance army" in South East Asia, despite its alliance with Japan and Germany: "[Nehru's] face was aglow, his eyes lit with emotion as the words came tumbling out like sparks: 'Netaji did very great things, extraordinary things, the successful way he organized the military, the Azad Hind Fauz and civilians alike. There he was like a God,'" Chattopadhyay recorded.[14] As fellow anticolonial socialists who frequently felt constrained by their loyalty to Gandhi, she and Nehru understood each other well.

In parting, Abdel Krim held both of Chattopadhyay's hands and bowed low, asking that she take his good wishes "to your people and your great leader." She described looking back at him through the rear window of her car, "a silent rock-like figure . . . so confident he would go back to a free Morocco. . . . As my car sped on the picture faded, like an epoch crowded with many stirring events."¹⁵

A short time later, Chattopadhyay departed for London, but she would meet Shaarawi again within weeks at the International Alliance of Women's conference in Copenhagen.

GATHERING STORMS

At a meeting in Beirut in 1938 (having been forced to cancel the planned women's conference in Bludan the previous year), Arab women from Syria, Lebanon, and Palestine wrote to Shaarawi and charged her with a mission: to represent the Palestinian cause in the international arena. There were several reasons why this made sense, notably the greater freedom of movement and access to international fora that Shaarawi enjoyed as an Egyptian national, compared to her colleagues in countries administered as Mandates. The experience of Bludan had made it woefully apparent how easily British and French authorities could quash women's efforts to organize, leaving to one side the matter of travel visas, which could be arbitrarily withheld. But the letter was also an expression of the profound level of trust and respect the women of the Levant had for Shaarawi, in her abilities as an orator and advocate, and in her staunch commitment to Palestine. Events in Copenhagen would prove that Shaarawi took their confidence immensely seriously and did her best to live out the responsibility with which she had been entrusted.

The thirteenth session of the International Alliance of Women was held in Copenhagen in the month of July. The conference took place under the unmistakable shadow of impending war, which prevented many national delegations from attending. The fascist countries were out, as were those under Nazi occupation. Russia did not send a delegation, and for the first time neither did the Americans. In marked contrast to the twelfth session in 1935, the only non-Western countries represented were Egypt, India, and Palestine—but from Palestine only the Jewish Women's Equal Rights Association (ERA) came; the Palestinian Arab affiliate of the IAW had been unable to send a representative owing to the ongoing political turmoil in the country, caused by the Arab Revolt. According to Saiza Nabarawi's report, the ERA used their opening statement to advance a claim to the Jewish people's inalienable right to the land of Palestine, as conferred in the Bible. This statement was immediately objected to by the Danish hosts, who reminded the IAW President that their government had only permitted the event to take place on the condition that it avoid "any political allusions."[16] Assuming that were true, the Danish government was in for several days of profound frustration—and they weren't the only ones.

As has been exhaustively laid out by historians including Margot Badran and Charlotte Weber, the Copenhagen congress devolved into a showdown between Western feminists and their sisters from the East—anticipating the conflicts of feminism's second wave, when the presumed universality of white middle-class paradigms for women's liberation would be challenged by Black and third-world feminists.[17] The background to the confrontation was the IAW's long-standing policy of neutrality on all issues deemed "purely national" in scope—a Westphalian clause intended to prevent the Alliance's entanglement in the domestic affairs of individual member states. For an organization explicitly committed to the legal and political enfranchisement of women within their respective countries, this was a pretension somewhat lacking in self-awareness; nevertheless, the leadership of the IAW strove to uphold its "neutrality" in matters of national politics.

The trouble was that by the summer of 1939, fewer and fewer subjects could be construed as apolitical. In Europe the battle lines were hardening; the ugly realities of Nazi occupation, including the dismissal of women from their jobs, the dissolution of women's organizations, and the forced deportation of untold thousands of Jews from their homes were impossible for the IAW to ignore. Meanwhile in the Middle East, four years of devastating bloodshed in Palestine had left the entire region in a state of shock, scandalized by the brutality of Britain's repression in a territory it supposedly held in trust. With many important delegations absent from the proceedings in Copenhagen, those present found themselves struggling to agree on what constituted "national politics," which were off limits, and what pertained more broadly to international peace and human rights, subjects the delegates were encouraged to address.

In their accounts, both Egyptian and Indian delegates to the conference criticized what they perceived as a double standard, by which the IAW used one definition of "political neutrality" in addressing the crisis in Europe and another for events in the colonized world, specifically Palestine. For example, delegates passed a resolution defining democracy as the ideal form of government. Another resolution, passed unanimously, called on states to ratify the League of Nations's convention on the rights of refugees. Expressions of sympathy and solidarity went out to women suffering under Nazi occupation. The general mood was apparent in an issue of the IAW's newsletter, *Jus Suffragii*, published shortly before the conference convened: "The Alliance is pledged to neutrality on all questions that are strictly national, but can it be claimed that the forcible taking over of one country by another, a country with a different race, culture and language, is purely a national question?" As Weber notes, "it was precisely the question Arab women had been asking all along."[18]

Seizing, then, on what she interpreted to be a more lax attitude toward the neutrality clause, and noting that the matter of Jewish displacement had a direct bearing on the peace and stability of Palestine, Shaarawi attempted to rouse her colleagues to a resolution or "expression of sympathy" for their absent Palestinian colleagues. This naturally placed the Egyptians at loggerheads with the Jewish women of the ERA, who objected to the language the Egyptians sought to include. The balance of sympathy fell in favor of the Zionists. As IAW President Margery Corbett-Ashby reflected years later, European delegates to the conference were impressed "by the vastness and immediacy of the Jewish problem whereas the Palestine problem was far off and concerned relatively few people" among the participants.[19]

Incensed, Shaarawi asked for clarification on a recent incident. Following the German invasion of Czechoslovakia the previous year, reports had circulated that the celebrated Jewish Czech feminist and IAW board member Františka Plamínková had been arrested by the Nazis. An all-call had gone out from the IAW for its members and affiliates to petition the German authorities for her release, which Shaarawi among many others had immediately done.[20] Yet around the same time, Sadhij Nassar—the President of the IAW's Arab Palestinian affiliate, who had led its delegation to the last conference in Istanbul—was arrested and imprisoned for her prominent role in the anticolonial movement in her country. There had been no comment from the IAW, no similar outreach to its members to petition British authorities. Shaarawi demanded to know why.

Corbett-Ashby tried to explain that IAW members had acted "in a personal capacity" on behalf of Plamínková but maintained that interceding in Nassar's case would have violated the IAW's bylaw of neutrality in matters of national politics. As Chattopadhyay would remark ruefully in her memoir, at Copenhagen "colonial problems were treated as "internal matters of the ruling country." In other words, the ruling country possessed a legal right to rule its colonies."[21]

Matters came to a head on the last day of the conference, when Egyptian delegates sought to introduce a resolution criticizing "forced immigration" as a barrier to peace, much as the conference had condemned forced deportations, and sought to address the European refugee crisis. Members of the IAW attempted to draft a compromise resolution that acknowledged the three interlocking crises as resulting from "the defaulting of all governments in regard to this immense human problem"—a concession, however bland, to the Egyptians' insistence that liberal democracies be held accountable for their share of blame alongside totalitarian regimes. As Badran recounts, this resolution sparked "a long and heated debate," with the ERA delegates demanding that the reference to "forced immigration" be struck. When the Egyptians asked that the resolution be put to a vote, their request was denied, and the resolution died on the floor.[22] Their options thus exhausted, the delegates rose from their seats and walked out of the chamber—four Egyptians, and at least one Indian. Chattopadhyay later recalled the conference with a mix of frustration and pride: "The International Women's Conference in Copenhagen proved a source of aggravation. While righteous wrath was directed against Nazism, a tight curtain was drawn over imperialism.... Madame Charaoui Pasha and I were again the only rightful representatives of our people. Utterly frustrated by our failure, we walked out of the Conference. I straightaway sent a strongly worded directive to the Indian Women's Conference to promptly disaffiliate itself from this international body, which it did."[23]

Julie Barbieri describes the report, which was authored jointly by Chattopadhyay and Dr. Malini Sukthankar, as "scathing." It denounced the majority of conference delegates as "obsessed by their own problems" and incapable of viewing Easterners "except as primitive and backward, needing the protective wing of some European power or other." In recommending that the All-India Women's Congress (AIWC) split with the International Alliance of Women (IAW), they suggested it should instead strengthen its links "with the Eastern countries ... and thus be able to form a solid block to be able to make its impact felt on the Alliance." In response, AIWC President Rani Lakshmibai Rajwade wrote a letter of complaint criticizing the IAW for appearing to uphold "such differences as Eastern and Western or Asian and European in a body which claims to be a world organization." At Chattopadhyay's insistence, the AIWC did, in fact, break with the IAW and did not formally rejoin the organization until 1966.[24]

For the All-India Women's Conference to have withdrawn its membership of a prominent international feminist organization is dramatic enough; what has not tended to be appreciated by feminist historians, Arab or Indian, is that, given the context of the debate, the decision of Chattopadhyay (and possibly Sukthankar) to walk out, then petition her home organization to break ties with the IAW, was clearly motivated by her solidarity with the Egyptian delegation, and at least by extension her sympathy with the Palestinian cause. It was a stunning act of Eastern and anticolonial solidarity, later underscored by the AIWC's passage of a resolution calling for the annulment of the Balfour Declaration at their first postwar conference in 1946.

This sheds new light on Shaarawi's own statement that it was the Copenhagen congress that convinced her that "it had become necessary to create an Eastern feminist union as a structure within which to consolidate our forces and help us to have an impact upon the women of the world."[25] In light of Chattopadhyay's contemporary statements and actions, an Eastern women's union was a likely subject of conversation between them during their time in Denmark. More concretely, in the staunch loyalty of their Indian sisters, perhaps the Egyptians perceived a viable alternative to the platitudes and equivocations of their European counterparts. Certainly, the connections between them would continue to deepen in the years to come.

There were a great many plans in the air that spring and summer, plans for future meetings, "next" conferences, and visits between friends. But of course, those plans—along with a hundred million other things—were not to be. Within months Europe was at war, and the world wasn't far behind.

PART IV THE EAST AT WAR

NINE

Hearts and Minds

> [The British] might well fight an army, but they could not stand against press propaganda.[1]
> —CHOUDHRY KHALIQUZZAMAN

FASCISTS OR IMPERIALISTS?

The cataclysms of the Second World War had a profound impact on nationalist politics across Egypt and India. In a war between European fascists and European imperialists, should the anticolonial East take sides? If so, which side? Nehru felt torn between his impulse to throw support behind the antifascist struggle and the opportunity presented by the crisis of war to finally force the issue of India's national liberation.[2] In this painful ambiguity, he was far from alone. Right from 1939 some leftists in the colonized East openly supported the Allied war effort, lending their services to the press and radio while others attempted to enlist. They were scorned by friends and former comrades as traitors or British stooges. In Palestine, a Muslim intellectual who had fought with the Republicans in Spain found himself expelled from the local Communist Party for publishing a book in which he used the Quran and Hadith to eviscerate Nazi doctrine.[3] In his memoirs he remarked that the Communists' policy of accommodation to Hitler in the early years of the war was "the beginning of the tragedy that befell the party. . . . They did not realize their big mistake until very late."[4]

Gandhi's uncompromising commitment to nonviolence had served in many cases to insulate him from the kind of moral agony often suffered by his more equivocal disciples; yet World War II seems to have sent even the Mahatma into a spiral of inner conflict and reversals. Willing, unwilling, then willing again to make concessions to the British war effort, as he witnessed its brutalizing impact on India's people and landscape—the slaughtering of cows for military rations, the destitution caused by famine, the drunkenness and promiscuity of foreign troops stationed in the cities—he grew disgusted and spoke with uncharacteristic venom about the British presence in his country.[5]

Even this stance was moderate compared to that of many of his colleagues. Gandhi's former rival Subhas Chandra Bose had grown estranged from the Congress Party following his forced resignation (before the eyes of the visiting Wafd delegates) at the Tripuri session in the spring of 1939. Bose was briefly imprisoned in 1940; upon his release he escaped, traveling to Afghanistan in disguise with the aid of German agents. In 1941 he arrived in Berlin, from where he began orchestrating pro-Axis propaganda and recruiting prisoners of war to his Indian Legion.

In Egypt, the Wafd's opposition to Nazism and Italian fascism predated the war, rooted in both a principled rejection of authoritarian rule and the increasingly fascist alignment of many of its domestic rivals. Like Nehru, the Communists and the progressive left in India, Nahas—a liberal capitalist—found himself unable to countenance an Axis victory, any more than he could accept the domestic threats he perceived as emanating from the palace, Islamists, and proto-fascist parties like Young Egypt.[6] Thus, "despite its historic opposition to British domination," as Beinin and Lockman observe, "in the particular conjuncture of the Second World War the Wafd became the most pro-British force in Egypt."[7]

As the international system convulsed with the war's many shocks and stunning reversals, political currents split and split again. Allied and Axis propaganda flooded the region, supported by Orientalist functionaries and anticolonial collaborators. In the chaos of war, many in Egypt and India perceived opportunities for the advancement of the national cause or the undermining of political allies, personal enrichment or worker's rights, solidarity across borders—or the forging of altogether new ones.

OUTBREAK

Beginning in 1935, a multiplicity of international conflagrations, from the Italian invasion of Abyssinia to the Munich Crisis, had given Britain ample cause to consider, and then reconsider, defensive arrangements for its empire. Each of these events had the effect of exposing a potential weakness or blind spot in

British planning, which Lampson and his Service Chiefs in Cairo then sought to address, often by appealing for additional men (from India) and materiel (from London). This earned Lampson, over time, the profound resentment of his colleagues in both Simla and Whitehall. Linlithgow, the Viceroy of India, deemed it "quite evident that Miles Lampson has been very unnecessarily hot and bothered over his position in Egypt."[8] Lieutenant-General Sir Henry Pownall of the War Office was more blunt, calling him "a great fat useless beggar who would be better employed in doing his own job of keeping up British prestige in Egypt."[9]

Notwithstanding his unpopularity, however, Lampson might have been forgiven a moment of personal vindication when, on the eve of war in early September 1939, the political and military apparatus he had fought so hard to engineer clicked, for the most part, smoothly into gear. Already by late summer, the Mediterranean Fleet was battle ready; Air Force squadrons were at their war stations; two battalions of reinforcements had arrived from Palestine; and the fixed defenses at Suez had been manned. Air patrols and mine sweeping had begun around Alexandria harbor, and the majority of British forces, with Egyptian support, had been moved to their forward position at Mersa Matruh, with the remainder concentrated in the Delta and Canal Zones.[10] Upon the outbreak of hostilities, the government of Ali Maher acknowledged that, in the words of the Anglo-Egyptian Treaty, a state of "apprehended international emergency" now existed. The government pledged to cooperate fully with Egypt's ally Great Britain, severed ties with Germany, and moved immediately to sequester German property and intern adult males. Nazi Party members were rounded up and interned in Alexandria at the Italian school, while non-Nazis were held at the German school in the Bulaq neighborhood of Cairo.[11] Martial law was declared under the aegis of the Egyptian Prime Minister, enabling the censorship of the press, post, radio, and telegraph, and Egypt's railways were placed at the disposal of the British Army. A more orderly and complete transition to war could scarcely have been dreamt of in the ambassadorial bedchamber... with one rather jarring exception. Ali Maher, while professing himself eager—in fact determined—to accomplish it, spent the month of September avoiding, by increasingly acrobatic feats, an Egyptian declaration of war on Germany.[12]

Most recent histories drawing on British archival sources have followed Lampson in attributing Maher's intransigence in the fall of 1939 to an affinity with the Axis powers[13]—or, as the High Commissioner put it at the time, of "keeping a foot in both camps."[14] More convincing is Charles Tripp's argument that Maher's refusal to declare war on Germany in 1939 formed part of his broader campaign to wrest mass popular support from the Wafd:

> No one yet knew what demands Great Britain would make of Egypt in the war. . . . Nor did anyone yet know the physical destruction which war might inflict on the population of Egypt, but Axis propaganda and the fears of aerial bombardment had convinced many, not only in Egypt, that it would be devastating. It was Ali Mahir's intention, therefore, to avoid the responsibility for the hardship which war would inevitably cause, and to maintain the King's image as a champion of national rights, by granting the British only that to which Egypt was demonstrably committed under the terms of a Treaty drawn up largely at the initiative of the Wafd. In this Treaty there was no specific commitment to declare war.[15]

Credence is leant to this argument by, among other things, the repeated requests made by both the King and his Prime Minister for increased British reinforcements and arms throughout the early phases of the crisis.[16] Had they wished for an Axis invasion to oust the British, this persistent (and relatively effective) lobbying would have been counterproductive. It seems clear that Maher's desire, at this early stage in the conflict, was for the maintenance of internal stability and the robust defense of Egypt from attack; any other eventuality threatened his own grasp on power. It was only later, as relations with Lampson and the British government came under increased strain, and as an Axis victory over the Allies began to appear inevitable, that Ali Maher and his patron Faruq sought to reinsure with the German and Italian governments.

On the far shores of the ocean in India that September, Britain's control of the central government meant there was little if any doubt that a declaration of war would be forthcoming once the British ultimatum to Germany had expired. But nationalist leaders, and Congress in particular, had anticipated some form of consultation with the central authorities, providing the opportunity for the country to be seen to enter the war of its own volition. That the Viceroy, Lord Linlithgow, brought India into the war immediately following Britain's formal declaration—without consulting any of the institutions of government that Indian nationalists had been persuaded, with deep reluctance, to participate in—fatally undermined their willingness to continue to do so. "India," Congress argued, "cannot associate itself in a war said to be for democratic freedom when that very freedom is denied her."[17]

Attempts to negotiate with the government yielded nothing, and so that autumn the Congress-dominated provincial governments of Madras, Bombay, Bihar, the United Provinces, Orissa, and the Central Provinces all resigned in protest. Linlithgow archly suggested their seats could be taken by the Muslim League. It was a cynical threat, but it spoke volumes about the approach the

Government of India would now adopt, actively stoking hostility between Congress and the Muslim League. Seizing the initiative, in a highly controversial move, Jinnah called for countrywide celebrations of the Congress resignations as a "Day of Deliverance" and was joined by a hodgepodge of other anti-Congress politicians, including the Dalit leader and opponent of Gandhi, B.R. Ambedkar.[18] Such theatrics were viewed not unfavorably by the British as keeping Indian nationalists safely divided. For, as Linlithgow explained to his new Secretary of State, Leo Amery (who replaced Zetland in the spring of 1940), the Muslim League was a valuable counterweight: "the only organized opposition to Congress"; "nor do I want to risk a combination against us of Congress and the Muslim League."[19] Instead, Linlithgow encouraged Jinnah to get more creative and develop a "constructive policy" for India's Muslims.[20] As Khaliquzzaman was at pains to point out in his memoir, the Viceroy did not make this suggestion in a vacuum—having already been alerted by Zetland to the Muslim League's growing interest in partition.[21]

Irrespective of the mixed political directives emanating from Delhi, Indian troops were already headed west. The first Indian reinforcements reached Cairo in August 1939. Ultimately over 2.5 million Indians would serve in World War II, many of them in the theaters of the Middle East and North Africa. In contrast to their Australian fellows—who were initially refused billeting by the Egyptian government on account of their infamous hooliganism during World War I[22]—most sepoys spent at least some of the war based in and around Allied Force Headquarters in Cairo. The Fourth and Fifth Indian Infantry Divisions were to become especially famous for their celebrated roles in the Desert War.[23] They would also play significant roles in the liberation of East Africa from Mussolini[24]—belatedly fulfilling calls first heard in the Indian Legislature in 1935.

Conversely, there were many in India, Egypt, and throughout the broader Middle East who found the Axis's vow to cast off the British yoke irresistible. Among them was Hajj Amin al-Husseini, who had left Beirut for Baghdad as war broke out in 1939. There he forged a close relationship with Rashid Ali al-Kaylani, a former Prime Minister, and other Iraqi nationalists who were, like the Mufti, interested in an anti-British alliance with Nazi Germany. Shortly after his arrival in February 1940, Hajj Amin wrote to Jinnah, whom he did not know personally, although he had of course met envoys of the Muslim League in Beirut the previous spring. The letter was not particularly personal; it outlined Palestinian grievances since the outbreak of the war and claimed that "hundreds" of men had been executed by the British authorities since the end of the revolt.[25] The letter was most likely part of a broader attempt by the Mufti to rally continued support for the Palestinian resistance from known sympathizers and supporters; evidently, the efforts of Siddiqi and Khaliquzzaman along these lines had not been forgotten. It is unclear whether Jinnah replied, although he did forward the correspondence on to the Governor General at Simla. Whether to protest the Palestinians' treatment or to keep British officials abreast of the seditious Mufti's activities is also unclear; by this juncture, either motive seems plausible.

JINNAH'S DEMAND

For Jinnah, the war years created a growing convergence of interests with the British government, beginning with Linlithgow's tip of the hat to the Muslim League in September 1939. The Viceroy's conscious elevation of Jinnah and his party as the Muslim counterargument to Congress drastically enhanced his prestige, and with it, his political ambition. The following spring at Lahore, Jinnah unveiled the League's new "constructive policy." It called for Muslim majority provinces in North India to be grouped into "autonomous and sovereign" states: "It has always been taken for granted mistakenly that the Mussalmans are a minority, and of course we have got used to it . . . these settled notions sometimes are very difficult to remove. The Mussalmans are not a minority. The Mussalmans are a nation by any definition. . . . The problem in India is not of an inter-communal character, but manifestly of an international one, and it must be treated as such."[26]

The Lahore Resolution thus formalized a shift in vocabulary away from the language of a spiritually bound "community" or "religious minority," which the Muslim League's advocates and Jinnah himself had still been pressing into service on behalf of the Palestinians as late as the spring of 1939. One year later, the rights they claimed were on behalf of Muslims as a "nation". Jinnah had accepted Khaliquzzaman's argument: they could not keep "talking on the old basis,"[27] for, as the Muslim League President acknowledged in a meaningful aside to his speech, "the word "nationalist" has now become the play of conjurers in politics."[28]

In the same speech Jinnah singled out Palestine as an ongoing subject of negotiation between the Muslim League and the British government: "We are told that endeavours, earnest endeavours, are being made to meet the reasonable, national demands, of the Arabs. Well, we cannot be satisfied by earnest endeavours, sincere endeavours, best endeavours. (*Laughter.*) We want that the British Government should in fact actually meet the demands of the Arabs in Palestine. (Hear, hear.)"[29]

The Lahore Resolution was seconded by Choudhry Khaliquzzaman. In the high-key public discussions and debates that followed its pronouncement, Palestine was apparently still on quite a few minds. Arguments about what a prospective Pakistan would (or would not) be able to do for the Palestinian people appeared in multiple treatises arguing for and against the creation of a Muslim state.[30] A set of semiofficial volumes, to which Jinnah provided the foreword, suggested that where Muslim efforts to defend Palestine had so far failed, a future Pakistan could and would do better.[31]

What is striking is the extent to which Jinnah and his votaries did not meaningfully distinguish between the categories of nation-state and empire, the unit of political organization with which they were, of course, infinitely more familiar. Indeed, the vision of Pakistan that gradually emerged in the wake of the Lahore Resolution took its cues from the realities and historical practices of the British Empire itself. Thus Jinnah cited the way British Commonwealth citizens moved through foreign waters and territories to reach different parts of their far-flung empire as an analogy for movement between East and West Pakistan. Even more tellingly, he evoked British intervention on behalf of Ottoman Christians in the nineteenth century: "If Britain in Gladstone's Time could intervene in Armenia in the name of protection of minorities, why should it not be right for us to do so in the case of our minorities in Hindustan—if they are oppressed?"[32]

This was the logic of an imperial world system in which religious communities sought patronage from foreign powers; it was the logic according to which the Khilafatists had brandished Britain's wartime guarantees for the "inviolability of Muslim holy places"; and it was the precise logic that the Muslim League had so recently seen dismissed at St James's. By "conjuring" the language of the nation-state, Jinnah and other Muslim Leaguers seemed to believe, the legitimacy of such claims might be revived. For if Pakistan were to come into existence, they could only envision it as a great power, one to whose flag the Muslims of other countries might also eventually rally. As Ambedkar observed in his widely read commentary on the prospect of a Muslim state (one of the earliest and most influential on the subject, and one which Jinnah himself encouraged people to read),[33] "there is nothing to prevent Pakistan from joining Afghanistan, Iran, Iraq, Arabia, Turkey and Egypt and forming a federation of Muslim countries constituting one Islamic State extending from Constantinople down to Lahore. A Mussalman must be really very stupid if he is not attracted by the glamour of this new destiny and be completely transformed in his view of the place of Muslims in the Indian cosmos."[34]

Pakistan as it was depicted in the early 1940s (and in radical contrast to its eventual manifest form) was thus profoundly Easternist. While maps (with varying borders) were drawn and (contradictory) treatises were written about it, it could and did still mean wildly different things to different people, depending on which of the many statements about it they chose to latch on to—and more to the point what they wished, or hoped, these statements could mean. These delusions were far from confined to the "masses" who found the vision of a Muslim homeland compelling; they sprang straight from the top—where Pakistan became the repository for a myriad of spiritual and temporal aspirations dashed on the shoals of Sèvres, Ankara, Mecca, London, and Geneva. This did not escape the notice of contemporary British commentators. Reginald Coupland, sent to India to study the prospects for its future governance (much as he had done as part of the Peel Commission in Palestine in 1937),[35] couldn't resist observing that "in looking forward to creating a political nexus between Pakistan and the Moslem countries of the Middle East . . . are not the Partitionists inviting a repetition of what happened 20 years ago? If Panislamism was dead then, can it be resuscitated now?"[36]

Jinnah may not have much cared for the term *pan-Islamism*, yet in nation-statehood he seemed to discern possibilities for great power status and prestige that were, in their implications, not dissimilar to those the Ottomans had enjoyed mere decades prior. In this sense Pakistan had become the vehicle for a set of Muslim cosmopolitan imaginaries he had once, as a younger man, dismissed out of hand.

THE FALL OF FRANCE

Between May and June 1940, Hitler launched his blitzkrieg invasion of Western Europe, utterly transforming the nature of the war. In the Egyptian capital, the fall of France and the Allied evacuation of the continent hit like a bombshell. Military defenses that had been relaxed following the initial excitement of the previous summer were once again placed on high alert. Thousands of children were evacuated from Alexandria, as the threat of aerial bombardment loomed.

Within a week of Dunkirk, Mussolini had entered the war on the side of the Axis, eager to claim a portion of the spoils of war. In 1939 there had been fewer than a thousand Germans resident in Egypt; by contrast, there were at least fifty-eight thousand Italians. While these were not all card-carrying Fascists, a contemporary British intelligence assessment noted that it was "unhealthy" for Italians in Egypt to express antifascist views.[37] In terms of physical geography, Germany had no colonies or known territorial objectives in the vicinity of the Eastern Mediterranean; Mussolini's forces were on Egypt's door in Libya and could control access to the Red Sea and the headwaters of the Blue Nile in Ethiopia, on which Egypt's fresh water supply depended. Moreover, Mussolini and his supporters had made little effort to disguise their goal of reconstituting the Roman Empire in North Africa, with Egypt at its heart. With the Italian entry into the war, the sense of direct threat to Egypt thus became palpable.

The fall of France appeared to spell disaster for the Allies, and many believed that British defeat was imminent. In this context, Ali Maher sought to signal to the Italians that his government was only fulfilling its commitments to the British under duress and bore the Axis no ill will. This was the message passed on from the Egyptian Minister in Rome to Count Ciano, the Fascist Foreign Minister, that spring when he hinted at Egyptian neutrality in the event of Italian entry.[38] Following the Italian declaration of war, Maher dragged his feet on internments. A week after the outbreak of hostilities, the staff of the Italian Legation was still at liberty in Cairo;[39] when Italian war planes bombed the Egyptian Army in the Western Desert, Maher glossed the attacks as "border incidents which can be settled by diplomatic means."[40] Alarmed by this lax attitude, Lampson met with King Faruq and requested the reinstatement of the Wafd under Nahas. At this, Faruq balked; he was well aware that the return of the Wafd would also usher in renewed attempts to curb his prerogative as sovereign. The eventual compromise was Hussein Sirri, an independent, who, though not enjoying much popular following, would prove exceptionally cooperative from the British perspective.

In India, the fall of France was perceived as a critical opening wherein the nationalists might finally force the issue of the country's postwar status. Congress now demanded the immediate formation of a representative national government; in response, Linlithgow (in concert with Churchill) issued what became known as the August Offer. It promised that, at the end of the war, "a body representative of the principal elements in India's national life" would be formed "with the least possible delay." As D.A. Low states frankly, the offer was of little substance—"scarcely worth the paper it was written on"—and contained nothing about Congress's central demand: independence.[41] It did, however, register for the first time the government's acknowledgement of the Lahore Resolution, when it stated "It goes without saying that they [His Majesty's Government] could not contemplate the transfer of their present responsibilities for the peace and welfare of India to any system of government whose authority is directly denied by large and powerful elements in India's national life. Nor could they be parties to the coercion of such elements into submission to such a Government."[42]

Jinnah seized on this support for his position; his relations with Congress rapidly deteriorated. And, in a formulation seemingly lifted from the text of the 1939 White Paper on Palestine, the Viceroy and the Indian Secretary became fond of saying that until Hindus and Muslims in India learned to get along, Britain could not possibly move the country toward self-government.

ECONOMIC CRISIS

Two years since its outbreak, war had begun to sink its teeth into Egyptian and Indian society. In addition to the barrage of bad news over the wireless, the fretting over loved ones who were far from home and in harm's way and the sense of fear and uncertainty pervading daily life, the rising cost of living had become a public menace. Initially, the industrial boom brought on by the outbreak of war had allowed wages in Egypt and India to keep pace with rising prices. But by 1941 inflation was beginning to outstrip increased earnings; as the war dragged on, the situation of the peasantry and urban laborers became desperate. In Egypt, daily industrial wages increased by 113 percent between 1939 and 1945, but the cost of living increased by 193 percent, resulting in a substantial decline in real wages.[43] In India, the spike in rates of inflation that began in 1941 particularly impacted the cost and availability of staple foodstuffs such as grain. This would contribute to a nightmarish confluence of factors culminating in the Bengal Famine of 1943.

By the summer of 1941 the Egyptian economy was in crisis, partially due to the disruption to shipping that had resulted, for the second year in a row, in a failure to export the Egyptian cotton crop.[44] In Cairo, the Joint Transport Federation, representing the city's tram and bus operators, called for a strike as the cost of living continued to soar. Although trade unions remained legally unrecognized in Egypt until 1942, on the cusp of war a high-profile campaign by labor activists had brought the issue briefly to national prominence. In May 1939 the General Federation, a coalition of labor unions from a variety of sectors, cited the failure of successive Egyptian administrations to take their cause seriously and announced that they would go on hunger strike until parliament granted full legal recognition to trade unions. Should the government fail to meet their demands, they claimed for themselves "the honor of martyrdom in the cause of serving the workers of the Kingdom of Egypt."[45] At that time, as Lockman and Beinin note, hunger strikes as political action were basically without precedent in Egypt. The trade unionists had been inspired by the example of the Mahatma's resort to fasting in the service of India's independence struggle. One prominent Egyptian labor activist, Mahmud al-Askari, referred to labor activists as "the successors of Gandhi in Egypt."

The strike was well organized and effective at garnering widespread press coverage and sympathy for the trade unionists' cause.[46] Activists broke their fast when it was announced that a bill on the legalization of unions would be debated in the Chamber of Deputies; however, the replacement of Muhammad Mahmud (who had been relatively sympathetic to the worker's plight) by Ali Maher as Prime Minister, and the onset of war in September, conspired to prevent the bill's passage. Nevertheless, by 1941 unions were reorganizing and remobilizing to address the crisis of inflation, and thanks to the hunger strike their platform and legitimacy were enhanced. A strike that September succeeded in forcing a 10 percent wage increase for all workers, a breakthrough victory for organized labor in Egypt.[47]

In India, where unions were legal, the Defense of India Act suspended normal mechanisms of dispute resolution and allowed the state to force strikers back to work. Across the subcontinent, grain, kerosene, cloth, and other basic goods grew scarcer, as the military snapped up an increasing share of what was available, and the cost of what remained drifted ever further out of reach for ordinary people. Though a state of famine did not crystallize in India until 1943, already by 1941 the warning signs were apparent. As the situation grew dire, Yasmin Khan notes, among the first to sound the alarm about the rising toll of inflation and economic insecurity in Indian villages weren't even physically there: they were soldiers of the Army of India serving in the Middle East.

By 1943, the steady trickle of worrying letters these men had begun to receive—describing high prices, hunger, and shortages of essential goods—had turned into a flood of despair. A representative letter from Bengal described how "many people can hardly get one meal a day and are almost half clad. If the war goes on for another few months many will die of starvation." Another was yet more dire: "People are dying of hunger and if this goes on for another two or three months then you won't find a single soul alive in our village. God knows when this wretched war will end." Military censors, infamous for their cold attitude toward the emotional pleas of families seeking remittances, were finally so overwhelmed by the sheer volume of desperate reports and the profound impact they were having on the men that they recommended a pay increase for Indian soldiers, less than a year after a similar raise had been granted.[48] Of course, this could do but little to assuage the rising tide of misery across the subcontinent, most tragically in Bengal.

SEPOYS IN CAIRO

Military authorities in Cairo had other concerns regarding the Indian troops now stationed there. For one thing, they were the targets of relentless Axis propaganda, in the form of leaflets dropped from airplanes and radio broadcasts in various Indian languages. On the model of Radio Bari, both Italy and Germany established radio stations targeting Indians: Radio Himalaya and Azad Hind Radio, respectively. The fifteen thousand to seventeen thousand Indian soldiers captured by the Axis in North Africa and the Mediterranean were well treated because they were seen as potential recruits.[49] The Indian Legion, founded by Subhas Chandra Bose in Germany in 1941, was the largest Axis unit formed by Indian prisoners of war, while the Battaglione Azad Hindoustan was led by Muhammad Iqbal Shedai—the same Punjabi who had arranged meetings for Siddiqi and Khaliquzzaman in Milan in 1939.

In addition to monitoring broadcasts and other Axis propaganda, British authorities in Cairo were worried about the unhealthy influence Egyptian nationalists might have on their officers. In an intelligence meeting held between liaisons from Middle East H.Q. and the Indian Intelligence Service, the two sides agreed that a detachment of security police should be sent out from India and stationed in Cairo.

At the end of the war, the commanding officer of the Indian security police in Cairo sent a letter of application for his men to receive the Africa Star for their service in Egypt. From this it can be confirmed that the unit arrived in Cairo between July and August 1940 and consisted of a staff of eight: two British officers, Major W.H.A. Richard and Captain P.J. Wilkinson; two subinspectors, Naurang Singh and Rashid Ahmed Khan; three foot constables, Khuda Baksh, Kartar Singh, and Mohammad Yunus; and a clerk, Kundan Singh Mall. With the exception of Singh Mall, who hailed from the United Provinces, all were officers of the Punjabi police. Richard, their commanding officer, was Assistant to the Deputy Inspector General of Police in the Criminal Investigations Department. The Punjabis remained in Egypt until the end of November 1941; it is unclear if another unit replaced them when they departed.[50] Among the principal objectives of the detachment was to monitor the activities of Indian sepoys and the sorts of friends they were making: "The Indian population in Egypt present a problem and contacts of Indian troops with Egyptians of the effendi class rendered a Field Security police unit very desirable. Information from Censorship confirmed this view. The general conclusion was that the proposed establishment might have to be increased. . . . Egypt emphasised the necessity of avoiding having to co-operate direct with the Egyptian Police. Co-operation, as may be necessary, will be done through Defence Security Office, Egypt."⁵¹

Given that the concern was over contacts between young, armed, educated men who might be susceptible to nationalist conversion, the desire to avoid unnecessary involvement with the Egyptian police force was perhaps understandable; however, authorities should have been more worried about the corrupting influence of Indian soldiers on their comrades from Britain and the Commonwealth. As one sergeant wrote home to his family in England, "I have met scores of these Indian troops in Cairo and have had drinks with many of them and would do so again. If India was composed chiefly of these kind of blokes I would say they deserve Home Rule and be glad to see them get it."⁵²

PREEMPTIVE STRIKES: IRAQ AND IRAN

In April 1941, Iraqi officers calling themselves the "Golden Square" orchestrated a coup that brought Rashid Ali al-Kaylani to power. In Cairo, Archibald Wavell, Commander in Chief of Middle East forces, was facing a German onslaught in the Western Desert and planning a major attack on Crete. He had no men to spare and even less interest in becoming embroiled in Iraq. Instead, he proposed that the crisis be dealt with by diplomatic means. In India, the Viceroy and his Commander in Chief, Claude Auchinleck, were horrified. They immediately cabled the Indian Secretary Leo Amery and, in words that would have been warmly familiar to their predecessors in the Great War, complained that Britain's man in Cairo had "quite failed to grasp politico-strategic significance of Iraq in existing Middle East complex or to grasp that India operating through [Persian] Gulf is natural base . . . for operations in that most important area." Wavell remained unmoved; thus Amery enlisted Winston Churchill's support to approve the dispatch of an Indian Army division to Basra.⁵³

By the time those forces arrived, al-Kaylani had reached out to Italy and Germany for military assistance. Joachim Ribbentrop, Hitler's Foreign Minister, put it to the Führer in terms equally reminiscent of the 1910s: from Iraq, he suggested, Germany could expand its network of agents throughout the Middle East, and "the whole Arab world shall then be aroused into rebellion against England from our centre in Iraq." This "constantly expanding insurrection of the Arab world could be of the greatest help in the preparation of our decisive advance towards Egypt." Hitler, much like Kaiser Wilhelm before him, was converted. Directives were given to prepare a German and Italian squadron for duty in Iraq. Money, arms, tanks, and artillery were made available, as well as strong-signal radio transmitters to broadcast propaganda into Arab countries.

Hitler sent his former Minister in Iraq, Fritz Grobba, back to Baghdad to make contact with al-Kaylani and his ally, Hajj Amin al-Husseini. Grobba reported that the Mufti was planning a major action in Palestine in the near future and requested more funds on his behalf, which were swiftly approved in Berlin. As the Nazis prepared to send major aid and reinforcements to Baghdad, General Wavell resisted the transfer of two relief units from Palestine to Iraq, on the grounds that this would leave the Mandate exposed. Extraordinarily, he was overruled by London. Iraq was reinforced before the Axis air squadrons could arrive. Within a month, Baghdad had surrendered, and al-Kaylani, Hajj Amin, and their supporters had fled the country, making their way to Berlin. Shortly thereafter, Auchinleck and Wavell were ordered to trade places: Auchinleck, much in favor with Churchill and the War Cabinet, moved into Wavell's office in Cairo, while Wavell was appointed Commander in Chief of the Army of India.[54]

The entry of the Soviet Union into the war on the side of the Allies following the launch of Operation Barbarossa brought Iran back to the top of the list of priorities for General Headquarters in Cairo and Simla. With the German push East, Iran was suddenly exposed to invasion from the north; in addition to the oilfields and refinery at Abadan, the country's railway system became crucial to the transport of war materials to and from the Soviet Union. In this context, British and Soviet forces coordinated a pincer movement to invade and occupy Iran before Germany could do the same.

In 1947, a cache of seized Nazi documents revealed that weeks before this operation took place, King Faruq had sent a telegram to his father-in-law, Youssef Zulficar Pasha, who was then serving as Egyptian Ambassador in Tehran. In the letter, Faruq shared details of the planned invasion of Iran and requested that Zulficar pass the information on to the German Minister, Erwin Ettel, as well as Reza Pahlavi, the Shah of Iran. In his meeting with Ettel, Faruq also asked Zulficar to express to the German Ministry of Foreign Affairs the King's "desire for open and loyal relations with Germany."[55]

Despite Faruq's efforts, however, the Allies successfully invaded Iran, interning all Germans, Italians, and their sympathizers, as well as those known to have supported Rashid Ali's coup in Iraq. The Shah was forced to abdicate in favor of his son Mohammad Reza Pahlavi, who also happened to be the husband of Faruq's sister Fawzia. According to Lampson, who had no knowledge of Faruq's telegram to Zulficar, the abdication made a strong impression on Egypt's young monarch, who appeared skittish and placating in its aftermath: "Fear of his throne is the card to play," Lampson concluded, "if we are faced with further backsliding, which I fear we may be."[56]

THE REACTIONARY EAST

It was probably just as well for Lampson's health that when it came to "backsliding" into a Nazi embrace, he didn't know the half of it. As most thoroughly documented by David Motadel, a host of militants, politicians, and intellectuals from across the Middle East and Asia were tempted into the German camp during World War II. From 1941 onward, the Nazi regime was more than willing to do business with "racially inferior" anticolonial activists who had the potential to destabilize the British Empire from within. In exchange, they hosted and bankrolled these exiled leaders and their entourages in Berlin, which became the center of a "reactionary cosmopolitanism."[57] Rashid Ali al-Kaylani, Hajj Amin al-Husseini, and the Palestinian militant leader Fawzi al-Quwuqji all arrived in Berlin in 1941, as did Subhas Chandra Bose, the former Congress leader from Calcutta, following a cloak-and-dagger escape from house arrest via Kabul and Moscow. "Germany may be a fascist or imperialist, ruthless or cruel" he mused, "but one cannot help admiring these [military] qualities of hers. . . . Could not these qualities be utilized for promoting a nobler cause?"[58] Bose, for one, was determined to believe so.

Mansour Daoud, a cousin of King Faruq, also surfaced in the German capital in 1942. That year saw the organization of an anticolonial solidarity conference between exiled Indians and Arabs under the auspices of the Nazi government in the heart of Berlin. "The room," Motadel tells us, "was packed with anticolonial nationalists and Axis functionaries." In a speech, al-Kaylani referred to the "global anti-imperial struggle" which connected the Arab world to India and Iran. "'Today India has the opportunity', he announced, 'to throw off the shackles of serfdom', and he expressed full solidarity with India's 'fight' for 'freedom, independence and sovereignty'. In response, Bose wished the 'Arab nation' all 'success' in its 'liberation struggle': 'Long live the free Arab nation! Long live the Tripartite Powers and their allies! Long live the free India!'"[59]

Among the common connecting threads between these movements was their rejection of the liberal internationalist order that had emerged from the 1919 Paris Peace Conference. Of course, the conference famously punished Germany for the war in the Treaty of Versailles, which had remained a key grievance for the Nazis. But as we saw in chapters 1 and 2, the conference was also responsible for the dissolution of the Ottoman Empire and the carving up of the Middle East into British and French mandates, ushering in state-backed Zionism in Palestine and sparking the Khilafat Crisis in India. Twenty years later, some Indians, Arabs, and Nazis found these shared grievances compelling grounds for alliance. Others were more motivated by the present (in particular, the pecuniary benefits of Nazi sponsorship). Still others, among them Subhas Chandra Bose, had their gaze fixed firmly on the future.

Traumatized, perhaps, by his experiences with the endlessly discursive politics of the INC, Bose was attracted by the authoritarian leadership and militant discipline that characterized the German, Italian, and Japanese regimes. This would come to be reflected in Bose's Azad Hind brigades, which he developed on rigidly hierarchical lines, himself assuming the role of supreme leader ("Netaji" to his many lieutenants). As Motadel observes, the "New India" of the postwar era was already on display in Germany in the early 1940s.[60] It was being broadcast to the subcontinent from Berlin, by shortwave radio transmissions modeled closely on the earlier Radio Bari broadcasts. German propaganda in Arabic was similarly rooted in the Bari playbook, promising to safeguard "Egypt's independence and sovereignty" and "liberate ... the whole of the Near East" from British oppression.[61]

INDIAN PROPAGANDA FOR THE MIDDLE EAST

Clearly, propaganda had become a battleground every bit as fierce as the Western Desert. Just as news of the coup in Iraq was making headlines in April 1941, Lampson submitted a memorandum to the Ministry of Information in London entitled "India and the War." An initiative of the British embassy in Cairo authored by Lampson and Reginald Davies, his Director of Publicity, the memorandum followed swiftly on the heels of a fact-finding mission Davies had undertaken earlier that spring across India and several Arab countries. It found that audiences in the Middle East had broadly accepted an "Axis portrayal" of India as a hotbed of anticolonial agitation, whose people were eager to use the pressures of war to extract concessions from the British. Simultaneously, Arab populations were said to hold "preconceived ideas" about India and Indians, which led them to underestimate the significance of the subcontinent to the war effort. At a time when Allied positions in both the Atlantic and the Far East were increasingly under siege, the Cairo memorandum argued, it was essential for local morale that Arabs (and, they underscored, particularly Egyptians) be persuaded that India—the source of their own defense—constituted a near-impregnable bulwark: "a vast reservoir of men and war material which can be drawn upon with little or no possibility of enemy interference."[62]

Lampson and Davies acknowledged that accomplishing this reversal in public opinion would be a tall order; however, they argued, "it is the business of publicity to modify preconceived ideas by playing adroitly on the susceptibilities of those holding them, and India provides much material with which to influence the people of the Middle East from a variety of angles."[63] They thus proposed a far-reaching propaganda campaign encompassing newspaper coverage, periodicals and illustrated digests, broadcast radio, cinema, and even publicity tours to educate Middle Eastern audiences about India's civilizational grandeur, its overwhelming potency as an imperial war machine, and the staunch anti-Axis attitudes of its prominent citizens.

The Cairo memorandum reflected consistency in Lampson's perception that Egyptians and Arabs held racialized prejudices "of India as a country of black men, to be regarded with condescension or even contempt."[64] Certainly this blunt appraisal was of a piece with his earlier petitions for Hindu sepoys to be excluded from the troops sent to defend Egypt on the grounds that their presence might hurt Egyptian pride.[65] The trajectory of the war had apparently caused Lampson to change tack: now that it was essential for Egypt, and much of the Middle East, to rely on Indian troops, Lampson sought to tackle the prejudicial attitudes themselves. Other officials in Iraq and India acknowledged that there was at least some truth in the Ambassador's characterization. As a 1943 circular from the Government of India's Publicity Office, titled *India and the Middle East*, admitted, "it is often pointed out that there is a prejudice against Indians in Middle Eastern countries and that the people of those countries do not want to hear about India. It would be useless to deny that such a prejudice has existed in the past and to a certain extent persists to-day."[66]

The High Commissioner in Palestine and the Ambassador in Iraq were both quick to express their enthusiasm for the proposals contained in the Cairo memorandum. However, they were less moved by the need to combat anti-Indian attitudes within their jurisdictions than they were concerned that Arabs might be "inspired" by—and liable to imitate—Indian anticolonial activism. As the High Commissioner of Palestine put it, "What Mohamedans of the Near East hear of India now is what enemy propaganda supplies namely stories of grave disaffection and attempts by their co-religionists and others to extract concessions while we are hard pressed. This naturally encourages the Arabs in the same way. . . . A corrective of the perspective is thus very desirable and should have a stabilising effect."[67]

Lampson and Davies's memorandum won support not only from officials in other parts of the Middle East but also from the Government of India's Department of External Affairs, which went so far as offering to match London's expenditures on the scheme up to £10,000, resulting in a proposed overall budget of £20,000 (equivalent to over £1 million adjusted for 2024 inflation). They proposed that the new organization be headquartered in Delhi, where it could easily coordinate with All-India Radio and existing Publicity Bureau efforts targeting Afghanistan and Persia. Underscoring their "full support" for the Cairo scheme, Simla noted that it "should go far both to add to India's own stature . . . and to define to the world in general the importance of India's war effort, now as in 1914–18, towards the defence and freedom of the Middle East."[68]

The timing of the Cairo memorandum coincided with the launch of a separate, better documented propaganda initiative orchestrated by Churchill to shape American public opinion about India. Whereas Lampson and Davies were keen to impress on Arab audiences the military strength and civilizational grandeur of the subcontinent, the campaign in the United States sought to undermine growing popular support for Indian independence. From their bureau in New York, British publicity depicted Indian nationalist leaders as ill-prepared for the responsibilities of statehood, emphasizing the "intricacies" of communal relations (which only the British understood) and the grave threat that independence would pose to the Allied war effort.[69] In short, the image of India being projected to Americans was of a house of cards that required Britain's steady hand lest it collapse into turmoil—dragging the Allies down with it. By contrast, the India to be pitched to Arab audiences was a solid and reliable powerhouse, invulnerable to attack and staunchly committed to the war effort.

A December 1941 newsreel perfectly embodied the image of the country that Cairo and the Government of India sought to project. Over live-action shots of turbaned sepoys carrying out martial drills in the shadow of the pyramids, the commentator praised their valor and solid constancy:

> Heroic and invaluable has been the fighting record of the Indian Army during its hundred and forty years of service under the Crown. In this war we have thrilled at the distinguished part played by the Indians in Egypt, Somaliland, Abyssinia, the Sudan, Eritrea. . . . No praise is too high for these fine men who are doing so much for the Empire; they rank among the staunchest in the world. . . . From every corner and province of India have come these gallant, sturdy warriors. We have every reason to be proud of these men, who are again helping so nobly in their *second* World War.[70]

The Government of India felt the need for an expanded Arabic-language campaign to promote this vision of the subcontinent was so urgent that they decided not to wait for its funding to be approved in London, instead telegramming the Indian Secretary: "We are prepared to defray the cost of any such measures ourselves, and do not think they should be delayed until the organisation to be created under Davies's scheme has been set up. At a later stage they could be absorbed."[71] Essentially from that moment in June 1941, the Government of India forged ahead with the production of films, newsreels, radio broadcasts, pamphlets, periodicals, and illustrated postcards in Arabic—without awaiting further instructions (or funds) from London.

UNITED PUBLICATIONS

The official charged with this campaign was Colonel Geoffery Wheeler, a linguist and intelligence agent who would go on to have a storied career, postwar, as a researcher and analyst of Central Asia. In the early 1940s, as head of the Publicity Office within the External Affairs Department of the Government of India, he undertook to produce foreign-language magazines, newsletters, pamphlets, and other printed material for the Middle East. His office alone produced over 300 tons of printed propaganda per year, contributing in no small measure to an acute shortage of paper on the subcontinent. By 1943, Wheeler had organized his titles under the label United Publications, with Arabic, Persian, English, and French titles catering to readerships in Egypt, Iraq, Palestine, Syria, Persia, the Arab Gulf, and Turkey. The United Publications moniker was intended to mask their origin as British government publicity: "Although there was never any intention of concealing the Government origin of any of the magazines, it was felt that the employment of an unofficial name would serve to prevent that natural feeling of irritation which is usually aroused in India when the Government is exposed as the originator of something undeniably good and useful."[72]

In a letter to the Middle East Section of the Ministry of Information, he elaborated on his "light touch" approach to wartime propaganda: "We find that the best mixture for our readers is rather small quantities of direct war propaganda diluted with cultural matter selected according to their particular tastes. This cultural matter should not, we consider, contain too much praise of British life and institutions."[73] This last line was a thinly veiled criticism of the material then being circulated by the Ministry of Information, some of which has been preserved in the archives. From these examples, it is clear that the Arabic propaganda produced in London was at pains to present Britain in a positive light[74]—something that Wheeler's office found tacky and possibly counterproductive.

The most popular magazine in Wheeler's stable was the illustrated monthly, *The Bugle*—published in French as *Le Clairon*, in Persian as *Shaipur*, and in Arabic as *al-Nafir*. Featuring eight pages in full color and at least five pages per issue "of special interest to women readers," demand for the *The Bugle* was estimated at "about 50% in excess of supply," and despite printing forty thousand copies a month, United Publications could not keep up with orders—particularly owing to the shortage of paper in India.[75] In 1942 the magazine began ramping up its "Indian content," until articles about India accounted for 25 percent of each issue. "Quite apart from this," wrote Wheeler in 1946, "the very fact of *The Bugle* originating from India has done much to raise the prestige of India in the eyes of the Middle East."[76]

Another periodical, *Al-Arab Weekly*, was acquired by United Publications on account of its established distribution network and readership in Arabia and the Persian Gulf. The title was then "remodeled" as a bimonthly illustrated journal: "Published in India, *Al Arab* endeavours to inform Arabic readers throughout the Middle East of India's ancient culture, of her modern achievements and of the part she is playing in the present war."[77]

Alongside these efforts, articles on India were distributed in existing publications. A regular newsletter about culture, society, and current affairs in India, *al-Mizan*, was distributed in Arabic, Persian, Turkish, French, and Russian. Shorts prepared by the Indian Film Board were dubbed into Arabic and Persian.[78] The extent of the Publicity Office's efforts to produce material in these languages was underscored by a 1943 progress report, which noted that the presses under contract to print Indian periodicals for the Middle East were wearing out their Arabic type pieces, and the government's Finance Department had had to advance them the funds to replace the machinery.[79] All of these endeavors, particularly *The Bugle* and *Al-Arab Weekly*, responded directly to the publicity agenda laid out by Davies and Lampson's Cairo memorandum. What is remarkable is that they were ultimately achieved entirely on the initiative—and on the dime—of the Government of India, without support or political oversight from London.

THE EAST ACCORDING TO THE NEW LEFT

Curiously, around the same moment in 1942 that Geoffery Wheeler began producing material about India in Arabic, the Cairo leftist review *al-Majalla al-Jadeeda* (The New Magazine) devoted a special issue to the people and politics of the subcontinent. At the time, Editor Salama Musa (author of one of the Arabic biographies of Gandhi that appeared in the wake of his 1931 voyage through the Suez Canal) was in the midst of transferring the review into new hands: Ramses Younane, among the leading lights of Art and Liberty, was to be the new man at the helm. It is therefore unsurprising to find members of the surrealist collective featured prominently among the contributors to the special issue, as well as other contemporaneous coverage of India in the pages of *al-Majalla al-Jadeeda*.[80]

It is worth appreciating the ways in which coverage of India in *al-Majalla al-Jadeeda* mirrored the pro-Indian propaganda first envisioned by Lampson and produced by Wheeler's office. According to Hala Halim, "the editorial line adopted in the special issue on India . . . combines the didactic aim of educating readers about that country with the promotion of Indian socialism."[81] The volume contained primers on the principal actors in what the review called the "Indian Drama," including Nehru, Jinnah, and Sir Stafford Cripps. Another article, "Ma Hiya al-Hind?" (What is India?) sought to inform Arabic audiences about Indian geography, culture, and politics. On a superficial level, at least, these articles would not have seemed out of place in any of Wheeler's publications. Of course in terms of editorial line, there was a significant divergence between the two outlets.

A twin set of articles in the special issue contrasted "Mashakil al-Hind al-Haqqa," the "real" problems of India, with "al-Mashakil al-Hindiyya al-Za'ifa," the "invented" problems of India, by which was meant intercommunal strife. Together, these articles argued that India's true difficulties were economic, political, and rooted in British colonialism, while tensions between Hindus and Muslims were "contrived"—presumably by the British—"for a covert purpose." This dovetailed neatly with the position of Nehru, whom *al-Majalla al-Jadeeda* championed as the leader of India's future.[82] India's Muslim League politicians would have strenuously disagreed with the analysis, of course; but then they had long struggled to find much sympathy for their point of view in Cairo.

In another issue of the magazine, Art and Liberty's Georges Henein wrote an admiring biography of Nehru, whose socialism, secularism, and pragmatic modernity were championed by the editors of *al-Majalla al-Jadeeda*.[83] In the special issue, Nehru was presented in flattering contrast to the traditionalism and religious idealism of an older generation of Indian leaders, including Iqbal, Tagore, and Gandhi. The latter, readers of the review were told, possessed "an exceedingly mystical quality which pervades [their] reformist opinions and humanist principles . . . to the extent that at times it may be construed as a sort of sterile imagination."[84]

Another article by Henein, "Bayn al-Wataniyya wa al-Duwaliyya" (Between nationalism and internationalism), outlined the author's vision for the ideal form of governance in the postwar world and highlights India as a model for "transforming nationalist sentiment into an instrument for international solidarity." Henein contrasted this with the narrower forms of nationalism that Art and Liberty had always rejected. According to the Egyptian surrealist, India's nationalism should proceed in keeping with its leading role "within an Eastern world brought together by solidarity, guarded by Turkey to the right and China to the left."[85]

In the pages of the 1942 Cairo review, we see the poetic East of the 1920s and early 1930s—that "ocean of idealism" embraced by figures like Gandhi, Tagore, and Ahmad Shawqi—eclipsed by the harder edged materialism of a younger anticolonial generation. Yet this new terrain was still, in Henein's articulation, characterized as an expansive East, broader and more inclusive than the boundaries of any one religion, language, or ethnicity. In this vision of the postwar order, national liberation would have the effect of empowering former colonies and subjugated peoples through closer cooperation than ever before, to end oppressive systems and rectify economic inequalities, ushering in a new era of true internationalism. This vision of the East was championed by the Cairo surrealists of Art and Liberty, the secular left editors and readership of *al-Majalla al-Jadeeda*, and progressive and socialist figures in India, of whom Jawaharlal Nehru remained the most paradigmatic.

This projection of a socialist East stood in partial overlap with its liberal cosmopolitan doppelganger, produced for Arab, Turkish, and Persian consumption by the Government of India. The image grows more complex placed alongside the Eastern imaginary shared by the anticolonial militants clustered in Berlin. Then there is Muhammad Ali Jinnah's Pakistan demand, which coopted the vocabulary of nationalism to make claims that appeared to many—both at the time and since—as echoing 1920s visions of Muslim cosmopolitanism. By the early 1940s, fragments of this kaleidoscopic East were not only moving further and further away from one other, they were also beginning to take on sharply divergent lives of their own.

TEN

No Way Back

Do or die.[1]
—GANDHI'S MANTRA FOR THE
QUIT INDIA CAMPAIGN, 1942

CATASTROPHE, AND REFUGEES

In February 1941 General Erwin Rommel took command of the German army in North Africa, signaling the onset of a new and—for the Allies—terrifying chapter in the Desert War. Within three weeks of his first offensive action in March, Rommel had pushed his adversaries 650 kilometers back, from El Agheila in Libya to the Egyptian border. Establishing air superiority from their bases in Libya and Sicily, the Luftwaffe and Regia Aeronautica ruled the skies, attacking British shipping and bombarding Malta relentlessly.[2]

Rommel's arrival in the Western Desert was particularly ill-timed for the Allies, as a significant portion of their troops had just been recalled from forward positions in Libya and sent to southeastern Europe to stave off the Axis advance there. By the middle of April, Allied positions on both sides of the Mediterranean were collapsing. Rommel seized as-Saloum, inside the Egyptian frontier; Yugoslavia surrendered to the Nazis; and the Greek government was evacuated from Athens in the teeth of the German advance.

They were not the only ones fleeing. As mainland Greece's defenses were overrun, many people sought to escape by the only route still open to them: the sea. In a Mediterranean sequel to Dunkirk, tugboats, cargo vessels, small steamers, and traditional fishing boats were all pressed into service as a makeshift evacuation fleet.³ They sailed south toward North Africa.

The first of the refugees began to arrive on the shores of Egypt in late April; they numbered at least five thousand.⁴ Ultimately tens of thousands of Europeans would find shelter in refugee camps across the Middle East and North Africa.⁵ Initially there was nowhere to put them other than in tents on the beaches, as most schools were already in use as hospitals or internment facilities for German and Italian citizens. British and Egyptian authorities were forced to requisition brothels to house the newcomers.

Adding to the spectacle of hungry and bedraggled Europeans, the refugees were joined at the end of May by the eighteen thousand survivors of the Allies' disastrous last stand on Crete (the remaining twelve thousand were taken prisoner). They were exhausted and traumatized by their ordeal, but there was no time for recuperation. A major offensive was scheduled for July in a desperate bid to force Rommel back across the Western Desert. The operation, code-named Battle Axe, was a near total defeat with heavy British casualties. By December, with Rommel's forces fanning out across the desert from Tunisia to the Egyptian border, the siege of Malta ongoing, and all of Europe under Axis occupation, the walls appeared to be closing in on Britain's position in Egypt.

In addition to the soldiers and refugees arriving in Alexandria, there were of course other Europeans making their way across the Mediterranean in rickety, overcrowded boats—the "illegals." Irrespective of the war, Britain continued to enforce the restrictions on Jewish immigration contained in the 1939 White Paper. Thus on the dark, silent beaches of Palestine, agents of the Yishuv would wait for the rhythmic flashes of light that signaled the approach of clandestine ships. Those lucky enough to escape from Europe, survive the perilous sea crossing, and elude the British coast guard were called the *maapilim*: the ones who had ascended. This illicit "alternative immigration" accounted for half of all new arrivals to Mandate Palestine between 1939 and 1944.⁶ Their numbers were infinitesimally small compared to the scale of need for safe haven.

Across the occupied continent of Europe, the sinews of mass deportation now snaked from the Atlantic coast to the Black Sea, conveying into the maw of the camps millions of Jews, Roma, Slavs, communists, queers—everyone deemed "defective" or "subhuman." The Final Solution began to take shape in 1941 in Eastern Europe, where the Nazis worked to colonize and depopulate the lands they conquered from the retreating Soviet army (what Hitler envisioned as a blitzkrieg rendition of America's westward expansion). Gas chambers had first been used inside Germany to euthanize the disabled, in a connected effort to cleanse the national bloodlines. Gradually the urgency of territorial conquest, the logic of racial liquidation, and the regime's many technological innovations congealed into a transnational apparatus of genocide.[7] The broad contours of these horrors were becoming discernible overseas, though accurate statistics and verifiable information were initially elusive. Still, Allied countries including Britain and the United States continued to severely restrict entry to desperate Jewish refugees. In the words of Louise London, "the problem of what to do with the Jews took precedence over saving them, whether from Nazi persecution or mass murder."[8]

It was at this moment in early 1942—with the Allies on their knees in North Africa, the whole of Europe under occupation, and the Holocaust accelerating—that Japan attacked Pearl Harbor and launched its lightning invasion of Southeast Asia. Within twenty-four hours of the attack on the American fleet in Hawaii, Japan had also invaded Thailand and British Malaya and begun aerial bombardments of Hong Kong, the Philippines, Shanghai, Singapore, Guam, and the Wake Islands. Within a week, Japanese soldiers were in Burma, on British India's northeastern frontier.

The fall of Singapore on 15 February 1942 was the largest surrender in British military history. Eighty thousand Allied troops—mostly Indian, Australian, and British servicemen—were taken prisoner. Another fifty thousand were captured in British Malaya. As with Pearl Harbor, the speed and devastation of the Japanese advance came as a bolt from the blue. Once again the very nature of the war had been utterly transformed, seemingly overnight.

Within forty-eight hours of the fall of Singapore, the order had been given to evacuate Rangoon, as Japanese forces continued their relentless drive through Burma toward the Indian frontier. The Desert War and ongoing campaigns in the Eastern Mediterranean and Persian Gulf were to some degree responsible for the failure of British defenses in Burma, as many of the Indian Army units that had stayed at home had been stripped of their best men and officers, shipped off to Cairo and Basra. The remaining troops were pared down and inexperienced.[9]

It was among the darkest hours in the history of the British Empire, in which India had become the sole bastion left standing on the Eurasian continent, as George Orwell acknowledged in an article published that February: "With the Japanese army in the Indian Ocean and the German armies in the Middle East, India becomes the centre of the war—it is hardly an exaggeration to say, the centre of the world. For a long time to come, possibly for years, it may have to act as a supply base from which men and munitions can be poured out in two directions, East and West."[10]

Even this analysis was, in a way, optimistic, assuming as it did that India would hold. After the fall of Singapore, Subhas Chandra Bose took to the airwaves on Azad Hind Radio to announce the impending collapse of "Anglo-American imperialism" and the coming liberation of India at the hands of Germany, Italy, and Japan.[11] Among those who did not fancy the Axis as liberators, there were still many who thought he was probably right.

In the north of India, hundreds of thousands of refugees now began arriving from Burma. They were Indian and European residents and retreating Allied soldiers, many at the end of a 900-mile overland journey from Rangoon, on foot, through jungle and mountainous terrain. Those who managed to survive arrived in India exhausted and emaciated from the treacherous journey, made nightmarish by the arrival of the monsoon in May.

Wealthier residents of Burma were, in some cases, able to purchase a more comfortable journey for themselves and their families, either by sea or airplane. Yet as the influx of refugees into India soared—ultimately over five hundred thousand would arrive—they brought with them stories of something more disturbing: a two-tiered evacuation policy where Europeans and Anglo-Indians were systematically prioritized, where police would allow some through but block the path to others. As one Indian escapee from Rangoon later recounted, his father had managed to purchase tickets for a steamer headed to Madras, as the Japanese approached the outskirts of the city. But on the assigned date, they were refused permission to board: "The then British government thought that only the lives of the British and Anglo-Indians were worth saving and allowed only them to board the steamer. The rest of us were thrown out to fend for ourselves." These reports were confirmed by other observers, including an American consular official in Rangoon, causing outrage in India.

Yasmin Khan argues convincingly for the overwhelming importance of the Burmese refugee crisis in contributing to a loss of faith in the British Raj among the Indian public. It confirmed, in the eyes of many, that the empire was coming apart at the seams and undermined any remaining sense of legitimacy or trustworthiness it could claim to possess.[12]

Gandhi in particular was appalled by the suffering of the refugees and enraged by their treatment at the hands of the authorities—who, it was revealed, even paid for a higher rate of care for non-Indians in displaced persons camps: "Hundreds, if not thousands, on their way from Burma perished without food or drink, and the wretched discrimination stared even these miserable people in the face. One route for the whites, another for the blacks! Provision of food and shelter for the whites, none for the blacks! And discrimination even on their arrival in India! ... India is being ground down to dust and humiliated. ... And so one fine morning I came to the decision to make this honest demand: for Heaven's sake leave India alone."[13] It was the straw that finally broken the camel's back. Out of the Burmese refugee crisis and discrimination scandal, Quit India was born.

GLOVES OFF

That same spring, on the opposite side of the globe, Zionist leaders convened an "Extraordinary Conference" at the Biltmore Hotel in New York City. The proceedings were grim and urgent. In Palestine, the Irgun, Lehi, and Hagana militias had already turned their weapons on the British—fed up with the White Paper's continuing restrictions on Jewish immigration while millions in Europe faced their deaths. More information about the horrors of the camps had begun to penetrate beyond Europe, but the United States and Britain refused to revise their policies on immigration or sanction the establishment of a formal Jewish fighting force. Overwhelmed with frustration, grief, and anger, even Jews who had long been skeptical of the Zionist project increasingly concluded that the extremists had been right all along: their community stood alone against the world. From here on out, it would have to build the capacity to defend itself.

It was at Biltmore that the youthful militant David Ben Gurion emerged victorious over the aging Chaim Weizmann, and a new, more radical policy was adopted. "Although it had once been possible for Zionists to debate the definition of the Jewish national home they sought to construct," notes Mark Tessler, by 1942 a powerful consensus had emerged that "this could mean nothing other than a fully sovereign Jewish state." The Biltmore Program committed the Zionist movement to an independent Jewish nation in the whole territory of Mandate Palestine: "Then and only then," its delegates affirmed, "will the age-old wrong to the Jewish people be righted."[14] The Biltmore Program thus crystallized the Zionist reconfiguration of Palestine as a form of reparation, in payment of which Europe could be redeemed for not only the present horrors of Nazism but many centuries of antisemitic persecution. The Biltmore Program did not mention the Palestinians. Having always been an inconvenience to Zionism, in the context of the Holocaust, they became irrelevant—just one more obstacle to overcome.

As 1942 progressed, the news only got worse for Britain. By the middle of the year, Allied H.Q. in Cairo was planning for the full-scale removal of its press and publicity operations to India as part of a larger anticipated evacuation. The specter of another Singapore haunted officials in the Department of Information and Broadcasting at Delhi, who offered the following advice to their colleagues in the Middle East: "If there is serious prospect of evacuation of Cairo question of immediate removal of Middle East equipment to India should receive most urgent attention. Experience at Singapore has taught that when emergency actually arises, it is too late to act."[15]

At one point the risk to Cairo was deemed imminent enough that thousands of sensitive documents were burned in the courtyard of the British embassy; days later Cairo's street vendors were still selling peanuts wrapped in half-charred state secrets.[16]

A young Edward Said and his family were among those streaming out of the Egyptian capital as the Germans closed in. He recalled his father's black Plymouth, its headlights blued out, pulling over again and again as convoys of British tanks and personnel carriers trundled in the opposite direction: "We made the long drive in complete silence right through the night. My father negotiated the unmarked Sinai roads after having crossed the Suez Canal without ceremony or fuss at the Qantara bridge; the customs post there was deserted." They made the long, harrowing night drive into Palestine in convoy with a Jewish Egyptian who rode in Said's father's tracks, "convinced he was running for his life."[17]

As Rommel crushed Britain's offensive efforts in the Western Desert and Singapore's defenses collapsed, Lampson faced mounting instances of pro-Axis resistance and anti-British subterfuge emanating from King Faruq and his closest allies, notably Ali Maher.

Whereas throughout the interwar years the palace and the British had shared an authoritarian impulse to reign in the more liberal parliament, the signature of the Anglo-Egyptian Treaty and the coming of war had together altered the calculus of Egypt's balance of power. Britain was obliged by the treaty to work with and through parliament to a greater degree, while liberal nationalists—including the Wafd and many independents—saw in Nazi Germany, its fascist allies, and their local admirers a more sinister threat than British imperialism. With the war going badly and the palace leaning ever further into the enemy camp, the Wafd began to appear, in British eyes, like a strong local "partner" whose authentic support could hold the country onside.

At the end of January 1942, Ali Maher attempted to stoke anti-British demonstrations, in concert with his long-term ally Sheikh Maraghi. Within twenty-four hours, before the riots could gather any momentum, Prime Minister Hussein Sirri resigned. On his way out, he advised the British Ambassador bluntly to "send for the Wafd."[18] Lampson told him it "was an instance of great minds thinking alike, for before coming to see him I had come to precisely the same conclusion."[19]

Predictably, Faruq was opposed to the return of the Wafd and sought to preempt the British embassy by appointing an interim government of his own choosing. Lampson rejected this solution as too easy for the palace to manipulate. He insisted that Nahas be consulted by Faruq on the nature of the government to be formed and set a time limit within which this meeting should take place. Nahas, for his part, communicated to the embassy his eagerness to come to an understanding with the British and against the palace. As he professed, "the spirit of the Treaty meant mutual cooperation on both sides in every sense. If Hussein Sirry had been of use to us [the British], Nahas would be of even more use. If Nahas had worked well with us in peacetime he would work tenfold as well in war time. But he must have a free hand especially with the Palace. What he wanted was real democracy and real cooperation with us, and the King stood against both. If we backed him with the King he would see it through."[20]

Here in stark language was a full articulation of the reversal in the Wafd's priorities. Nahas was impatient with his party's long exile from government, alarmed at the advance of fascism both on the battlefield and in the streets of Cairo, and above all suspicious of what he perceived as the King's authoritarian tendencies. Together these factors convinced him that backing Great Britain, and even coming to power under the cover of a British ultimatum, was justifiable—perhaps even necessary—to protect Egypt's liberal democracy.

The total novelty of the situation from both Lampson's and Nahas's perspectives is attested by the frequent instances of both parties seeking verification and reassurance from one another, in the lead-up to Lampson's fateful meeting with Faruq. In one interview the day before the British ultimatum expired, Lampson told Nahas's close ally and advisor, Amin Osman, that he "hoped there was no question of Nahas wriggling out?—Amin said none whatever. Nahas had been asking the same question about us and Amin had assured him that we were in grim earnest."[21] The next day, mere hours before he was scheduled to leave for the palace, Lampson took Osman aside in an empty room. "Was I still safe in relying completely on Nahas if I carried on? Amin said he would bet his bottom dollar on Nahas being firm."[22]

What then transpired is among the better-known episodes of World War II in Egypt. Having consulted with the Service Chiefs in Cairo and the Foreign Office, Lampson instructed his staff to prepare contingencies for a military standoff with the Egyptian monarch. Faruq's abdication letter was drafted by, in Lampson's estimation, the ideal man for the job: Walter Monckton, the recently arrived Director of Propaganda and Information Services, who had been advisor to Edward VIII in 1936 and crafted his renunciation of the British throne.[23] The ultimatum to Faruq having expired, Lampson and General Oliver Stone made the short drive from the embassy to Abdin Palace, accompanied by an escort of

British officer cadets and armored vehicles. Approximately six hundred British troops surrounded Midan Abdin and sealed off all routes in and out of the palace.

THE KING AND I

In Lampson's detailed (and at times romantic) account of his nocturnal audience with the King of Egypt, he refers several times to the presence of British tanks outside the palace. Ian Weston Smith, an officer of the Scots Guard who participated in the action that evening, has disputed this claim, suggesting that Lampson mistook armored cars for tanks.[24] This being as it may, Lampson's excitement caused him to imagine himself and the scene around him in epic terms, as is clear from the uncharacteristic lyricism of his report to the Foreign Office: "I arrived at the Palace accompanied by General Stone and an impressive array of specially picked stalwart military officers armed to the teeth. On the way we passed through lines of military transport looming up through the darkened streets. . . . Whilst we waited upstairs I could hear the rumble of tanks and armoured cars taking up their positions round the Palace. . . . This caused no little stir and added to the growing anticipation of coming events."

Entering the King's room, Lampson found Faruq still attempting to stall over the British ultimatum regarding Nahas. Lampson interrupted and read him "with full emphasis and increasing anger" a prepared statement, which concluded, "Having failed to secure a Coalition Government, Your Majesty has refused to entrust the Government to the leader of the political party which, by commanding the general support of the country, is thus alone in a position to ensure the continued execution of the Treaty in the spirit of friendship in which it was conceived. Such recklessness and irresponsibility on the part of the Sovereign endanger the security of Egypt and of the Allied Forces. They make it clear that Your Majesty is no longer fit to occupy the Throne."

Lampson then served the King with the instrument of abdication, which had been scribbled out by hand on a piece of British embassy stationary. As an afterthought, the letterhead had been torn off.[25] Lampson, who clearly relished his formulation, told Faruq "that he must sign it at once or I should have something else and more unpleasant with which to confront him."[26]

At this point the Royal Chamberlain, Ahmed Hassanein Pasha, who had been with Faruq when the British "visitors" were announced and had remained in the room throughout the proceedings, intervened. Hassanein had, at one time, been the monarch's tutor, and he spoke to him now, briefly and urgently, in Arabic. While Lampson could not understand what was said, its effect was immediately apparent: "After a tense pause King Farouk, who was by this time completely cowed, looked up and asked almost pathetically and with none of his previous bravado if I would not give him one more chance."[27]

As is apparent from his diary, Lampson was terribly disappointed by this folding of the King's hand. He had been eager to see the thing through; a ship was on standby to whisk Faruq to the Seychelles, and for days afterward the Ambassador would ruminate on this turning point in the interview, when he might have, in his own evocative phrasing, "turf[ed] the boy out"[28] once and for all. But at dinner earlier that evening, Lampson had been forced to agree with the Minister of State, Oliver Lyttleton, that if Faruq was finally willing to concede the appointment of a Wafd government, it would be difficult to insist on his removal. Thus Lampson found himself constrained to withdraw the abdication letter and accept the King's undertaking to call on Nahas immediately to form a government.

As he turned to leave, thus having been denied his ultimate satisfaction, Lampson comforted himself with the impressiveness of the British martial display: the entire palace was "filled with military officers . . . grim armed British soldiers in their steel helmets with their rifles and Tommy guns at the ready. . . . As we drove out of the Courtyard we passed dim shapes of tanks and armoured cars, drawn up and ready for action."[29]

After months of nothing but bad news from the front, the projected strength and competence of these men and their machines appear to have acted as a soothing balm on the diplomat's frayed nerves. Abdin was a deeply personal event—not only for Faruq, whose humiliation would poison the rest of his reign, and not just for the Egyptian people, whose shock and resentment would prove of far greater consequence. It was also personal for Lampson, who briefly glimpsed himself within reach of a momentous role in history—the protagonist in a great drama. After all, as he recorded in his diary that night, "it doesn't often come one's way to be pushing a Monarch off the Throne."[30]

Returning to the embassy, the spell was broken by a phone call from Hassanein: Might the troops now be called off, to allow Nahas's car to reach the palace . . . ?

THE AFTERMATH

Reactions to Lampson's actions within the British administration were intensely mixed. Many shared the Ambassador's sense of breathlessness. Duff Cooper recalled that he and his wife, who were staying with the Lampsons, "found most of the principal actors in the hall of the Embassy discussing the evening as people discuss the first night of the play, when nobody is sure whether it has been a success or a failure."[31] Mrs. Cooper remarked that later in the evening Lampson emerged from his den "arm in arm with Nahas Pasha, both grinning themselves in two."[32] Surely this was the apotheosis of the collaborative moment ushered in by the Anglo-Egyptian Treaty in 1936; contained within it was the poison that would spell ruin for the Wafd, to say nothing of the British presence in Egypt.

Among the greatest miscalculations appears to have been the belief, if not on the part of Lampson then certainly on the part of Nahas, that the proceedings of the evening could remain a secret—or at least, be somehow delinked from his own accession to the premiership. Within days, however, "it was being generally said that Nahas had come in supported by British bayonets."[33] This was, of course, perfectly true and thus difficult to refute, although the Wafd and the embassy certainly tried. As word leaked out, Egyptians reacted with shock, dismay—and anger. In his memoirs, one prominent Egyptian trade unionist recalled the slow trickle of rumors and reports that first alerted the Egyptian people to the compromised nature of Nahas's new government: "When the incident of February 4, 1942 occurred we didn't know that it was the English who returned al-Nahas and we went out in demonstrations to support al-Nahas Pasha. Afterwards we learned that what happened was an act of aggression against us and the King. Not the corrupt King, the King simply as a symbol of Egypt."[34]

Muhammad Neguib, later a member of the Free Officers and the first President of postrevolutionary Egypt, attempted to resign from his post as lieutenant colonel in the Egyptian Army in 1942, so humiliated was he by its failure to defend the King against this naked threat of British force. From where his unit was stationed in the Sudan, another soldier, Gamal Abdel Nasser, wrote, "Until now the officers only talked of how to enjoy themselves; now they are speaking of sacrificing their lives for their honor. . . . This event—this blow, has put life into some. It has taught them there is something called dignity which has to be defended."[35]

Abdin was the loudest shot never fired in Cairo. While Faruq remained on the throne and Nahas returned to power, both were forever tainted by that night: the King for his cowardice in caving to British demands and the leader of the Wafd for his complicity in the nation's humiliation. When the Free Officers seized control of the country in 1952, they appointed as their Prime Minister Ali Maher—the royal favorite whose "evil influence" on the King had precipitated the abdication crisis. As Charles Tripp notes, in 1942 Maher "went down as a martyr in the nationalist myth he had sought to exploit, leaving the field clear

FIGURE 17   Miles Lampson and Mustafa al-Nahas "grinning themselves in two." Cairo, 1936.
ASSOCIATED PRESS / ALAMY

for those who saw in the events of February 1942 justification for the belief that the political method endorsed by Ali Maher [i.e., authoritarian rule] represented the only valid course if Egypt's national aspirations were finally to be realised."[36]

However, the Egyptian Revolution of 1952 was still ten years away. In the more immediate future, the Wafd had once again found its way back into office after a long political exile.

EASTERN ECHOES

In the Wafd administration of 1942–44, we glimpse for the first time the influence of Nehru and the INC on the Wafd as the governing part of Egypt. This is particularly evident in two shifts in policy: one in the realm of external affairs and the other in the realm of labor relations.

In *Redefining the Egyptian Nation*, Israel Gershoni and James Jankowski note the important "international repercussions of the Wafdist ministry of 1942–1944," for during its brief wartime tenure in office, "Egypt's leading political party committed the country to an institutionalized role in the political life of the surrounding Arab world"—ultimately resulting in the founding of the Arab League under Egyptian auspices, with Cairo as its headquarters. They suggest that this pivot outward—depicted as a break with the insular, territorial nationalist stance of the 1920s and 1930s—was a spontaneous reaction to the difficult new domestic political situation the Wafd inherited in 1942.[37]

They cite, as an example of this "new turn" in the Wafd's orientation, a speech by Nahas on 13 November 1942 when he evoked "the need for 'Arab and Eastern' countries to band together to form 'a strong and cohesive block' in the postwar world." Another benchmark took place one year later, in November 1943, when the Wafd hosted a party conference for the first time since 1935, the tone of which was overtly internationalist and pan-Arab.[38]

By now it is hopefully apparent that this outward-facing orientation, which placed Egypt in a leading role within an "Arab and Eastern" community of nations, was by no means a new idea for Nahas and his colleagues in 1942. The plans Nahas had divulged to Nehru for a Wafd Party conference in November 1938 already articulated the "wider Oriental stamp over and above its local character" that he intended it to have, with invitations issued to representatives from India, Palestine, and other "oppressed people of the Near East."[39] The 1938 conference was banned by Faruq's allies in government, but in this context the overtly internationalist, pan-Arab tone of the 1943 meeting was not a new departure for Nahas; rather, it was the realization of a long-cherished dream that had been inspired, in no small part, by his burgeoning friendship with Nehru.

The second notable shift in Wafd policy in 1942 was its promotion of labor legislation, and in particular the legalization of trade unions. Zachary Lockman and Joel Beinin ascribe this shift to changes in British attitudes to labor rights over the course of the war: "By the middle of the war . . . British colonial policy makers began to encourage the enactment of labor legislation, including the legalisation of trade unions. Since Egypt was not formally a British colony, such a measure could not be unilaterally undertaken there. Although there is no direct evidence available indicating a preponderant British role in the formulation and development of the Egyptian government's labor policy during World War II, there can be no doubt that the Wafd's approach to this question was substantively influenced by the new British attitude toward colonial labor movements."[40] This is undoubtedly part of the explanation, but Jawaharlal Nehru may also be cited as an influence, given his long interview with the leadership of the Wafd in 1938, touching on precisely this issue. At that meeting, he presented Congress as an example of a nationalist movement based on strong ties with workers and rural peasantry, zeroing in on the illegality of trade unions specifically and the Wafd's lack of mass popular organization more broadly as its greatest weakness.[41]

In his subsequent correspondence with Nahas, Nehru sought to address this shortcoming, which he perceived as emanating from the Wafd's political backwardness and lack of international exposure. He encouraged Nahas toward international conferences and organized people's movements, like the socialist-leaning Rassemblement Universel pour la Paix.[42] And of course, the 1939 labor strike that had called public attention to the issue of trade union legalization in Egypt also took its cues from the methods of Gandhian satyagraha. Thus we can perceive the echoes of Indian-Egyptian ties in the policies of the wartime Wafd ministry well after the records of direct interaction between the two movements go cold.

A BELATED GESTURE

1942 was also a year of uncommon significance for the national movement in India. The opening of the war in the Pacific and the relentless advance of the Japanese; the collapse of British defenses in Hong Kong, Malaya, Burma, and above all Singapore; and the Burmese refugee crisis, with its attendant revelations of systematic discrimination, together shook the foundations of British authority in India to their core. In this context, Churchill—the infamous diehard—found himself backed into a corner by Indian petitions, parliamentary questions, and British public opinion. In March, he announced that a political mission headed by Sir Stafford Cripps, the Lord Privy Seal, was to travel to India and consult with national leaders, with the aim of drafting a declaration on future British policy. The offer was said to "reiterate" (although it was in fact a very new formulation) the British government's commitment to Dominion status for India "as soon as possible after the war."[43] It had finally been conceded in London that—

with disaster bearing down from all directions—something had to be conceded to Indian demands. Leo Amery, the Secretary of State, compared it to being forced into a proposal for financial reasons.[44]

Cripps was the consummate diplomat: a well-traveled and thoughtful man whose political star was on the ascendant (he had recently been made Leader of the House of Commons). By most accounts he was enthusiastic and genuine in pursuit of his aim, but he lacked support from either Churchill, who hoped the mission would fail, or Linlithgow, who remained studiously aloof from its proceedings. Both Congress and the Muslim League also hedged; Nehru—whose passionate commitment to the struggles both for independence and against fascism caused him no end of agony during these years—expressed his earnest desire to work with Cripps and, in private, his conviction that it was far too late for such a compromise.[45]

Cripps came to India armed with a proposal that transferred most ministerial portfolios, including Home and Finance, into Indian hands. The sole exception was responsibility for Defense. This was to remain under British control. Negotiations on this point were inconclusive; the details could not be agreed. Finally Congress leadership stated publicly that they did not believe Britain was, in fact, willing to countenance the reality of an Indian national government. Particularly in the context of 1942, they had a point, for as Yasmin Khan observes, "the legal, economic, and social structure of the Raj was at that moment completely dominated and geared to defence"; indeed, "under the Defence of India Act, defence and power had become synonymous."[46] Gandhi described the proposal as a "post-dated check," leaving others to reflect on the state of Britain's credit.

The mission's collapse would prove to be a momentous turning point both for British-Indian wartime relations, and for Indian domestic and intercommunal politics. They signaled the death of the last vestiges of goodwill between the imperial state and Indian nationalists. His "forced proposal" refused, Amery breathed a deep sigh of relief: "We can now go ahead with the war with a clear conscience."[47] There would be no further conciliatory gestures to local sensitivities. Years of progressive devolution in India were swept aside in favor of more straightforward, extractive colonial praxis. In the face of the simultaneous Japanese and German advances, the subcontinent was to be squeezed for all she was worth in the name of defending the empire. Any further voices of dissent were to be crushed.

Nationalist positions also hardened. The obvious lack of buy-in to the Cripps Mission on the part of key players like Churchill, Amery, and Linlithgow made the entire process seem like a publicity stunt that no one had intended to see through. And indeed, as Churchill wrote Cripps in a consolatory note upon his departure from India, "the effect of our proposals has been most beneficial in the United States and in large circles here"—perhaps the mission had been a success, after all.[48] On 14 July, after long and agonized debate, the Congress Working Committee hammered out a resolution calling for a voluntary British withdrawal and complete independence for India, and acknowledging Gandhi's leadership of a nonviolent mass movement toward that end. The resolution was slated for adoption the following month, at the All-India Congress meeting in Bombay. At that meeting, on 7 August, the Quit India Movement was formally launched.

In his speech Gandhi was at pains to stress that he did not wish to undermine the war effort. He made a special appeal to the foreign reporters covering his momentous pronouncement: "I do not want them [the Allies] to accept nonviolence and disarm today. There is a fundamental difference between Fascism and even this imperialism which I am fighting. . . . Think what difference it would make if India was to participate as a free ally [in the war]. That freedom, if it is to come, must come today."[49]

Much like Nahas and in stark contrast to his young rival Bose, Gandhi was under no illusions that an Axis victory could liberate India. Yet he rejected the logic of acquiescence to British rule as the price of fighting fascism. In his determination to defeat both colonialism in India and fascism in the world he was prepared to concede even his dearest moral principle: nonviolence. "Free India," he told the British and American press, "that we may together defeat fascism as equals." "For him this was an astonishing change," remarked Nehru in 1946, "involving suffering of the mind and pain of the spirit": "In the conflict between that principle of non-violence which had become his very life-blood and meaning of existence, and India's freedom which was a dominating and consuming passion for him, the scales inclined towards the latter. That did not mean, of course, that he weakened in his faith in non-violence. But it did mean that he was prepared to agree to the Congress not applying it in this war. The practical statesman took precedence over the uncompromising prophet."[50]

This monumental concession went unacknowledged, perhaps even unrecognized, by the British. Two days later, on the morning of 9 August, police and plainclothes intelligence officers knocked on doors across the length and breadth of the country. Members of the Congress Working Committee were arrested; trains had been requisitioned to transport them to prison, where they would remain for the duration of the war. One detainee described boarding his assigned train to find Nehru and the rest of the Congress high command in the dining car, ordering breakfast.[51]

As word of the arrests spread, India's masses took to the streets. They were led by the youth—students, urban workers, the sons and daughters of elite households, villagers. Cut off from the Congress's older, more statesmanlike leadership and Gandhi's strictly nonviolent influence, these young people assumed the mantle of the popular movement and shaped Quit India according to their own ethics and beliefs. Swiftly descending into largescale violence and destruction of infrastructure, in some places the movement approached wholesale insurrection.[52]

"I am engaged here in meeting by far the most serious rebellion since the repression of the 1857 uprising," Linlithgow telegraphed Churchill (the phantoms of an earlier era breathing down his neck), "the gravity and extent of which we have so far concealed from the world for reasons of military security." In the first four days after Gandhi's arrest, the police killed thirty-three people. They were the first of thousands, as Britain brought the full weight of the wartime security apparatus—including fighter planes, gas, and mortars—to bear on the country's rebellious youth.[53]

The imprisonment of Congress leaders in August 1942 also removed the final hurdle to Jinnah's political ascendancy. Since unveiling the demand for Pakistan in 1940, he had been consolidating his position within Muslim political circles, silencing rivals, and gaining support among northern tribesmen and university students alike. His promotion as the government's principal Muslim interlocutor by officials and particularly Churchill (who relished in the growing acrimony between India's Muslims and Hindus) further burnished his reputation. Above all, however, it was the silencing of Congress leadership in 1942 that enabled the meteoric rise of other, more hardline voices—notably the militant nationalist Bose and the Muslim nationalist Jinnah.[54]

As in Egypt, the breakdown of diplomacy and reversion to "hard" imperial power had been occasioned by the British perception of existential threat; unlike in Egypt, the Congress leadership chose exile over capitulation. Their imprisonment sparked a national uprising, over which, the British authorities soon discovered, Congress was prevented from exercising its trademark moderating influence. Across the subcontinent, protesters went for broke, torching government buildings, sabotaging rail networks, and destroying communications infrastructure. Subhas Chandra Bose's voice blared across Indian radio waves, and communal tensions rose steadily, stoked by the rising profile of the Muslim League and the demand for Pakistan. All went uncontested by Gandhi, Nehru, and their imprisoned comrades.

In Egypt, the false start of Abdin resulted in no immediate eruption; the people's bitterness and resentment would simmer beneath the surface for a decade before boiling over in July 1952. Yet as elsewhere, by the time Egypt's youth were confronting the British in the streets, the traditional forces of nationalism—the aging liberals of the Wafd—were in no position to contain their revolutionary zeal. The fragments of a once expansive East had become mass movements of their own.

EPILOGUE

Midnight in Delhi

Standing on this watershed which divides two epochs of human history and endeavor, we can look back at our long past and look forward to the future that is taking shape before our eyes.... When the history of our present time is written, this event may well stand out as a landmark which divides the past of Asia from the future. And because we are participating in this making of history something of the greatness of historic events comes to us all.[1]

—JAWAHARLAL NEHRU'S INAUGURAL ADDRESS TO
THE ASIAN RELATIONS CONFERENCE, 23 MARCH 1947

Everywhere [partition] has left an unending trail of strife, violence [and] despair, as in Ireland, Palestine ... the entire region is caught in the coils of a vicious ghost, from which it is never able to extricate itself.[2]

—KAMALADEVI CHATTOPADHYAY, WRITING IN 1986

The arrival of delegates to Purana Qila, the Old Fort in Delhi, was a suitably grand occasion. Thousands of Indian and foreign participants, members of the press and international observers, made their way up the ramparts to the Bada Darwaza gate, alongside accredited delegates from over thirty countries.[3] The immense turrets and red brick facade of the fortress—witness to five centuries of Delhi's storied past—dwarfed them all. Even as they gathered beneath the great tents erected in the courtyard (complete with wicker-back chairs and overhead fans), history was on the march. In her opening address as Conference President, Sarojini Naidu waxed poetic on the theme of Asia's cultural diversity and spiritual unity: "To-day India has beckoned to her kindred of Asia to come and understand the new message of hope to the world. Out of the diversity of Asia's culture is born that unity of the Asian people. Who wants a uniform culture? Who wants a colorless culture? It is rather richness, variety, diversity, and sometimes conflict of one culture with another that is a guarantee and prophecy of real, abiding, dynamic unity and that is what I want, what Nehru wants, what Gandhi wants and what my people want."[4]

Nehru no less eloquently spoke of "this mother continent of ours," whose children had been drawn to the ancient city of Delhi not only by an invitation but by "some deeper urge" that connected them all. Within the first minute or two of his delivery, Nehru had singled out Egypt as his country's special, not-quite-Asian guest: "If we view the millennia of history, this continent of Asia, with which Egypt has been so intimately connected in cultural fellowship, has played a mighty role in the evolution of humanity." "Egypt and the Arab countries of Western Asia" were welcomed first among the countries who had sent delegations, and Saad Zaghlul was honored as one of the "great architects of Asian freedom," alongside Sun Yat Sen, Mustafa Kemal Ataturk, and Gandhi.[5]

Nehru linked the impetus for the conference to his earlier experiences of pan-Asian solidarity, notably the League Against Imperialism.[6] "Strong winds are blowing all over Asia," he intoned, fifteen years ahead of British Prime Minister Harold MacMillan's speech at Cape Town. "Let us not be afraid of them but welcome them, for only with their help can we build the Asia of our dreams."[7] These were fine, familiar sentiments, but by the time they were uttered, the humanist and cosmopolitan impulses underpinning them were already under siege.

Although it took place months before India's formal independence was achieved in August, the Asian Relations Conference struggled to make itself heard amid partition's rising din. Intercommunal violence was already spilling into the streets of the Indian capital; at some moments it threatened to consume the neighborhoods surrounding the conference venue. The fate of millions would be sealed mere weeks later, when Congress voted in favor of India's partition into Hindu and Muslim majority states on 14 June. Kamaladevi Chattopadhyay, a member of Congress's transitional government cabinet, looked on in horror as her colleagues voted for divorce from their Muslim relations: "After having lived together for centuries, we had to pretend that we could not continue to do so. The partition had to provide credibility to a lie. . . . When the proposition was put to the vote, I could not even reconcile myself to remain neutral. Something within me warned me that . . . if I did not record my belief I would live with a sense of

ASSEMBLING AT THE PURANA KILA FORT FOR SAFETY: MUSLIMS FLEEING FROM NEW DELHI AWAIT ADMITTANCE TO THE CAMP, WHERE THOUSANDS ARE ALREADY GATHERED.

FIGURE 18   Muslim refugees awaiting transfer to Pakistan, August 1947.
MARY EVANS PICTURE LIBRARY

heinous guilt. So I raised my hand in opposition. With that I broke my link with this political life."[8]

The Congress vote for partition mirrored the broader postwar tone, in which the nation-state had become the single viable unit of international society. The decision was a major blow to Easternism. As fuzzy and intangible as it had always been, if it stood for anything it was the basic cohesion, the viability, of the East as a heterogeneous space. Though Congress had long ago accepted the model of the nation-state, for decades it had also insisted on the inviolability of the Indian subcontinent as a unitary, heterodox space; in 1947, it conceded on this point in exchange for the prize of political independence from Britain. In doing so, the East lost one of its most powerful institutional champions. By September of that year, the Purana Qila's red brick facades had morphed from the picturesque venue of an international conference into a sprawling refugee camp, where thousands of Muslims displaced by communal violence awaited transfer to Pakistan.[9]

Many years after the fact, Choudhry Khaliquzzaman would acknowledge the role he had played in the creation of the new state. But as Pakistan morphed from a rhetorical utopia into a stark political reality, he could not imagine leaving his beloved city of Lucknow. Like many Muslims in August 1947, he wished to remain in India—part of the familiar, cosmopolitan East he had grown up in, rather than the modern Islamic nation being conjured somewhere else. On the eve of independence, as Nehru completed his famous "tryst with destiny" speech to parliament, the next speaker to take the dais in celebration of India's independence was Khaliquzzaman. In seconding Nehru's motion, his former political adversary spoke of the new challenges awaiting the nascent country, which were "not to be fought against any outsider, but . . . settled among our own selves." Whereas the previous decades had called for protest, resistance, and competition, the new struggle required new tactics: in particular, "no communal considerations would be allowed to prevail." As Khaliquzzaman concluded his remarks, Nehru stood and embraced him.[10] It was an evening of deep emotion and high hopes. And of course, it could not last.

Late on 16 August, as the pageantry of independence celebrations wound down, senior Indian and Pakistani government officials were summoned to the Viceregal Lodge. With most of the British civil service and armed forces already departed, they were given two hours to study maps outlining the (almost entirely arbitrary) borders of their newly separate countries.[11] The next morning, 360 million people awoke to the news of which state they now lived in. Millions discovered, to their horror, that they were suddenly on the "wrong" side of a national frontier. Communal violence had of course been anticipated; in truth it had been going on for months. But the scale of the massacres that ensued were beyond even the worst fears of the political elite in Delhi. The Muslim League and Congress may have been proverbial enemies, but in practice they were longtime colleagues, personally intertwined in social and even familial networks, notwithstanding their political disagreements. Thus they struggled to fathom the extent of the hatreds partition had unleashed. The violence tore through the fine fabric of their genteel existences; both Khaliquzzaman in Lucknow and Abdurrahman Siddiqi in Calcutta were quickly forced to abandon their homes. They and their families became, alongside millions of others, reluctant refugees in the new state they had helped usher into existence.

The Asian Relations Conference that preceded India's partition also revealed the deep cleavages emerging between Eastern countries. Already by the spring of 1947, transnational solidarities that had long been aligned against imperialism were shifting tracks, as the emerging national interests of soon-to-be independent states diverged. Nehru's appeals for Asian unity came under attack from delegates from Southeast Asia who were concerned by the echoes of Imperial Japan's Greater East Asia Co-Prosperity Sphere and suspicious that India was making a bid for its own form of cultural hegemony. A delegate from Burma, which had direct experience of both, insisted that "it was a terrible thing to be ruled by a Western power, but it was even more so to be ruled by an Asian power."[12] The Vietnamese delegation pressed India to make good on its claims of anticolonial solidarity through material and diplomatic support for its ongoing guerrilla war against the French. With his eyes on India's future bilateral relations with France, Nehru demurred; an independent India would offer only "moral support" to brother Asian countries.[13]

The chill of US-Soviet competition had also begun to set in. Several Central Asian Soviet republics attended the Asian Relations Conference, in a distant echo of the 1920 Congress of Peoples of the East in Baku, and of course the League Against Imperialism—founded during an era when Moscow still appeared as a gleaming beacon of anticolonial ideals. For many conference organizers and attendees, the luster had certainly worn off by 1947. The Stalinist terrors of the 1930s, the Molotov-Ribbentrop Pact, and the similarly unorthodox wartime alliance with capitalist Britain and the United States had brought many early enthusiasts of the Soviet Union back down to Earth. While listening to delegates from Georgia and Azerbaijan rehearse the party line, Nehru, Naidu, and Chattopadhyay may have thought of their beloved Chatto, who had been such an important link among them and instrumental in their interwar explorations of socialism and global anti-imperial networks in Europe. As the Nazi grip closed over Germany in 1933, Chatto left Berlin for Leningrad, where he secured a faculty position at the Academy of Sciences. His status as a department chair and his sincere commitment to communism were, however, no match for Stalin's paranoia; as with so many other party faithful in the late 1930s, Chatto was arrested by the secret police in 1937 and forcibly disappeared. He was never seen or heard from again.[14]

In the lead-up to the Asian Relations Conference, there had also been some debate among the countries of the recently formed Arab League about attending. Hot on the heels of Nehru's invitations, letters had arrived in Arab capitals from Muhammad Ali Jinnah, urging representatives to stay away. In the press,

FIGURE 19   Pomp and circumstance: Muhammad Ali Jinnah in 1947.
WORLD HISTORY ARCHIVE / ALAMY

the Muslim League described the 1947 conference as an "Asian Fraud," nothing more than Nehru's latest vanity project. Touring Arab countries in 1946, Jinnah had gone so far as to claim that only the creation of Pakistan could act as a check on "Hindu imperialism," which otherwise threatened to swallow not only South Asia but the Middle East as well. Jinnah singled out Egypt, the home of Congress's closest regional allies, as particularly at risk.[15]

Given that Congress and the Muslim League tended to envision their states-in-waiting as global powers comparable in influence to the imperial Raj they would replace,[16] Jinnah was both extrapolating and projecting; still, at least some of his Arab listeners appeared to be listening. Syria, Lebanon, Yemen, and Saudi

Arabia all declined to participate in the Asian Relations Conference, apparently dissuaded by Jinnah's appeals. But by 1947, Egyptian nationalists and feminists had maintained ties with the INC for the better part of thirty years; they also understood the dynamics of Indian domestic politics well enough to come to their own conclusions about the nature of the conference, and Nehru's intentions in hosting it. The Egyptians came to Delhi, as did a small collection of Hebrew University professors from what was still, for a few months longer, called Palestine. Led by the socialist Dr. Samuel Bergmann, the Zionist delegation had worked hard, lobbying through their American intermediaries, to score an invitation.[17] An Easternist of sorts himself, Bergmann viewed his delegation's presence in Delhi as part of a larger homecoming for the Jewish people, which had been "driven from its Asiatic Motherland eighteen hundred years ago by the force of the Roman Sword":

> The Asian system of multi-racial, multi-religious, and multi-cultural political organisations has stood the test of time. . . . This lesson Europe was unable to teach us. We do not want to be ungrateful to Europe. We have learned very important lessons there. We learned to appreciate logical reasoning and methodical thinking. We have learned in Europe and trans-planted to Palestine the teaching and way of life of modern socialism.
>
> But one thing we could not learn from Europe: Mutual co-operation of groups of men belonging to different races and creeds. We have been everywhere a persecuted minority; and during the last war six millions of our brethren . . . have been ruthlessly murdered in gas-chambers. This last lesson of Europe to us we shall never forget.
>
> . . . It is our hope that Palestine, notwithstanding her present differences, will not go the European way of 'solving', so to speak, problems, by dispossessing populations, but, by a common effort to use the results of science and research to make room for more people, will mean more good neighbours, more co-operation and more reciprocal help.[18]

Sincere and well-intentioned as these remarks certainly were, in depicting Jews in monolithic terms, Bergmann overlooked the presence of indigenous Jewish communities in many of the countries represented at the conference, whose histories and experiences of intercommunal relations differed greatly from those of the Jews of Europe.[19] This point was made by Karima al-Said of Egypt, one of Huda Shaarawi's young protégés. Interrupting the proceedings, al-Said asked Nehru to afford her the opportunity to respond to Bergmann's remarks: "Madame Karima . . . made the point that there had been no controversy in Palestine between Arabs and Jews. What the Arabs did not want was European Zionists coming under British protection to claim a separate state."[20] This and other incidents (including a rather stern rebuke from Gandhi) left the Zionist delegation unsettled; some members were consoled that at least Hindu revivalists appeared "open to relations and bold connections with our enterprise in Palestine," apparently on the basis of a common alignment against Muslims.[21] By contrast Bergmann, a prominent binationalist, was "disturbed" that, notwithstanding Sarojini Naidu's opening remarks, delegates appeared unanimous in their view "that in every country a homogenous unity should be created out of the existing groups, minorities and religions. . . . We pointed out . . . that this could not apply to Palestine since in this country two different nations are living together, neither of which was prepared to assimilate or amalgamate itself to the other."[22]

The United Nations would respond to this conundrum later the same year, when in November—as India and Pakistan reeled from the displacement of over 10 million people and the murder of a million more—it opted to repeat the experiment of partition in Palestine. The territory of the former British Mandate was to be sliced into six neat, noncontiguous triangles that kissed each other on the map: three Arab and three Jewish. It was unclear how residents were to move between these geometric parcels of land; perhaps there would be tunnels and overpasses so that Jews and Arabs could be funneled through the same intersections without ever brushing shoulders or locking eyes. India served on the United Nations Special Committee on Palestine; in a rare instance of accord, both India and Pakistan (and every other Arab and Asian country but one)[23] voted against partition in the General Assembly. In these earliest days of decolonization, they were outnumbered by the Western and Soviet blocs. The Egyptian representative to the United Nations, former Prime Minister Mahmud Fahmi al-Nuqrashi, wept in his seat as the results were read out.

The partition of Palestine triggered a grim closing of ranks among the Arabs, as opposition to the new state of Israel overshadowed all other foreign policy considerations. Following the trajectory of the late 1930s, this expanded Egypt's role in regional politics; Cairo became the headquarters of the newly created Arab League, with Mustafa al-Nahas its first President. Simultaneously, however, the mounting conflict in Israel-Palestine foreclosed some of the broader transnational projects in which Egyptian politicians and activists had previously been implicated. Arab nationalism replaced Easternism definitively as the Egyptian frame of reference in external affairs. Following the Arab-Israeli war in 1948 and the Nakba, or "catastrophe" of mass Palestinian expulsion,[24] popular anger over the war's conduct contributed to a coup in Egypt. This brought to power a group of veterans, the Free Officers, and resulted in the life-term presidency of Gamal Abdel Nasser. In Arab nationalist Egypt, little space remained for the *mutamassirun*; by the late 1950s the country's Greek, Jewish, French, Italian, and British communities had dwindled into oblivion. Inspired by Nasser and the Free Officers, a wave of Arab nationalist coups swept the region. The emphasis of these new regimes were the twin pillars of armed opposition to Israel and economic "parity" with the West. Liberal democracy, political pluralism, and religious freedom were all perceived as potential threats to these imperatives, and so they were systematically curtailed over the course of coming decades.

In India, while liberal democracy survived, the dilemma posed by independent principalities and, above all, the bitter legacies of partition prompted a sea change within Congress, liberated from the moral imperative of nonviolence by the assassination of Gandhi in 1948. Beginning that year and under Nehru's leadership, India launched a series of military annexations against its smaller neighbors, utilizing a variety of legal and political pretexts worthy of Lord Dalhousie himself. "As a rash of crises broke out over the princely states of Junagadh, Hyderabad and above all Kashmir," Srinath Raghavan has observed, "officers and men, companies and battalions, regiments and formations that had fought together in the Second World War were now ranged on opposite sides. . . . By the time the First Kashmir War ended in December 1948, India and Pakistan were locked in a rivalry that persists to this day."[25]

Both in the Middle East and in India, 1947 signaled the triumph of statism over more expansive, universalist imaginations of a heterodox postcolonial order. In this climate, lands no less than ideas had to be emptied of their human contradictions, ironed into politically legible "units of analysis." Others have called the Asian Relations Conference a precursor to the summit at Bandung in 1955, but in truth it was more like a wake: the final celebration of an era and an ideal which had already been overtaken by events. With the partitions of India and Palestine, the "unity of the East" as a humanist, cosmopolitan rallying cry had been definitively discarded in favor of other models. The profoundly statist priorities of participants at Bandung less than a decade later only underscored the evaporation of former activists' high ideals, now replaced by the realpolitik of long-term incumbents.[26]

What the crises of the late 1930s and above all the existential peril of the war years did was force choices and increase polarization between the many conflicting impulses that had animated interwar politics in places like Egypt and India. Were you an anticolonial or an antifascist? Were you a territorial nationalist or a spiritual universalist? Did you prioritize the needs and interests of your community above all else or espouse principled solidarity with oppressed peoples everywhere? Crucially, what were you willing to sacrifice, or barter away, in the service of these commitments? In their radically different answers to these questions, which became rapidly less abstract after 1935, a broad range of connected movements and former allies definitively parted company.

By the time of the Abyssinian Crisis, the basic contours of these divisions were already apparent, as illustrated in the contrasting positions of Subhas Chandra Bose and Jawaharlal Nehru, or Shakib Arslan and Muhammad Lutfi Gomaa. As we have seen, these divisions resurfaced in much starker form during World War II.

For Egypt's sometimes Prime Minister, Mustafa al-Nahas, the priority that took precedence over all others was, in the end, the protection of Egyptian liberalism. Rightly or wrongly, Nahas estimated that the nationalist Wafd could survive under British rule but not under the thumb of an authoritarian palace. The British High Commissioner, Miles Lampson, appears to have reached the same conclusion in reverse: that Britain could tolerate the principled nationalism of the Wafd more easily than the pro-Axis machinations of the young King. To maintain the possibility of constitutional democracy after independence, Nahas was willing to come to power under the threat of British arms. What he had not properly accounted for was the inevitability of this becoming known, and the consequent undermining of not only his and the Wafd's reputations but the legitimacy of liberalism itself in Egyptian eyes.

For Subhas Chandra Bose, anticolonialism was above all defined by the struggle against Britain; any expedient that could hasten its departure from India was fair game. Similarly, by the time of the Arab Revolt, Amin al-Husseini had concluded that rescuing Palestine from the twin threats of British and Zionist colonization justified any means—including armed revolt and, as with Bose, Nazi patronage.

The Muslim League and the Zionist Yishuv occupied the ideological void between these positions: protection of their large, disparate, and vulnerable communities seemed to require a perpetual shifting of alliances (what Walid Jumblatt, the Lebanese Druze leader, once described as the sharp right and left turns required to keep a vehicle steady on a winding mountain road). Thus the Muslim Leaguers and the Zionists could feasibly and *did* work with anyone—the British, anticolonial militants, Fascist Italy, the USSR, even the Nazi government itself—if it served their immediate needs. Naturally, these alliances were immensely contingent and often short-lived. In both cases, however, the primacy of communal interest fed into the logic of partition—construed in many, if not most, circles as yet another "temporary" expedient.[27]

Confronted with partition as the cost of independence, Gandhi and Nehru folded, as did many other Congress luminaries who had for decades insisted on India's territorial and intercommunal indivisibility. "We were tired men and we were getting on in years," admitted Nehru in 1960. "The plan for partition offered a way out and we took it."[28] Zionists fought hard for partition while Palestinians rejected it, as they had always done. They were overruled. In the shameful wreckage of the Holocaust, Western states accepted the terms of the Biltmore Program: (someone else's) land in exchange for absolution. The nation-state could do that too.

In 1946 Huda Shaarawi traveled to Interlaken, Switzerland, for the first postwar conference of the IAW (her Indian colleagues didn't make it). Margery Corbett-Ashby, among Shaarawi's staunchest friends and allies, announced her resignation in order to focus on domestic affairs in Britain: "Feminist efforts in the international scene were increasingly running foul of the national politics of different countries, and seemed fated to encounter fruitless complications," she observed.[29] It was an astute, if depressing appraisal.

Undaunted, though increasingly frail, Huda deputized her youthful successors to attend international conferences on her behalf. She sent Amina al-Said to the Indian Women's Conference in Hyderabad in late 1945, while Hawa Idris and Karima al-Said went to the Asian Relations Conference as her representatives (and did their best to speak up for Palestine, as their mentor had taught them to do). Shaarawi was still campaigning against the partition of Palestine from her bed in December 1947 when she finally succumbed to a failing heart. Her death formed part of a wave of loss, for in the mid-1940s, so it seemed, champions of the expansive East either became something else—nation-statists, bureaucrats, strictly apolitical—or they didn't survive. The hyphenations that the interwar years had made possible (and indeed encouraged) were, in the new context of the postwar order, apparently lethal.

The marriage between Walter Smart, the British Oriental Secretary, and Amy Nimr, a Syrian surrealist artist connected to Art and Liberty, had been emblematic of more flexible interwar social, political, and cultural alliances. Their only child, Max, was killed in 1942 when he stumbled upon an unexploded landmine during a family picnic near Giza. Amy's brother-in-law, George Antonius, another living metaphor for Anglo-Arab hybridity (and indefatigable champion of the Palestinians at St James's), also died in 1942 at his home in Jerusalem—a casualty of the war years rather than the war itself.

Gandhi was assassinated by a Hindu nationalist in Delhi the month after Huda Shaarawi's death in Cairo; he died chanting God's name. Jinnah lived only until September 1948, victim of his own success. Having contracted tuberculosis, he hid his diagnosis and ignored his doctors' warnings to protect his singular role at the helm of the Pakistan project. When he died, there was no one comparable to assume the national mantle, let alone the enormous responsibilities he had fiercely guarded for himself. As President of the Pakistan Muslim League, Khaliquzzaman made another tour of the Middle East in 1949. He found Arab leaders painfully ignorant and uncurious about Pakistan: "Our services to the Palestine cause and our anxiety to see Muslims of the Middle East countries strong and independent was hardly known to our Arab brethren. . . . The writer found the Arab people completely ignorant of all that we had done for Palestine and other Muslim countries. In fact up to that time we had no satisfactory credential to convince our Arab brethren of our capacity to exist." He called it "the end of my hopes of seeing in my life time a well-knit Islamic Polity."[30]

Despite his role in the founding of the Arab League, Nahas was to run afoul of both King Faruq and the Free Officers; he and his wife were placed under house arrest in 1953. That year Georges Henein wrote to the exiled Ramses Younane, opining that the revolution had had an unsalutary effect on Cairo's young painters: they were becoming fervent nationalists. A forthcoming exhibition by Art and Liberty's new generation proposed to exclude a Hungarian veteran of the movement because he failed "to express the quintessence of Egyptian life": "Here you go," Henein seethed, "now one must paint a goat or a walnut tree, a *sakia* [ancient water wheel], a class of *Kouttab* [Muslim scribes]. All the rest is taxed with accusations of cosmopolitanism."[31]

As India's first Prime Minister—an office he held until his death in 1964—Nehru was one of the many anticolonial activists turned government officials to discover just how greatly the wielding of state power diverged from the challenging of it. Sarojini Naidu was another. In 1948 she rebuffed the organizers of a pan-Asian women's conference who had hoped to win her support for it to take place in Calcutta: "At the present time I see no necessity for the functioning of women's organizations," Naidu told them. "Every dream and every desire of the women of India has been realized. Every individual must rely upon herself to attain her ends. One needn't look far for an example: I . . . have become a governor of a large province."[32] Already in 1948, the feminist poet had been reincarnated as a sated bureaucrat.

Naidu's sister-in-law chose a different path. Following the body blow of Congress's vote for partition, Kamaladevi Chattopadhyay withdrew from the party and India's transitional government. In the wake of Gandhi's death she followed through on a project they had discussed to resettle partition refugees on a collective farm on the outskirts of Delhi. This evolved into the township of Faridabad, which ultimately rehabilitated over fifty thousand refugees, mostly from the North West Frontier, without state assistance. In later years, Chattopadhyay devoted herself to the preservation of indigenous arts and handicrafts, establishing a series of museums and cultural institutions for which she received international recognition and multiple honors. She never reentered politics.

In her autobiography, Chattopadhyay recalled one of her final meetings with Gandhi, in the immediate aftermath of Congress's fateful acceptance of partition in June 1947.

> I had never seen him look so pale and dispirited . . . There was a kind of despair in his tone that I found hard to take. I feared I might break down. 'Why did you let it happen', I almost cried out. 'You had once said [of partition, that] we were striking at the very root of our nation. [. . .] Even now if you refuse to accept this monstrous decision, the people will support you. You have only to give the word', I went on breathlessly for a while . . . He made a heart-breaking figure, he who had challenged and humbled the mighty British empire . . . here was the indomitable man who had shaken global foundations, looking beaten.
>
> 'It is too late. If it had been ten years earlier . . .' The voice trailed off for a while, as though lost in some thought, then he resumed: 'You see my colleagues came to me when they were still in their prime of life, giving up their bright careers, plunging into an unknown destiny'.[33]

In many ways this has been a book about dreams and plans envisioned but never quite enacted, the future of a world that ultimately failed to materialize. The East as a universalist, heterodox space lost its capital with Cairo's absorption into the Arab nationalist bloc, as geopolitics pivoted to a focus on discrete "Areas" of the globe—drawn with increasingly thick, rigid frontiers. This did as much as anything, in the second half of the twentieth century, to erase our collective memory of the kinds of interconnections that bound much of the world together mere decades prior.

As for the East, though a case might be made for Delhi or Bandung as the inheritor of Cairo, it is perhaps truer to say that it remained homeless throughout the early years of the Cold War, awaiting the rise of a new generation of anticolonial idealists who began to resurrect aspects of borderless interconnection and resistance in the late 1950s, now constellated around the Global South. It was a vision that the intervening decade had rendered yet more militant and uncompromising, as the stakes of the nuclear age and superpower competition seemingly demanded. Perhaps by then Algiers had emerged as a new capital of the East, or Havana, reflecting the shift of political gravity across the Atlantic. What is certain is that by 1960, both India and Egypt had receded into the hazy middle distance, becoming regionally important players in global affairs . . . as indeed had Britain itself.

If they could have done it all over—Gandhi and his colleagues, Huda Shaarawi and hers, Jinnah and the Muslim League, the Palestinian leadership, the surrealists of Cairo, Nehru and Nahas—how might it have turned out differently, if they'd taken it once more from the top? From back when they were all still, as Gandhi had it, bright young things full of unspent enthusiasm, who had not yet been exhausted by the world?

These are not questions historians can answer.

But that shouldn't stop us from asking.

DRAMATIS PERSONAE

THE OLD GUARD

Jamal al-Din al-Afghani: Nineteenth-century anticolonial firebrand, itinerant scholar, and Islamist-Easternist revolutionary whose teachings and exhortations inspired generations of Arab, Indian, and Muslim disciples.

Syed Ahmad Khan: Nineteenth-century Muslim educational reformer and founder of the Muhammadan Anglo-Oriental College (after 1920, Aligarh Muslim University), Khan believed Indian Muslim advancement required cooperation with the British to counterbalance the cultural, social, and numerical advantages enjoyed by Indian Hindus.

Mustafa Kamil: Editor of the anticolonial *al-Liwa* magazine and founder, with Muhammad Farid and Ahmad Lutfi al-Sayyid, of the Egyptian Watani Party— the forerunner of the country's interwar nationalist movement.

Abd al-Aziz Jawish: Kamil's successor at *al-Liwa*, under whose editorship it became associated with anti-Copt, Islamist, and pro-Ottoman sentiments.

Gopal Krishna Gokhale: Senior leader of the Indian National Congress, originator of the nationalist Swadeshi movement, and Gandhi's political mentor.

Bal Gangadhar Tilak: Known to British officials as the "father of Indian unrest," he famously broke with Gokhale and split the Congress Party in 1907 between "moderates" committed to constitutional methods and those, like Tilak, who called for armed resistance. Sometimes considered a Hindu nationalist, he was represented at his sedition trials by a youthful Muhammad Ali Jinnah.

THE WAFDISTS

Saad Zaghlul: Figurehead of the 1919 Egyptian Revolution and first Prime Minister of Egypt.

Mustafa al-Nahas: Zaghlul's successor, he served five nonconsecutive terms as Prime Minister and one term of house arrest under Nasser.

Makram Ebeid: A highly influential Wafd minister and Secretary-General of the Party from 1936-42. Often described as the brains of the operation.

Mahmud Abul Fat'h: Gandhi's 1931 interviewer for the Egyptian newspaper *al-Ahram* and chronicler of the Wafd's 1939 embassy to India.

Ahmad Qasim Gouda: A member of the 1939 Wafd embassy, he later authored a memoir about his time in India.

Muhammad Ali Alluba: A member of the Wafd in 1919, by the mid-1930s he had split with the party. As a Liberal Constitutionalist, he became a key figure in pro-Palestinian activism, organizing the 1938 World Congress in Cairo and forging close working relations with the Muslim League. In 1948 he became Egypt's first Ambassador to Pakistan.

THE CONGRESSWALLAHS

Mohandas Karamchand Mahatma Gandhi: A devout Hindu, hand-spinning evangelist, and firm believer in nonviolence.

Motilal Nehru: Among the first Indian graduates of Cambridge University and twice-elected President of the Indian National Congress, he renounced an opulent lifestyle to follow Gandhi.

Jawaharlal Nehru: Motilal's son, a senior Congress Party leader, and first Prime Minister of India. An admirer of socialist revolution, Gandhian satyagraha and rational pragmatism, he struggled throughout his life to reconcile them all.

Abul Kalam (Ahmad) Azad: The most influential Muslim within the Indian National Congress, his book on Gandhi's movement and alliance with Khilafat leaders was translated into Arabic in 1922.

Subhas Chandra Bose: A one-time Congress President from the party's socialist wing, he ultimately grew impatient with gradualism and nonviolence.

Kamaladevi Chattopadhyay: A socialist-feminist satyagrahi, Congress luminary and senior leader of the Seva Dal who renounced politics on the eve of India's independence and devoted the rest of her life to charitable, artistic, and cultural endeavors.

Sarojini Naidu: A renowned poet, feminist, and satyagrahi who later became the Governor of a Large Province.

THE MUSLIM LEAGUERS

Sultan Mahomed Shah, Aga Khan III: Leader of the Ismaili community, first President of the All-India Muslim League, breeder of champion racehorses, and noted mango enthusiast.

Mohamed Ali Jauhar: A poet, anticolonial nationalist, Muslim cosmopolitan and leader of the Khilafat movement, he did much to forge ties between Indian Muslims and Palestine.

Shawkat Ali: Another leading figure of the Khilafat movement, he sought to carry forward his brother Mohamed's legacy after his death.

Choudhry Khaliquzzaman: A friend and ally of the Ali brothers whose sense of Muslim solidarity propelled him on many adventures. He holds the distinction of having seconded both Jinnah's 1940 Lahore Resolution and Nehru's 1947 "tryst with destiny" speech.

Abdurrahman Siddiqi: Khaliquzzaman's friend and colleague who shared his many voyages, from a volunteer medical mission to the Ottoman Empire to their rather less voluntary migration to the new state of Pakistan.

Muhammad Ali Jinnah: A man of strong opinions, excellent taste, and enormous ambition, with a lawyer's appreciation for the power of language.

THE EGYPTIAN FEMINISTS

Huda Shaarawi: Founder and President of the Egyptian Feminist's Union (EFU), founder of the Eastern feminist journal *L'Egyptienne*, and tireless campaigner for democracy, women's rights, and the Palestinian cause.

Saiza Nabarawi: Founding member of the EFU, journalist, and editor of *L'Egyptienne*.

Hawa Idriss: A member of the EFU and youthful protegée of Shaarawi who attended the Asian Relations Conference in 1947 and later wrote about it in her memoir.

Karima al-Said: A youthful EFU member who attended the Asian Relations Conference and spoke on behalf of the absent Palestinians.

THE POETS

Ahmad Shawqi: Egypt's "Prince of Poets," who drew on ancient Egyptian and modern nationalist themes and wrote a poetic tribute to Gandhi in 1931.

Rabindranath Tagore: Messenger of a "Spiritual East" and the first non-European winner of a Nobel Prize, his focus in later years was the founding of a university, Visva-Bharati, for the "study of humanity somewhere beyond the limits of nation and geography."

Muhammad Iqbal: The "Poet of the East," a Muslim cosmopolitan and, like Tagore, a staunch antinationalist. Jinnah claimed he was the true originator of the Pakistan idea; Iqbal denied having anything to do with it.

THE SURREALISTS

Georges Henein: The communist-inspired founder and moving spirit behind Art and Liberty, who picked fights with Italian futurists; rejected Stalinism, Egyptian nationalism, and British imperialism; and believed surrealism had the power to change the world.

Ramses Younane: A celebrated painter and one of Henein's closest friends and collaborators, he was briefly imprisoned after the war and spent a decade in exile in Paris. Eventually he returned to Cairo, having been fired from his job with a French broadcaster for refusing to condemn the Nasser regime during the 1956 Suez Crisis.

Kamel el-Telmissany: Another founding member of Art and Liberty, and a disciple of both Karl Marx and Charlie Chaplin. After the war he became an avant-garde filmmaker in Lebanon.

Amy Nimr: The daughter of a Syrian newspaper magnate with a fine arts background, a husband in the British Embassy, and an eclectic group of friends.

Inji Efflatoun: A politically engaged teenager when she began exhibiting with Art and Liberty, she would later develop a unique painting style during her years of imprisonment by the Nasser regime—emerging as one of the great Egyptian artists of the twentieth century.

THE PALESTINIANS

Jamal al-Husseini: Founding member of the Arab Higher Committee and its official representative at the 1939 St James's Conference on Palestine. An advocate of Gandhian nonviolence, until he wasn't.

Hajj Amin al-Husseini (the Mufti): Influential leader of the Arab Revolt, longtime thorn in the side of the British Mandate administration, wartime resident of Berlin.

Nijati Sidqi: Introduced to Communism by Jewish colleagues, he studied in Moscow and fought with the Republicans in the Spanish Civil War before being kicked out of the party for his vehement opposition to Nazism.

Sadhij Nassar: Cofounder of the Arab Women's Union of Haifa and prominent leader of the General Strike that initiated the Arab Revolt. The first Palestinian woman to be arrested and imprisoned by the British for her nationalist activities.

THE ZIONISTS

Chaim Weizmann: Russian-born Professor of Biochemistry at Manchester University, recognized "father" of industrial fermentation and many British policies on Palestine. President of the World Zionist Congress and, subsequently, Israel.

David Ben Gurion: Polish-born socialist, failed student of Arabic, leader of the wartime British Yishuv, and first Prime Minister of Israel.

Ze'ev Jabotinsky: Odessan Jewish militant and poet. Founder of the Revisionist Zionist movement, which ranged itself against the "peace mongers" of mainstream Zionism.

Hugo Samuel Bergmann: Czech-born philosopher, professor at the Hebrew University, and leader of the Zionist delegation to the 1947 Asian Relations Conference. Binationalist peace monger.

THE REGIONAL LEADERS

Mustafa Kemal Ataturk: The Turkish general who won back in the field what the Paris Peace Conference had allocated to Greece, thus forcing the Treaty of Lausanne. Founder of the modern Turkish Republic, he abolished the Ottoman Caliphate in 1924.

Abbas Hilmi II: The last Khedive of Egypt, he supported Mustafa Kamil's Watani Party and was deposed by the British at the outset of World War I.

King Fuad: Hilmi's successor as ruler of Egypt. Proud Circassian and aspiring caliph.

King Faruq: Fuad's son, who ascended the throne in 1937. His father's former aides, especially Sheikh Maraghi of al-Azhar, capitalized on the youthful monarch's popularity to briefly revive the bid for a caliphate in Egypt.

Ali Maher: Prime Minister of Egypt at the outset of World War II., and again following the Free Officer's Coup in 1952. Among Faruq's closest allies and advisors.

Sharif Hussein of Mecca: Hashemite ruler of the Hijaz and one half of the Hussein-McMahon correspondence. Agreed to instigate a revolt against the Ottomans during World War I in exchange for hereditary rule of an independent Arab Kingdom at war's end.

Prince Faisal: Hussein's son, he led the 1917–18 Arab Revolt in the Hijaz and was eventually made ruler of British Mandate Iraq.

Ibn Saud: In 1926 he defeated Sherif Hussein of Mecca to become King of Arabia and Guardian of the Two Holy Places (Mecca and Medina)—titles his family has retained.

Rashid Ali al-Kaylani: One-time Prime Minister of Iraq and leader of a pro-Axis coup during World War II.

Reza Shah Pahlavi: Another military general-turned-nationalist modernizer, he abolished Iran's Qajar dynasty in 1925; unlike Ataturk, he founded a new royal lineage. Amidst Axis intrigue, the British forced him to abdicate in favor of his son (the brother-in-law of King Faruq) in 1941. Mohammad Reza Pahlavi would remain on the throne as Shah of Iran until 1979, when the Islamic Revolution forced him into exile.

THE IMPERIALISTS

Thomas Edward Lawrence: British archaeologist, wartime intelligence officer, noted desert sartorialist, and Prince Faisal's translator at the Paris Peace Conference.

Edwin Montagu: Liberal Member of Parliament for Cambridgeshire, Secretary of State for India during and immediately following World War I, anti-Zionist Jew.

Herbert Samuel: First British High Commissioner to Palestine, and Montagu's cousin.

Leo Amery: As a Secretary in the War Cabinet during World War I, he was a key framer of the Balfour Declaration. Later he served as Secretary of State for India during World War II.

Miles Lampson: British High Commissioner (1934-36) and subsequently Ambassador to Egypt, 1936-46. Mediocre golfer, decent shot, and prolific diarist with atrocious penmanship.

Walter Smart: Britain's Oriental Secretary in Cairo and Amy Nemr's husband.

Edward Wood, First Earl of Halifax: Viceroy of India from 1926–31, he served as Foreign Secretary at the height of the Arab Revolt and the descent to war in Europe, from 1938–40.

Malcolm MacDonald: As Secretary of State for the Colonies, he oversaw the repeal of the British government's policy of partition in Palestine, the 1939 St James's Conference, and the unilateral adoption of the 1939 White Paper.

Victor Hope, Second Marquess of Linlithgow: Viceroy of India, 1936–43, initially tasked with implementing the 1935 India Act. His other contributions to Indian political life included encouraging the breakdown in relations between Congress and the Muslim League.

Lawrence Dundas, Second Marquess of Zetland: Governor of Bengal, 1917-22, and Secretary of State for India, 1935–40. Zetland played an important role in negotiating the 1935 India Act, opposed by Churchill and Conservative diehards. When Churchill became Prime Minister in 1940, Zetland tendered his resignation.

Richard Stafford Cripps: A former Labour Member of Parliament, expelled for advocating a popular front against the policy of appeasement. As wartime British Ambassador to the USSR, he was instrumental in forging an alliance with Stalin.

His popularity soared, and he was appointed Leader of the House of Commons in 1942. It has been suggested that Churchill sent him to India to check his meteoric rise.

THE FREE AGENTS

Shakib Arslan: The "Prince of Eloquence," among the most widely read columnists of the interwar Arabic press. Infamous apologist for Italy's invasion of Ethiopia.

Rashid Rida: A hugely influential Muslim scholar and editor of Cairo's *al-Manar*, he supported Ibn Saud's caliphal bid and established Salafism as a major current of political Islam.

Muhammad Lutfi Gomaa: A lawyer, popular Egyptian journalist, and passionate advocate of Eastern universalism.

Virendranath Chattopadhyaya (Chatto): Friend of Nehru, brother of Kamaladevi Chattopadhyay and Sarojini Naidu. Connected Indian nationalists to socialist and communist movements in Europe. Disappeared during the Stalinist terror.

George Antonius: Freelance diplomat, political science researcher perpetually behind on his deadlines, and Amy Nimr's brother-in-law. He served as Secretary to the Arab Delegation at the St James's Conference, ahead of which he published a reassessment and full translation of the Hussein-McMahon correspondence. His account and analysis of the emergence of Arab nationalism has remained influential.

NOTES

Introduction

1. The letter appears as an appendix in A.Q. Gouda, *Marid min al-Sharq* (Cairo, 1950), 50–52.

2. S. Bose, *A Hundred Horizons: The Indian Ocean in the Age of Global Empire* (Cambridge, 2006); G.F. Hourani and J. Carswell, *Arab Seafaring in the Indian Ocean in Ancient and Early Modern Times* (Princeton, 1995); S.E. Sidebotham, *Berenike and the Ancient Maritime Spice Route* (Berkeley, 2011).

3. E. Dal Lago, R. Healy, and G. Barry, eds., *1916 in Global Context: An Anti-Imperial Moment* (New York, 2018); P. Gopal, *Insurgent Empire: Anticolonial Resistance and British Dissent* (New York, 2019).

4. M. Hawas, "World Literature and the Question of History," in *The Routledge Companion to World Literature*, ed. T. D'haen, D. Damrosch, and D. Kadir (London, 2018), 228.

5. I. Gershoni and J. Jankowski, *Redefining the Egyptian Nation, 1930–1945* (Cambridge, 2002); J. Whidden, *Monarchy and Modernity in Egypt: Politics, Islam and Neocolonialism between the Wars* (New York, 2013).

6. M. Badran, *Feminists, Islam, and Nation: Gender and the Making of Modern Egypt* (Princeton, 1995); E.L. Fleischmann, *The Nation and Its "New" Women: The Palestinian Women's Movement, 1920–1948* (Berkeley, 2003).

7. J. Darwin, *The Empire Project* (Cambridge, 2010); V. Huber, *Channelling Mobilities: Migration and Globalisation in the Suez Canal Region and Beyond, 1869–1914* (Cambridge, 2013); S. Morewood, *The British Defence of Egypt 1935–1940: Conflict and Crisis in the Eastern Mediterranean* (London, 2005).

8. R.J. Blyth, *The Empire of the Raj: India, Eastern Africa and the Middle East 1858–1947* (Basingstoke, 2003); P. Satia, *Spies in Arabia: The Great War and the Cultural Foundation of Britain's Covert Empire in the Middle East* (Oxford, 2008), 45–46; B. Westrate,

The Arab Bureau: British Policy in the Middle East, 1916–1920 (University Park, 1992), 24–26.

9. A. Ayalon, *The Press in the Arab Middle East: A History* (Oxford, 1995); Z.B.D. Benite, "'Nine Years in Egypt': Al-Azhar University and the Arabization of Chinese Islam," *Hagar* 8:1 (2008); J.T. Chen, "Re-orientation: The Chinese Azharites between Umma and Third World, 1938–55," *Comparative Studies of South Asia, Africa and the Middle East* 34:1 (2014); R. Cormack, *Midnight in Cairo: The Female Stars of Egypt's Roaring '20s*, (London, 2021); Z. Fahmy, *Ordinary Egyptians: Creating the Modern Nation through Popular Culture* (Stanford, 2011); J. Gelvin and N. Green, eds., *Global Muslims in the Age of Steam and Print* (Berkeley, 2013); N. Green, *How Asia Found Herself: A Story of Intercultural Understanding* (New Haven, 2022), 18; E. Rogan, *The Arabs: A History* (London, 2012), 240.

10. A. Asseraf, *Electric News in Colonial Algeria* (Oxford, 2019); Z. Fahmy, *Ordinary Egyptians*; S.J. Potter, *Wireless Internationalism and Distant Listening: Britain, Propaganda, and the Invention of Global Radio, 1920–1939* (Oxford, 2020); A.L. Stanton, *"This Is Jerusalem Calling": State Radio in Mandate Palestine* (Austin, 2013); A.L. Stanton, "Can Imperial Radio Be Transnational? British-Affiliated Arabic Radio Broadcasting in the Interwar Period," *History Compass* 18:1 (2020).

11. Accounts of this transformation are heavily indebted to Benedict Anderson, who emphasized the role of print capitalism in the emergence of national consciousness between the late nineteenth and early twentieth centuries; with the advent of commercial radio after World War I, aural media greatly expanded the reach and penetration of ideas formerly carried by print. B. Anderson, *Imagined Communities: Reflections on the Origins and Spread of Nationalism* (London, 1983). For the Egyptian context, see esp. Z. Fahmy, *Ordinary Egyptians*; on the symbiotic nature of these transformations across colonial cities, see for example P. Kidambi, "Nationalism and the City in Colonial India: Bombay 1890–1940," *Journal of Urban History* 38:5 (2012); S.L. Lewis, *Cities in Motion: Urban Life and Cosmopolitanism in Southeast Asia, 1920–1940* (Cambridge, 2016); C.A. Lin, "Nation, Race, and Language: Discussing Transnational Identities in Colonial Singapore circa 1930," *Modern Asian Studies* 46:2 (2012); R. Parr, *Citizens of Everywhere: Indian Women, Nationalism and Cosmopolitanism, 1920–1952* (Cambridge, 2022); S. Rahnama, *The Future Is Feminist: Women and Social Change in Interwar Algeria* (Ithaca, 2022).

12. This is the central argument of Gershoni and Jankowski, *Redefining the Egyptian Nation*.

13. B. Baron, *The Women's Awakening in Egypt: Culture, Society, and the Press* (New Haven, 1997).

14. J. Beinin and Z. Lockman, *Workers on the Nile: Nationalism, Communism, Islam, and the Egyptian Working Class, 1882–1954* (Cairo, 1998).

15. S. Bardaouil, *Egyptian Surrealism: Modernism and the Art and Liberty Group* (London, 2017).

16. As documented most comprehensively by Noor Khan. N.A.I. Khan, *Egyptian-Indian Nationalist Collaboration and the British Empire* (New York, 2011).

17. Easternism has been placed under the academic microscope a handful of times,

most notably by James Jankowski and Israel Gershoni in *Redefining the Egyptian Nation*. They depict it as a nebulous current of thought distinct from pan-Islam and pan-Arabism, which preceded these ultimately more consequential movements and served as a short-lived conduit toward them in the early 1930s. While I don't necessarily disagree, in what follows I use *Easternism* to mean something slightly different. For my purposes, *Easternism* serves as the umbrella term for perceived connections and affinities between Egypt and India, with plenty of space for territorial nationalisms, pan-Arabism, pan-Asianism, pan-Islam, socialism, anticolonialism, feminism, and other isms to compete and coexist beneath its canopy. Defined in this way, Easternism has a longer and more interesting trajectory, as this book seeks to demonstrate.

18. As first and most indelibly captured by Edward W. Said in *Orientalism* (New York, 1978).

19. This is the subject of works such as S. Alavi, *Muslim Cosmopolitanism in the Age of Empire* (Cambridge, MA, 2015); C. Aydin, *The Politics of Anti-Westernism in Asia: Visions of World Order in Pan-Islamic and Pan-Asian Thought* (New York, 2007); T. Harper, *Underground Asia: Global Revolutionaries and the Assault on Empire* (London, 2020); M.L. Louro, *Comrades against Imperialism: Nehru, India, and Interwar Internationalism* (Cambridge, 2018); P. Mishra, *From the Ruins of Empire: The Revolt Against the West and the Remaking of Asia* (London, 2012); M. Ramnath, *Haj to Utopia: How the Ghadar Movement Charted Global Radicalism and Attempted to Overthrow the British Empire* (Berkeley, 2011).

20. Emblematic of scholarship on Rabindranath Tagore and Kakuzo Okakura. See R. Barucha, *Another Asia: Rabindranath Tagore and Okakura Tenshin* (New Delhi, 2006); M.R. Frost, "'That Great Ocean of Idealism': Calcutta, the Tagore Circle, and the Idea of Asia, 1900–1920," in *Indian Ocean Studies: Cultural, Social, and Political Perspectives*, ed. S. Moorthy and A. Jamal (New York, 2009); I. Shigemi, "Okakura Kakuzo's Nostalgic Journey to India and the Invention of Asia," in *Nostalgic Journeys: Literary Pilgrimages between Japan and the West*, ed. S. Fisher (Vancouver, 2006).

21. C. Aydin, *The Idea of the Muslim World: A Global Intellectual History* (London, 2017); J.M. Landau, *Pan-Islam: History and Politics* (New York, 2015). On the growth and significance of Muslim cosmopolitan imaginaries in colonial India, see esp. F. Devji, *Muslim Zion: Pakistan as a Political Idea* (London, 2013); M. Hasan, ed., *Communal and Pan-Islamic Trends in Colonial India* (New Delhi, 1981); G. Minault, *The Khilafat Movement: Religious Symbolism and Political Mobilization in India* (New York, 1982); Y. Saikia, "Hijrat and Azadi in Indian Muslim Imagination and Practice: Connecting Nationalism, Internationalism, and Cosmopolitanism," *Comparative Studies of South Asia, Africa and the Middle East* 37:2 (2017).

22. This is particularly evident in popular histories of the ancient and medieval periods; see commentary in Green, *How Asia Found Herself*, 10–20.

23. I see this framing as equally applicable to conceptions of the British Raj as a semiautonomous Indian Ocean empire, as it is to the nonaligned bloc in the mid-twentieth century. On the former, see Blyth, *Empire of the Raj*; G. Crouzet, *Inventing the Middle East: Britain and the Persian Gulf in the Age of Global Imperialism* (Montreal, 2022); J. Onley, *The Arabian Frontier of the British Raj: Merchants, Rulers, and the Brit-*

ish in the *Nineteenth-Century Gulf* (Oxford, 2007). On the latter, see N. Miskovic, H. Fischer-Tiné, and N. Boskovska, eds., *The Non-Aligned Movement and the Cold War: Delhi-Bandung-Belgrade* (London, 2014).

24. A. Khan, *World Enough and Time: The Memoirs of Aga Khan* (New York, 1954), 181. Not coincidentally, this vision bears a striking resemblance to some of the rhetoric that swirled around the idea of Pakistan in the early 1940s. See V. Dhulipala, *Creating a New Medina: State Power, Islam, and the Quest for Pakistan in Late Colonial North India* (Cambridge, 2015).

25. Ahmad Qasim Gouda's memoir (*Marid min al-Sharq*, 1950) about his travels in India as a member of the 1939 Wafd embassy is a case in point. Published in 1950, it is replete with fanciful illustrations of snake charmers, elephants, and dancing girls—the publisher's attempt, perhaps, to liven up Gouda's account of their many political meetings.

26. On Egyptian Islamists' admiration for Gandhi, see R.B. Sadeh, "Debating Gandhi in al-Manar during the 1920s and 1930s," *Comparative Studies of South Asia, Africa and the Middle East* 38:3 (2018); N.A.I. Khan, *Egyptian-Indian Nationalist Collaboration*, 114–23; on Tagore and Japan, see my note 20.

27. N.A.I. Khan, *Egyptian-Indian Nationalist Collaboration*, 110; E. Elhalaby, "Empire and Arab Indology," *Modern Intellectual History* 19:4 (2022); C. Stolte, "'The Asiatic Hour': New Perspectives on the Asian Relations Conference, New Delhi, 1947," in Miskovic et al., *Non-Aligned Movement*, 75–93.

28. I am immensely grateful to Mattias Olesen for sharing his PhD dissertation with me and look forward to his forthcoming book on interwar Easternism in Egypt. M.G. Olesen, "The Future Is Eastern: Muhammad Lutfi Jum'a (1886–1953) and the *Drang nach Osten* in Interwar Egypt" (PhD diss., Aarhus University, 2023).

29. Priya Satia delivered the 2024 Nehru Memorial Lecture at King's College, London, while I was in the final weeks of revising this manuscript. Her lucid insights into Nehru's pragmatism, and the ways in which it limited him, helped me articulate what I was struggling to get at in a generation of his political contemporaries.

30. This book is part of a much broader wave of new transnational work on the entanglement of interwar Arab and South Asian histories, many focused on the 1947/48 partitions as connected events. See esp. A. Dubnov and L. Dobson, eds., *Partitions: A Transnational History of Twentieth-Century Territorial Separatism* (Stanford, 2019); M. Birnbaum, "Entangled Empire: Religion and the Transnational History of Pakistan and Israel," *Millennium* 50:2 (2022); Devji, *Muslim Zion*; V. Kattan and A. Ranjan, eds., *The Breakup of India and Palestine: The Causes and Legacies of Partition* (Manchester, 2023); P. Sinanoglou, *Partitioning Palestine: British Policymaking at the End of Empire* (Chicago, 2019).

31. On Indra's Net and global history see E.M.B. O'Halloran, "From Imperial History to Global Histories of Empire: Writing in and for the 21st Century," *Past and Present Blog*, Past and Present Society, 21 October 2020, https://pastandpresent.org.uk/from-imperial-history-to-global-histories-of-empire-writing-in-and-for-the-21st-century.

32. Mishra, *From the Ruins*, 1–11; Aydin, *Politics of Anti-Westernism*, chap. 4.

33. This is revealed in the pathbreaking scholarship of Zvi Ben-Dor Benite and John Chen: Benite, "Nine Years in Egypt"; Chen, "Re-Orientation."

34. On India's sphere of influence see Blyth, *Empire of the Raj*; on Nehru's pan-Asianism see Louro, *Comrades against Imperialism*.

35. On the emergence of pan-Islamic discourses as a political response to Western colonialism see Aydin, *Idea of the Muslim World*, and Mishra, *From the Ruins*, chap. 2.

36. An Azharite delegation sent to India met with Gandhi and produced a semiofficial report on Muslim life in India, portions of which were reprinted in the press. The contents of the report were deemed patronizing and disparaging toward Indian Muslims, causing some consternation. *Dirasat li-Hawal al-Tawa'if wa al-Hayat al-Islamiyya bi al-Hind* (Cairo, 1937); "Azhar: Missions to Various Countries," n.d. FO 141/649.

37. A similar point is made by Green in *How Asia Found Herself*, 7.

38. An early connection was made in Robert Tignor's article on the "Indianization" of Egypt's administration at the hands of British civil servants imported from the raj in the late nineteenth and early twentieth centuries. Roger Owen made a similar point about Lord Cromer in 1965 (a subject recently elaborated on and theorized by Aaron Jakes). Several years later Sudha Rao and Zaheer Quraishi offered Indian perspectives on Middle Eastern history, though without engaging transnational methodologies; the first article on Egyptian-Indian nationalist links in the interwar period, by Miloslav Krása, appeared around the same time, in 1973. Together these form the only scholarly works on Egyptian-Indian ties predating Noor Khan's groundbreaking 2011 book. R.L. Tignor, "Indianization of the Egyptian Administration under British Rule," *American Historical Review* 68:3 (1963); R. Owen, "The Influence of Lord Cromer's Indian Experience on British Policy in Egypt, 1883–1907," *Middle Eastern Affairs* 4 (1965); Z.M. Quraishi, *Liberal Nationalism in Egypt: Rise and Fall of the Wafd Party* (Allahabad, 1970); S.V. Rao, *The Arab-Israeli Conflict: The Indian View* (Delhi, 1972); M. Krása, "Relations between the Indian National Congress and the Wafd Party of Egypt in the Thirties," *Archiv Orientalni* 41 (1973); A.G. Jakes, *Egypt's Occupation: Colonial Economism and the Crisis of Capital* (Stanford, 2020).

39. N.A.I. Khan, *Egyptian-Indian Nationalist Collaboration*, 11.

40. R. Ginat, *Egypt and the Struggle for Power in Sudan: From World War II to Nasserism* (Cambridge, 2017); E.M. Troutt Powell, *A Different Shade of Colonialism: Egypt, Great Britain, and the Mastery of the Sudan* (Berkeley, 2003).

41. My thinking on interwar alternatives to the nation-state owes significant debts to (among others) Bardaouil, *Egyptian Surrealism*; Devji, *Muslim Zion*; P. Satia, *Time's Monster: How History Makes History* (Cambridge, MA, 2020).

42. N.A.I. Khan, *Egyptian-Indian Nationalist Collaboration*, 8.

Chapter One: Morning in Cairo

1. M. Iqbal, *Pas Chih Bayad Kard ay Aqwam-i-Mashriq ma'a Musafir* (Karachi, 1936), lines 18–20.

2. S. Bose and A. Jalal, *Modern South Asia: History, Culture, Political Economy*, 2nd ed. (London, 2014), 52–53.

3. On the EIC, see W. Dalrymple, *The Anarchy: The Relentless Rise of the East India Company* (London, 2019); P.J. Stern, *The Company-State: Corporate Sovereignty and the Early Modern Foundations of the British Empire in India* (Oxford, 2011); J. Wilson,

The Domination of Strangers: Modern Governance in Eastern India, 1780–1835 (London, 2008).

4. K. Wagner, *Rumours and Rebels: A New History of the Indian Uprising of 1857* (Oxford, 2017).

5. The literature on the rebellion is vast, as illustrated by and documented in C. Bates, ed., *Mutiny at the Margins: New Perspectives on the Indian Uprising of 1857*, vol. 6, *Perception, Narration and Reinvention: The Pedagogy and Historiography of the Indian Uprising* (London, 2014).

6. P. Deshpande, "The Making of an Indian Nationalist Archive: Lakshmibai, Jhansi, and 1857," *Journal of Asian Studies* 67:3 (2008).

7. Mishra, *From the Ruins*, 56–59; T. Metcalf, *The Aftermath of Revolt: India 1857–1970* (Princeton, 1964), 296–303.

8. See esp. K. Fahmy, *All the Pasha's Men: Mehmed Ali, His Army and the Making of Modern Egypt* (Cambridge, 1997).

9. Mishra, *From the Ruins*, 74–76; on the canal, see Huber, *Channelling Mobilities*; Aaron Jakes's forthcoming *Tilted Waters: The World the Suez Canal Made* also promises to break new ground.

10. J. Abu-Lughod, "Tale of Two Cities: The Origins of Modern Cairo," *Comparative Studies in Society and History* 7:4 (1965).

11. Jakes, *Egypt's Occupation*, 37.

12. On the Urabi Revolt, see J.R. Cole, *Colonialism and Revolution in the Middle East: Social and Cultural Origins of Egypt's 'Urabi Movement* (Cairo, 1999).

13. Owen, "Influence of Lord Cromer"; Tignor, "Indianization of the Egyptian Administration"; see also Jakes, *Egypt's Occupation*.

14. H.A.H. Omar, "Empire, Islam, and the Invention of 'Politics' in Egypt, 1867–1914" (DPhil thesis, University of Oxford, 2016), chap. 3.

15. Z. Fahmy, "Francophone Egyptian Nationalists, Anti-British Discourse, and European Public Opinion, 1885–1910: The Case of Mustafa Kamil and Ya'qub Sannu," *Comparative Studies of South Asia, Africa and the Middle East* 28:1(2008).

16. Jakes, *Egypt's Occupation*, 130–35; N.A.I. Khan, *Egyptian-Indian Nationalist Collaboration*, 22–26.

17. N.A.I. Khan, *Egyptian-Indian Nationalist Collaboration*, 25.

18. N.A.I. Khan, 28.

19. N. Sengupta, *Bengal Divided: The Unmaking of a Nation, 1905–1971* (London, 2007), 16.

20. B.R. Nanda, *Gokhale: The Indian Moderates and the British Raj* (Delhi, 1999), vol. 3, chaps. 22–23.

21. Sengupta, *Bengal Divided*, 15–18.

22. Sengupta, 15–18.

23. On the evolution of British airpower in the Middle East, see esp. Satia, *Spies in Arabia*; P. Satia, "The Defense of Inhumanity: Air Control and the British idea of Arabia," *American Historical Review* 111:1 (2006).

24. This intentionally visceral metaphor crops up frequently in the archives and was a favorite expression of the British High Commissioner (later Ambassador) to Egypt,

Miles Lampson. See esp. the Diaries of Lord Killearn (hereafter Lampson Diaries), St Antony's College, Middle East Centre Archive; see also J. Darwin, "Imperialism in Decline? Tendencies in British Imperial Policy between the Wars," *Historical Journal* 23 (1980): 668.

25. Jakes, *Egypt's Occupation*, 135.

26. Bose and Jalal, *Modern South Asia*, 102.

27. B.R. Nanda, *Gandhi: Pan-Islamism, Imperialism, and Nationalism in India* (Bombay, 1989), 188.

28. C. Markovits, "Making Sense of the War (India)," in *International Encyclopedia of the First World War*, ed. U. Daniel et al. (Berlin, 2014).

29. K. Chattopadhyay, *Inner Recesses, Outer Spaces: Memoirs* (New Delhi, 1986), 48.

30. Hussein Omar and Jonathan Wyrtzen, among others, have pushed back against depictions of Woodrow Wilson as the "inspiration" behind postwar calls for self-determination, in Egypt and elsewhere—a thesis attributed to E. Manela, *The Wilsonian Moment: Self-Determination and the International Origins of Anti-colonial Nationalism* (Oxford, 2007). H.A.H. Omar, "Arabic Thought in the Liberal Cage," in *Islam after Liberalism*, ed. F. Devji and Z. Kazmi (London, 2019); H.A.H. Omar, "The Arab Spring of 1919," *LRB Blog*, London Review of Books, 4 April 2019, https://www.lrb.co.uk/blog/2019/april/the-arab-spring-of-1919; J. Wyrtzen, *Worldmaking in the Long Great War: How Local and Colonial Struggles Shaped the Modern Middle East* (Columbia, 2022).

31. H. Sha'arawi, *Harem Years*, trans. Margot Badran (London, 1986).

32. H. Sha'arawi, *Harem Years*.

33. A fuller account of this incident appears in D.M. Reid, *Contesting Antiquity in Egypt: Archaeologies, Museums and the Struggle for Identities from World War I to Nasser* (Cairo, 2015), 51–74.

34. A. Shawqi, *al-Shawqiyyat*, vol. 2 (Cairo, 1946), 159–60, qtd. Reid, *Contesting Antiquity*, 71–72.

35. Qtd. Reid, *Contesting Antiquity*, 48.

36. S.S. Hasan, *Christians versus Muslims in Modern Egypt: The Century-Long Struggle for Coptic Equality* (Oxford, 2003), 4.

37. Z. Fahmy, *Ordinary Egyptians*, 31.

38. Qtd. J. Abu-Lughod, *Cairo: 1001 Years of the City Victorious* (Princeton, 1971), 430.

39. Abu-Lughod, "Tale of Two Cities," 430.

40. Z. Fahmy, *Ordinary Egyptians*, 33–34.

41. On the various competing modes of time in colonial Egypt, see esp. O. Barak, *On Time: Technology and Temporality in Modern Egypt* (Berkeley, 2013).

42. I am grateful to Roy Bar Sadeh for sharing with me his images of *Islami Dunya* issues held in the collection of the British Library.

43. B.D. Cannon, *Symbolism and Folk Imagery in Early Egyptian Political Caricatures: The Wafd Election Campaign, 1920–1923* (Salt Lake City, 2019), chap. 6; on feminine depictions of the nation, see B. Baron, *Egypt as a Woman: Nationalism, Gender and Politics* (Berkeley, 2007).

44. For a fuller discussion, see M. Eppel, "Note about the Term *Effendiyya* in the History of the Middle East," *International Journal of Middle East Studies* 41:3 (2009);

L. Ryzova, *The Age of the Efendiyya: Passages to Modernity in National-Colonial Egypt* (Oxford, 2014).

45. Cannon, *Symbolism and Folk Imagery*, chap. 6.

46. Troutt Powell, *Different Shade*, 7; Ginat, *Egypt and the Struggle for Power*, chap. 2.

47. H. Lüthy, "India and East Africa: Imperial Partnership at the End of the First World War," *Journal of Contemporary History* 6:2 (1971).

48. A. Khan, *India in Transition: A Study in Political Evolution* (Bombay, 1918), 127.

49. Qtd. Lüthy, "India and East Africa," 84.

50. A.D. Barder, "Scientific Racism, Race War and the Global Racial Imaginary," *Third World Quarterly* 40:2 (2019); M. Lake and H. Reynolds, *Drawing the Global Colour Line: White Men's Countries and the International Challenge of Racial Equality* (Cambridge, 2008); L.J. Weaver, "The Laboratory of Scientific Racism: India and the Origins of Anthropology," *Annual Review of Anthropology* 51 (2022).

51. The scholarly debate over Gandhi's racist statements and pro-imperialist activities during his time in South Africa is productively engaged in A. Burton et al., "The South African Gandhi: Stretcher-Bearer of Empire," *Journal of Natal and Zulu History* 32:1 (2018).

52. See also Troutt Powell, *Different Shade*; Lüthy, "India and East Africa," and M.A. Rhett, *The Global History of the Balfour Declaration* (New York, 2016), chap. 6.

53. On the mandates system, see esp. S. Pedersen, *The Guardians: The League of Nations and the Crisis of Empire* (Oxford, 2015).

54. P. Andrew, *America's Forgotten Middle East Initiative: The King-Crane Commission of 1919* (London, 2015).

55. M. Tessler, *A History of the Israeli-Palestinian Conflict*, 2nd ed. (Bloomington, 2009), 145–55.

56. S. Avineri, *The Making of Modern Zionism: The Intellectual Origins of the Jewish State* (London, 2017); W. Laqueur, *A History of Zionism* (London, 2003).

57. M. Macmillan, *Paris 1919: Six Months That Changed the World* (New York, 2003), 410.

58. Tessler, *History of the Israeli-Palestinian Conflict*, 150; Macmillan, *Paris*, 410–20.

59. A.F. Khater, *Sources in the History of the Modern Middle East*, 2nd ed. (Boston, 2010), 155.

60. Macmillan, *Paris*, 416.

61. Great Britain, contributor, and League of Nations, author, *Mandate for Palestine and Memorandum by the British Government Relating to Its Application to Transjordan* (Geneva, 1922).

62. MacMillan, *Paris*, 420; Rhett, *Global History*, 160.

63. Montagu, "The Anti-Semitism of the Present Government," 23 August 1917, CAB 21/58. On Montagu's anti-Zionism, see esp. Rhett, *Global History*.

64. Chattopadhyay, *Inner Recesses*, 48.

65. N.A.I. Khan, *Egyptian-Indian Nationalist Collaboration*, 29–30; see also M. Goebel, *Anti-Imperial Metropolis: Interwar Paris and the Seeds of Third World Nationalism* (Cambridge, 2015).

66. A.K. Ahmad, *Thawrat al-Hind al-Siyasiyya: Ithr Tarikha wa Wassaf Haqiqa*, trans. A.R. al-Malihi (Cairo, 1922).

67. M.D. Rida, *Abtal al-Wataniyya: Mustafa Kamil, Sa'ad Zaghlul, Mustafa Kemal, Mahatma Ghandi, Mudabbaja bi-Aqlam Uzuma Munshi Hadha al-Asr* (Cairo, 1923); N.A.I. Khan, *Egyptian-Indian Nationalist Collaboration*, 113.

68. A. Shawqi, *al-Mosua' ash-Shawqiyya: al-'Amaal al-Kamila li-'Ameer ash-Shua'ara' Ahmad Shawqi*, vol. 3, ed. I. al-Ibyaari (Beirut, 1994).

69. F. Radwan, *al-Mahatma Ghandi: Hayatahu wa Jihadhu* (Cairo, 1934), qtd. N.A.I. Khan, *Egyptian-Indian Nationalist Collaboration*, 120.

70. N.A.I. Khan, *Egyptian-Indian Nationalist Collaboration*, 112.

71. R. Guha, *Gandhi 1914–1948: The Years That Changed the World* (London, 2018), 474–75.

72. A. Youssef, *Independent Egypt* (London, 1940), 199.

73. Qtd. Guha, *Gandhi*, 474–75.

74. The image appears in H. Wassef and N. Wassef, eds., *Daughters of the Nile: Photographs of the Egyptian Women's Movement, 1900–1960* (Cairo, 2001).

75. S. Sharawi Lafranchi, *Casting Off the Veil: The Life of Huda Shaarawi* (London, 2012), 176.

76. N.A.I. Khan, *Egyptian-Indian Nationalist Collaboration*.

77. Louro, *Comrades against Imperialism*.

Chapter Two: Whose Caliphate?

1. A. Shawqi, *al-Shawqiyyat*, vol. 1 (Cairo, 1946), 116.

2. M.A. Jauhar, *Kalam-e-Jauhar* (Delhi, 1936).

3. Qtd. I. Gershoni and J. Jankowski, *Egypt, Islam, and the Arabs: The Search for Egyptian Nationhood, 1900–1930* (Oxford, 1986), 72. Reproduced with the permission of Oxford University Press through PLSclear.

4. On the Silk Letters conspiracy see E.M.B. O'Halloran, "A Tempest in a British Teapot: The Arab Question in Cairo and Delhi," in *1916 in Global Context: An Anti-Imperial Moment*, ed. E. Dal Lago, R. Healy, and G. Barry (London, 2018), 103–16.

5. "We are devoted and loyal subjects of the British Government," wrote Syed Ahmad Khan. "We are not the subjects of Sultan Abdul Hamid II. . . . He neither had, nor can have any spiritual jurisdiction over us as Khalifa." Qtd. P. Dixit, "Political Objectives of the Khilafat Movement in India," in M. Hasan, *Communal and Pan-Islamic Trends*.

6. D.S. Lelyveld, *Aligarh's First Generation: Muslim Solidarity and English Education in Northern India, 1875–1900* (Chicago,1975).

7. Khaliquzzaman, *Pathway to Pakistan* (London, 1961), 14.

8. In 1920, at the height of the Khilafat Movement, a group of prominent Aligarh alumni would go so far as to establish an alternative, nationalist institution, the Jamia Millia Islamia (National Muslim University)—initially located, in insurrectionary fashion, on the grounds of Aligarh itself. The college had been closed by its board of trustees in an attempt to suppress nationalist strike action initiated by students and faculty. S.H. Haider, "Jamia Millia Islamia: The Formative Phase (1920–1947)" (PhD thesis, Aligarh Muslim University, 2012).

9. B. Akçapar, *People's Mission to the Ottoman Empire: M. A. Ansari and the Indian Medical Mission, 1912–13* (Oxford, 2014). In his description of the mission, Khaliquzzaman recalled the difficulties they encountered in communicating with their hosts: "Not knowing the Turkish language we felt very awkward in meeting people and talking to them only in broken phrases, composed of English, Urdu and a few words of Persian and Arabic." Khaliquzzaman, *Pathway to Pakistan*, 21.

10. N.R. Keddie, *Sayyid Jamaluddin al-Afghani: A Political Biography* (Berkley, 1972); N.R. Keddie, *An Islamic Response to Imperialism: Political and Religious Writings of Sayyid Jamāl ad-Dīn "al-Afghānī"* (Berkeley, 1983); A. Hourani, *Arabic Thought in the Liberal Age, 1798–1939* (Cambridge, 2012), chap. 5; Mishra, *From the Ruins*, chap. 2.

11. Cole, *Colonialism and Revolution*, 195; P. Gopal, *Insurgent Empire*, 141–43, 148–50.

12. M. Hasan, "Religion and Politics in India: The Ulama and the Khilafat Movement," in M. Hasan, *Communal and Pan-Islamic Trends*, 7; Keddie, *Islamic Response*, 59, 101; Mishra, *From the Ruins*, 94–98.

13. On the rather nebulous history of caliphs and caliphates, see Aydin, *Idea of the Muslim World*, 19–24.

14. In an appreciation of Indian domestic politics for the *Arab Bulletin* in 1916, a political agent of the raj explained: "When we were pro-Turk and anti-Russian we, too, rallied Indian Moslems to the Prophet's Standard, filling their minds with novel ideas regarding the Ottoman Caliphate. . . . Until a few years ago, Great Britain was regarded as the champion of Turkey and of the Ottoman Caliphate." *Arab Bulletin*, 522–23.

15. *The Comrade*, Calpack hat advertisement, 10 October 1914, 283.

16. M. Hasan, "Religion and Politics in India," in M. Hasan, *Communal and Pan-Islamic Trends*, 26.

17. *The Comrade*, "Indian Moslems and the War," 7 November 1914, 344.

18. "Statement of Indian Muslim Views on Palestine," 14 February 1939, CO 733/408/13.

19. F. Zaman, "Futurity and the Political Thought of North Indian Muslims, c. 1900–1925" (DPhil thesis, University of Cambridge), 179–80.

20. On the complex encounter between Indian sepoys and "enemy" in Ottoman lands see S. Das, "'Their Lives Have Become Ours': Counter-Encounters in Mesopotamia, 1915–1918," in *Militarized Cultural Encounters in the Long Nineteenth Century: War, Culture and Society, 1750–1850*, ed. J. Clarke and J. Horne (London, 2018).

21. Hasan, "Religion and Politics," 17.

22. Translation of address by Muhammad Ali, written by the extra assistant commissioner Abdus Subhan Khan, 30 May 1919. Qtd. Zaman, "Futurity," 180.

23. A. Özcan, *Pan-Islamism: Indian Muslims, the Ottomans and Britain, 1877–1924*, vol. 12 (Leiden, 1997), 155–56.

24. A. Fatima, "Maulana Muhammad Ali Jauhar: A Man Who Chose the Pen above the Sword," *Dawn* 4 (January 2015).

25. "Mairay boorhay hathon mein abhi bhi itni jaan hai kay mein tumhara gala daba doon." Fatima, "Maulana Muhammad Ali Jauhar."

26. Qtd. V. Menon, *Indian Women and Nationalism: The U.P. Story* (New Delhi, 2003), 61.

27. Khaliquzzaman, *Pathway to Pakistan*, 33.

28. Bose and Jalal, *Modern South Asia*, 114–16.

29. Madihah Akhter notes that purdah was interpreted by some of its practitioners as an anticolonial and nationalist expression, because it was a custom untainted by and in defiance of Western-imperial value systems. This context is important to place alongside the observation that, in both Egypt and India, it was the urgent requirements of the nationalist movements that began to pull women out of seclusion and into the public sphere. See M. Akhter, "In Her Own Right: Sovereignty and Gender in Princely Bhopal" (PhD diss., Stanford University, 2020); also G. Minault, "Purdah Politics," in *Separate Worlds: Studies of Purdah in South Asia*, ed. H. Papaneck and G. Minault (New Delhi, 1982).

30. Qtd. Menon, *Indian Women*, 67.

31. S. Muhammad, *Freedom Movement in India: The Role of the Ali Brothers* (New Delhi, 1979), 160.

32. Menon, *Indian Women*, 68. It is speculated that Bi Amman's punishing schedule of tours and speaking engagements—across the Punjab, Bombay, Bihar, and her native United Province—hastened her demise; she died alongside hopes for the Khilafat Movement itself in 1924.

33. Qtd. Minault, "Urdu Political Poetry during the Khilafat Movement," *Modern Asian Studies* 8:4 (1974): 470–71.

34. Qtd. M.A. Forster, "The Resignation of Montagu," *Round Table* 58:231 (1968): 328.

35. Devji, *Muslim Zion*, 82–83; see also A. Jalal, *The Sole Spokesman: Jinnah, the Muslim League and the Demand for Pakistan* (Cambridge, 1994), 8–10.

36. Nanda, *Gandhi*, 372.

37. S. Amin, *Event, Metaphor, Memory: Chauri Chaura, 1922–1992* (Berkeley, 1995).

38. A. Khan, *World Enough*, 197–98.

39. P.B. Kinross, *The Ottoman Centuries: The Rise and Fall of the Turkish Empire* (London, 1977), 384.

40. B. Lewis, *The Emergence of Modern Turkey* (Oxford, 1961), 263; see also "Ameer Ali's Letter with the Aga Khan to His Excellency Ghazi Ismat Pasha, The Prime Minister of Turkey," in *The Right Honourable Syed Ameer Ali: Political Writings*, ed. S. Muhammad (New Delhi, 1989), 288–90.

41. B.M. Nafi, "The Abolition of the Caliphate: Causes and Consequences," in *The Different Aspects of Islamic Culture*, vol. 6, part 1, *Islam in the World Today*, ed. A. Ali, I.D. Thiam, and Y.A. Talib (Paris, 2016), 185.

42. C. Nallino, "La fine del cosiddetto califatto ottomano," *Oriente Moderno* 4:3 (15 March 1924): 141–42.

43. M.H. Muhammad, *al-Lttijahat al-Wataniyya fi al-Adab al-Mu'asir* (Cairo, 1954).

44. *Al-Siyasa*, 5 March 1924, 4. On the contours of the caliphate debate in the Egyptian press, see "Egypt and the Caliphate Question, 1924–1926," in Gershoni and Jankowski, *Egypt, Islam, and the Arabs*, 55–74.

45. Another prominent admirer of Ibn Saud was Rashid Rida in Cairo. For a comparative analysis of his reaction to the caliphate crisis and that of the INC leader Abul

Kalam Azad, see J. Willis, "Debating the Caliphate: Islam and Nation in the Work of Rashid Rida and Abul Kalam Azad," *International History Review* 32:4 (2010): 711–32.

46. J. Teitelbaum, "Hashemites, Egyptians and Saudis: The Tripartite Struggle for the Pilgrimage in the Shadow of Ottoman Defeat," *Middle Eastern Studies* 56:1 (2020): 43–44.

47. *Al-Akhbar*, 19 March 1924, 3.

48. Qtd. Gershoni and Jankowski, *Egypt, Islam, and the Arabs*, 58, 71.

49. For a full account of these machinations, see Teitelbaum, "Hashemites, Egyptians and Saudis," 36–47.

50. Gershoni and Jankowski, *Egypt, Islam, and the Arabs*.

51. A.R.A. al-Sanhuri, *Le Califat: Son évolution vers une société des nations orientales* (Paris, 1926). Mattias Olesen offers a rich analysis of Sanhuri's intriguing thesis—see Olesen, "The Future Is Eastern," 90–96.

52. B.M. Nafi, "The General Islamic Congress of Jerusalem Reconsidered," *Muslim World* 86:3-4 (1996): 270.

53. A. Khan, *World Enough*, 181, 191. Despite his apparent wistfulness for the "missed opportunity" of a Muslim or Eastern federation, the Aga Khan's memoir glosses over his involvement with the Khilafat Movement. It may be inferred that his personal role in catalyzing the Caliphate's dissolution was not among the scenes of his life which the Aga Khan was eager to relive.

54. Muhammad Ali called for a Supreme Islamic Council composed of international representatives from across the Muslim world. See esp. J.M. Willis, "Burying Mohamed Ali Jauhar: The Life and Death of the Meccan Republic," *International Journal of Archaeology and Social Sciences in the Arabian Peninsula* 17 (2023); M.S. Kramer, *Islam Assembled: The Advent of the Muslim Congresses* (New York, 1986), 124.

55. Rida's proposal during the Mecca conference for a *mithaq isalmi* (Islamic pact) would have bound Muslim governments to resolve disputes among themselves through arbitration, conducted by an international body at Mecca—what Kramer describes as a "league of Muslim states." See Kramer, *Islam Assembled*, 115.

56. *Al-Muqattam*, 21 May 1926; Gershoni and Jankowski, *Egypt, Islam, and the Arabs*, 70.

57. They were Nashashibis, a fact that proved significant to the contours of future regional alliances. Hajj Amin al-Husseini, leader of the rival (dominant) Palestinian faction, did not come to Cairo but attended the congress in Mecca where he forged alliances with Egyptian nationalists and Indian Khilafatists. Nafi, "General Islamic Congress," 256.

58. Kramer, *Islam Assembled*, 93.

59. At the World Islamic Congress in Mecca, Muhammad Ali told Sheikh Muhammad al-Ahmadi al-Zawahiri that Britain's continued presence in Egypt formed the major stumbling block to Indian support for a caliphate there: "Were it not for this, they would have bound all their hopes to Egypt," Zawahiri recorded. Report by Sheikh Muhammad al-Ahmadi al-Zawahiri, n.d., as translated by Kramer, *Islam Assembled*, 109; see also M.N. Qureshi, *Pan-Islam in British Indian Politics: A Study of the Khilafat Movement, 1918–1924* (Leiden, 1999), 400.

60. Nafi, "Abolition," 190.

61. On Soviet involvement in the conference, see R.B. Sadeh, "Worldmaking in the Hijaz: Muslims between South Asian and Soviet Visions of Managing Difference, 1919–1926," *Comparative Studies in Society and History* 66:1 (2024).

62. Report by Sheikh Muhammad al-Ahmadi al-Zawahiri, n.d., qtd. Kramer, *Islam Assembled*, 109.

63. Willis, "Burying Mohamed Ali Jauhar."

64. H. Wahba, *Jazirat al-Arab fi al Qarn al-Ashreen* (Cairo, 1956), 157–58; see also Wahba's letter to Amin Bey, 22 October 1926, in which he describes a growing affinity between Indians and Egyptians in opposition to Ibn Saud. Excerpted in Kramer, *Islam Assembled*, 120.

Chapter Three: The Poetic East

1. R. Tagore, *Gitanjali: Song Offerings*, ed. W.B. Yeats (London, 1914).

2. A. Shawqi, *al-Mosua' ash-Shawqiyya: al-'Amaal al-Kamila li-'Ameer ash-Shua'ara' Ahmad Shawqi*, vol. 3 (Beirut, 1994).

3. As quoted in M.A. Jauhar, speech to the Fourth Plenary Session of the First Round Table Conference, London, 19 November 1930. G. Allana, ed., *Pakistan Movement Historical Documents* (Karachi, 1969), 67.

4. *Egyptian Gazette*, "Rabindranath Tagore at the Alhambra," 29 November 1926: 3.

5. *Egyptian Gazette*, 3.

6. *Egyptian Gazette*, "Sir Rabindranath Tagore: Lecture in Cairo," 2 December 1926, 3.

7. T. Hussein, *The Days: His Autobiography in Three Parts*, trans. E.H. Paxton, H. Wayment, and K. Cragg (Cairo, 1997), 383–84.

8. Hawas, "World Literature," 228.

9. In the same issue of the *Egyptian Gazette* that reported on Tagore's lecture, the cinemas of Alexandria advertised *The Mystic*, starring Aileen Pringle as Zara, a turbaned psychic and charlatan.

10. *Egyptian Gazette*, "Rabindranath Tagore: A Great Personality," 30 November 1926, 3.

11. Hasan, " Khilafat Movement," 7; Keddie, *Islamic Response*, 59, 101; Mishra, *From the Ruins*, 94–98.

12. A. 'Abd al-Raziq, "Khusum al-Rabita al-Sharqiyya min al-Sharqiyyin," *Majallat al-Rabita al-Sharqiyya* 2:4 (1930): 27.

13. Jankowski, "Eastern Idea," 661.

14. Jankowski, 655.

15. This point has also been made by Khan, who notes that Indians made up almost one-third of the foreign visitors hosted by the Eastern Bond Society and its leading members in Cairo during the 1920s. N.A.I. Khan, *Egyptian-Indian Nationalist Collaboration*, 103.

16. Jankowski, "Eastern Idea," is representative.

17. "Madame Soumé Tcheng," *L'Egyptienne* (October 1927); J. Marques, "Ferdinand Duchene et la situation de la femme Kabyle," *L'Egyptienne* (August 1927): 14–21; "Ex-

trait des mémoires de Halide Edib," *L'Egyptienne* (April 1927): 14–16; J. Marques, "Un nouvel aspect du génie de M. Magre: 'Le roman de Confucius,'" *L'Egyptienne* (July 1927), 8–13; Enrique Gomez Carillo, "Les femmes et la loi juive," *L'Egyptienne* (July 1927): 26–28; C.A. Lazarides, "Organisation de l'empire pharaonique d'Asie à l'époque de Tel el Amarna," *L'Egyptienne* (October 1927): 2–9.

18. Nehru's engagement with the League Against Imperialism has been documented most extensively in Louro, *Comrades against Imperialism*.

19. Louro, *Comrades against Imperialism*; J. Brown, *Nehru: A Political Life* (New Haven, 2003); B. Zachariah, *Nehru*, Routledge Historical Biographies (London, 2004).

20. J. Nehru, "Report on the Brussels Congress," in *Selected Works of Jawaharlal Nehru*, ed. S. Gopal, vol. 2 (New Delhi, 1972), 278–97.

21. Nehru, "Report on the Brussels Congress," 2:278–97; Louro, *Comrades against Imperialism*, 51.

22. "A Foreign Policy for India," 13 September 1927, in S. Gopal, *Selected Works of Jawaharlal Nehru*, 2:348–64.

23. M.A. Jauhar, speech to the Fourth Plenary Session of the First Round Table Conference, 19 November 1930. Allana, *Pakistan Movement*, 69.

24. Qtd. Hawas, "World Literature," 228–29.

25. Described most evocatively by Mishra, *From the Ruins*, prologue.

26. C. Aydin, "A Global Anti-Western Moment? The Russo-Japanese War, Decolonization, and Asian Modernity," in *Competing Visions of World Order: Global Moments and Movements, 1880s–1930s*, ed. S. Conrad and D. Sachsenmaier (New York, 2007).

27. R. Tagore, *Nationalism* (1917, reprint, London, 2010), 7; see also Frost, "Great Ocean."

28. Rida began writing about Japan's conversion in the months following the victory at Tsushima in May 1905; see for example, "Da'wat al-Yaban ila al-Islam," *al-Manar*, 8:18 (November 13, 1905); "Da'wat al-Islam fi al-Yaban," *al-Manar* 9:1 (February 24, 1906).

29. Okakura, "Ideals of the East," qtd. Frost, "Great Ocean," 267–68.

30. Nehru, "Report on the Brussels Congress," 2:278–97. On the romanticizing of Arabs and Arabia see Satia, *Spies in Arabia*, chap. 5.

31. W. Armbrust, "The Ubiquitous Non-Presence of India: Peripheral Visions from Egyptian Popular Culture," in *Global Bollywood: Travels of Hindi Song and Dance*, ed. S. Gopal and S. Moorti (Minneapolis, 2008), 200–220.

32. A similar point is made by Armbrust, "Ubiquitous Non-Presence," 206–7.

33. The idea originated with the High Commissioner Herbert Samuel. See N.E. Roberts, "Making Jerusalem the Centre of the Muslim World: Pan-Islam and the World Islamic Congress of 1931," *Contemporary Levant* 4:1 (2019): 4–5.

34. It is said that Prophet Muhammad was taken to the site by the winged horse Buraq on his Night Journey, and from there ascended to heaven. The Haram al-Sharif is also sometimes called "First Qibla," as Muslims initially oriented themselves toward Jerusalem to pray, before God instructed Muhammad to face Mecca instead.

35. S. Chawla, "The Palestine Issue in Indian Politics in the 1920s," in M. Hasan, *Communal and Pan-Islamic Trends*, 28.

36. Chawla, "Palestine Issue," 31.

37. P. Mattar, *The Mufti of Jerusalem: Al-Hajj Amin al-Husayni and the Palestinian National Movement*, 2nd ed. (New York, 1992), 29–30.

38. I. Pappé, "Hajj Amin and the Buraq Revolt," *Jerusalem Quarterly* 18 (2003): 8.

39. Pappé, "Hajj Amin," 8.

40. H.A. al-Husseini, "General Appeal to the Muslim World," as translated by the Government of Mandate Palestine, qtd. Roberts, "Making Jerusalem the Centre," 5.

41. Nafi, "General Islamic Congress," 244.

42. Roberts, "Making Jerusalem the Centre," 7.

43. Chawla, "Palestine Issue," 33–34.

44. M.A. Jauhar, speech to the Fourth Plenary Session of the First Round Table Conference, London, 19 November 1930. Allana, *Pakistan Movement*, 61–75.

45. M. Azaryahu and Y. Reiter, "The Geopolitics of Interment: An Inquiry into the Burial of Muhammad Ali in Jerusalem, 1931," *Israel Studies* 20:1 (2015): 37–38, 41.

46. *Al-Jamia al-Arabiyya*, 8 January 1931, qtd. Azaryahu and Reiter, "Geopolitics," 39.

47. O. Khalidi, "Indian Muslims and Palestinian Awqaf," *Jerusalem Quarterly* 40 (2009), 53.

48. Azaryahu and Reiter, "Geopolitics," 46–48.

49. Chancellor to Passfield, "Funeral of the Late Maulana Mohammad Ali," 24 January 1931 FO 371/15330.

50. For the early history of the Arab Women's Association, see Fleischmann, *The Nation*, 108–9.

51. A. Nuwayhid, *Rijal min Filastin ma Bayna Bidayat al-Qarn Hatta 'am 1948* (Beirut, 1981), 369.

52. Elhalaby, "Empire and Arab Indology," 13.

53. *Mira'at al-Sharq*, qtd. Azaryahu and Reiter, "Geopolitics," 39.

54. Reid, *Contesting Antiquity*, 310; R.M. Coury, "The Politics of the Funereal: The Tomb of Saad Zaghlul," *Journal of the American Research Center in Egypt* 29 (1992): 191–200.

55. As related by Zaghlul's great-nephew: H.A.H. Omar, "Pharaohs on Parade," *LRB Blog*, London Review of Books, 6 April 2021, https://www.lrb.co.uk/blog/2021/april/pharaohs-on-parade. For a slightly different versions of events, see Coury, "Politics of the Funereal," 193; Reid, *Contesting Antiquity*, 310–11.

56. N. Pothen, *Glittering Decades: New Delhi in Love and War* (New Delhi, 2012), 37.

57. U.C. Bhattacharya and S.S. Chakravarty, eds., *Pandit Motilal Nehru: His Life and Work*, 3rd ed. (Calcutta, 1934), 52.

58. Even if the design was influenced as much by Classical architecture as pharaonic. See Reid, *Contesting Antiquity*, 310.

59. Bhattacharya and Chakravarty, *Pandit Motilal Nehru*, 53–54; this volume is somewhat hagiographic, but it is nevertheless a valuable and relatively exhaustive collection of the elder Nehru's papers, speeches, etc., lovingly compiled. I do not think it is terribly important whether the phrasing of Gandhi's remarks at the pyre is exact—it is obviously his tone and style, and as the first edition appeared in 1931, it was likely transcribed from contemporary newspaper reports.

60. Gandhi Films Foundation / GandhiServe, *Mahatma Gandhi Embarking on SS 'Ra-*

jputana' at Bombay on August 29, 1931, https://www.youtube.com/watch?v=zWW35no1vrk.

61. D. Sumbul, "A Living History," *Newsline*, August 2017.

62. I am grateful to Ashish Jaiswal for sharing this anecdote with Faisal Devji and me. Also see S.Y. Azim, "The Baby in Gandhi's Lap," *Dawn*, 26 February 2017.

63. Gandhi Films Foundation / GandhiServe, Mahatma Gandhi *Embarking*.

64. N.A.I. Khan, *Egyptian-Indian Nationalist Collaboration*, 115.

65. Youssef, *Independent Egypt*, 199.

66. Youssef, 199.

67. Nahas was not permitted to be among them, something he would continue to lament years later (as related in chap. 7). J. Nehru, "A Letter from the Mediterranean," in S. Gopal, *Selected Works of Jawaharlal Nehru*, 9:11–12.

68. Nabaraoui, Ceza. "Après le passage de Mahatma Gandhi," *L'Egyptienne*, December 1931, 2–5.

69. I. Mazhar, trans., *Mahatma Ghandi, Siratahu Kama Katabaha bi-Qalamihi* (Cairo, 1934); S. Musa, *Ghandi wa al-Haraka al-Hindiyya* (Cairo, 1934); Radwan, *al-Mahatma Ghandi*.

70. Rida, *Abtal al-Wataniyya*.

71. Nabaraouii, "Après le passage de Mahatma Gandhi," 2.

72. There is much debate on this point among the conference's organizers and participants, some of whom claim that the idea predated Jauhar's funeral; nevertheless it is clear that the two events were connected, at least insofar as Shawkat Ali's involvement as coorganizer can be traced to his brother's funeral and a publicity tour he subsequently made around Palestine. For a summary of the competing versions of the debate, see Nafi, "General Islamic Congress."

73. For a detailed description of al-Husseini's efforts to overcome official Egyptian reservations to the conference, see T. Mayer, "Egypt and the General Islamic Conference of Jerusalem in 1931," *Middle Eastern Studies* 18:3 (1982): 311–22.

74. Y. Porath, *The Palestine Arab National Movement*, vol. 2, *From Riots to Rebellion* (London, 1977), 12. Freas offers an alternative interpretation of the congress's pro-Christian utterances; see E. Freas, "Hajj Amin al-Husayni and the Haram al-Sharif: A Pan-Islamic or Palestinian Nationalist Cause?" *British Journal of Middle Eastern Studies*, 39:1 (2012): 42, 44.

75. Nafi, "General Islamic Congress," 257.

76. Nafi, 261, 257.

77. Nafi, 265.

78. Nafi, 265.

79. W.C. Matthews, "Pan-Islam or Arab Nationalism? The Meaning of the 1931 Jerusalem Islamic Congress Reconsidered," *International Journal of Middle East Studies* 35:1 (2003): 14.

80. Nabaraoui, "Après le passage de Mahatma Gandhi," 3.

81. "Al-'Atizirat wa Kalimat lil Shu'ara," *al-Ahram*, 5 December 1932, 2 (with deepest thanks to Chihab El Khachab, who helped me locate and access this article during lockdown).

82. "Al-'Atizirat," *al-Ahram*.

Chapter Four: Abyssinia in the Headlines

1. M. Iqbal, *Dharb-i-Kalim* (Karachi, 1936), 173.
2. "'Aoudat al-Mufawadh al-Sami'," *al-Ahram*, 1 October 1935.
3. M.E. Yapp, ed., *Politics and Diplomacy in Egypt: The Diaries of Sir Miles Lampson, 1935–1937* (London, 1997), 305–6.
4. On British interwar internationalism, see H. McCarthy, *The British People and the League of Nations: Democracy, Citizenship and Internationalism, c. 1918–45* (Manchester, 2016).
5. On the prosecution of the Second Italo-Ethiopian War and global reactions to Italian atrocities, see R. Pankhurst, "Italian Fascist War Crimes in Ethiopia: A History of Their Discussion, from the League of Nations to the United Nations (1936–1949)," *Northeast African Studies* 6:1–2 (1999); A. Sbacchi, "Poison Gas and Atrocities in the Italo-Ethiopian War (1935–1936)," in *Italian Colonialism*, ed. R. Ben-Ghiat and M. Fuller, Italian and Italian American Studies (London, 2005); N. Gordon and N. Perugini, *Human Shields: A History of People in the Line of Fire* (Berkeley, 2020).
6. Kuwait Intelligence summary, 16–29 September 1935, IOR L/PS/12/1514.
7. Ormsby-Gore to Baldwin, 8 September 1935, Cambridge University Library, Baldwin papers.
8. Official Report of the Indian Legislative Assembly Debate, 3 September 1935, IOR/L/PS/12/1521.
9. S. Morewood, "This Silly African Business: The Military Dimension of Britain's Response to the Abyssinian Crisis," in *Collision of Empires: Italy's Invasion of Ethiopia and Its International Impact*, ed. B. Strang (Farnham, 2013), 96.
10. Morewood, "Silly African Business," 94–95.
11. On British nonintervention in the Abyssinian Crisis, see Morewood, "Silly African Business"; A. Holt, "'No More Hoares to Paris': British Foreign Policymaking and the Abyssinian Crisis, 1935," *Review of International Studies* 37:3, 2011.
12. The significance of the Singapore Strategy in World War II has been usefully problematized by Bell; it nevertheless remains crucial to understanding British defensive planning in the mid-1930s. See C.M. Bell, *The Royal Navy, Seapower and Strategy between the Wars* (Basingstoke, 2000); L.R. Pratt, *East of Malta, West of Suez: Britain's Mediterranean Crisis 1936–1939* (Cambridge, 2008).
13. C. Brown, "This Changing World," *Washington Evening Star*, December 1935, qtd. N. Mulder, *The Economic Weapon: The Rise of Sanctions as a Tool of Modern War* (New Haven, 2022), 223.
14. Drummond to Eden, 18 March 1936, IOR/L/PS/12/1521.
15. Morewood, *British Defence of Egypt*, 39–40, 58.
16. This emerges in a note by General J.D. Coleridge, then Military Secretary to the India Office, who was present at a War Office meeting on 2 October where Lampson's telegram was read aloud. See Coleridge to C. in C. India, 3 October 1935, IOR/L/MIL/7/19496.
17. CIGS to C. in C. India, 3 October 1935, IOR/L/MIL/7/19496.
18. On Mussolini's vision of a reconstituted Italian empire, see N. Arielli, *Fascist Italy and the Middle East, 1933–1940* (London, 2013), 32–34; R. Pergher, *Mussolini's*

Nation-Empire: Sovereignty and Settlement in Italy's Borderlands, 1922–1943 (Cambridge, 2018), 37–40.

19. Arielli, *Fascist Italy*, 59–60; Bardaouil, *Egyptian Surrealism*, 61, 68–69.

20. Arielli, *Fascist Italy*, 59.

21. Lampson to the Government of India, Army Dept., 5 October 1935, IOR/L/MIL/7/19496.

22. "Indian Publicity in the Middle East—Proposals of the Ambassador at Cairo," 25 April 1941, IOR/L/I/1/790. This statement, and the proposal it appears in, are discussed further in chap. 9 of the present volume.

23. Official Report of the Indian Legislative Assembly Debate, 3 September 1935, IOR/L/PS/12/1521.

24. Official Report, 3 September 1935.

25. "A Note Regarding the Despatch of Reinforcements from India to Egypt in Case of Emergency," October 1935, IOR/L/MIL/7/19496.

26. Marginalia, IOR/L/MIL/7/19496.

27. Arielli, *Fascist Italy*; F. Cavarocchi, *Avanguardie dello spirito: Il fascismo e la propaganda culturale all'estero* (Rome, 2010); C.A. MacDonald, "Radio Bari: Italian Wireless Propaganda in the Middle East and British Countermeasures 1934–38," *Middle Eastern Studies*, 13:2 (1977): 195–207; A. Marzano, *Onde fasciste: La propaganda araba di Radio Bari (1934–43)* (Rome, 2015); M.A. Williams, *Mussolini's Propaganda Abroad: Subversion in the Mediterranean and the Middle East, 1935–1940* (Abingdon, 2006).

28. Italian lire figures appear in Arielli, *Fascist Italy*, 46.

29. "Anis Daoud Effendi," 4 September 1935, FO 141/659.

30. Ministry of the Interior, European Department to the Foreign Office, 19 November 1935, FO 141/659.

31. *L'Abyssinie et l'esclavage*, n.d. (1935), FO 141/659.

32. Williams, *Mussolini's Propaganda Abroad*, 83.

33. MacDonald, "Radio Bari," 195.

34. "Transcript of Bari Broadcast," 15 June 1935, FO 141/659.

35. Metcalfe to Rumbold, 11 June 1937, IOR/L/PS/12/25.

36. A. Buelli, "The Hands Off Ethiopia Campaign, Racial Solidarities and Intercolonial Antifascism in South Asia (1935–36)," *Journal of Global History* 18 (2022): 56.

37. Hamilton to Macann, 28 April 1937, IOR/L/PS/12/25.

38. Italian overtures to Rabindranath Tagore likewise failed to gloss over the colonial violence of the campaign in Ethiopia. See M. Prayer, "Italian Fascist Regime and Nationalist India, 1929–1945," *International Studies* 28:3 (1991), 266–67; G. Procacci, *Dalla parte dell'Etiopia: L'aggressione italiana vista dai movimenti anticolonialisti d'Asia, d'Africa, d'America* (Milan, 1984), 48–58.

39. Arielli, *Fascist Italy*, 48.

40. M. Hauner, *India in the Axis Strategy* (Stuttgart, 1981), 251–52, 366; see also D. Motadel, "The Global Authoritarian Moment and the Revolt against Empire," *American Historical Review* 124:3 (2019).

41. See esp. Gershoni and Jankowski, *Confronting Fascism*; Buelli, "Hands Off Ethi-

opia." See also Arielli, *Fascist Italy*; MacDonald, "Radio Bari"; Marzano, *Onde fasciste*; Williams, *Mussolini's Propaganda Abroad*.

42. Olesen, "The Future Is Eastern," 160; see also H. Erlich, "The Tiger and the Lion: Fascism and Ethiopia in Arab Eyes," in *Arab Responses to Fascism and Nazism: Attraction and Repulsion*, ed. I. Gershoni (Austin, 2014).

43. Arielli, *Fascist Italy*, 57.

44. Gershoni and Jankowski, *Confronting Fascism*, 60–62.

45. See esp. Morewood, "Appeasement from Strength"; chap. 5 in Morewood, *British Defence of Egypt*, and Kolinsky, *Britain's War in the Middle East* (London, 1999), 29–31. For a fuller explanation of this historiography and my divergence from it, see my note 77.

46. "Ma Yishghul Intibha Misr wa Madha Tirrid," *al-Jihad*, 6 October 1935.

47. "E.D. Saleh," 20 September 1935, FO 141/659.

48. "E.D. Saleh."

49. Buelli, "Hands Off Ethiopia," 56.

50. H. de Kerillis, "Le conflit Italie-Éthiopie: Au cours d'une interview sensationelle, M. Mussolini précis ses vues," *L'Echo de Paris*, 21 Juillet 1935.

51. FO 141/659.

52. H.A. Ibrahim, *The 1936 Anglo-Egyptian Treaty* (Khartoum, 1976), 52–56.

53. Gershoni and Jankowski, *Confronting Fascism*, 62.

54. J. Nehru, "Reply to Italian Consul-General (8 May, 1936)," in S. Gopal, *Selected Works of Jawaharlal Nehru*, 7:567.

55. M. Iqbal, *"Mussolini," Dharb i-Kalim* 171, trans. International Iqbal Society.

56. Buelli, "Hands Off Ethiopia," 56.

57. "Anis Daoud Effendi," 4 September 1935, FO 141/659.

58. W.L. Cleveland, *Islam against the West: Shakib Arslan and the Campaign for Islamic Nationalism* (Austin, 1985), xxi.

59. Arielli, *Fascist Italy*, 50–51.

60. Drummond to British consul-general in Milan, 17 December 1936, IOR/L/PS/12/2151; see also Arielli, *Fascist Italy*, 50–51; Buelli, "Hands Off Ethiopia," 63–64.

61. Buelli, "Hands Off Ethiopia," 58–59.

62. Arielli, *Fascist Italy*, 70–71.

63. Arielli, 72–73.

64. Arielli, 70.

65. M.L. Gomaa, *Bayna al-Asad al-Ifriqi wa al-Nimr al-Itali* (Cairo, 1935), 13, 21. As discussed in Erlich, "The Tiger and the Lion," 280–60; Olesen, "The Future Is Eastern," 160.

66. Olesen, "The Future Is Eastern," 161; see also M.L. Gomaa, "Nasib al-Sharq fi Nahdat al-Insaniyya fi al-Mustaqbal: Inhiyar al-Hadara al-Madiyya wa-Inti'ash al-Haya al-Ruhiyya," *al-Rabita al-'Arabiyya*, 8 August 1937, in Gomaa, *Mabahith fi al-Tarikh* (Cairo, 2001), 82.

67. Holt, "No More Hoares," 1384.

68. *Egyptian Gazette*, "Franco-British Peace Plan," 10 December 1935, 5.

69. *Egyptian Gazette*, "Storm of Criticism for Peace Plan," 14 December 1935, 7.
70. D. Cooper, *Old Men Forget* (London, 1953), 192–93.
71. Pedersen, *Guardians*, 297.
72. Mulder, *Economic Weapon*, 221–24.
73. Morewood, "Appeasement from Strength," 106.
74. Qtd. Pratt, *East of Malta*, 3.
75. Lampson Diaries, 26 May 1936.
76. Morewood, "Appeasement from Strength," 549.
77. Gershoni and Jankowski, *Redefining the Egyptian Nation*, 155.

78. As the treaty negotiations are peripheral to the subject of the present volume, I have refrained from excessive detail; however it should be acknowledged that my presentation of the treaty's significance is at odds with much of the British imperial and military historiography. These accounts tend to depict the Anglo-Egyptian Treaty as a coup by Lampson and his team against an Egyptian delegation "forced" to the negotiating table by their fear of Italian aggression. By contrast, historians of interwar Egyptian politics have generally taken for granted that the Wafd had long desired the reopening of negotiations and used the Italian invasion of Ethiopia to force Britain into negotiations and major concessions. The military historiography remains extremely valuable despite these differences in interpretation; see in particular Morewood, "Appeasement from Strength"; Morewood, *British Defence of Egypt*; Kolinsky, and *Britain's War in the Middle East*. For Egyptian perspectives that accord with my own, see A.D. al-Hadidy, "Mustapha al-Nahhas and Political Leadership," and M. el-Feki, "Makram Ebeid: Politician of the Majority Party," both in *Contemporary Egypt: Through Egyptian Eyes*, ed. C. Tripp (London, 1993); Ibrahim, *1936 Anglo-Egyptian Treaty*; M.Y. Zayid, *Egypt's Struggle for Independence* (Beirut, 1965). Unique among British historians of empire, John Darwin tends to accord with the Egyptian view; see *Empire Project*, 472–74. For Egyptian reactions to the Anglo-Egyptian Treaty, see Gershoni and Jankowski, *Redefining the Egyptian Nation*, 155–56.

79. On the India Act, see esp. A. Muldoon, *Empire, Politics and the Creation of the 1935 India Act: Last Act of the Raj* (Abingdon, 2009).

80. D.A. Low, *Britain and Indian Nationalism: The Imprint of Ambiguity 1929–1942* (Cambridge, 1997), 246.

81. Shaarawi distributed scathing antitreaty pamphlets and wrote open letters to Nahas and Members of Parliament calling for a referendum prior to the Anglo-Egyptian Treaty's ratification and demanding that women be permitted to vote in it. One of her principal concerns was that a defensive alliance with Britain would prejudice Egypt's freedom of action in support of "revolutionary Palestine" and could even force Egypt to take up arms against its neighbor. According to Margot Badran, "the question of the 1936 treaty further intensified the feminists' desire for the vote." Badran, *Feminists, Islam, and Nation*, 214–15.

82. J.M. Brown, *Modern India: The Origins of an Asian Democracy* (Oxford, 1994), 296.
83. Darwin, *Empire Project*, 468.
84. Gershoni and Jankowski, *Redefining the Egyptian Nation*, 178.

Chapter Five: Palestine HQ

Parts of chapter 5 are developed from E.M.B. O'Halloran, "India, the Arabs and Britain's Problem in Palestine," *International History Review* 43:3 (2020). Reprinted by permission of Taylor and Francis.

1. Women's Committee at Acre to Huda Shaarawi, 14 July 1937, FO 141/676 (retranslation mine).

2. S. Abdul Vahid, ed., *Thoughts and Reflections of Iqbal* (Lahore, 1992), 373–74.

3. On the triangulated conflict between the Foreign, Indian, and Colonial Offices over British policy during the Arab Revolt, see O'Halloran, "India, the Arabs, and Britain's Problem."

4. Dubnov and Robson, *Partitions*, 8–10; Tessler, *History of the Israeli-Palestinian Conflict*, 185–218.

5. Tessler, *History of the Israeli-Palestinian Conflict*, 174.

6. Tessler, 177, 212; Dubnov and Robson, *Partitions*, 8–10.

7. J. Buggle et al., "The Refugee's Dilemma: Evidence from Jewish Migration out of Nazi Germany," CEPR Discussion Paper 15533 (2020); H.A. Strauss, "Jewish Emigration from Germany: Nazi Policies and Jewish Responses," *Leo Baeck Institute Year Book* 25:1 (1980): 313–61.

8. F.R. Nicosia, *Zionism and Anti-Semitism in Nazi Germany* (Cambridge, 2008), 78–89; Tessler, *History of the Israeli-Palestinian Conflict*, 208–9.

9. Calculated using immigration data collated by Tessler, *History of the Israeli-Palestinian Conflict*, 40–41, 61, 170, 208. As Tessler notes, 1930s immigrants to Palestine came in large numbers from Poland and other European countries as well as Germany.

10. Tessler, *History of the Israeli-Palestinian Conflict*, 230–31.

11. On the importation to Mandate Palestine of innovators in colonial violence from India and Ireland and the tactics they employed, see C. Elkins, *Legacy of Violence: A History of the British Empire* (London, 2023), 193–239. Scholarship on the Arab Revolt is extensive and evolving; see in particular C.W. Anderson, "Other Laboratories: The Great Revolt, Civil Resistance, and the Social History of Palestine," *Journal of Palestine Studies* 50:3 (2021); M. Hughes, *Britain's Pacification of Palestine: The British Army, the Colonial State, and the Arab Revolt, 1936–1939* (Cambridge, 2019); M. Hughes, "The Banality of Brutality: British Armed Forces and the Repression of the Arab Revolt in Palestine," *English Historical Review* 124:507 (2009); G. Kanafani, *The Revolution of 1936–1939 in Palestine*, trans. H. Jamjoum (New York, 2023); S.F. al-Nimr, *The Arab Revolt of 1936–1939 in Palestine: A Study Based on Oral Sources* (London, 1990); L. Parsons, *The Commander: Fawzi al-Qawuqji and the Fight for Arab Independence 1914–1948* (London, 2017); T. Swedenburg, *Memories of Revolt: The 1936–1939 Rebellion and the Palestinian National Past* (Fayetteville, 2003).

12. On the Peel Commission, see esp. L. Parsons, "The Secret Testimony of the Peel Commission (Part I)," *Journal of Palestine Studies* 49:1–2 (2019–20).

13. P. Partner, *Arab Voices: The BBC Arabic Service, 1938–1988* (London, 1988), 5.

14. L. Allday, "The Establishment of BBC Arabic & Egyptian 'Nahwy,'" *Asian and African Studies Blog*, British Library, 4 October 2017, https://blogs.bl.uk/asian-and-african/2017/10/the-establishment-of-bbc-arabic-egyptian-nahwy.html.

15. Partner, *Arab Voices*, 17.
16. R. Bullard, *The Camels Must Go: An Autobiography* (London, 1961), 206.
17. Partner, *Arab Voices*, 21.
18. This quote is still featured on the BBC's website as a proud moment in its history of resistance to government oversight. See "Newswatch: The History of BBC News | 1930s," http://news.bbc.co.uk/1/shared/spl/hi/newswatch/history/noflash/html/1930s.stm.
19. Potter, *Wireless Internationalism*, 115.
20. Leeper to Graves, 18 Jan 1938, FO 395/558, as cited in Potter, *Wireless Internationalism*, 119–20.
21. Potter, *Wireless Internationalism*, 116–20; see also FO 395/557, 558, 559.
22. Lampson to Rendel, January 1938, FO 395/557.
23. Gershoni and Jankowski, *Redefining the Egyptian Nation*, 170, 180.
24. *Timhu min al-wujud*, literally "erase from existence."
25. The telegram was forwarded by Huda Shaarawi to Miles Lampson alongside her own appeal for Britain to reject the partition of Palestine; to his credit, Lampson sent a lengthy, strongly worded (and laboriously drafted) letter to his government echoing many of her talking points. Women's Committee at Acre to Huda Shaarawi, 14 July 1937, FO 141/676.
26. Badran, *Feminists, Islam, and Nation*, 225–26.
27. Gershoni and Jankowski, *Redefining the Egyptian Nation*, 170.
28. Qtd. Gershoni and Jankowski, 171.
29. Gershoni and Jankowski, 171.
30. Qtd. Rogan, *The Arabs*, 255.
31. Lampson to Eden, 12 August 1936, FO 371/20023.
32. Gershoni and Jankowski, *Redefining the Egyptian Nation*, 171–72.
33. Gershoni and Jankowski, 177.
34. E. Rossi, "Il Congresso interparlamentare arabo e musulmano pro Palestina al Cairo, 7–11 ottobre," *Oriente Moderno* 18:11 (November 1938), 588.
35. Badran, *Feminists, Islam, and Nation*, 227–28.
36. Badran, 227–28.
37. MacKereth to Halifax, 2 July 1938, FO 371/E4049.
38. Fleischmann, *The Nation*, 184, 296n47.
39. Khaliquzzaman, *Pathway to Pakistan*, 198.
40. *Egyptian Gazette*, "Arab Congress in Cairo," 8 October 1938.
41. *Egyptian Gazette*, "Sabean Odours," 8 October 1938.
42. C.E. Weber, "Making Common Cause? Western and Middle Eastern Women in the International Feminist Movement, 1911–1948" (PhD diss., Ohio State University, 2003), 206.
43. Rossi, "Il Congresso," 590.
44. Charaoui to Chamberlain, 30 September 1938, FO 371/22008.
45. *Egyptian Gazette*, "Arab Congress in Cairo," 8 October 1938.
46. Khaliquzzaman, *Pathway to Pakistan*, 199.
47. The Azharite delegation sent to India met with Gandhi and produced a semi-official report on Muslim life in India, portions of which were reprinted in the press.

The contents of the report were deemed patronizing and disparaging toward Indian Muslims, apparently causing some consternation. *Dirasat li-Hawal al-Tawa'if wa al-Hayat al-Islamiyya bi al-Hind* (Cairo, 1937); "Azhar: Missions to Various Countries," n.d., FO 141/649.

48. Khaliquzzaman, *Pathway to Pakistan*, 199–200.
49. Gershoni and Jankowski, *Redefining the Egyptian Nation*, 184–85.
50. Gershoni and Jankowski, 185.
51. Khaliquzzaman, *Pathway to Pakistan*, 198–99.
52. Devji cites this anecdote as illustrative of the complex and in some ways contradictory thinking within the Muslim League regarding relations between minorities and the state; see Devji, *Muslim Zion*, 17.
53. Qtd. Badran, *Feminists, Islam, and Nation*, 231.
54. Badran, 231.
55. Badran, 231.
56. Lampson to FO, 24 October 1938, FO 371/E6432.
57. Gershoni and Jankowski, *Redefining the Egyptian Nation*, 186.
58. Y. Henein et al., *Vive l'art dégénéré: Manifesto du 22 Décembre* (Cairo, 1938).
59. D. LaCoss, "Egyptian Surrealism and 'Degenerate Art' in 1939," *Arab Studies Journal* 18:1 (Spring 2010): 81, 83–84.
60. "Art et liberté," *Clé: Bulletin mensuel de la Fédération internationale de l'art révolutionnaire indépendant* 2 (February 1939): 12.
61. This is a central thesis of Bardaouil, *Egyptian Surrealism*.
62. Qtd. "Art et liberté," 99.
63. See chap. 1.
64. K. el-Telmissany, "al-Insaniyya wa al-Fann al-Hadith," *al-Tatawwur* (February 1940), qtd. Bardaouil, *Egyptian Surrealism*, 136, 138.
65. Bardaouil, *Egyptian Surrealism*, 15.
66. Bardaouil, 69.
67. M.E. Paniconi, "Italian Futurism in Cairo: The Language(s) of Nelson Morpurgo across the Mediterranean," *Philological Encounters* 2:1–2 (2017): 174–75.
68. Bardaouil, *Egyptian Surrealism*, 22.
69. Bardaouil, 82–83.
70. The phrase is Martin Luther King Jr.'s. M.L. King Jr., "Beyond Vietnam: A Time to Break Silence," speech, Riverside Church, Manhattan, 4 April 1967.
71. There are many potential comparisons and perhaps even connections to be drawn between Cairo's Art and Liberty and the much larger Progressive Writer's Association in India, founded in 1936; I regret that I ran out of time and space to attempt it here. See M. Ramnath, "The Progressive Writers Association," *Oxford Research Encyclopedia of Asian History* (Oxford, 2019); Satia, *Time's Monster*, chap. 5.

Chapter Six: The Diplomats

Parts of chapter 6 are developed from E.M.B. O'Halloran, "India, the Arabs, and Britain's Problem in Palestine," *International History Review* 43:3 (2020). Reprinted by permission of Taylor and Francis.

1. Khaliquzzaman, *Pathway to Pakistan*, 203.
2. George Antonius Collection (hereafter GAC), St Antony's College, Middle East Centre Archive, 2/5/1, draft notes of the seventh meeting, held at St James's Palace, 16 February 1939, E3.
3. Viceroy's house to Clauson, 29 October 1938, IOR/L/I/1/604.
4. Linlithgow to Zetland, 11 September 1938, IOR/L/I/1/604.
5. Creasy to Clauson, 21 September 1938, IOR/L/I/1/604,
6. For the military and strategic background to the announcement of the St James's Conference, see Rogan, *The Arabs*, 257–58; Kolinsky, *Britain's War*, 71–73.
7. Zetland to Linlithgow, 31 October 1938, IOR/L/I/1/604.
8. Zetland to Linlithgow.
9. Linlithgow to Zetland, 4 November 1938, IOR/L/I/1/604.
10. Zetland to Linlithgow, 15 November 1938, IOR/L/I/1/604.
11. Zetland to Linlithgow, 29 November 1938, IOR/L/I/1/604.
12. Siddiqi to Creasy, 29 November 29 1938, CO 733/372/15.
13. "Representation of A.R. Siddiqi," marginalia, November–December 1938, CO 733/372/15.
14. India Office to Luke, 10 December 1938, CO 733/372/15.
15. MacDonald to Zetland, 23 December 1938, CO 733/372/15.
16. The fullest articulation of the second Khilafat argument is probably contained in Siddiqi and Khaliquzzaman's "Statement of Indian Muslim Views on Palestine," n.d. (1939), CO 733/408/13. Gandhi and Nehru were also alive to this logic. See Chawla, "Palestine Issue," 46, 51; L. Chester, "'Close Parallels?': Interrelated Discussions of Partition in South Asia and the Palestine Mandate (1936–1948)," in Dubnov and Robson, *Partitions*, 133; Panter-Brick, *Gandhi*, 134.
17. A similar appreciation, focused on the Indian Army, appears in an early 1939 report to Cabinet: "The interest of the Muslims in the Army . . . discourages them from participation in [Congress] propaganda against recruiting or against India participating in the war. But sympathy with the Arabs of Palestine . . . would make the [Muslim] League hostile to the Army being used for purposes considered to be prejudicial to Islam." "Quarterly Survey of the Political and Constitutional Position in British India," 31 January 31 1939, CAB 24/284.
18. MacDonald to Zetland, 23 December 1938, CO 733/372/15.
19. MacDonald to Zetland.
20. Khaliquzzaman, *Pathway to Pakistan*, 200.
21. Madras presidency, Muslim League to S. of S. India, 14 December 1938, CO 733/408/13.
22. R. Khalidi, *The Iron Cage: The Story of the Palestinian Struggle for Statehood* (Boston, 2006), 115.
23. A.R. Takriti, "Before BDS: Lineages of Boycott in Palestine," *Radical History Review* 134 (2019), 69.
24. Draft notes of the seventh meeting held at St James's Palace, 16 February 1939, E3, GAC 2/5/1. A summary of the conference's proceedings was also published at

the time by Chatham House. See H.G.L and H.L., "The Palestine Conferences in London," *Bulletin of International News* 16:4 (25 February 1939), 3–13.

25. "Secret: Sheikh Fuad el-Khatib," 2 February 1939, CO 733/410/2.
26. Draft minutes of meetings, February–March 1939, GAC 2/5/1.
27. Parsons, "Secret Testimony of the Peel Commission (Part I)," 11.
28. At the St James's Conference, these two countries were put forward by the Arab delegates again and again as models for Palestinian statehood. See GAC 2/1 and 2/5/1.
29. "Meeting of MacDonald with Siddiqui and Khaliquzzaman," 25 January 1939, CO 733/372/15.
30. Jinnah to MacDonald, 30 January 1939, CO 733/408/13.
31. "Viceroy's Draft," 30 January 1938, CO 733/408/13; Clauson to Creasy, 3 February 1939, CO 733/408/13.
32. "Memorandum of the Committee on Palestine," 30 January 1939, CAB 24/283/2.
33. *First Qiblah* alludes to the Haram el-Sharif in Jerusalem, which, according to tradition, was the original point of orientation for Muslim prayer, before Prophet Muhammad received divine guidance to face Mecca instead.
34. Clauson to Creasy, 8 February 1939, CO 733/408/13.
35. The classic account is Jalal, *Sole Spokesman*, 8–9.
36. A further invocation of Britain's wartime pledge to protect the sanctity of Islam's holy places.
37. Siddiqi to Zetland, 29 January 1939, CO 733/408/13.
38. "Statement of Indian Muslim Views on Palestine," 1939, CO 733/408/13.
39. C. Khaliquzzaman, *Only If They Knew It?* (Karachi, 1965), 17–18.
40. Aga Khan to the Viceroy, 3 April 1939, IOR/L/I/1/604.
41. Zetland to Linlithgow, 28 March 1939, Mss EUR/D/609/11. As described in Khaliquzzaman, *Pathway to Pakistan*, 204–7.
42. Khaliquzzaman, *Only If They Knew It*, 18.
43. Muhammad Iqbal Shedai, an Indian revolutionary anti-imperialist, became a consultant on Indian and Middle Eastern affairs for Mussolini's government. During World War II, he served as a propagandist for Italy's *Radio Himalaya* and was appointed commissar of the Battaglione Azad Hindoustan, comprised of Indian POWs.
44. Gian Galeazzo Ciano was Foreign Minister of Fascist Italy 1936–43.
45. Khaliquzzaman, *Only If They Knew It*, 18. His account is confirmed by the Italian foreign ministry archives. See R. De Felice, *Il fascismo e l'Oriente: Arabi, ebrei e indiani nella politica di Mussolini* (Bologna, 1988), 203–4.
46. De Felice, *Il fascismo e l'Oriente*, 203–4n.
47. Khaliquzzaman, *Pathway to Pakistan*, 210.
48. Khalidi, *Iron Cage*, 115–16.
49. Historians have tended to dismiss this voluminous body of written and verbal protest as so much "lip service" to a Muslim cause, a consensus I sought to challenge in O'Halloran, "India, the Arabs, and Britain's Problem."
50. M.A. Jinnah, presidential address to the All-India Muslim League, March 1940,

in *Foundations of Pakistan: The All-India Muslim League Documents: 1906–1947*, ed. S.S. Pirzada, vol. 2 (Karachi, 1970), 335.

51. Having planned to attend, the Aga Khan was absent from the proceedings due to illness. Aga Khan to Zetland, 18 May 1938, IOR/L/I/1/604.
52. Lampson to Foreign Office, 1 May 1939, CO 733/410/16.
53. "Procés-verbaux," 17 May 1939, CO 733/4102.
54. Khaliquzzaman, *Only If They Knew It*, 17–18.
55. Phipps to FO, 26 May 1939, CO 733/408/75872/30.
56. Porath, *Palestinian Arab National Movement*, 292.
57. For fans of archival shade-throwing: someone at the Foreign Office took the trouble to translate the full article and then forwarded it, without comment, to the CO. "Al Jezireh," 1 June 1939, CO 733/408/12.
58. Lampson Diaries, 5 May 1939.
59. Lampson Diaries, 27 April 1939.
60. "Palestine: Press in India," 26 May 1939, CO 733/408/13.
61. Khalidi, *Iron Cage*, 116–17.
62. I. Tannous, *The Palestinians: A Detailed Documented Eyewitness History of Palestine under the British Mandate* (New York, 1988), 309.
63. The key source of this argument is Bayan Nuwayhit al-Hut's 1982 history of Mandate Palestine, which cites the papers of 'Izzat al-Tannous and 'Auni Abdal-Hadi to argue that the Arab Higher Committee would have accepted the White Paper, if not for the Mufti's refusal. See B.N. al-Hut, *al-Qiyadat wa al-Mu'assasat al-Siyasiyya fi Filastin, 1917–1948* (Beirut, 1982), 296–98. Similar interpretations appear in G. Achcar, *The Arabs and the Holocaust: The Arab-Israeli War of Narratives*, trans. G.M. Goshgarian (Beirut, 2010), 138–39; M.J. Cohen, *Britain's Moment in Palestine: Retrospect and Perspectives, 1917–48* (Abingdon, 2014), 304; Z. Elpeleg, *The Grand Mufti: Haj Amin al-Hussaini, Founder of the Palestinian National Movement*, trans. D. Harvey (London, 1993), 51–52, 54–55; and Khalidi, *Iron Cage*, 114–17. See also Tannous, *Palestinians*, 309–10. Tannous's account has been contested, notably by the Mufti himself, and by 'Izzat Darwaza, another member of the Arab Higher Committee present during the consultations that led to the White Paper's rejection. See M.A. al-Husseini, *Haqa'iq 'an Qadiyyat Filastin* (Cairo: 1954), 48; I. Darwaza, *Hawla al-Harakah al-'Arabiyyah al-Hadithan* (Saida, 1950), 246.
64. Khaliquzzaman, *Pathway to Pakistan*, 210–11.
65. Khaliquzzaman, 210–11.

Chapter Seven: The Delegation

1. J. Nehru, "A Letter from the Mediterranean," in S. Gopal, *Selected Works of Jawaharlal Nehru*, 9:12–13.
2. J. Nehru, "To Nahas Pasha," in S. Gopal, *Selected Works of Jawaharlal Nehru*, 9:175–79.
3. The same ship was chartered the previous October to transport a thousand British troops from India to Palestine, to suppress the ongoing Arab Revolt.
4. Gouda, *Marid min al-Sharq*, 9–10.
5. Initially it was recounted by Gouda, a member of the Egyptian delegation, in the

travel memoir *Marid min al-Sharq*; later it was covered by historians Miloslav Krása, in "Relations between the Indian National Congress and the Wafd Party of Egypt in the Thirties," and Noor Khan, in *Egyptian-Indian Nationalist Collaboration and the British Empire*. Most recently Michele Louro discussed some aspects of the visit and Nehru's relationship with Mustafa al-Nahas in *Comrades against Imperialism*. Chattopadhyay also mentions the Wafd's visit with Gandhi in her 1986 memoir, in which we discover that she was present at their meeting: *Inner Recesses*, 218.

6. N.A.I. Khan, *Egyptian-Indian Nationalist Collaboration*, 125–27.
7. Nehru, "A Letter from the Mediterranean," 10–11.
8. Nehru, 11–12.
9. Nehru, 11–12.
10. Nehru, 11–12.
11. Nehru, 11–12.
12. Nehru, 12–13.
13. Krása, "Relations," 215–16, 225.
14. J. Nehru, *Jawaharlal Nehru: An Autobiography* (Delhi, 1985 [1936]), 601.
15. J. Nehru, "On the Morale of Spain," *Hindustan Times*, 19 June 1938.
16. Nehru, "To Nahas," 175–79.
17. J. Nehru, *Bunch of Old Letters* (Delhi, 1988), 292.
18. Gershoni and Jankowski, *Redefining the Egyptian Nation*, 145.
19. Dhulipala, *Creating a New Medina*, 51; M. Hasan, "The Muslim Mass Contact Campaign: An Attempt at Political Mobilisation," *South Asia: Journal of South Asian Studies* 7:1 (1984): 67.
20. Dhulipala, *Creating a New Medina*, 115–16.
21. Nehru, "To Nahas," 175–79.
22. Qtd. Badran, *Feminists, Islam, and Nation*, 231.
23. S. Gandhi, ed., *Freedom's Daughter: Letters between Indira Gandhi and Jawaharlal Nehru* (London, 1989), 408–9; N.A.I. Khan, *Egyptian-Indian Nationalist Collaboration*, 124.
24. S.K. Bose and S. Bose, eds., *Netaji: Collected Works*, vol. 9, *Congress President* (Delhi, 1995), 284.
25. Smart to Ewart, 15 February 1938, FO 371/23363/758.
26. "Egyptian Delegation to Indian National Congress," marginalia, 27 February 1939, FO 371/23363/758.
27. "Wafd Delegation's Visit to India," 8 May 1939, FO 371/23363/758.
28. "Egyptian Delegation to Indian National Congress," marginalia, 27 February 1939, FO 371/23363/758.
29. Bose and Bose, *Netaji*, 91. Bose claimed elsewhere to have met Nahas in Egypt, possibly during a flight layover between Vienna and India in 1934, although this is difficult to verify. S.C. Bose, *The Indian Struggle, 1920–1934* (London, 1935).
30. "Cairo City Police Report on the Wafd Delegation's Recent Visit to India," 19 April 1939, FO 371/23363/758.
31. "Wafd Delegation's Visit to India," 8 May 1939, FO 371/23363/758.
32. Lampson to Halifax, 15 May 1939, FO 371/23363/758.

33. "Memorandum by Abul Fath," 14 August 1939, FO 371/23363/758 (retranslation mine).
34. "Cairo City Police Report on the Wafd Delegation's Recent Visit to India," 19 April 1939, FO 371/23363/758.
35. Lampson to Halifax, 15 May 1939, FO 371/23363/758.
36. Lampson to Halifax.
37. Nehru to Bose, 1 March 1939, in Bose and Bose, *Netaji*, 190.
38. Bose to Ag. General Secretary, 28 February 1939, in Bose and Bose, *Netaji*, 285.
39. Chattopadhyay, *Inner Recesses*, 218.
40. No mention of Chattopadhyay, whether by name or otherwise, is present in the relevant intelligence files (FO 371/23363/758), nor is it referenced in the report subsequently prepared by Abul Fat'h, nor does Chattopadhyay appear in Gouda, *Marid min al-Sharq*.
41. Lampson to Halifax, 15 May 1939, FO 371/23363/758.
42. "Memorandum by Abul Fath," 14 August 1939, FO 371/23363/758.
43. Abul Fat'h reportedly told the British press officer in Cairo that Nahas had been "very impressed" by Gandhi's statement of loyalty to Britain in the event of war. Smart to Ewart, 5 May 1939, FO 371/23363/758.
44. "Memorandum by Abul Fath," 14 August 1939, FO 371/23363/758; Lampson to Halifax, 15 May 1939, FO 371/23363/758.
45. Nehru to Bose, 16 March 1939, in Bose and Bose, *Netaji*, 192.
46. Lampson to Halifax, 15 May 1939, FO 371/23363/758.
47. Lampson to Halifax.
48. Nehru, "A Letter from the Mediterranean," 13.
49. Gouda, *Marid min al-Sharq*.
50. Gouda, *Marid min al-Sharq*, 9–10.
51. Lampson to Halifax, 15 May 1939, FO 371/23363/758
52. Lampson to Halifax.
53. Khaliquzzaman, *Only If They Knew It*, 30.

Chapter Eight: The Feminists
1. C. Nabaraoui, "Impressions du Congrès," *L'Égyptienne*, 1 October 1929, 12.
2. No mention is made of Chattopadhyay or her visit in Louro, *Comrades against Imperialism*; N.A.I. Khan, *Egyptian-Indian Nationalist Collaboration*; or Krása, "Relations between the Indian National Congress and the Wafd Party," the studies directly concerned with ties between Egyptian and Indian nationalists in the 1930s. Badran quotes Chattopadhyay's memoir in passing in *Feminists, Islam, and Nation* to depict breakfast at Huda Shaarawi's home, though without discussing the context of the visit or the depth of the relationship between the two feminist leaders. Biographical studies of Chattopadhyay are alive to her many international engagements but vague on her connections with the Middle East; a partial exception is J.L. Barbieri, "Kamaladevi Chattopadhyaya: Anti-Imperialist and Women's Rights Activist, 1939–1941" (master's thesis, Miami University, 2008).
3. Chattopadhyay, *Inner Recesses*, 153–54.
4. Chattopadhyay, 157–58.

5. Chattopadhyay, 149–51.
6. Chattopadhyay, 126.
7. Chattopadhyay, 126–27.
8. C. Nabaraoui, "Impressions du Congrès," *L'Egyptienne*, October 1929, 12.
9. Chattopadhyay, *Inner Recesses*, 125–28.
10. Chattopadhyay, 218.
11. Chattopadhyay, 219–20.
12. M. Er, "Abd-el-Krim al Khattabi: The Unknown Mentor of Che Guevera," *Terrorism and Political Violence* 29:1 (2017); M.R. de Madriaga, *Abd-el-Krim el Jatabi: La lucha por la independencia* (Madrid, 2009).
13. M.P. Ortiz, "'Spain! Why?' Jawaharlal Nehru, Non-Intervention and the Spanish Civil War," *European History Quarterly* 49:3 (2019): 451.
14. Chattopadhyay, *Inner Recesses*, 212.
15. Chattopadhyay, 220–21.
16. C. Nabaraoui, "La délégation Egyptienne au Congrès de Copenhague," *L'Egyptienne*, July–August 1939, 3–4.
17. The account of the conference presented here is based largely on the research of Badran and Weber. See Weber, "Making Common Cause," 169, 206–17; M. Badran, "Rosa Manus in Cairo, 1935, and Copenhagen, 1939: Encounters with Egyptians," in *Rosa Manus (1881–1942): The International Life and Legacy of a Jewish Dutch Feminist*, ed. M. Everard and F. de Haan (Leiden, 2016); Badran, *Feminists, Islam, and Nation*, 232–36.
18. "Czechoslovakia," *Jus Suffragii* 33:7 (April 1939), as cited in Weber, "Making Common Cause," 207.
19. Badran, *Feminists, Islam, and Nation*, 236.
20. Reports of the arrest may have been mistaken; Nabarawi implies as much, and Plamínková's biographers make no mention of an arrest in 1938. Plamínková participated in the Copenhagen conference and would likely have been in the room when Shaarawi raised the matter with the board. Concerns for her safety were, however, well-founded: she was arrested and ultimately executed by the Nazis following the outbreak of World War II. See B. Reinfeld, "Františka Plamínková (1875–1942), Czech Feminist and Patriot," *Nationalities Papers* 25:1 (1997): 13–33.
21. Chattopadhyay, *Inner Recesses*, 230.
22. Badran, *Feminists, Islam, and Nation*, 234–35.
23. Chattopadhyay, *Inner Recesses*, 230.
24. K. Chattopadhyay and M. Sukthankar, "The International Women's Congress at Copenhagen. Our Impressions," 18 July 1939, All-India Women's Conference files; Rani Lakshmibai Rajwade to Mrs. Corbett Ashby, 21 September 1939, All-India Women's Conference files. As cited by Barbieri, "Kamaladevi Chattopadhyaya," 14.
25. Qtd. Badran, *Feminists, Islam, and Nation*, 238.

Chapter Nine: Hearts and Minds

1. Khaliquzzaman, *Pathway to Pakistan*, 203.
2. Louro, *Comrades against Imperialism*, 257.
3. Sidqi, *al-Taqalid*. For more on Sidqi's antifascist crusade see M. Kabha, "A Bold

Voice Raised above the Raging Waves: Palestinian Intellectual Najati Sidqi and His Battle with Nazi Doctrine at the Time of World War II," in Bashir and Goldberg, eds., *The Holocaust and the Nakba: A New Grammar of Trauma and History* (New York, 2019), chap. 7.

4. Sidqi, *Mudhakkirat Najati Sidqi: Hikayat Ishtrakiyya* (Beirut, 2002), 167. Qtd. Kabha, "Bold Voice," 165.

5. Y. Khan, *Raj at War*, 177–78.

6. Israel Gershoni and James Jankowski have rightly challenged the characterization of these Egyptian factions as explicitly fascist in the context of the interwar years; here these ideological nuances are treated as less relevant than wartime allegiance to Italy and Germany. See Gershoni and Jankowski, *Confronting Fascism*.

7. Beinin and Lockman, *Workers on the Nile*, 286.

8. Linlithgow to Zetland, 21 October 1935, IOR Mss Eur D609/7.

9. Qtd. Morewood, *British Defence of Egypt*, 124.

10. Qtd. Morewood, 134.

11. A. Cooper, *Cairo in the War, 1939–1945* (London, 1989), 45.

12. C. Tripp, "'Ali Mahir Pasha and the Palace in Egyptian Politics, 1936–42: Seeking Mass Enthusiasm for Autocracy" (PhD thesis, University of London, School of Oriental and African Studies, 1984); Lampson Diaries, 1939; A.R. 'Azaam, *Mudhakkirat* (Cairo, 1977).

13. See for example Cooper, *Cairo in the War*; Moorewood, *British Defence*; Kolinsky, *Britain's War*.

14. Lampson Diaries, 16 September 1939.

15. Tripp, "'Ali Mahir Pasha," 327.

16. See for example Lampson Diaries, 30 August, 2 September, and 4 September, 1939; Morewood, *British Defence of Egypt*, 166–67.

17. M. Gwyer and A. Apadorai, eds., *Speeches and Documents on the Indian Constitution 1921–1947*, vol. 2 (London, 1957), 504–5.

18. S. Raghavan, *India's War: World War II and the Making of Modern South Asia* (New York, 2016), 25.

19. Qtd. D.A. Low, "The Mediator's Moment: Sir Tej Bahadur Sapru and the Antecedents to the Cripps Mission to India, 1940–1942," *Journal of Imperial and Commonwealth History* 2:2 (1984): 148.

20. Qtd. Raghavan, *India's War*, 30.

21. Khaliquzzaman, *Pathway to Pakistan*, 207.

22. Cooper, *Cairo in the War*, 46.

23. Raghavan, *India's War*; Y. Khan, *Raj at War*, 35–36.

24. Raghavan, 117–21.

25. Governor General to Secretary of State for India, 11 June 1940, CO 733/426/8.

26. Jinnah, presidential address, 332–35.

27. Khaliquzzaman, *Pathway to Pakistan*, 210–11.

28. Jinnah, presidential address, 335.

29. Jinnah, 332–35.

30. Dhulipala, *Creating a New Medina*, 168, 201, 259, 286.

31. M.S. Toosy, *Pakistan and Muslim India* (Bombay, 1942), 184; see also Dhulipala, *Creating a New Medina*, 168.

32. Dhulipala, 172, 175–76.

33. S. Kapila, "Ambedkar's Agonism: Sovereign Violence and Pakistan as Peace," *Comparative Studies of South Asia, Africa and the Middle East*, 39:1 (2019); Devji, *Muslim Zion*; D. Keer, *Dr. Ambedkar: Life and Mission* (Bombay, 1962), 336.

34. B.R. Ambedkar, *Thoughts on Pakistan* (Bombay, 1941), 333.

35. A. Dubnov, "The Architect of Two Partitions or a Federalist Daydreamer? The Curious Case of Reginald Coupland," in Dubnov and Robson, *Partitions*; Birnbaum, "Entangled Empire."

36. R. Coupland, *The Future of India* (Oxford, 1943), 106; Birnbaum, "Entangled Empire," 579.

37. "Situation Regarding Italian Nationals in Egypt and Steps for Their Control in Emergency," January 1939, WO 186/2018A.

38. Tripp, "'Ali Mahir Pasha," 335.

39. Kolinsky, *Britain's War*, 127.

40. Tripp, "'Ali Mahir Pasha," 336–37.

41. Low, "Mediator's Moment," 149.

42. Gwyer and Apadorai, *Speeches and Documents*, 485.

43. Beinin and Lockman, *Workers on the Nile*, 268.

44. "Egypt: Review of Political Situation between October 1941 and March 1942," FO 371/31570.

45. Qtd. Beinin and Lockman, *Workers on the Nile*, 235.

46. Qtd. Beinin and Lockman, 235–36.

47. Qtd. Beinin and Lockman, 248–49.

48. Y. Khan, *Raj at War*, 87, 90, 203–4.

49. Khan, 77.

50. W.H.A. Rich to the inspector general of police, Punjab, 2 January 1945, IOR Mss Eur F 161/213.

51. "Provision of a Section of Indian Security Police," WO 106/2050.

52. Qtd. Y. Khan, *Raj at War*, 72.

53. Kolinsky, *Britain's War*, 156.

54. Kolinsky, 157–59.

55. Qtd. Cooper, *Cairo in the War*, 140.

56. Lampson Diaries, 4 October 1941.

57. Motadel, "Global Authoritarian Movement," 845–48.

58. Qtd. J. Kuhlmann, *Netaji in Europe* (New Delhi, 2012), 19

59. Motadel, "Global Authoritarian Movement," 867, paraphrasing "Araber und Inder in gemeinsamer Front," *Völkischer Beobachter* (Berlin), September 24, 1942.

60. Motadel, "Global Authoritarian Movement," 861–63.

61. Motadel, 852.

62. "Indian Publicity in the Middle East—Proposals of the Ambassador at Cairo," 25 April 1941, IOR/L/I/1/790.

63. "Indian Publicity."

64. "Indian Publicity."
65. See chap. 4.
66. "India and the Middle East," n.d., IOR/L/I/1/790.
67. High Commissioner, Palestine, to Secretary of State for the colonies, 26 May 1941, IOR/L/I/1/790.
68. GOI External Affairs to Secretary of State for India, 16 June 1941, IOR/L/I/1/790.
69. A. Weigold, *Churchill, Roosevelt, and India: Propaganda During World War II* (New York, 2008), 41–42.
70. British Pathé, *Indian Troops in Africa (1941)*, newsreel, 11 December 1941, https://www.britishpathe.com/asset/67019.
71. GOI External Affairs to Secretary of State for India, 16 June 1941, IOR/L/I/1/790.
72. G.E. Wheeler, "United Publications," *Journal of the Royal Central Asian Society* 33:2 (1946): 207.
73. Wheeler to Lloyd, 27 July 1942, IOR/L/I/1/790.
74. See for example Welch, *Persuading the People*; L. Allday, "For the Sake of Freedom: British World War II Propaganda Posters in Arabic," *Untold Lives Blog*, British Library, 5 February 2014, https://blogs.bl.uk/untoldlives/2014/02/for-the-sake-of-freedom-british-world-war-ii-propaganda-posters-in-arabic.html; L. Allday, "An A–Z of Arabic Propaganda," *Asian and African Studies Blog*, British Library, 28 April 2016, https://blogs.bl.uk/asian-and-african/2016/04/an-a-z-of-arabic-propaganda.html.
75. Extract of Progress Report No. 8, 1 July 1943, IOR/L/I/1/790; Wheeler, "United Publications," 204.
76. Wheeler, "United Publications," 204.
77. United Publications catalogue, n.d., IOR/L/I/1/790.
78. Extract of Progress Report No. 8, 1 July 1943, IOR/L/I/1/790.
79. Extract of Progress Report.
80. H. Halim, "'A Theatre—or, More Aptly, a Laboratory': India in the 1940s Egyptian Left as an Antecedent of Bandung Internationalism," *Comparative Literature Studies*, 59:1 (2022). Halim's article is based on a privately held collection of *al-Majalla al-Jadeeda* back issues, which forms the basis of my discussion. The special issue on India is *al-Majalla al-Jadeeda* 401 (April 14, 1942).
81. Halim, "A Theatre," 56.
82. Halim, "A Theatre," 56–59.
83. G. Henein, "Shakhsiyyat al-'Addad: Jawaharlal Nehru," *al-Majalla al-Jadeeda* 399 (25 January 1942), qtd. Halim, "A Theatre," 56.
84. M.K. Munib, "Bayn Uduba'a al-Tali'a al-Hunud," *al-Majalla al-Jadeeda* 401 (April 14, 1942), qtd. Halim, "A Theatre," 62–63.
85. G. Henein, "Bayn al-Wataniyya wa al-Duwaliyya," *al-Majalla al-Jadeeda* 401 (April 14, 1942), qtd. Halim, "A Theatre," 60.

Chapter Ten: No Way Back

1. M. Gandhi, "Quit India," speech, Bombay, 8 August 1942.
2. J. Holland, *Fortress Malta: An Island under Siege, 1940–1943* (London, 2003).

3. Cooper, *Cairo in the War*, 79.

4. Lampson Diaries, 21 April and 23 April 1941. Significant numbers of Mediterranean refugees also made their way to India, including six hundred Maltese who traveled overland through Turkey; Greek and Maltese refugees were housed in dormitories on the grounds of a college in Coimbatore, Tamil Nadu. See Y. Khan, *Raj at War*, 123.

5. The El Shatt Camp in Egypt alone became home to thirty thousand displaced Yugoslavs. See F. Bieber, "Building Yugoslavia in the Sand? Dalmatian Refugees in Egypt, 1944–1946," *Slavic Review* 79:2 (2020): 298–99.

6. Bashir and Goldberg, *Holocaust and the Nakba*, 10; Tessler, *History of the Israeli-Palestinian Conflict*, 249, 256.

7. H. Friedlander, *The Origins of Nazi Genocide: From Euthanasia to the Final Solution* (Chapel Hill, 1997); C. Gerlach, *The Extermination of European Jews* (Cambridge, 2016); M. Mazower, *Hitler's Empire: Nazi Rule in Occupied Europe* (London, 2008). On Hitler's obsession with American history and racial segregation see E.B. Westermann, *Hitler's Ostkrieg and the Indian Wars: Comparing Genocide and Conquest* (Norman, 2016); J.Q. Whitman, *Hitler's American Model: The United States and the Making of Nazi Race Law* (Princeton, 2017).

8. L. London, *Whitehall and the Jews, 1933–1948: British Immigration Policy, Jewish Refugees and the Holocaust* (Cambridge, 2003), 2; see also S.S. Friedman, *No Haven for the Oppressed: United States Policy toward Jewish Refugees, 1938–1945* (Detroit, 2017); D.S. Wyman, *The Abandonment of the Jews: America and the Holocaust, 1941–1945* (New York, 2007).

9. Y. Khan, *Raj at War*, 99.

10. G. Orwell, "India Next," *The Observer*, 22 February 1942.

11. Bose and Bose, *Azad Hind*, 74.

12. Khan, 120–21.

13. Khan, 107.

14. Tessler, *History of the Israeli-Palestinian Conflict*, 250–51; A. Berman, *Nazism, the Jews and American Zionism, 1933–1988* (Detroit, 1992), chap. 4; "The Biltmore Program," in *The Israel-Arab Reader: A Documentary History of the Middle East Conflict*, ed. W. Laqueur and B. Rubin (New York, 1984), 77–79.

15. Government of India, Department of Information and Broadcasting, to S of S India, 22 August 1942, IOR/L/I/1/790.

16. Raghavan, *India's War*, 376.

17. E.W. Said, *Out of Place* (London, 1999), 25.

18. Lampson Diaries, 1 February 1942.

19. Lampson Diaries, 1 February 1942.

20. Lampson Diaries, 3 February 1942.

21. Lampson Diaries, 3 February 1942.

22. Lampson Diaries, 4 February 1942.

23. Lampson Diaries, 4 February 1942.

24. A. Timpson and A. Gibbson-Watt, *In Rommel's Backyard: A Memoir of the Long-range Desert Group* (Barnsley, 2000), 170.

25. Cooper, *Cairo in the War*, 175.

26. Lampson Diaries, 4 February 1942.
27. Lampson Diaries, 4 February 1942.
28. Lampson Diaries, 5 February 1942.
29. Lampson Diaries, 4 February 1942.
30. Lampson Diaries, 4 February 1942.
31. Cooper, *Old Men Forget*, 308.
32. Qtd. Cooper, *Cairo in the War*, 176–77.
33. Lampson Diaries, 5 February 1942.
34. Qtd. Beinin and Lockman, *Workers on the Nile*, 288.
35. Qtd. P. Mansfield, *Nasser*, Makers of the Modern World (London, 1969), 35.
36. Tripp, "'Ali Mahir Pasha," 376.
37. Gershoni and Jankowski, *Redefining the Egyptian Nation*, 192, 196.
38. Gershoni and Jankowski, 196–97.
39. Nehru, *Bunch*, 292.
40. Lockman and Beinin, *Workers on the Nile*, 287.
41. Nehru, "Letter from the Mediterranean," 12–13.
42. Krása, "Relations," 228.
43. Qtd. Low, "Mediator's Moment," 158.
44. Diary entry for April 10–11, 1942, in *The Empire at Bay: The Leo Amery Diaries 1929–1945*, ed. J. Barnes and D. Nicholson (London, 1988), 794.
45. Barnes and Nicholson, *Empire at Bay*, 157; Raghavan, *India's War*, 235.
46. Y. Khan, *Raj at War*, 134.
47. Qtd. Y. Khan, *Raj at War*, 135.
48. Qtd. Raghavan, *India's War*, 235.
49. Gandhi, "Quit India," 187.
50. J. Nehru, *The Discovery of India* (London, 1946), 383–84, with thanks to Priya Satia for directing me to this passage.
51. Y. Khan, *Raj at War*, 179.
52. Raghavan, *India's War*, 271–72.
53. The numbers of deaths and detainees remain difficult to establish; Y. Khan cites Hutchens's reproduction of official figures, citing 1,600–2,500 recorded deaths; she also notes 60,000–90,000 interned in the latter half of 1942. Khan and Raghavan concur that attacks took place in which crowds were machine-gunned from the air. See Khan, *Raj at War*, 193–94; Raghavan, *India's War*, 273; F.G. Hutchens, *India's Revolution: Gandhi and the Quit India Movement* (Cambridge, MA, 1973), 230–32.
54. Y. Khan, *Raj at War*, 190–94, 218–21; Raghavan, *India's War*, 272–73.

Epilogue: Midnight in Delhi

1. J. Nehru, inaugural speech to the Asian Relations Conference, 23 March 1947.
2. K. Chattopadhyay, *Inner Recesses, Outer Spaces: Memoirs*, 2nd ed. (New Delhi, 2014), 303. Reprinted with permission of Niyogi Books.
3. Invitations were issued to the heads of thirty-two Asian countries and Egypt, soliciting national delegations of up to sixteen individuals. Delegates were to be selected by academic or research associations in each country. The full list of countries invited

to participate included Turkey, Syria, Lebanon, Palestine, Transjordan, Egypt, Saudi Arabia, Yemen, Iraq, Azerbaijan, Iran, Kirghizia, Kazakhstan, Turkmenistan, Uzbekistan, Tajikistan, Afghanistan, Mongolia, Tibet, Nepal, Bhutan, China, Japan, Korea, the Philippines, Burma (Myanmar), Siam (Thailand), Cambodia, Vietnam, Malaya, Singapore, Indonesia, and Ceylon (Sri Lanka). Observers also attended from institutes of international affairs in Canada, the United States, the United Kingdom, Australia, and New Zealand. Most of these countries sent delegates, observers, or both; Syria, Lebanon, Yemen, and Saudi Arabia declined. See "List of Countries Invited to the Inter-Asian Relations Conference," IOR/L/I/1/152.

4. "Asian Relations Conference (Mrs Naidu's Address of Welcome)," New Delhi, 24 April 1937, IOR/L/I/1/152.

5. "Opening of Asian Conference: Inaugural Address by Pandit Nehru," IOR/L/I/1/152.

6. V. Thakur, "An Asian Drama: The Asian Relations Conference, 1947," *International History Review* 41:3 (2019): 677.

7. D. Gopal, ed., *Asian Relations: Being a Report of the Proceedings and Documentation of the First Asian Relations Conference, New Delhi, March–April, 1947* (New Delhi, 1948).

8. Chattopadhyay, *Inner Recesses*, 303, 305.

9. A. Chandra, "Potential of the 'Un-Exchangeable Monument'": Delhi's Purana Qila in the Time of Partition, c. 1947–63," *International Journal of Islamic Architecture* 2:1 (2013): 101–23.

10. Khaliquzzaman, *Pathway to Pakistan*.

11. On the boundary commission, see J. Chatterji, "The Fashioning of a Frontier: The Radcliffe Line and Bengal's Border Landscape, 1947–52," *Modern Asian Studies* 33:1 (1999); L.P. Chester, *Borders and Conflict in South Asia: The Radcliffe Boundary Commission and the Partition of Punjab* (Manchester, 2017).

12. D. Gopal, *Asian Relations*, 96.

13. Thakur, "Asian Drama," 680.

14. Louro, *Comrades against Imperialism*, 260.

15. Stolte, "Asiatic Hour"; Thakur, "Asian Drama." On Jinnah's claim that Hindu imperialism could threaten Egypt and the Arab East, see Dhulipala, *Creating a New Medina*, 19, 176.

16. By 1946 Nehru was pressing for independent India's membership of the United Nations Security Council on the grounds that, as a prospective great power, it would hold the balance of Middle Eastern and Southeast Asian security in the new world order: "It is India that counts in the security and defence of both these regions far more than any other country." As Raghavan has demonstrated, this assessment was rooted both in the military and strategic realities of World War II and the preceding 150 years of de facto Indian imperial influence extending across much of the Asian continent. See *India's War*, esp. 445–46; on India's "empire," see also Blyth, *Empire of the Raj*.

17. R.G. Stern and A. Dubnov, "'A Part of Asia or Apart from Asia?' Zionist Perceptions of Asia, 1947–1956," in *Unacknowledged Kinships: Postcolonial Studies and the Historiography of Zionism*, ed. S. Vogt, D. Penslar, and A. Saposnik (Waltham, 2023), 243.

18. "Asian Relations Conference (Summary of Speeches)," New Delhi, 23 March 1947, IOR/L/I/1/152.

19. In an article written during the conference, Zionist delegates Bracha Habas and David Hacohen claimed that Asian countries didn't "have any contact with Jews," revealing their ignorance of the well-established Jewish communities of Iraq, Iran, Egypt, and their host country. See Stern and Dubnov, "Part of Asia," 248.

20. "Asian Relations Conference (Summary of Speeches)," New Delhi, 23 March 1947. IOR/L/I/1/152.

21. Stern and Dubnov, "Part of Asia," 247–49.

22. Stern and Dubnov, 259.

23. The sole exception was the Philippines, which voted with the United States.

24. The term *al-Nakba* was originally used by Constantine Zuraiq. See C. Zuraiq, *Ma'na al-Nakba* (Beirut, 1948); see also N. Masalha, *The Palestine Nakba: Decolonising History, Narrating the Subaltern, Reclaiming Memory* (London, 2012); I. Pappé, *The Ethnic Cleansing of Palestine* (New York, 2007); E. Rogan and A. Shlaim, eds., *The War for Palestine: Rewriting the History of 1948* (Cambridge, 2001).

25. Raghavan, *India's War*, 460–61.

26. Similar critiques of Bandung and its participants appear as early as 1956. See C. Romulo, *The Meaning of Bandung* (Chapel Hill, 1956); G.H. Jansen, *Afro-Asia and Non-Alignment* (London, 1966), 182; Stern and Dubnov, "Part of Asia," 253.

27. Debates continue to rage as to whether Pakistan was conceived as the ultimate goal of negotiations, a "bargaining counter," or an interim arrangement that could lead to eventual federation with India. It was certainly hoped by many Indians of all communities that the separation would not prove final. B. Chakrabarty, "An Alternative to Partition: The United Bengal Scheme," *South Asia* 26:2 (2003); Devji, *Muslim Zion*; Dhulipala, *Creating a New Medina*; Jalal, *Sole Spokesman*; Y. Khan, *Great Partition*; J. Singh, *Jinnah: India, Partition, Independence* (Oxford, 2010). On the poetic afterlives of the heterodox East in postpartition India, see esp. P. Satia, "Poets of Partition: The Recovery of Lost Causes," in Dubnov and Robson, *Partitions*; Satia, *Time's Monster*, chap. 5. The Yishuv's position was more straightforward: both in 1937 and again ten years later, internal dissent was overcome and partition formally accepted, whether as an "indispensable minimum" or a stepping stone toward Jewish sovereignty in all of Mandate Palestine. Dubnov and Robson, *Partitions*, 11–12; A.S. Klieman, "In the Public Domain: The Controversy over Partition for Palestine," *Jewish Social Studies* 42:2 (1980); C. Shindler, "Opposing Partition: The Zionist Predicament after the Shoah," *Israel Studies* 14:2 (2009); Tessler, *History of the Israeli-Palestinian Conflict*, 251, 259.

28. Qtd. Y. Khan, *Great Partition*, 85.

29. Sharawi Lafranchi, *Casting Off the Veil*, 270.

30. Khaliquzzaman, *Only If They Knew It*, 31–32.

31. Qtd. Bardaouil, *Egyptian Surrealism*, 234.

32. Qtd. E. Armstrong, "Before Bandung: The Anti-Imperialist Women's Movement in Asia and the Women's International Democratic Federation," *Signs: Journal of Women in Culture and Society* 41:2 (2016): 314.

33. Chattopadhyay, *Inner Recesses*, 303–4.

BIBLIOGRAPHY

Public Records
British Library
India Office Records (IOR)

British National Archives, Kew
Cabinet Papers (CAB)
Committee of Imperial Defence, Middle East Subcommittee
Colonial Office (CO)
Foreign Office Confidential Print: Egypt and Eastern Departments (FO)
War Office (WO)

Middle East Centre Archive, St Antony's College
Diaries of Lord Killearn (Lampson Diaries)
George Antonius Collection (GAC)

Press
al-Ahram (Cairo)
The Comrade (Delhi)
Dawn (Karachi)
L'Écho de Paris (Paris)
Egyptian Gazette (Cairo)
L'Egyptienne (Cairo)
Giornale d'Oriente (Alexandria)
Hindustan Times (Delhi)
Islami Dunya (Cairo)
al-Jihad (Cairo)
Jus Suffragii (Geneva)

Kawkab al-Sharq (Cairo)
al-Majalla al-Jadeeda (Cairo)
Majallat al-Rabita al-Sharqiyya (Cairo)
al-Manar (Cairo)
al-Muqattam (Cairo)
al-Musawwar (Cairo)
The Observer (London)
Oriente Moderno (Cairo)
Ruz al-Youssef (Cairo)
The Statesman (Delhi)
al-Tatawwur (Cairo)
The Times (London)

Memoirs and Published Primary Sources

'Abd al-Raziq, A. *al-Islam wa Usl al-Hukm.* 3rd ed. Cairo, 1925.
Abdul Vahid, S., ed. *Thoughts and Reflections of Iqbal.* Lahore, 1992.
Aga Khan, M.A. *India in Transition: A Study in Political Evolution.* Bombay, 1918.
———. *World Enough and Time: The Memoirs of Aga Khan.* New York, 1954.
Ahmad, A.K.A. *Thawrat al-Hind al-Siyasiyya: Ithr Tarikha wa Wassaf Haqiqa.* Translated by A.R. al-Malihi. Cairo, 1922.
Ahmad, J., ed. *Speeches and Writings of Mr. Jinnah.* Lahore, 1964.
Ali, M., ed. *Jinnah on World Affairs: Select Documents, 1908–1948.* Karachi, 2007.
Allana, G., ed. *Pakistan Movement: Historic Documents.* 4th ed. Lahore, 1988.
Ambedkar, B.R. *Thoughts on Pakistan.* Bombay, 1941.
'Azaam, A.R. *Mudhakkirat.* Cairo, 1977.
Barnes, J., and D. Nicholson, eds. *The Empire at Bay: The Leo Amery Diaries 1929–1945.* London, 1988.
Bhattacharya, U.C., and S.S. Chakravarty, eds. *Pandit Motilal Nehru: His Life and Work.* 3rd ed. Calcutta, 1934.
Bose, S.C. *The Indian Struggle, 1920–1934.* London, 1935.
Bose, S.K., and S. Bose, eds. *Azad Hind: Subhas Chandra Bose Writings and Speeches, 1914–1943.* London, 2004.
———. *Netaji: Collected Works.* Vol. 9, *Congress President.* Delhi, 1995.
Bullard, R. *The Camels Must Go: An Autobiography.* London, 1961.
Chattopadhyay, K. *Inner Recesses, Outer Spaces: Memoirs.* New Delhi, 1986, 2014.
Cooper, D. *Old Men Forget.* London, 1953.
Darwaza, M.I. *Hawla al-Harakah al-'Arabiyyah al-Hadithan.* Vol. 3. Saida, 1950.
Gandhi, S., ed. *Freedom's Daughter: Letters between Indira Gandhi and Jawaharlal Nehru.* London, 1989.
Glendevon, J. *The Viceroy at Bay: Lord Linlithgow in India, 1936–1943.* London, 1971.
Gomaa, M.L. *Bayna al-Asad al-Ifriqi wa al-Nimr al-Itali.* Cairo, 1935.
———. *Mabahith fi al-Tarikh.* Cairo, 2001.
Gopal, D., ed. *Asian Relations: Being a Report of the Proceedings and Documentation of the First Asian Relations Conference, New Delhi, March–April, 1947.* New Delhi, 1948.

Gopal, S., ed. *Selected Works of Jawaharlal Nehru*, vols. 1–9. New Delhi, 1972.
Gouda, A.Q. *Marid min al-Sharq*. Cairo, 1950.
Government of India. *The Tiger Strikes: India's Fight in the Middle East*. Calcutta, 1943.
Great Britain, contributor, and League of Nations, author. *Mandate for Palestine and Memorandum by the British Government Relating to Its Application to Transjordan*. Geneva, 1922.
Gwyer, M., and A. Apadorai, eds. *Speeches and Documents on the Indian Constitution 1921–1947*. Vol. 2. London, 1957.
Henein, Y., et al. *Vive l'art dégénéré: Manifesto du 22 Décembre*. Cairo, 1938.
Hussein, T. *Mustaqbal al-Thaqafa fi Misr*. Cairo, 1938.
———. *The Days: His Autobiography in Three Parts*. Translated by E.H. Paxton, H. Wayment, and K. Cragg. Cairo, 1997.
al-Husseini, M.A. *Haqa'iq 'an Qadiyyat Filastin*. Cairo, 1954.
al-Hut, B.N. *al-Qiyadat wa al-Mu'assasat al-Siyasiyya fi Filastin, 1917–1948*. Beirut, 1982.
Iqbal, M. *Dharb-i-Kalim*. Karachi, 1935.
———. *Pas Chih Bayad Kard ay Aqwam-i-Mashriq ma'a Musafir*. Karachi, 1936.
'Izz al-Din, A., ed. *Mudhakkirat Mustafa al-Nahhas*. 2 vols. Cairo, 2000.
Kanafani, G. *The Revolution of 1936–1939 in Palestine*. Translated by H. Jamjoum. New York, 2023.
Khaliquzzaman, C. *Only If They Knew It*. Karachi, 1965.
———. *Pathway to Pakistan*. London, 1961.
King, M.L., Jr. "Beyond Vietnam: A Time to Break Silence." Speech, Riverside Church, Manhattan, 4 April 1967.
Mahfouz, N. *The Cairo Trilogy*. Translation by William Maynard Hutchins. New York, 1992.
———. *Midaq Alley*. Translation by Humphrey Davis. Cairo, 2015.
Manley, D., ed. *A Cairo Anthology: 200 Years of Travel Writing*. Cairo, 2013.
Manning, O. *The Levant Trilogy*. London, 2003.
Mazhar, I., trans. *Mahatma Ghandi, Siratahu Kama Katabaha bi-Qalamihi*. Cairo, 1934.
Muhammad, M.H. *al-Ittijahat al-Wataniyya fi al-Adab al-Mu'asir*. Cairo, 1954.
Muhammad, S., ed. *The Right Honourable Syed Ameer Ali: Political Writings*. New Delhi, 1989.
Musa, S. *Ghandi wa al-Haraka al-Hindiyya*. Cairo, 1934.
Nallino, C. "La fine del cosiddetto califatto ottomano." *Oriente Moderno* 4:3 (15 March 1924).
Nehru, J. *Bunch of Old Letters*. Delhi, 1988.
———. *The Discovery of India*. London, 1946.
———. *Jawaharlal Nehru: An Autobiography*. Delhi, 1985. First published 1936.
Nuwayhid, A. *Rijal min Filastin ma Bayna Bidayat al-Qarn Hatta 'am 1948*. Beirut, 1981.
Parel, A.J., ed. *Gandhi: 'Hind Swaraj' and Other Writings*. Cambridge, 1997.
Pirzada, S.S., ed. *Foundations of Pakistan: The All-India Muslim League Documents: 1906–1947*. Vol. 2. Karachi, 1970.
Quaroni, P. *Il mondo di ambasciatore*. Milan, 1956.
Radwan, F. *al-Mahatma Ghandi: Hayatahu wa Jihadhu*. Cairo, 1934.

———. *Tarikh Ghandi*. Cairo, 1932.
Rida, M.D. *Abtal al-Wataniyya: Mustapha Kamil, Sa'ad Zaghlul, Mustapha Kemal, Mahatma Ghandi, Mudabbaja bi-Aqlam Uzuma Munshi Hadha al-Asr*. Cairo, 1923.
al-Sanhuri, A.R.A. *Le Califat: Son évolution vers une société des nations orientales*. Paris, 1926.
al-Sayyid, A.L. *al-Muntakhabat*. 2 vols. Cairo, 1945.
———. *Qissat Hiyati*. Cairo, 1962.
Sha'arawi, H. *Harem Years*. Translated by M. Badran. London, 1986.
Shawqi, A. *al-Mosua' ash-Shawqiyya: al-'Amaal al-Kamila li-'Ameer ash-Shua'ara' Ahmad Shawqi*. Vol. 3. Edited by I. al-Ibyaari. Beirut, 1994.
Sidqi, N. *Mudhakkirat Najati Sidqi: Hikayat Ishtrakiyya*. Beirut, 2002.
———. *al-Taqalid al-Islamiyya wa al-Mabadi' al-Naziyya, Hal Tatafaqan?*. Beirut, 1940.
Tagore, R. *Gitanjali: Song Offerings*. Edited by W.B. Yeats. London, 1914.
———. *Nationalism*. 1917. Reprint, London, 2010.
Tannous, I. *The Palestinians: A Detailed Documented Eyewitness History of Palestine under the British Mandate*. New York, 1988.
Timpson, A., and A. Gibbson-Watt. *In Rommel's Backyard: A Memoir of the Long-Range Desert Group*. Barnsley, 2000.
Toosy, M.S. (M.R.T.). *Pakistan and Muslim India*. Bombay, 1942.
Wahba, H. *Jazirat al-Arab fi al Qarn al-Ashreen*. Cairo, 1956.
Wheeler, G.E. "United Publications," *Journal of the Royal Central Asian Society* 33:2 (1946).
Yapp, M.E., ed. *Politics and Diplomacy in Egypt: The Diaries of Sir Miles Lampson, 1935–1937*. London, 1997.
Youssef, A. *Independent Egypt*. London, 1940.
Zuraiq, C. *Ma'na al-Nakba*. Beirut, 1948.

Secondary Literature

Abu-Lughod, J. *Cairo: 1001 Years of the City Victorious*. Princeton, 1971.
———. "Tale of Two Cities: The Origins of Modern Cairo." *Comparative Studies in Society and History*, 7:4 (1965).
Achcar, G. *The Arabs and the Holocaust: The Arab-Israeli War of Narratives*. Translated by G.M. Goshgarian. Beirut, 2010.
D'Agostino, A. *The Rise of Global Powers: International Politics in the Era of the World Wars*. Cambridge, 2012.
Akçapar, B. *People's Mission to the Ottoman Empire: M. A. Ansari and the Indian Medical Mission, 1912–13*. Oxford, 2014.
Alavi, S. *Muslim Cosmopolitanism in the Age of Empire*. Cambridge, MA, 2015.
Ali, A., I.D. Thiam, and Y.A. Talib, eds. *The Different Aspects of Islamic Culture*. Vol. 6, part 1, *Islam in the World Today*. Retrospective of the Evolution of Islam and the Muslim World. Paris, 2016.
Allday, L. "The Establishment of BBC Arabic and Egyptian 'Nahwy.'" *Asian and African Studies Blog*. British Library, 4 October 2017. https://blogs.bl.uk/asian-and-african/2017/10/the-establishment-of-bbc-arabic-egyptian-nahwy.html.

Amin, S. *Event, Metaphor, Memory: Chauri Chaura, 1922–1992*. Berkeley, 1995.
Anderson, B. *Imagined Communities: Reflections on the Origins and Spread of Nationalism*. London, 1983.
Anderson, C.W. "Other Laboratories: The Great Revolt, Civil Resistance, and the Social History of Palestine." *Journal of Palestine Studies*, 50:3 (2021).
Andrew, P. *America's Forgotten Middle East Initiative: The King-Crane Commission of 1919*. London, 2015.
Arielli, N. *Fascist Italy and the Middle East, 1933–1940*. Basingstoke, 2010.
Armbrust, W. "The Ubiquitous Non-Presence of India: Peripheral Visions from Egyptian Popular Culture." In *Global Bollywood: Travels of Hindi Song and Dance*, edited by S. Gopal and S. Moorti. Minneapolis, 2008.
Armstrong, E. "Before Bandung: The Anti-Imperialist Women's Movement in Asia and the Women's International Democratic Federation." *Signs: Journal of Women in Culture and Society* 41:2 (2016).
Asseraf, A. *Electric News in Colonial Algeria*. Oxford, 2019.
Avineri, S. *The Making of Modern Zionism: The Intellectual Origins of the Jewish State*. London, 2017.
el-Awaisi, A.F.M. *The Muslim Brothers and the Palestine Question, 1928–1947*. London, 1998.
Ayalon, A. *The Press in the Arab Middle East: A History*. Oxford, 1995.
Aydin, C. "A Global Anti-Western Moment? The Russo-Japanese War, Decolonization, and Asian Modernity." In *Competing Visions of World Order: Global Moments and Movements, 1880s–1930s*, edited by S. Conrad and D. Sachsenmaier. New York, 2007.
———. *The Idea of the Muslim World: A Global Intellectual History*. London, 2017.
———. *The Politics of Anti-Westernism in Asia: Visions of World Order in Pan-Islamic and Pan-Asian Thought*. New York, 2007.
Azaryahu, M., and Y. Reiter, "The Geopolitics of Interment: An Inquiry into the Burial of Muhammad Ali in Jerusalem, 1931." *Israel Studies* 20:1 (2015).
Badran, M. *Feminists, Islam, and Nation: Gender and the Making of Modern Egypt*. Princeton, 1995.
Barak, O. *On Time: Technology and Temporality in Modern Egypt*. Berkeley, 2013.
Bardaouil, S. *Egyptian Surrealism: Modernism and the Art and Liberty Group*. London, 2017.
Barder, A.D. "Scientific Racism, Race War and the Global Racial Imaginary." *Third World Quarterly* 40:2 (2019).
Baron, B. *Egypt as a Woman: Nationalism, Gender and Politics*. Berkeley, 2007.
———. *The Women's Awakening in Egypt: Culture, Society, and the Press*. New Haven, 1997.
Barucha, R. *Another Asia: Rabindranath Tagore and Okakura Tenshin*. New Delhi, 2006.
Bashir, B., and A. Goldberg, eds. *The Holocaust and the Nakba: A New Grammar of Trauma and History*. New York, 2019.
Bates, C., ed. *Beyond Representation: Constructions of Identity in Colonial and Postcolonial India*. New Delhi, 2005.

———. *Mutiny at the Margins: New Perspectives on the Indian Uprising of 1857*. Vol. 6, *Perception, Narration and Reinvention: The Pedagogy and Historiography of the Indian Uprising*. London, 2014.

Beinin, J., and Z. Lockman. *Workers on the Nile: Nationalism, Communism, Islam, and the Egyptian Working Class, 1882–1954*. Cairo, 1998.

Bell, C.M. *The Royal Navy, Seapower and Strategy between the Wars*. Basingstoke, 2000.

Ben-Ghiat, R., and M. Fuller, eds. *Italian Colonialism*. Italian and Italian American Studies. London, 2005.

Benite, Z.B.D. "'Nine Years in Egypt': Al-Azhar University and the Arabization of Chinese Islam." *Hagar* 8:1 (2008).

Berman, A. *Nazism, the Jews and American Zionism, 1933–1988*. Detroit, 1992.

Birnbaum, M. "Entangled Empire: Religion and the Transnational History of Pakistan and Israel." *Millennium* 50:2 (2022).

Blyth, R.J. *The Empire of the Raj: India, Eastern Africa and the Middle East 1858–1947*. Basingstoke, 2003.

Bose, S. *A Hundred Horizons: The Indian Ocean in the Age of Global Empire*. Cambridge, 2006.

Bose, S., and A. Jalal. *Modern South Asia: History, Culture, Political Economy*. 2nd ed. London, 2014.

Brown, J.M. *Modern India: The Origins of an Asian Democracy*. Oxford, 1994.

———. *Nehru: A Political Life*. New Haven, 2003.

Buelli, A. "The Hands Off Ethiopia Campaign, Racial Solidarities and Intercolonial Antifascism in South Asia (1935–36)." *Journal of Global History* 18 (2022).

Buggle, J., M. Thoenig, T. Mayer, and S.O. Sakalli. "The Refugee's Dilemma: Evidence from Jewish Migration out of Nazi Germany." *CEPR Discussion Paper* 15533 (2020).

Burton, A., F. Devji, M.J. Soske, A. Desai, and G. Vahed. "The South African Gandhi: Stretcher-Bearer of Empire," *Journal of Natal and Zulu History*, 32:1 (2018).

Busch, B.C. *Britain, India and the Arabs, 1914–1921*. London, 1971.

Cannon, B.D. *Symbolism and Folk Imagery in Early Egyptian Political Caricatures: The Wafd Election Campaign, 1920–1923*. Salt Lake City, 2019.

Cavarocchi, F. *Avanguardie dello spirito: Il fascismo e la propaganda culturale all'estero*. Rome, 2010.

Chakrabarty, B. "An Alternative to Partition: The United Bengal Scheme." *South Asia* 26:2 (2003).

Chandra, A. "Potential of the 'Un-Exchangeable Monument': Delhi's Purana Qila in the Time of Partition, c. 1947–63." *International Journal of Islamic Architecture* 2:1 (2013).

Chandra, B., M. Mukherjee, A. Mukherjee, K.N. Panikkar, and S. Mahajan. *India's Struggle for Independence, 1857–1947*. London, 1989.

Chatterji, J. "The Fashioning of a Frontier: The Radcliffe Line and Bengal's Border Landscape, 1947–52." *Modern Asian Studies* 33:1 (1999).

Chatterjee, P. "Nationalism, Internationalism, and Cosmopolitanism: Some Observations from Modern Indian History." *Comparative Studies of South Asia, Africa, and the Middle East* 36:2 (2016).

Chawla, S. "The Palestine Issue in Indian Politics in the 1920s." In *Communal and Pan-Islamic trends in Colonial India*, edited by M. Hasan. New Delhi, 1985.

Chen, J.T. "Re-orientation: The Chinese Azharites between Umma and Third World, 1938–55." *Comparative Studies of South Asia, Africa and the Middle East* 34:1 (2014).

Chester, L.P. *Borders and Conflict in South Asia: The Radcliffe Boundary Commission and the Partition of Punjab*. Manchester, 2017.

———. "'Close Parallels?': Interrelated Discussions of Partition in South Asia and the Palestine Mandate (1936–1948)." In *Partitions: A Transnational History of Twentieth-Century Territorial Separatism*, edited by L. Dobson and A. Dubnov. Stanford, 2019.

Clarke, P.F. *The Last Thousand Days of the British Empire*. London, 2007.

Cleveland, W.L. *Islam against the West: Shakib Arslan and the Campaign for Islamic Nationalism*. Austin, 1985.

Cohen, M.J. *Britain's Moment in Palestine: Retrospect and Perspectives, 1917–48*. Abingdon, 2014.

Cohen, M.J., and M. Kolinsky, eds. *Britain and the Middle East in the 1930s*. London, 1992.

Cole, J.R. *Colonialism and Revolution in the Middle East: Social and Cultural Origins of Egypt's 'Urabi Movement*. Cairo, 1999.

Colombe, M. *L'Evolution de l'Egypte, 1924–1950*. Paris, 1951.

Cooper, A. *Cairo in the War, 1939–1945*. London, 1989.

Cooper, F., and A.L. Stoler, eds. *Tensions of Empire: Colonial Cultures in a Bourgeois World*. Berkeley, 1997.

Cormack, R.M. *Midnight in Cairo: The Female Stars of Egypt's Roaring '20s*. London, 2021.

Coury, R.M. "The Politics of the Funereal: The Tomb of Saad Zaghlul." *Journal of the American Research Center in Egypt* 29 (1992).

Crouzet, G. *Inventing the Middle East: Britain and the Persian Gulf in the Age of Global Imperialism*. Montreal, 2022.

Dalrymple, W. *The Anarchy: The Relentless Rise of the East India Company*. London, 2019.

Dann, U., ed. *The Great Powers in the Middle East, 1919–1939*. Tel Aviv, 1988.

Darwin, J. *Britain, Egypt and the Middle East: Imperial Policy in the Aftermath of the War 1918–1922*. London, 1981.

———. *The Empire Project*. Cambridge, 2010.

———. "Imperialism in Decline? Tendencies in British Imperial Policy between the Wars." *Historical Journal*, 23 (1980).

Das, S. "'Their Lives Have Become Ours': Counter-Encounters in Mesopotamia, 1915–1918." In *Militarized Cultural Encounters in the Long Nineteenth Century: War, Culture and Society, 1750–1850*, edited by J. Clarke and J. Horne. London, 2018.

Deshpande, P. "The Making of an Indian Nationalist Archive: Lakshmibai, Jhansi, and 1857." *Journal of Asian Studies* 67:3 (2008).

Devji, F. *Muslim Zion*. London, 2013.

Dhulipala, V. *Creating a New Medina: State Power, Islam, and the Quest for Pakistan in Late Colonial North India*. Cambridge, 2015.

Dixit, P. "Political Objectives of the Khilafat Movement in India." In M. Hasan, *Communal and Pan-Islamic Trends*.

Dubnov, A., and L. Dobson, eds. *Partitions: A Transnational History of Twentieth-Century Territorial Separatism*. Stanford, 2019.

Elhalaby, E. "Empire and Arab Indology." *Modern Intellectual History* 19:4 (2022).

Elkins, C. *Legacy of Violence: A History of the British Empire*. London, 2023.

Elpeleg, Z. *The Grand Mufti: Haj Amin al-Hussaini, Founder of the Palestinian National Movement*. Translated by D. Harvey. London, 1993.

Eppel, M. "Note about the Term *Effendiyya* in the History of the Middle East." *International Journal of Middle East Studies* 41:3 (2009).

Er, M. "Abd-el-Krim al Khattabi: The Unknown Mentor of Che Guevera." *Terrorism and Political Violence* 29:1 (2017).

Erlich, H. "The Tiger and the Lion: Fascism and Ethiopia in Arab Eyes." In *Arab Responses to Fascism and Nazism: Attraction and Repulsion*, edited by I. Gershoni. Austin, 2014.

Everard, M., and F. de Haan, eds. *Rosa Manus (1881–1942): The International Life and Legacy of a Jewish Dutch Feminist*. Leiden, 2016.

Fahmy, K. *All the Pasha's Men: Mehmed Ali, His Army and the Making of Modern Egypt*. Cairo, 1997.

———. "For Cavafy, with Love and Squalor: Some Critical Notes on the History and Historiography of Modern Alexandria." In *Alexandria Real and Imagined*, edited by A. Hirst and M. Silk. London, 2004.

Fahmy, Z. "Francophone Egyptian Nationalists, Anti-British Discourse, and European Public Opinion, 1885–1910: The Case of Mustafa Kamil and Ya'qub Sannu'." *Comparative Studies of South Asia, Africa and the Middle East* 28:1 (2008).

———. *Ordinary Egyptians: Creating the Modern Nation through Popular Culture*. Stanford, 2011.

el-Feki, M. "Makram Ebeid: Politician of the Majority Party." In *Contemporary Egypt: Through Egyptian Eyes*, edited by C. Tripp. London, 1993.

de Felice, R. *Il fascismo e l'Oriente: Arabi, ebrei e indiani nella politica di Mussolini*. Bologna, 1988.

Fieldhouse, D.K. *Western Imperialism in the Middle East*. Oxford, 2006.

Fleischmann, E.L. *The Nation and Its "New" Women: The Palestinian Women's Movement 1920–1948*. Berkeley, 2003.

Forster, M.A. "The Resignation of Montagu." *The Round Table* 58:231 (1968).

Freas, E. "Hajj Amin al-Husayni and the Haram al-Sharif: A Pan-Islamic or Palestinian Nationalist Cause?." *British Journal of Middle Eastern Studies* 39:1 (2012).

Friedlander, H. *The Origins of Nazi Genocide: From Euthanasia to the Final Solution*. Chapel Hill, 1997.

Friedman, S.S. *No Haven for the Oppressed: United States Policy toward Jewish Refugees, 1938–1945*. Detroit, 2017.

Frost, M.R. "'That Great Ocean of Idealism': Calcutta, the Tagore Circle, and the Idea of Asia, 1900–1920." In *Indian Ocean Studies: Cultural, Social, and Political Perspectives*, edited by S. Moorthy and A. Jamal. New York, 2009.

Gelvin, J., and N. Green, eds. *Global Muslims in the Age of Steam and Print*. Berkeley, 2013.

Gerlach, C. *The Extermination of European Jews*. Cambridge, 2016.
Gershoni, I. *The Emergence of Pan-Arabism in Egypt*. Tel Aviv, 1981.
Gershoni, I., and J. Jankowski. *Confronting Fascism in Egypt: Dictatorship vs. Democracy in the 1930s*. Stanford, 2010.
———. *Egypt, Islam, and the Arabs: The Search for Egyptian Nationhood, 1900–1930*. Oxford, 1986.
———. *Redefining the Egyptian Nation, 1930–1945*. Cambridge, 2002.
Ginat, R. *Egypt and the Struggle for Power in Sudan: From World War II to Nasserism*. Cambridge, 2017.
Goebel, M. *Anti-Imperial Metropolis: Interwar Paris and the Seeds of Third World Nationalism*. Cambridge, 2015.
Goldschmidt, A. *Modern Egypt: The Formation of a Nation-State*. Boulder, 1988.
Gordon, N., and N. Perugini. *Human Shields: A History of People in the Line of Fire*. Berkeley, 2020.
Gopal, P. *Insurgent Empire: Anticolonial Resistance and British Dissent*. London, 2019.
Green, N. *How Asia Found Herself: A Story of Intercultural Understanding*. New Haven, 2022.
Guha, R. *Gandhi 1914–1948: The Years That Changed the World*. London, 2018.
al-Hadidy, A.D. "Mustafa al-Nahhas and Political Leadership." In *Contemporary Egypt: Through Egyptian Eyes*, edited by C. Tripp. London, 1993.
Halim, H. "'A Theatre—or, More Aptly, a Laboratory': India in the 1940s Egyptian Left as an Antecedent of Bandung Internationalism." *Comparative Literature Studies* 59:1 (2022).
Harper, T. *Underground Asia: Global Revolutionaries and the Assault on Empire*. London, 2020.
Hasan, M., ed. *Communal and Pan-Islamic Trends in Colonial India*. New Delhi, 1981.
———. "The Muslim Mass Contact Campaign: An Attempt at Political Mobilisation." *South Asia: Journal of South Asian Studies* 7:1 (1984).
———. "Religion and Politics in India: The Ulama and the Khilafat Movement," in M. Hasan, *Communal and Pan-Islamic Trends*.
Hasan, S.S. *Christians versus Muslims in Modern Egypt: The Century-Long Struggle for Coptic Equality*. Oxford, 2003.
Hauner, M. *India in the Axis Strategy*. Stuttgart, 1981.
Hawas, M. "World Literature and the Question of History." In *The Routledge Companion to World Literature*, edited by T. D'haen, D. Damrosch, and D. Kadir. London, 2018.
Holland, J. *Fortress Malta: An Island under Siege, 1940–1943*. London, 2003.
Holt, A. "'No More Hoares to Paris': British Foreign Policymaking and the Abyssinian Crisis, 1935." *Review of International Studies*, 37:3 (2011).
Hourani, A. *Arabic Thought in the Liberal Age, 1798–1939*. Oxford, 1962.
Hourani, G.F., and J. Carswell. *Arab Seafaring in the Indian Ocean in Ancient and Early Modern Times*. Princeton, 1995.
Huber, V. *Channelling Mobilities: Migration and Globalisation in the Suez Canal Region and Beyond, 1869–1914*. Cambridge, 2013.

Hughes, M. "The Banality of Brutality: British Armed Forces and the Repression of the Arab Revolt in Palestine." *English Historical Review* 124:507 (2009).

———. *Britain's Pacification of Palestine: The British Army, the Colonial State, and the Arab Revolt, 1936–1939*. Cambridge, 2019.

Hutchens, F.G. *India's Revolution: Gandhi and the Quit India Movement*. Cambridge, MA, 1973.

Ibrahim, H.A. *The 1936 Anglo-Egyptian Treaty*. Khartoum, 1976.

Jabbarah, T. *al-Muslimun al-Hunud wa Qadiyat Filastin*. Amman, 1998.

Jakes, A.G. *Egypt's Occupation: Colonial Economism and the Crises of Capitalism in Egypt*. Stanford, 2020.

Jalal, A. *The Sole Spokesman: Jinnah, the Muslim League and the Demand for Pakistan*. Cambridge, 1994.

Jankowski, J. "The Eastern Idea and the Eastern Union in Interwar Egypt." *International Journal of African Historical Studies* 14:4 (1981).

———. "Egyptian Regional Policy." In *Britain and the Middle East in the 1930s*, edited by M.J. Cohen and M. Kolinsky. London, 1992.

Jansen, G.H. *Afro-Asia and Non-Alignment*. London, 1966.

Kapila, S. "Ambedkar's Agonism: Sovereign Violence and Pakistan as Peace." *Comparative Studies of South Asia, Africa and the Middle East* 39:1 (2019).

Kattan, V., and A. Ranjan, eds. *The Breakup of India and Palestine: The Causes and Legacies of Partition*. Manchester, 2023.

Keddie, N.R. *An Islamic Response to Imperialism: Political and Religious Writings of Sayyid Jamāl ad-Dīn "al-Afghānī"*. Berkeley, 1983.

———. *Sayyid Jamaluddin al-Afghani: A Political Biography*. Berkley, 1972.

Kedourie, E. *The Chatham House Version and Other Middle Eastern Studies*. London, 1984.

———. "Great Britain, the Other Powers, and the Middle East before and after World War I." In *The Great Powers in the Middle East, 1919–1939*, edited by U. Dann. Tel Aviv, 1988.

Keer, D. *Dr. Ambedkar: Life and Mission*. Bombay, 1962.

Kelly, M.K. *The Crime of Nationalism: Britain, Palestine, and Nation-Building on the Fringe of Empire*. Berkeley, 2017.

Khalidi, O. "Indian Muslims and Palestinian Awqaf." *Jerusalem Quarterly* 40 (2009).

Khalidi, R. *The Iron Cage: The Story of the Palestinian Struggle for Statehood*. Boston, 2006.

Khan, N.A.I. *Egyptian-Indian Nationalist Collaboration and the British Empire*. New York, 2011.

Khan, Y. *The Great Partition: The Making of India and Pakistan*. New Haven, 2007.

———. *The Raj at War: A People's History of India's Second World War*. London, 2015.

Khater, A.F. *Sources in the History of the Modern Middle East*. 2nd ed. Boston, 2010.

Khuri-Makdisi, I. *The Eastern Mediterranean and the Making of Global Radicalism, 1860–1914*. Berkeley, 2013.

Kidambi, P. "Nationalism and the City in Colonial India: Bombay 1890–1940." *Journal of Urban History* 38:5. 2012.

Kinross, P.B. *The Ottoman Centuries: The Rise and Fall of the Turkish Empire*. London, 1977.
Klieman, A.S. "The Divisiveness of Palestine: Foreign Office versus Colonial Office on the Issue of Partition, 1937." *Historical Journal* 22:2 (June 1979).
———. "In the Public Domain: The Controversy over Partition for Palestine." *Jewish Social Studies* 42:2 (1980).
Kolinsky, M. *Britain's War in the Middle East: Strategy and Diplomacy, 1936–1942*. London, 1999.
Kozma et al., eds. *A Global Middle East: Mobility, Materiality and Culture in the Modern Age, 1880–1940*. London, 2015.
Kramer, M.S. *Islam Assembled: The Advent of the Muslim Congresses*. New York, 1986.
Krása, M. "Relations between the Indian National Congress and the Wafd Party of Egypt in the Thirties." *Archiv Orientalni* 41 (1973).
LaCoss, D. "Egyptian Surrealism and 'Degenerate Art' in 1939." *Arab Studies Journal* 18:1 (Spring 2010).
Lake, M., and H. Reynolds. *Drawing the Global Colour Line: White Men's Countries and the International Challenge of Racial Equality*. Cambridge, 2008.
Landau, J.M. *Pan-Islam: History and Politics*. New York, 2015.
Laqueur, W. *A History of Zionism*. London, 2003.
Laqueur, W., and B. Rubin, eds. *The Israel-Arab Reader: A Documentary History of the Middle East Conflict*. New York, 1984.
Latham, M. *The Right Kind of Revolution: Modernization, Development, and U.S. Foreign Policy from the Cold War to the Present*. Ithaca, 2011.
Lelyveld, D.S. *Aligarh's First Generation: Muslim Solidarity and English Education in Northern India, 1875–1900*. Chicago, 1975.
Lewis, B. *The Emergence of Modern Turkey*. Oxford, 1961.
Lewis, S.L. *Cities in Motion: Urban Life and Cosmopolitanism in Southeast Asia, 1920–1940*. Cambridge, 2016.
Lin, C.A. "Nation, Race, and Language: Discussing Transnational Identities in Colonial Singapore circa 1930." *Modern Asian Studies* 46:2 (2012).
London, L. *Whitehall and the Jews, 1933–1948: British Immigration Policy, Jewish Refugees and the Holocaust*. Cambridge, 2003.
Low, D.A. *Britain and Indian Nationalism: The Imprint of Ambiguity 1929–1942*. Cambridge, 1997.
———. "The Mediator's Moment: Sir Tej Bahadur Sapru and the Antecedents to the Cripps Mission to India, 1940–1942." *Journal of Imperial and Commonwealth History* 2:2 (1984).
Louro, M.L. *Comrades against Imperialism: Nehru, India, and Interwar Internationalism* (Cambridge, 2018).
Lüthy, H. "India and East Africa: Imperial Partnership at the End of the First World War." *Journal of Contemporary History* 6:2 (1971).
MacDonald, C.A. "Radio Bari: Italian Wireless Propaganda in the Middle East and British Countermeasures 1934–38." *Middle Eastern Studies* 13:2 (May 1977).
MacLean, D.N., and S.K. Ahmed, eds. *Cosmopolitanisms in Muslim Contexts: Perspectives from the Past*. Edinburgh, 2012.

Macmillan, M. *Paris 1919: Six Months That Changed the World.* New York, 2003.
de Madriaga, M.R. *Abd-el-Krim el Jatabi: La lucha por la independencia.* Madrid, 2009.
Manela, E. *The Wilsonian Moment: Self-Determination and the International Origins of Anti- Colonial Nationalism.* Oxford, 2007.
Mansfield, P. *Nasser.* Makers of the Modern World. London, 1969.
Markovits, C. "Making Sense of the War (India)." In *International Encyclopedia of the First World War*, ed. U. Daniel et al. Berlin, 2014.
Marzano, A. *Onde fasciste: La propaganda araba di Radio Bari (1934–43).* Rome, 2015.
Masalha, N. *The Palestine Nakba: Decolonising History, Narrating the Subaltern, Reclaiming Memory.* London, 2012.
Mattar, P. *The Mufti of Jerusalem: Al-Hajj Amin al-Husayni and the Palestinian National Movement.* 2nd ed. New York, 1992.
Matthews, W.C. "Pan-Islam or Arab Nationalism? The Meaning of the 1931 Jerusalem Islamic Congress Reconsidered." *International Journal of Middle East Studies* 35:1 (2003).
Mayer, T. "Egypt and the General Islamic Conference of Jerusalem in 1931." *Middle Eastern Studies* 18:3 (1982).
Mazower, M. *Hitler's Empire: Nazi Rule in Occupied Europe.* London, 2008.
McCarthy, H. *The British People and the League of Nations: Democracy, Citizenship and Internationalism, c.1918–45.* Manchester, 2016.
Menon, V. *Indian Women and Nationalism: The U.P. Story.* New Delhi, 2003.
Metcalf, T. *The Aftermath of Revolt: India 1857–1970.* Princeton, 1964.
Minault, G. *The Khilafat Movement: Religious Symbolism and Political Mobilization in India.* New York, 1982.
———. "Purdah Politics." In *Separate Worlds: Studies of Purdah in South Asia*, edited by H. Papaneck and G. Minault. New Delhi, 1982.
———. "Urdu Political Poetry during the Khilafat Movement." *Modern Asian Studies* 8:4 (1974).
Mishra, P. *From the Ruins of Empire: The Revolt against the West and the Remaking of Asia.* London, 2012.
Miskovic, N., H. Fischer-Tiné, and N. Boskovska, eds. *The Non-Aligned Movement and the Cold War: Delhi-Bandung-Belgrade.* London, 2014.
Mitchell, R.P. *The Society of the Muslim Brothers.* Oxford, 1993.
Monroe, E. *Britain's Moment in the Middle East.* Oxford, 1963.
Morewood, S. "Appeasement from Strength: The Making of the 1936 Anglo-Egyptian Treaty of Friendship and Alliance." *Diplomacy and Statecraft* 7:3 (1996).
———. *The British Defence of Egypt 1935–1940: Conflict and Crisis in the Eastern Mediterranean.* London, 2005.
———. "This Silly African Business: The Military Dimension of Britain's Response to the Abyssinian Crisis." In *Collision of Empires: Italy's Invasion of Ethiopia and Its International Impact*, edited by B. Strang. Farnham, 2013.
Motadel, D. "The Global Authoritarian Moment and the Revolt against Empire." *American Historical Review* 124:3 (2019).
Muhammad, M.H. *al-Lttijahat al-Wataniyya fi al-Adab al-Mu'asir.* Cairo, 1954.

Muhammad, S. *Freedom Movement in India: The Role of the Ali Brothers.* New Delhi, 1979.

Mulder, N. *The Economic Weapon: The Rise of Sanctions as a Tool of Modern War.* New Haven, 2022.

Muldoon, A. *Empire, Politics and the Creation of the 1935 India Act: Last Act of the Raj.* Abingdon, 2009.

Nafi, B.M. "The Abolition of the Caliphate: Causes and Consequences." In Ali et al., *Different Aspects of Islamic Culture.* Vol. 6, part 1.

———. "The General Islamic Congress of Jerusalem Reconsidered." *Muslim World* 86:3–4 (1996).

Nanda, B.R. *Gandhi: Pan-Islamism, Imperialism, and Nationalism in India.* Bombay, 1989.

———. *Gokhale: The Indian Moderates and the British Raj.* Vol. 3. Delhi, 1999.

Nicosia, F.R. *Zionism and Anti-Semitism in Nazi Germany.* Cambridge, 2008.

al-Nimr, S.F. *The Arab Revolt of 1936–1939 in Palestine: A Study Based on Oral Sources.* London, 1990.

O'Halloran, E.M.B. "From Imperial History to Global Histories of Empire: Writing in and for the 21st Century." *Past and Present Blog.* Past and Present Society, 21 October 2020. https://pastandpresent.org.uk/from-imperial-history-to-global-histories-of-empire-writing-in-and-for-the-21st-century.

———. "India, the Arabs, and Britain's Problem in Palestine." *International History Review* 43:3 (2020).

———. "A Tempest in a British Teapot: The Arab Question in Cairo and Delhi." In *1916 in Global Context: An Anti-Imperial Moment*, edited by E. Dal Lago, R. Healy, and G. Barry. New York, 2018.

Omar, H.A.H. "Arabic Thought in the Liberal Cage." In *Islam after Liberalism*, edited by F. Devji and Z. Kazmi. London, 2019.

———. "The Arab Spring of 1919." *LRB Blog.* London Review of Books, 4 April 2019. https://www.lrb.co.uk/blog/2019/april/the-arab-spring-of-1919.

———. "Pharaohs on Parade." *LRB Blog.* London Review of Books, 6 April 2021. https://www.lrb.co.uk/blog/2021/april/pharaohs-on-parade.

Onley, J. *The Arabian Frontier of the British Raj: Merchants, Rulers, and the British in the Nineteenth-Century Gulf.* Oxford, 2007.

Ortiz, M.P. "'Spain! Why?' Jawaharlal Nehru, Non-Intervention and the Spanish Civil War." *European History Quarterly* 49:3 (2019).

Owen, R. "The Influence of Lord Cromer's Indian Experience on British Policy in Egypt, 1883–1907," *Middle Eastern Affairs* 4 (1965).

Özcan, A. *Pan-Islamism: Indian Muslims, the Ottomans and Britain, 1877–1924.* Vol. 12. Leiden, 1997.

Paniconi, M.E. "Italian Futurism in Cairo: The Language(s) of Nelson Morpurgo across the Mediterranean." *Philological Encounters* 2:1–2 (2017).

Pankhurst, R. "Italian Fascist War Crimes in Ethiopia: A History of Their Discussion, from the League of Nations to the United Nations (1936–1949)." *Northeast African Studies* 6:1–2 (1999).

Pappé, I. *The Ethnic Cleansing of Palestine*. New York, 2007.

———. "Hajj Amin and the Buraq Revolt." *Jerusalem Quarterly* 18 (2003).

Parr, R. *Citizens of Everywhere: Indian Women, Nationalism and Cosmopolitanism, 1920–1952*. Cambridge, 2022.

Parsons, L. *The Commander: Fawzi al-Qawuqji and the Fight for Arab Independence 1914–1948*. London, 2017.

———. "The Secret Testimony of the Peel Commission (Part I): Underbelly of Empire." *Journal of Palestine Studies* 49:1 (2019).

———. "The Secret Testimony of the Peel Commission (Part II): Partition." *Journal of Palestine Studies* 49:2 (2020).

Partner, P. *Arab Voices: The BBC Arabic Service, 1938–1988*. London, 1988.

Pedersen, S. *The Guardians: The League of Nations and the Crisis of Empire*. Oxford, 2015.

Pergher, R. *Mussolini's Nation-Empire: Sovereignty and Settlement in Italy's Borderlands, 1922–1943*. Cambridge, 2018.

Porath, Y. *The Palestine Arab National Movement*. Volume 2, *From Riots to Rebellion*. London, 1977.

Pothen, N. *Glittering Decades: New Delhi in Love and War*. New Delhi, 2012.

Potter, S.J. *Wireless Internationalism and Distant Listening: Britain, Propaganda, and the Invention of Global Radio, 1920–1939*. Oxford, 2020.

Pratt, L.R. *East of Malta, West of Suez: Britain's Mediterranean Crisis 1936–1939*. Cambridge, 1975.

Prayer, M. "Italian Fascist Regime and Nationalist India, 1929–1945." *International Studies* 28:3 (1991).

Procacci, G. *Dalla parte dell'Etiopia: L'aggressione italiana vista dai movimenti anticolonialisti d'Asia, d'Africa, d'America*. Milan, 1984.

Qureshi, M.N. *Pan-Islam in British Indian Politics: A Study of the Khilafat Movement, 1918–1924*. Leiden, 1999.

Quraishi, Z.M. *Liberal Nationalism in Egypt: Rise and Fall of the Wafd Party*. Allahabad, 1970.

Raghavan, S. *India's War: World War II and the Making of Modern South Asia*. New York, 2016.

———. *The Future Is Feminist: Women and Social Change in Interwar Algeria*. Ithaca, 2022.

Ramnath, M. *Haj to Utopia: How the Ghadar Movement Charted Global Radicalism and Attempted to Overthrow the British Empire*. Berkeley, 2011.

———. "The Progressive Writers Association." *Oxford Research Encyclopedia of Asian History*. Oxford, 2019.

Rao, S.V. *The Arab-Israeli Conflict: The Indian View*. Delhi, 1972.

Reid, D.M. *Contesting Antiquity in Egypt: Archaeologies, Museums and the Struggle for Identities from World War I to Nasser*. Cairo, 2015.

Reinfeld, B. "Františka Plamínková (1875–1942), Czech Feminist and Patriot." *Nationalities Papers*, 25:1 (1997).

Reynolds, D. *Britannia Overruled*. London, 2011.

Rhett, M.A. *The Global History of the Balfour Declaration*. New York, 2016.

Roberts, N.E. "Making Jerusalem the Centre of the Muslim World: Pan-Islam and the World Islamic Congress of 1931." *Contemporary Levant* 4:1 (2019).
Robinson, F. "The British Empire and the Muslim World." In *The Oxford History of the British Empire. Volume 4, The Twentieth Century*, edited by J.M. Brown and W.M. Louis. Oxford, 1999.
Rogan, E. *The Arabs: A History*. London, 2012.
Rogan, E., and A. Shlaim, eds. *The War for Palestine: Rewriting the History of 1948*. Cambridge, 2001.
Romulo, C.P. *The Meaning of Bandung*. Chapel Hill, 1956.
Ryzova, L. *The Age of the Efendiyya: Passages to Modernity in National-Colonial Egypt*. Oxford, 2014.
Sadeh, R.B. "Debating Gandhi in al-Manar during the 1920s and 1930s." *Comparative Studies of South Asia, Africa and the Middle East* 38:3 (2018).
———. "Worldmaking in the Hijaz: Muslims between South Asian and Soviet Visions of Managing Difference, 1919–1926." *Comparative Studies in Society and History* 66:1 (2024).
Said, E.W. *Orientalism*. New York, 1978.
———. *Out of Place: A Memoir*. London, 1999.
Saikia, Y. "Hijrat and Azadi in Indian Muslim Imagination and Practice: Connecting Nationalism, Internationalism, and Cosmopolitanism," *Comparative Studies of South Asia, Africa and the Middle East* 37:2 (2017).
Satia, P. "The Defense of Inhumanity: Air Control and the British Idea of Arabia." *American Historical Review* 111:1 (2006).
———. *Spies in Arabia: The Great War and the Cultural Foundation of Britain's Covert Empire in the Middle East*. Oxford, 2008.
———. *Time's Monster: How History Makes History*. Cambridge, MA, 2020.
al-Sayyid-Marsot, A.L. *Egypt's Liberal Experiment, 1922–1936*. Berkeley, 1977.
Sbacchi, A. "Poison Gas and Atrocities in the Italo-Ethiopian War (1935–1936)." In *Italian Colonialism*, edited by R. Ben-Ghiat and M. Fuller. Italian and Italian American Studies. London, 2005.
Seal, A. *The Emergence of Indian Nationalism: Competition and Collaboration in the Later Nineteenth Century*. Cambridge, 1968.
Sengupta, N. *Bengal Divided: The Unmaking of a Nation, 1905–1971*. London, 2007.
Sharawi Lafranchi, S. *Casting Off the Veil: The Life of Huda Shaarawi, Egypt's First Feminist*. London, 2012.
Shigemi, I. "Okakura Kakuzo's Nostalgic Journey to India and the Invention of Asia." In *Nostalgic Journeys: Literary Pilgrimages between Japan and the West*, edited by S. Fisher. Vancouver, 2006.
Shindler, C. "Opposing Partition: The Zionist Predicament after the Shoah." *Israel Studies* 14:2 (2009).
Sidebotham, S.E. *Berenike and the Ancient Maritime Spice Route*. Berkeley, 2011.
Sinanoglu, P. "British Plans for the Partition of Palestine." *Historical Journal* 52:1 (2009).
———. *Partitioning Palestine: British Policymaking at the End of Empire*. Chicago, 2019.
Singh, J. *Jinnah: India, Partition, Independence*. Oxford, 2010.

Slight, J. *The British Empire and the Hajj, 1865–1956*. Cambridge, MA, 2015.

———. *Jinnah: India, Partition, Independence*. Oxford, 2010.

Stanton, A.L. "Can Imperial Radio Be Transnational? British-Affiliated Arabic Radio Broadcasting in the Interwar Period." *History Compass* 18:1 (2020).

———. *"This Is Jerusalem Calling": State Radio in Mandate Palestine*. Austin, 2013.

Stern, P.J. *The Company-State: Corporate Sovereignty and the Early Modern Foundations of the British Empire in India*. Oxford, 2011.

Stern, R.G., and A. Dubnov. "'A Part of Asia or Apart from Asia?' Zionist Perceptions of Asia, 1947–1956." In *Unacknowledged Kinships: Postcolonial Studies and the Historiography of Zionism*, edited by S. Vogt, D. Penslar, and A. Saposnik. Waltham, 2023.

Stolte, C. "'The Asiatic Hour': New Perspectives on the Asian Relations Conference, New Delhi, 1947." In *The Non-Aligned Movement and the Cold War: Delhi-Bandung-Belgrade*, edited by N. Miskovic, H. Fischer-Tiné, and N. Boskovska. London, 2014.

Strauss, H.A. "Jewish Emigration from Germany: Nazi Policies and Jewish Responses." *Leo Baeck Institute Year Book* 25:1 (1980).

Streets, H. *Martial Races: The Military, Race and Masculinity in British Imperial Culture, 1857–1914*. Manchester, 2010.

Swedenburg, T. *Memories of Revolt: The 1936–1939 Rebellion and the Palestinian National Past*. Fayetteville, 2003.

Takriti, A.R. "Before BDS: Lineages of Boycott in Palestine." *Radical History Review* 134 (2019).

Teitelbaum, J. "Hashemites, Egyptians and Saudis: the Tripartite Struggle for the Pilgrimage in the Shadow of Ottoman Defeat." *Middle Eastern Studies* 56:1 (2020).

Tessler, M. *A History of the Israeli-Palestinian Conflict*, 2nd ed. (Bloomington, 2009).

Thakur, V. "An Asian Drama: The Asian Relations Conference, 1947." *International History Review* 41:3 (2019).

Tignor, R.L. "Indianization of the Egyptian Administration under British Rule." *American Historical Review* 68:3 (1963).

Timpson, A., and A. Gibbson-Watt. *In Rommel's Backyard: A Memoir of the Long-range Desert Group*. Barnsley, 2000.

Tripp, C., ed. *Contemporary Egypt: Through Egyptian Eyes*. London, 1993.

Troutt Powell, E.M. *A Different Shade of Colonialism: Egypt, Great Britain, and the Mastery of the Sudan*. Berkeley, 2003.

Vink, M.P.M. "Indian Ocean Studies and the 'New Thalassology.'" *Journal of Global History* 2:1 (2007).

Volait, M. "Making Cairo Modern (1870–1950): Multiple Models for a "European-style" Urbanism." In *Urbanism: Imported or Exported? Native Aspirations and Foreign Plans*, edited by J. Nasr and M. Volait. Chichester, 2003.

Wagner, K. *Rumours and Rebels: A New History of the Indian Uprising of 1857*. Oxford, 2017.

Warburg, G.R. *Egypt and the Sudan: Studies in History and Politics*. London, 1985.

Wassef, H., and N. Wassef, eds. *Daughters of the Nile: Photographs of the Egyptian Women's Movement, 1900–1960*. Cairo, 2001.

Watenpaugh, K.D. *Being Modern in the Middle East: Revolution, Nationalism, Colonialism, and the Arab Middle Class*. Princeton, 2006.

Weaver, L.J. "The Laboratory of Scientific Racism: India and the Origins of Anthropology." *Annual Review of Anthropology* 51 (2022).
Weigold, A. *Churchill, Roosevelt, and India: Propaganda during World War II*. New York, 2008.
Welch, D. *Persuading the People*. Berkeley, 2016.
Westermann, E.B. *Hitler's Ostkrieg and the Indian Wars: Comparing Genocide and Conquest*. Norman, 2016.
Westrate, B. *The Arab Bureau: British Policy in the Middle East 1916–1920*. Philadelphia, 1992.
Whidden, J. *Monarchy and Modernity in Egypt: Politics, Islam and Neocolonialism between the Wars*. New York, 2013.
Whitman, J.Q. *Hitler's American Model: The United States and the Making of Nazi Race Law*. Princeton, 2017.
Wick, A. *The Red Sea: In Search of Lost Space*. Berkeley, 2016.
Williams, M.A. *Mussolini's Propaganda Abroad: Subversion in the Mediterranean and the Middle East, 1935–1940*. Abingdon, 2006.
Willis, J. "Debating the Caliphate: Islam and Nation in the Work of Rashid Rida and Abul Kalam Azad." *International History Review* 32:4 (2010).
Willis, J.M. "Burying Mohamed Ali Jauhar: The Life and Death of the Meccan Republic." *International Journal of Archaeology and Social Sciences in the Arabian Peninsula* 17 (2023).
Wilson, J. *The Domination of Strangers: Modern Governance in Eastern India, 1780–1835*. London, 2008.
Wyman, D.S. *The Abandonment of the Jews: America and the Holocaust, 1941–1945*. New York, 2007.
Wyrtzen, J. *Worldmaking in the Long Great War: How Local and Colonial Struggles Shaped the Modern Middle East*. Columbia, 2022.
Zachariah, B. *Nehru*. Routledge Historical Biographies. London, 2004.
Zayid, M.Y. *Egypt's Struggle for Independence*. Beirut, 1965.

Unpublished Scholarly Works

Akhter, M. "In Her Own Right: Sovereignty and Gender in Princely Bhopal." PhD diss., Stanford University, 2020.
Barbieri, J.L. "Kamaladevi Chattopadhyaya: Anti-Imperialist and Women's Rights Activist, 1939–1941." Master's thesis, Miami University, 2008.
Haider, S.H. "Jamia Millia Islamia: The Formative Phase (1920–1947)." PhD thesis, Aligarh Muslim University, 2012.
Olesen, M.G. "The Future Is Eastern: Muhammad Lutfi Jum'a (1886–1953) and the *Drang nach Osten* in Interwar Egypt." PhD diss., Aarhus University, 2023.
Omar, H.A.H. "Empire, Islam, and the Invention of 'Politics' in Egypt, 1867–1914." DPhil thesis, University of Oxford, 2016.
Tripp, C. "'Ali Mahir Pasha and the Palace in Egyptian Politics, 1936–42: Seeking Mass Enthusiasm for Autocracy." PhD thesis, University of London, School of Oriental and African Studies, 1984.

Weber, C.E. "Making Common Cause? Western and Middle Eastern Women in the International Feminist Movement, 1911–1948." PhD diss., Ohio State University, 2003.

Zaman, F. "Futurity and the Political Thought of North Indian Muslims, c. 1900–1925." DPhil thesis, University of Cambridge, 2015.

Audiovisual Media

British Pathé. *Asiatic Conference (1940)*. Newsreel. 1947?. https://www.britishpathe.com/asset/94977.

———. *Indian Troops in Africa (1941)*. Newsreel. 11 December 1941. https://www.britishpathe.com/asset/67019.

Gandhi Films Foundation / GandhiServe. *Mahatma Gandhi Embarking on SS 'Rajputana' at Bombay on August 29, 1931*. https://www.youtube.com/watch?v=zWW35o1vrk.

INDEX

Note: Page numbers in italics indicate illustrative material.

Abadi Begum (Bi Amman), 40, 46–48, 253n32
Abbas Hilmi II, Khedive of Egypt, 18, 53
Abdallah, King of Transjordan, 115
Abdel Krim, 172–73
Abdulmecid II, 50, 51
Abul Fat'h, Mahmud, 150, 153, 161–62, 163, *164*, 270n43
Abu-Lughod, Janet, 26
Abyssinian Crisis (1935): debates on British intervention in, 85–87; Eastern solidarity with Ethiopia, 5, 94–95, 99; and Hoare-Laval Pact, 100–101; Indian military support during, 86, 88–91; Italian propaganda, 91–93, 98; Italian propaganda, counters to, 95, 96; mentioned, 7, 10; as opportunity for anticolonial nationalists, 95–99; as threat to British control in Egypt, 84, 87–88; and 1930s 'world struggle', 106–7, 156
al-Afghani, Jamal al-Din, 41–42, 60
Afghanistan, in Italian propaganda, 93
al-Afifi, Hafez, 94–95
Aga Khan III, Sultan Mahomed Shah: on Indian colonization of Africa, 29–30; and dissolution of the Ottoman Caliphate, 50–51, 254n53; and League of Eastern Nations proposal, 53; and Palestinian cause, 132–33, 140–41, 148, 268n51; on Treaty of Lausanne, 49; and Easternism, 4
al-Ahram (newspaper), 52, 73, 83, 96–97
Akhter, Madihah, 253n29
el-Alaily, Iqbal, 125
al-Alami, Musa, 146
Ali, Amir, 50
Ali, Mehmed, 16
Ali brothers. *See* Jauhar, Mohamed Ali; Shawkat Ali
Aligarh (Muhammadan Anglo-Oriental College), 41, 46, 47, 49, 76, 251n8
All-India Muslim League: and Asian Relations Conference, 226; and Congress resignations, 184–85; and Congress-Wafd alliance, 151, 164–65; connections with Egyptians and Arabs, 121–22; goals of, 8–9, 20; and Indian partition proposal, 142, 149, 185, 186–87; and Khilafat campaign, 49; and Palestinian cause, 110, 117, 129, 134, 137, 138, *139*, 157, 159, 186–87; primacy of communal interest, 230; and satyagraha campaign, 35

297

All-India Radio, 198
All-India Women's Conference (AIWC), 168–69, 176
Alluba, Muhammad Ali, 117–18, *122*, 123, 134
Ambedkar, B.R., 185, 187
Amery, Leo, 32, 185, 193, 216
Amjadi Begum, 47, 68–69, *69*
Anderson, Benedict, 244n11
Anglo-Egyptian Treaty (1936): approval of, 102; criticism of, 103, 262n81; negotiations over, 97, 115; scholarship on, 262n78; Wafd weakened by, 154; in World War II, 183, 184, 208, 209, 212
Anjuman-i Khuddam-i Kaaba (Society of the Servants of the Kaaba), 46
Ansari, Ahmed, 109
Ansari, Mukhtar Ahmed, 41, 42, 54
anticolonial nationalism: Abyssinian Crisis as stoking, 95–99; *vs.* anti-imperialism, 8–9; Arab insurrections during World War II, 185–86, 193–94, 195–96; and the East, 4–6, 9, 53, 59, 60–63, 77, 85, 99, 167, 172, 176, 181, 195, 202; ideological alignment between Egyptian and Indian, 35–37; ideological differences between Egyptian and Indian, 37–38; international coalition in support of Palestine, 65–6, 69–71, 76–77; rise in Egypt, 17–19; rise in India, 19–20. *See also* All-India Muslim League; Arab Revolt; Khilafat campaign; Wafd Party
Anti-Comintern Pact (1936), 101
anti-imperialism *vs.* anticolonial nationalism, 8–9
Antonius, George, 136, 141, 231
al-Aqsa mosque, 65, 70
Al Arab (journal), 200
Arab Bureau, 21
Arab-Israeli War (1948), 228
Arab League, 214, 225–27, 228
Arab Revolt (1936–39): overview, 107–10; and British foreign-language broadcasts, 110–13; Egyptian diplomatic response to, 104, 114–16; Indian diplomatic response to, 129–30, 156–57; joint Arab declaration, 115–16; and exile of the Mufti, 146–49; pan-Arab conferences in response to, 117–22, 135–36, 158–59; White Paper on Palestine, 139–41, 142–46, 147–49. *See also* St James's Conference
Arab Society of Damascus, 122
Arielli, Nir, 94
Arslan, Shakib, 98–99
Art and Liberty (artist collective), 123–26, *126*, 201–2, 232
Asianism, *see* Pan-Asianism
Asian Relations Conference (1947), 221–22, 225–28, 229
al-Askari, Mahmud, 190
Asquith, Herbert, 45
Ataturk, Mustafa Kemal, 222
Auchinleck, Claude, 193, 194
August Offer, 189
Australia, 86, 185
Azad, Abul Kalam, 35, 53, 158
Azad Hind Brigades, 192, 196
Azad Hind Radio, 93, 192, 206
al-Azhar University, 114, 117, 120
Aziz Fatima, 72, *73*
al-Azmah, Bahirah, 118

Badran, Margot, 103, 118, 174, 176, 262n81, 270n2
Baksh, Khuda, 192
Baldwin, Stanley, 85
Balfour, Arthur, 31
Balfour Declaration, 32–33, 176
al-Banna, Hasan, 94
Bardaouil, Sam, 124, 125, 247n41
Barker, Henry, 58, 59
al-Bassiouni, Mahmoud, 150, 153, 159
Battaglione Azad Hindoustan. *See* Azad Hind brigades
Beinin, Joel, 182, 190, 214–15
Beitar movement, 65–66

Bengal: famine in, 190, 191; in Italian propaganda, 92–93; and Palestinian cause, 129–30; partition of, 19–20
Ben Gurion, David, 207
Bergmann, Samuel, 227, 228
Bergson, Henri, 169
Bi Amman. *See* Abadi Begum
Biltmore Program, 207, 231
Bludan Conference (Syria, 1937), 117–18, 173
Bose, Subhas Chandra: admiration of Mussolini, 98; Nehru's admiration of, 172; fall-out with the INC, 161–2, 182; Axis alliance during WWII, 182, 192, 195–6, 206; anticolonial rationale, 98, 217, 230; during Quit India Movement, 218; Radio Bari as inspiration for, 93; and Wafd visit to India, 159, 160–62. *See also* Azad Hind Brigades, Azad Hind Radio.
Bova Scoppa, R., 142
boycotts, 19, 34, 37, 47, 135
Brelvi, Abdullah, 149
Britain. *See* United Kingdom
British Broadcasting Corporation (BBC), 84, 95, 110–13
British East India Company (EIC), 14–15, 16
British Malaya, Japanese invasion of, 205
Brown, Constantine, 86–87
Buddhism, 4, 53, 64, 172
Bugle, The (magazine), 200
Bullard, Reader, 111–12, 113
Buraq Revolt (1929), 65–66
Burma, Japanese invasion of, 205, 206, 225
al-Bustani, Wadih, 69

Cairo: British evacuation of, 207–8; as diplomatic center of Arab world, 122, 228; emergence as global metropole, 2–3, 25–26; European infrastructure, 16, 26; multiethnic residents, 27–28; Old Cairo, 26–27; significance to British imperialism, 21

Cairo City Police, 151, 161, 162, 193
Caisse de la Dette, 16, 17
Caliph, as title, 42
Caliphate: Egyptian bid for, 2, 51–54, 55, 117, 120; Indian affinity with Ottoman, 40–45, Saudi bid for, 51–52, 54–55; Turkish dissolution of Ottoman, 50–51. *See also* Khilafat campaign
Calpack hats, 42, *43*, *44*
Calvert, A.S., 113
Carnarvon, Lord, 24
Carter, Howard, 24
Chamberlain, Neville, 119
charkha (spinning wheel) as symbol, 37, *38*
Chatfield, Admiral, 86, 101
Chattopadhyay, Kamaladevi, *170*; as activist philosopher, 5–6; and Gandhi, 34, 163, 168, 233; emergence as leading feminist, 168–71; ideological alignment with Egyptian feminists, 167, 169, 170, 176–77; involvement in satyagraha campaign, 34, 163, 168; opposition to India's partition, 222–23; post-independence career, 232–33; tour in Egypt, 170–72; in World War I, 21–22
Chattopadhyaya, Virendranath ("Chatto"), 37, 169, 225
Chelmsford, Lord, 33
China: at the Asian Relations Conference, 276–7n3; as part of the East, 61–62, 202; and League of Nations sanctions, 101; Chinese Muslims in Egypt, 3, 7, 27; at the World Interparliamentary Congress on Palestine, 118; and 1930s 'world struggle', 106–7, 156
Christians: and Abyssinian Crisis, 94, 98, 99; Coptic, 25, 39, 94, 124; holy lands, 33; and interfaith cooperation, 69–70; Levantine, 94
Churchill, Winston, 102–3, 189, 193, 194, 198, 215, 217, 218
civil disobedience, 34, 35, 37, 47, 135, 168, 190–91, 217

civilizational hierarchy, 28–30
Clark, J.B., 112
Coleridge, J.D., 259n16
Communist Party, 181
Company Rule, 14
Comrade, The (newspaper), 42, 44–45
Congress of Peoples of the East (Baku, 1920), 225
Congress of the Muslim World (Mecca, 1926), 54–55, 66, 254n59
Congress Party. *See* Indian National Congress
Cooper, Duff, 100, 211–12
Coptic Christians, 25, 39, 94, 124
Corbett-Ashby, Margery, 175, 231
cosmopolitanism: as accusation, 124, 232; in Cairo, 25–28, 124–25; and Easternism, 4, 61, 222, 224, 229; and disappointment, 55, 79, 232; among Indian Muslims, 40–46, 50, 54, 78, 99, 188, 202; among reactionaries in WWII, 195–6
cotton industry, 21, 190
Coupland, Reginald, 188
Cousins, Margaret, 169
Creasy, Gerald, 131, 133
Criminal Investigations Department (CID), 93, 192. *See also* Indian Intelligence Bureau
Cripps, Stafford, 215–17
Cromer, Evelyn Baring, First Earl of, 17, 18
Cunningham, Andrew, 86

Dadone, Ugo, 91–92, 98, 99
Dalhousie, Lord, 14, 229
Daoud, Mansour, 195
Daoud Effendi, Anis, 98
Darwin, John, 103, 262n78
Darwish, Sayyid, 25, 28
Davies, Reginald, 196–97
De Felice, Renzo, 142, 267n45
Defense of India Act (1939), 191
Devji, Faisal, 121, 247n41, 265n52

Dillon, John, 18
al-Din, Kamal, 65
Doctrine of Lapse, 14, 15
Dome of the Rock. *See* Haram al-Sharif mosque complex
Drummond, Eric, 87
Dyer, Reginald, 34

East Africa: Indian claims to, 29–30; liberation from Italy, 185. *See also* Abyssinian Crisis
Easternism, 3–5, 7, 9–10, 64, 65, 78, 223, 244–45n17, 246n28
Eastern Women's Conference (Cairo, 1938), 118–20, 121–22
Ebeid, Makram, 153, 160
Eden, Anthony, 87
Edib, Halide, 61
Efflatoun, Inji, 125
Egypt: Abyssinian Crisis as threat to British control in, 87–88; bid for Caliphate, 51–54, 55, 117, 120; British imperialism in, origins, 16–17; colonial ambitions, 28–29; economic struggles, 16, 21, 190–91; League of Nations membership, 94–95, 96, 102, 104, 115; Pharaonism, 24–25, 28, 29, 70–71, 124; refugees in during World War II, 203–4; response to Arab Revolt, 104, 114–16; response to Palestine partition, 228–29; revolution (1919), 22, 23–24; revolution (1952), 213; rise of anticolonial nationalism in, 17–19; and World War I, 20–21, 22. *See also* Anglo-Egyptian Treaty; Cairo; *specific political parties*
Egyptian Feminist's Union (EFU): admiration for Gandhi, 37, 74–75; and Palestinian cause, 114–15, 121–22. *See also* feminists and women's organizations; Shaarawi, Huda; Wafdist Women's Central Committee
Egyptian Gazette (newspaper), 58, 119, 120

Egyptian-Indian relations, scholarship on, 8–9, 151, 167, 247n38, 268–69n5, 270n2
Egyptian Museum, 24, 71, 124
Egyptian Revolution (1919), 22, 23–24
Egyptian Revolution (1952), 213
Egyptienne, L' (magazine), 4, 61, 74–75, 169, 172
Egyptology, 24–25
Elhalaby, Esmat, 69
England. *See* United Kingdom
Enver Pasha, 42, *43*
Ethiopia. *See* Abyssinian Crisis
Ettel, Erwin, 194

Fahmy, Ziad, 25–26, 27
Faisal I of Iraq, 31, 32
Farid, Muhammad, 19
Faruq I, King of Egypt: abdication crisis, 209–12; bid for Caliphate, 120; pro-Axis position in World War II, 194–95; and religious coronation proposal, 117; rise to power, 101, 114; vs. Wafd Party, 114, 117, 152, 189, 208–9
fellaheen (Egyptian rural peasantry), 21, 22, 25, 154
feminist and women's organizations: admiration for Gandhi, 34, 37, 74–75; and Anglo-Egyptian Treaty, 103, 262n81; ideological alignment between Egyptian and Indian feminists, 37, 167, 169, 170, 176–77; and Palestinian cause, 114–15, 118, 119–20, 121–22, 173, 231; Western vs. Eastern, 173–77
First Round Table Conference (1930), 66–67
Fisher, Admiral, 86
France: financial oversight in Egypt, 16; Mandates, 32; and Vietnam, 225; in World War II, 188
Fuad I, King of Egypt, 51–52, 54, 55, 65, 75, 88, 89, 101
Furness, Robert, 110–11

Gandhi, Indira, 159
Gandhi, Mohandas K., *37, 73, 164*; admiration for Egyptian nationalists, 36, 71; and Ali family, 46, 47, 72, 77; at Asian Relations Conference, 228; assassination of, 229, 231; and Chattopadhyay, 34, 163, 168, 233; and Cripps Mission, 216; criticism of British wartime dealings, 182, 206–7; Egyptian admiration for, 35, 37, 72–75, 153, 163, 190; fixed ideals of, 5–6, 181–82, 201; and India Act, 103; influence in Congress, 161–62; on materialism, 37, 59; mentioned, 146, 152, 222; at Motilal Nehru's funeral, 71–72; passages via Suez Canal, 35, 72–75, 77, 153, 201; poem by Ahmad Shawqi, 35, 57; and Quit India Movement, 217–18; on religious communalism, 39; and First Round Table, 67, 69; and Second Round Table, 72, 74; satyagraha campaign, 34, 35, 37, 47, 49; speech at Aden, 72; Tagore compared to, 59, 64; visit with Wafd in Delhi, 151, 163–64
George, Lloyd, 32
Germany: alliance with Eastern anticolonial activists, 185, 193–94, 195–96; alliance with Japan, 101; British anticipation of conflict with, 86, 101, 183; censorship, 123; declarations of war against, 183–84; Holocaust, 204–5, 207; invasion of Czechoslovakia, 175; invasion of France, 188; in Iraq and Iran, 193–94; Mediterranean advance, 203–4; Nazi rise to power in, 108; and Paris Peace Conference, 195; propaganda campaigns, 192, 196
Gershoni, Israel, 116, 117, 122, 214, 245n17, 272n6
Ghali, Wasif Butrus, 104, 117
Ginat, Rami, 8
Giornale d'Oriente (newspaper), 91
Gokhale, Gopal Krishna, 20, 29, 30, 39

Gomaa, Muhammad Lutfi, 94, 99, 100, 230
Gorst, Eldon, 18
Gouda, Ahmad Qasim, 150, 165, 246n25
Government of India Act (1935), 102–3, 129
Graves, Cecil, 112
Greater East Asia Co-Prosperity Sphere, 225
Greece, German invasion of, 203–4
Grey, Edward, 18
Grobba, Fritz, 194
Guam, Japanese invasion of, 205

Haavara Agreement (1933), 108
Habas, Bracha, 278n19
Hacohen, David, 278n19
Halim, Hala, 201
Hamza, Ahmad, 150
Haram al-Sharif mosque complex, 65–66, 67–70, 267n33
Hasan, Mushirul, 45–46
Hashemites, 31, 52
Hassanein, Ahmed, 210–11
Hawas, May, 2
HaYarden (newspaper), 99
Haykal, Muhammad Hussein, 51, 102
Henein, Georges, 125, *126*, 201–2, 232
Hijaz, 52, 54–55
Hilali, Naguib, 153
Hindu-Muslim collaboration: Khilafat-satyagraha alliance, 46–47, 49; as threat to British imperialism, 15–16, 134; as threat to Muslim League, 130, 134, 139; at World Islamic Congress, 77. *See also* Indian National Congress-Wafd alliance
Hindustan, 15
Hitler, Adolf. *See* Germany
Hoare, Samuel, 100
Hoare-Laval Pact (1935), 100–101
Holocaust, 204–5, 207
holy lands or places: Christian, 31, 33; and Easternism, 10, 59, 78; Hindu, 71–2; Jewish, 31, 33, 65–66, 68, 78; Muslim, 33, 43, 45–46, 48, 51, 54–6, 65–66, 68, 76, 78, 114, 137–38, 187, 256n34, 267n33. *See also* sacred geography
Hong Kong, Japanese invasion of, 205
hunger strikes, 49, 190–91
Hussein, Sharif of Mecca, 31, 51–52, 70
Hussein, Taha, 58
al-Husseini, Hajj Amin, Mufti of Jerusalem, 69, *143*; and Abyssinian Crisis, 98–99; and Ali brothers, 55, 66–67, 68, 69, 70, 76; exclusion from St James's Conference, 132, 135, 141, 148; exile, 146–49; fundraising campaign for Haram al-Sharif, 65, 66; internationalization of Palestinian cause, 66, 70, 71, 76, 254n57; and White Paper on Palestine, 141–44, 148–49, 268n63; at World Islamic Congress, 75–76; during World War II, 185–86, 194–95, 230
al-Husseini, Jamal, 65, 66, 135, 146

Ibn Saud, King of Saudi Arabia, 51–52, 54–55, 111–12, 115
Ibrahim, Hassan Ahmad, 96
India: colonial ambitions, 29–30; Cripps Mission to, 215–17; early British imperialism in, overview, 14–16; economic struggles, 21, 190, 191; Government of India Act (1935), 102–3, 129; independence of, 222, 223, 224; in Italian propaganda, 92–93; military during Abyssinian Crisis, 86, 88–91; military during World War II, 185, 191, 192–93; partition of, 121, 141–42, 149, 185, 186–88, 222–24, *223*; partition of Bengal, 19–20; pro-Indian propaganda campaigns, 196–202; Quit India Movement, 217–18; rebellion (1857–58), 14–16, 41, 46; refugees in, after partition, 206, 275n4; refugees in, World War II, 206, 275n4; response to Arab Revolt, 129–30,

156–57; rise of anticolonial nationalism in, 19–20; Round Table Conference, First (1930), 66–67; Round Table Conference, Second (1931), 72, 74; satyagraha campaign, 34, 35, 37, 47, 49; territorial conflict with Pakistan, 229; and United Nations Security Council membership, 277n16; and World War I, 21–22, 44–45, 48; World War II as opportunity for independence, 186–87, 189–90, 192–93, 195, 196, 206. *See also* All-India Muslim League; Indian National Congress (INC); Khilafat campaign; Muslim Indians

Indian-Egyptian relations, scholarship on, 8–9, 151, 167, 247n38, 268–69n5, 270n2

Indian Intelligence Bureau, 151, 161, 163, 164, 165, 192

Indian Legion, 192

Indian National Congress (INC): calls for Hindu-Muslim collaboration, 72; establishment and goals, 19; ideological divisions, 19–20; and India Act, 103; and Khilafat campaign, 47, 49; and LAI affiliation, 61; Mass Contact campaign, 158; mutual admiration between Wafd and, 35; and Palestinian cause, 134, 156–57; partition approval, 222–23, 231; provincial resignations following war declaration, 184–85; and Quit India Movement, 217–18; and Round Table, First, 69; and Round Table, Second, 72, 74; Second Round Table Conference (1931), 72, 74

Indian National Congress-Wafd alliance: delegation tour in Egypt, 167, 170–72; delegation tour in India, 150–51, 159–66, *164*; Nehru-Nahas correspondence, 157–59, 215; Nehru-Nahas meeting in Alexandria, 152–55, *156*

Indian Rebellion (1857–58), 14–16, 41, 46, 218

influenza pandemic (1918), 21

International Alliance of Women (IAW), 37–38, 167, 169, 173–77, 231

Iqbal, Muhammad, *106*; and Abyssinian Crisis, 93, 97; fixed ideals of, 5–6, 201; and Khilafat campaign, 49; New Year's address (1938), 105–7; and Shawqi, 77; at World Islamic Congress, 75

Iran: and Palestinian cause, 118; in World War II, 194–95

Iraq: as British Mandate, 32; constitution, 136; independence of, 96; and Palestinian cause, 115, 135–36; in World War II, 193–94

Islamic Caliphate Congress (Cairo, 1926), 52–54, 55

Islamic conferences: Congress of the Muslim World (Mecca, 1926), 54–55, 66, 254n59; Islamic Caliphate Congress (Cairo, 1926), 52–54, 55; World Islamic Congress (Jerusalem, 1931), 75–77

Islami Dunya (newspaper), 28

Ismail, Khedive of Egypt, 16

Ismet Pasha, 50

Israel, founding of, 228–29, 231. *See also* Palestine

Italy: antisemitism in, 125; and Palestinian cause, 142; propaganda campaigns, 91–93, 98, 110, 192, 267n43; propaganda campaigns, counters to, 95, 96; in World War II, 188–89, 193, 194. *See also* Abyssinian Crisis

Ittihad Party, 120

Jabotinsky, Ze'ev, 99

al-Jamaa al-Islamiyya (newspaper), 98

Jamia Millia Islamia (National Muslim University), 251n8

Jamiyyat al-Rabita al-Sharqiyya (Society of the Eastern Bond), 59–60, 76, 255n15

Jankowski, James, 116, 117, 122, 214, 245n17, 272n6

Japan: alliance with Germany, 101; alliance with Subhas Chandra Bose, 172, 196, 206; British anticipation of conflict with, 84, 86, 101; Eastern affinity with, 7, 63–64; Greater East Asia Co-Prosperity Sphere, 225; at the IAW Congress in Berlin, 169; students in Cairo, 3; and Pan-Asianism, 4, 62, in World War II, 10, 205, 215

al-Jarida (newspaper), 19

Jauhar, Mohamed Ali, *44*; and Caliphate Crisis, 52, 53, 54–55, 254n59; death and burial, 67–70, 71; expansive conception of the East, 62; at First Round Table, 66–67, 74; and Khilafat campaign, 46, 47; and League of Eastern Nations proposal, 53, 254n54; and Palestinian cause, 66, 68, 109

Jawish, Sheikh Abd al-Aziz, 19

Jewish Colonial Association, 107

Jewish National Fund, 107

Jewish Women's Equal Rights Association (ERA), 173, 175–76

Jews: and Asian Relations Conference, 227–28, 278n19; in Egypt, 22, 27, 103, 116, 121, 124–25, 208; in Germany, 108, 123; Holocaust, 204–5, 207; holy lands, 31, 33, 65–66, 68; at IAW Copenhagen congress, 173, 175; immigration to Palestine, 32, 107, 108, 136, 139–40, 145, 204; in Italy, 125; as indigenous to Asia and North Africa, 31–33, 94, 227, 278n19; St James's Conference delegation, 131, 138. *See also* Zionism

al-Jezireh (newspaper), 146, 148

al-Jihad (newspaper), 94, 96

Jinnah, Muhammad Ali, *226*; and Asian Relations Conference, 225–27; and Congress-Wafd alliance, 164–65; death of, 231–32; and Indian partition proposal, 149, 185, 186–87; and Khilafat campaign, 49; Lahore Resolution, 186–87, 189; and Palestinian cause, 66, 110, 117, 130, 133, 137–38, 144, 185, 186–87; and Quit India Movement, 218

Jumblatt, Walid, 230

Kahlo, Frida, 124

Kamil, Mustafa, 18, 19, 35, 36

Kar, Ida, 125

Kawkab al-Sharq (newspaper), 96, 98

al-Kaylani, Rashid Ali, 185, 193–94, 195

Kemal, Mustafa, 50–51

Khalidi, Rashid, 143, 148

Khaliquzzaman, Choudhry, *122*, *139*, *143*; and Abyssinian Crisis, 90; and Ali brothers, 46, 47; and Congress-Wafd alliance, 166; disillusionment with Arab leaders, 232; and Egyptian bid for Caliphate, 120; Indian partition proposal, 121, 141–42, 149, 186, 187, 224; and disagreement with Nahas, 121, 166; nationalist activism, 40–41, 42, 252n9; and Palestinian cause, 118–19, 123, 130, 133–35, 138–40, 142–44; *Only If They Knew It*, 140; *Pathway to Pakistan*, 119

Khan, Ajmal, 54

Khan, Noor Aiman I., 8–9, 35, 151, 159

Khan, Rashid Ahmed, 192

Khan, Syed Ahmad, 41, 251n5

Khan, Yasmin, 191, 216, 276n53

Khilafat movement: Ali family's prominence in, 46–48; alliance with satyagraha campaign, 46–47, 49; and bids for Caliphate, 54–55, 56; and British support, 48–49; concern for Muslim holy sites, 45–46, 66, 68; prospect of revival ('Second Khilafat'), 130, 134, 138, 139, 266n16; and Turkish dissolution of the Caliphate, 50–51

Krása, Miloslav, 247n38

Krishak Praja Party, 129

labor unions, 190–91, 214–15

Lahore Resolution, 186–87, 189

Lakshmibai, the Rani of Jhansi, 15
Lampson, Miles, 213; and abdication crisis, 209–12; and Abyssinian Crisis, 83–84, 88–89; and Anglo-Egyptian Treaty, 102, 262n78; anticipation of conflict with Germany, 183; and Arab Revolt, 113, 116, 147, 148, 264n25; and Mufti pardon, 146, 147, 148; propaganda campaign proposal, 196–97; and uncertainty of Egypt's position during World War II, 189, 194–95, 208–9
Lausanne, Treaty of, 49
Laval, Pierre, 100
Lawrence, Thomas Edward, 31
League Against Imperialism (LAI), 61, 155, 222, 225
League of Eastern Nations, proposal for, 53, 55
League of Nations: and Abyssinian Crisis, 84, 85, 94, 100–101; and Arab Revolt, 136, 142; Egyptian membership in, 94–95, 96, 102, 104, 115
Lebanon: and Asian Relations Conference, 226–27; as French Mandate, 32
Leeper, Rex, 112–13
Lesseps, Ferdinand de, 16
Levantine Christians, solidarity with Ethiopia, 94
Liberal Constitutionalist Party, 38, 51, 54, 60, 117
Libya, Italian colonization of, 90, 188–89
Linlithgow, Victor Hope, Second Marquess of, 131–32, 142, 183, 189, 216, 218
al-Liwa (newspaper), 18, 19
Lockman, Zachary, 182, 190, 214–15
London, Louise, 205
Louro, Michele, 61
Low, D.A., 189
Lutfi al-Sayyid, Ahmad, 18, 19
Lutfi Bey Said, 58
Lyttleton, Oliver, 211

MacDonald, J. Ramsay, 18
MacDonald, Malcolm, 131, 132–34, 137
MacMillan, Harold, 222
MacMillan, Margaret, 32
Maher, Ali: as Faruq's advisor, 114, 117; mentioned, 191; and Palestinian cause, 144–45, 146; post-revolution return as Prime Minister, 212–13; and World War II, 183–84, 189, 208
Mahmud, Muhammad, 117, 120–21, 145, 146–47, 148
al-Majalla al-Jadeeda (magazine), 200–202
Majallat al-Rabita al-Sharqiyya (journal), 60
al-Manar (magazine), 35
Mandates, 30–33
Manifesto della Razza (1938), 125
al-Maraghi, Mustafa, 52, 114, 117, 120, 208
Marinetti, Filippo Tommaso, 125
materialism, 37, 59, 99, 126, 202
McMahon, Henry, 31
media. See press and media
Milner Commission, 36
Minault, Gail, 48
Misr el-Fatah (Young Egypt), 98, 114
al-Mizan (newsletter), 200
Mohani, Hasrat, 109
Mokhtar, Mahmud, 28, 124; Nihdat Misr, 25
Monckton, Walter, 209
Montagu, Edwin Samuel, 33–34, 48, 138
Montgomery-Massingberd, Archibald, 87–88, 95
Motadel, David, 195, 196
al-Muayyad (newspaper), 18
Mufti. See al-Husseini, Hajj Amin, Mufti of Jerusalem
Muhammad, Prophet, 55, 256n34, 267n33
Muhammad, Shan, 47–48
Mulder, Nicholas, 100
Munich Crisis, 129, 131, 182
al-Muqattam (newspaper), 52, 53

Musa, Salama, 94, 201
al-Musawwar (newspaper), 96
Muslim Brotherhood, 94, 96, 109, 114, 120
Muslim holy lands, 33, 45–46, 55, 65–66, 137–38, 256n34, 267n33
Muslim Indians: and bids for Caliphate, 53, 54–55, 56, 120; in Italian propaganda, 92–93; loyalty to British vs. Ottomans, 41–42, 44–45; and Palestinian cause, 66–68, 109–10, 119, 129–31, 133–34, 137–41, 142–44, 186, 266n17; and partition of Bengal, 19–20; and partition of India, 121, 141–42, 149, 185, 186–88, 222–24, *223*; solidarity with Ethiopia, 90; support for Ottoman Empire, 40, 41, 42, 44–45. *See also* All-India Muslim League; Hindu-Muslim collaboration; Khilafat campaign
Mussolini, Arnaldo, 142
Mussolini, Benito. *See* Abyssinian Crisis; Italy
mutamassirun (European Cairenes), 27, 229

Nabarawi, Saiza (Céza Nabaraoui), 74–75, 77, 167, 169, 173, 271n20
Nafi, Basheer, 54
al-Nahas, Mustafa, *213*; and Abyssinian Crisis, 88, 96; as Arab League president, 228; and Congress-Wafd alliance, Alexandria meeting, 152–55, *156*; and Congress-Wafd alliance, correspondence with Nehru, 157–59, 215; and Congress-Wafd alliance, Egyptian delegation tour in India, 160–61, 166; cooperation with the British during World War II, 209, 212, 230; and Gandhi, 72, 74, 153; internationalist sentiments, 157, 214; and Palestinian cause, 115–16, 117, 121, 152, 157–58; treaty negotiations with the British, 95–96, 97, 101–2

Naidu, Sarojini, 34, 37, 169, 222, 228, 232
Nashashibis, 254n57
Nassar, Sadhij, 119, 175
Nasser, Gamal Abdel, 212, 229
nationalism. *See* anticolonial nationalism
Nationalist Party (Watani Party), 18–19
Nazi Germany. *See* Germany
Neguib, Muhammad, 212
Nehru, Jawaharlal: and Abyssinian Crisis, 97; at Asian Relations Conference, 222, 225, 227; Alexandria meeting with the Wafd, 152–55, *156*; correspondence with Nahas, 157–59, 215; and Wafd tour of India, 160, 163, 164, 165; Egyptian admiration for, 201; expansive conception of the East, 61–62, 64; and India Act, 103; and Indian partition proposal, 231; internationalist sentiments, 61–62, 156–57, 172, 215, 222; and labor policy, 215; mentioned, 37; at Motilal Nehru's funeral, 71; and Palestinian cause, 156–58; as Prime Minister, 232; and Quit India Movement, 217; and United Nations Security Council membership, 277n16
Nehru, Motilal, 71–72
Nem ya Khufu [Sleep, O Khufu], 25
New Zealand, 86
Nimr, Amy, 125, 231
nonviolent resistance, 34, 35, 37, 47, 135, 168, 190–91, 217
al-Nuqrashi, Mahmud Fahmi, 228

Okakura Tenshin, *The Ideals of the East*, 63–64
Olesen, Mattias, 99, 246n28, 254n51
Omar, Hussein, 249n30
Operation Barbarossa, 194
Operation Battle Axe, 204
Orientalism, 4, 64, 245n18. *See also* Said, Edward
Ormsby-Gore, William, 85
Orwell, George, 205
Osman, Amin, 209

Osman Ali Khan, Nizam of Hyderabad, 65
Ottoman Empire: dissolution of, 45–46, 50; Egypt as province of, 16, 17; vs. Egyptian nationalism, 19; Indian Muslim support for, 40, 41, 42, 44–45; in World War I, 20–21
Owen, Roger, 17, 247n38

Pahlavi, Mohammad Reza, Shah of Iran, 194
Pakistan: establishment of, 222–24, 226; proposal for, 135, 187–88; territorial conflict with India, 229. *See also* Lahore Resolution
Palestine: and Asian Relations Conference, 227–28; and Biltmore Program, 207; as British Mandate, 31–33, 65; Buraq Revolt, 65–66; international coalition in support of, 6, 65, 66, 69–70, 71, 76–77; participation in Islamic conferences, 52, 55, 75–76; Jewish immigration to, 32, 107, 108, 136, 139–40, 145, 204; partition of, 116, 121, 131–32, 228–29, 231; and 1930s 'world struggle', 106–7, 156; in World War I, 45; in World War II 185–86, 194, 195. *See also* Arab Revolt; holy lands
Palestinian Arab Women's Committee, 114–15
Pan-Asianism, 4, 7, 61–64, 232
Pan-Islamism, 3–5, 8, 9, 46, 51, 55, 56, 62, 76, 137, 158, 188, 232, 245n19, 247n35; and Easternism, 4, 7–8, 53, 55, 56, 60, 64, 77
Paris Peace Conference (1919), 22, 23–24, 30, 45, 195–96
Parsons, Laila, 136
Partner, Peter, 110
Pearl Harbor attack (1941), 205
Pedersen, Susan, 100
Peel Commission Report, 108–9, 130
Petrie, David, 108
Pharaonism, 24–25, 28, 29, 70–71, 124

Philippines: Japanese invasion of, 205; at the Asian Relations Conference, 276–77n3; as sole Asian vote for the partition of Palestine, 278n23
Phipps, Eric, 146, 148
Picot, Georges, 31
Plamínková, Františka, 175, 271n20
Plassey, Battle of (1757), 14
Poetic East, expansive conceptions of the East, 59–64, 202
Potter, Simon, 112
Powell, Eve Troutt, 8, 29
Pownall, Henry, 183
Prasad, Rajendra, 162
press and media: British foreign-language programming and propaganda campaigns, 110–13, 196–200; Cairo's dominance in, 2–3, 26; German propaganda campaigns, 192, 196; Italian propaganda, counters to, 95, 96; Italian propaganda campaigns, 91–93, 98, 110, 192, 267n43
Publicity Office, India, 198, 199–200
pyramids, 24, 25, 27, 28, 37, 153, 198

al-Qassam, Izzedine, 108
Quit India Movement, 217–18
Quraishi, Zaheer, 247n38
Qureshi, Shuaib and Gulnar, 72
al-Quwuqji, Fawzi, 195

racial discourse: and Burmese refugee crisis, 206–7; among Egyptians and Indians, 28–30, 89, 197; and the League of Nations, 30–31, 95
Radio Bari, 92, 93, 98, 110, 196
Radio Himalaya, 192
Radwan, Fathi, 35
Raghavan, Srinath, 229, 276n53, 277n16
Rahmat Ali, Choudhry, 135
Rajwade, Rani Lakshmibai, 176
Ramayana (Hindu epic), 37
Rao, Sudha, 247n38
Reading, Lord, 48

refugees: in Egypt, 203–4; in India, after partition, 206, 275n4; in India, World War II, 206, 275n4; Jewish, 108, 174–75, 204
Reith, John, 111, 112
religious plurality, 38–39
Ribbentrop, Joachim, 193
Richard, W.H.A., 192
Rida, Mohi al-Din, 75; *Abtal al-Wataniyya*, 35
Rida, Rashid, 35, 53, 64, 75, 254n45, 254n55
Rif War, 172
Rivera, Diego, 124
Roberts, N.E., 66
Rommel, Erwin, 203, 204
Rose, P.L., 161
Round Table Conferences, 66–67, 72, 74
Rowlatt, Sidney, 33
Rowlatt Act (1919), 33–34
Russo-Japanese War, 64

Saadist Party, 114, 120
sacred geography, 43, 45, 59, 65, 68, 71, 78. *See also* holy lands
Said, Edward, 208, 245n18
al-Said, Amina, 231
al-Said, Karima, 227
al-Said, Nuri, 115, 136
Saleh, E.D., 95
Salimullah, Nawab, 20
Salt March (1931), 168
Samuel, Herbert, 33, 65
al-Sanhuri, Abd al-Razzaq Ahmad, *Le Califat: Son évolution vers une société des nations orientales*, 53
Satia, Priya, 246n29
satyagraha campaign, 34, 35, 37, 47, 49
Saudi Arabia: and Asian Relations Conference, 226–27; bid for Caliphate, 51–52, 54–55; mended relations with Egypt, 114; and Palestinian cause, 115, 135–36, *139*

Second Round Table Conference (1931), 72, 74
Selassie, Haile, 84, 100
Seva Dal, 168
Shaarawi, Ali, 22
Shaarawi, Huda, *23*; and Anglo-Egyptian Treaty, 103, 262n81; background, 22–23; fixed ideals of, 5–6; ideological alignment with Indian feminists, 37, 167, 169, 170, 176–77; and Palestinian cause, 114, 118, 119–20, 121–22, 173, 175, 231, 264n25; view of Easternism, 4
Shanghai, Japanese invasion of, 205
Sharq, as term, 5, 59, 60, 61
Shaw, George Bernard, 18
Shawkat Ali: and Abyssinian Crisis, 90; and Caliphate Crisis, 52, 53, 55; fallout with the Mufti, 70, 76; at First Round Table, 66–67; at Jauhar's funeral, *69*, 69–70; and Khilafat campaign, 46, 47; and Palestinian cause, 66, 68, 76–77, 110; at World Islamic Congress, 75, 76–77, 258n72
Shawqi, Ahmad: death and eulogies, 77–78; poem for Gandhi, 35, 75; at Jauhar's funeral, 69–70; mentioned, 28, and Tagore, 58, 60; "Tutankhamun and the Parliament," 24
Shedai, Muhammad Iqbal, 93, 142, 192, 267n43
Shuckburgh, John, 133
Siddiqi, Abdurrahman, *122*, *143*; Indian partition proposal, 141–42, 149, 224; nationalist activism, 41, 42; and Palestinian cause, 119, 130, 133–35, 138–40, 142–44
Sidqi, Ismail, 70–71, 74, 79, 96
Simon Commission, 36
Singapore: Japanese invasion of, 205; in British naval strategy, 86, 259n12
Singh, Kartar, 192
Singh, Naurang, 192
Singh, Sardar Mandal, 90

Singh Mall, Kundan, 192
Sirri, Hussein, 189, 208
Smart, Walter, 95, 144, 159, 231
Smith, Ian Weston, 210
Society of the Eastern Bond (Jamiyyat al-Rabita al-Sharqiyya), 59–60, 76, 255n15
el-Solh, Riad, 76
Soviet Union: disillusionment with, 125, 225; vote to partition Palestine, 228; in World War II, 194, 204
Spain: and 1930s 'world struggle', 106–7, 156
Spanish Morocco: and Palestinian cause, 118; Rif War, 172
sphinx symbolism, 25, 37
Spiritual East, as concept, 4
St James's Conference (London, 1939): Arab joint strategy, 135–36; British offer (White Paper), 139–41, 142–43, 144–46, 147–49; Cairo Interparliamentary Congress as prelude to, 121; call for, 131–32; Indian representation at, 131, 133–35, 137–39
Stone, Oliver, 209
Strategic East, 4, 202
strikes, hunger, 190–91
Sudan, Egyptian claims to, 28–29
Suez Canal: and Abyssinian Crisis, 86; building of, 16; international ownership of, 53; significance to British imperialism, 17, 31
Sukthankar, Malini, 176
Sun Yat Sen, 222
Surour, Ahmad Kamal, 111
surrealism, 123–26, *126*, 201–2, 232. *See also* Art and Liberty
al-Suwaydi, Tawfiq, 145
Swadeshi movement, 19, 36, *37*
Sykes, Mark, 31
Syria: and Asian Relations Conference, 226–27; as French Mandate, 32; and Palestinian cause, 115

Tagore, Rabindranath, *63*; admiration for Shawqi, 77–78; Egyptian admiration for, 57–59; expansive conception of the East, 62–64; mentioned, 201
Tcheng, Soumé, 61
Tegart, Charles, 108
el-Telmissany, Kamel, 124, *126*
Temple Mount, 65–66, 68. *See also* Haram al-Sharif mosque complex
Tessler, Mark, 207
Tewfik, Khedive of Egypt, 17
Thailand, Japanese invasion of, 205
Thawrat al-Hind al-Siyasiyya (India's Political Revolution), 35
Tignor, Robert, 17, 247n38
Tilak, Bal Gangadhar, 20
trade unions, 190–91, 214–15
Transjordan, and Palestinian cause, 115, 135–36
Tripp, Charles, 183–84, 212–13
Trotsky, Leon, 124
Turkey: dissolution of Ottoman Caliphate, 50–51; and Palestinian cause, 118; republic of, establishment, 49–50
Tutankhamun, Pharaoh, 24

Umma Party (People's Party), 18–19
unions, trade, 190–91, 214–15
United Kingdom: Abyssinian Crisis, as threat to control in Egypt, 87–88; Abyssinian Crisis, debating intervention in, 85–87; Cripps Mission in India, 215–17; early imperialism in India, overview, 14–16; foreign-language programming and propaganda campaigns, 110–13, 196–200; imperialism in Egypt, origins, 16–17; in Italian propaganda, 92–93, 110; political rift between India Office and London, 33–34, 48; and Quit India Movement, 217–18; restrictions on Jewish immigration, 108, 205, 207; treaty negotiations with the Wafd,

United Kingdom (*cont*)
95–96, 97, 101–2, 115, 262n78; World War II, anticipation of conflict with Germany, 86, 101, 183; World War II, anticolonial insurrections during, 185–86, 193–94, 195–96; World War II, as threat to control in Egypt, 183–84, 189, 192–93, 194–95, 207–8; World War II, as threat to control in India, 186–87, 189–90, 192–93, 195, 196, 205–6

United Nations, 228

United Publications, 199–200

United States: and British naval defense, 86; British propaganda targeting, 31, 198, 217; India compared to revolutionary, 15, 17; delegates at St James's Conference, 138; and Palestinian cause, 118; restrictions on Jewish immigration, 108, 205, 207; wartime alliance with USSR, 225;

Universal Peace Congress (Brussels, 1936), 115

Urabi, Ahmad Bey, 17

Urabi Revolt (1879–82), 17, 41

de Valera, Éamonn, 146

Vansittart, Robert, 83, 160

Victoria, Queen of the United Kingdom, 16

Vietnam, war against France, 225

Wafd Party: and Abyssinian Crisis, 88; admiration for Gandhi, 35, 74, 75; communal diversity, 38–39; Coptic Christians in, 25, 39; and Egyptian bid for Caliphate, 52, 54; *vs.* Faruq, 114, 117, 152, 189, 208–9; and Jamiyyat al-Rabita al-Sharqiyya, 60; and Palestinian cause, 115–16, 117, 152, 157–58; and Paris Peace Conference, 22, 23–24; and Pharaonism, 24–25, 28, 29, 70; pro-British position during World War II, 182, 208; resignation from government, 70; treaty negotiations with the British, 95–96, 97, 101–2, 115, 262n78; Indian influence on wartime policies, 214–15. *See also* Indian National Congress-Wafd alliance

Wafdist Women's Central Committee, 23

Wahhabi Islam, 52, 54, 55

Wake Islands, Japanese invasion of, 205

Watani Party (Nationalist Party), 18–19

Wavell, Archibald, 193, 194

Weber, Charlotte, 174, 175

Weizmann, Chaim, 32, 207

Wheeler, Geoffery, 199–200

White Paper on Palestine (1939), 139–41, 142–46, 147–49

Wilkinson, P.J., 192

Willis, John, 54–55

Wilson, Woodrow, 22, 30, 249n30

Wingate, Reginald, 22

women's organizations. *See* feminists and women's organizations

Woodhead Report, 131

World Interparliamentary Congress of Arab and Muslim Countries for the Defense of Palestine (Cairo, 1938), 117, 118–19, 120–21, 158–59

World Islamic Congress (Jerusalem, 1931), 75–77

World War I, 20–22, 40–41, 43, 44–45

World War II: Arab insurrections during, 193–95; British anticipation of conflict, 86, 101, 183; economic impact, 190–91; fall of France, Eastern reactions to, 188–90; Holocaust, 204–5, 207; Indian military support during, 185, 191, 192–93; outbreak of, Eastern reactions to, 182–86; propaganda campaigns, 182, 195, 196–202

World Zionist Organization, 31, 32

Wyrtzen, Jonathan, 249n30

Yeats, W.B., 18

Yemen: and Asian Relations Conference, 226–27, 276–77n3; and Palestinian cause, *139*, 111, 118, 135–36

Yishuv: and Abyssinian Crisis, 99; during interwar period, 107–108; and WWII refugees, 204; shifting alliances of, 230. *See also* Jews, Zionism

Younane, Ramses, *126*, 201, 232

Young Egypt (Misr el-Fatah), 35, 96, 98, 114

Young Men's Muslim Association (YMMA), 76, 109, 114, 120

Youssef, Amine, 73–74

Yugoslavia: German invasion of, 203; and Palestinian cause, 118

Yunus, Mohammad, 192

Zaghlul, Saad: call for Egyptian independence, 22, 222; death and burial, 70–71; and Egyptian bid for Caliphate, 52, 54; elected Prime Minister, 24; and Gandhi, 36, 75; and Pharaonism, 25, 28, *29*, 70–71; and Tagore, 58, 60

al-Zawahiri, Muhammad al-Ahmadi, 54, 254n59

Zetland, Lawrence Dundas, Second Marquess of: and Indian Muslim engagement with Palestine, 131–34, 137–38, 140; and proposal for India's partition, 141–42, 149, 185

Ziadeh, May, 58

Zionism: and Balfour Declaration, 31–3, 48; debates at Biltmore, 207; Western support for, 31–2, 66, 76, 136, 228; criticisms of, 33, 227–28; at IAW Copenhagen congress, 173–75; and Indian Muslim nationalism, 68, 138, 144, 230; impact on Palestine, 65, 70, 75, 78, 107–8, 207, 231; at Paris Peace Conference, 32, 196. *See also* Jews; Yishuv

Zulficar, Youssef, 194

STANFORD BRITISH HISTORIES

Edited by Priya Satia

Stanford British Histories publishes new works of scholarship that expand our understanding of British culture, society, and power from regional to global scales. This series highlights histories of Britain and its empire that attend to the roles of institutions, systemic forces, and global historical forces such as capitalism, imperialism, and globalization, but that also recognize and value individual agency and lived experience. The series aims to bridge the early modern/late modern divide, and is particularly interested in projects that prioritize the voices of historical subjects who have previously been elided, including imperial subjects, the working classes, and other marginalized groups. At the same time, books in the series take seriously the material impact of institutions such as the military and imperial administration. Topics of interest include, but are not limited to, histories of ecology and the environment; military history and the history of war; violence and resistance; infrastructure and resource extraction; foodways and human-animal studies; histories of economic life; education; science, medicine, information, intelligence, technology, and knowledge production; intellectual history and the history of political movements; and the history of gender, race, and class.

KATE IMY
Losing Hearts and Minds: Race, War, and Empire in Singapore and Malaya, 1915–1960 **2024**

The authorized representative in the EU for product safety and compliance is:
Mare Nostrum Group B.V.
Mauritskade 21D
1091 GC Amsterdam
The Netherlands
Email address: gpsr@mare-nostrum.co.uk

KVK chamber of commerce number: 96249943

The authorized representative in the EU for product safety and compliance is:
Mare Nostrum Group
B.V Doelen 72
4831 GR Breda
The Netherlands

www.ingramcontent.com/pod-product-compliance
Lightning Source LLC
Chambersburg PA
CBHW031756220426
43662CB00007B/425